THE
SIGINT SECRETS

ALSO BY NIGEL WEST

Spy! (with Richard Deacon)
MI5: British Security Service Operations 1909–45
A Matter of Trust: MI5 1945–72
MI6: British Secret Intelligence Service Operations 1909–45
Unreliable Witness: Espionage Myths of the Second World War
GARBO (with Juan Pujol)

THE
SIGINT SECRETS

THE SIGNALS INTELLIGENCE WAR, 1900 TO TODAY

Including the Persecution of Gordon Welchman

Nigel West

Quill
William Morrow
New York

Recognizing the importance of preserving what has been written, it is the policy of William Morrow and Company, Inc., and its imprints and affiliates to have the books it publishes printed on acid-free paper, and we exert our best efforts to that end.

Library of Congress Cataloging-in-Publication Data

West, Nigel.
    The SIGINT secrets : the signals intelligence war, 1900 to today : including the persecution of Gordon Welchman / Nigel West.
        p.   cm.
    Reprint. Originally published: New York : W. Morrow, c1988.
    ISBN 0-688-09515-1
    1. Military intelligence—Great Britain—History—20th century.
2. Electronic surveillance—Great Britain—History. 3. Great
Britain. Government Communications Headquarters—History.
I. Title.
UB251.G7W486   1990
355.3'432'0941—dc20   89-27504
                                                                                    CIP

Printed in the United States of America

First Quill Edition

1   2   3   4   5   6   7   8   9   10

BOOK DESIGN BY NICOLA MAZZELLA

The very highest priority in personnel and material should be assigned to what may be called the Radio sphere. This demands scientists, wireless experts, and many classes of highly skilled labour and high-grade material. On the progress made much of the winning of the war and our future strategy, especially naval, depends.

WINSTON CHURCHILL, *Their Finest Hour*, October 15, 1940

Contents

Illustrations

9

(*Unless otherwise indicated, all photographs belong to the author's
    collection*)

Acknowledgments

I owe a debt of gratitude to the following:

Lord Sandhurst, for access to his father's records of the Radio Security Service and Special Communications Unit 1; Jürgen Rohwer; Donald Shirreff; Ralph Erskine; Roy Rodwell of the Marconi Company; Barbara Tuchman; David Kahn; Pat Hawker; Gerry Openshaw; all the former members of RSS who kindly gave their help; and the Radio Society of Great Britain.

The staff of the Public Records Office in Kew; the British Museum; the Imperial War Museum; Churchill College, Cambridge; King's College, London; the GPO Archives, London; the Royal Signals Museum, Blandford; the Intelligence Corps Museum, Ashford.

Abbreviations

AFSA	Armed Forces Security Agency
AGI	Auxiliary Vessel, Intelligence Gatherer
AI	Air Intelligence
ASA	Army Security Agency
BEF	British Expeditionary Force
BRUSA	Britain–United States of America Security Pact
CBME	Combined Bureau Middle East
CIA	American Central Intelligence Agency
CID	Committee of Imperial Defense
CSDIC	Combined Services Detailed Interrogation Center
CSE	Canadian Communications Security Establishment
DF	Direction-finding
DMI	Director of Military Intelligence
DNI	Director of Naval Intelligence
DSD	Australian Defense Signals Directorate
DWS	Diplomatic Wireless Service
FBI	American Federal Bureau of Investigation
FECB	Far East Combined Bureau
GC&CS	Government Code and Cypher School
GCHQ	Government Communications Headquarters
GPO	General Post Office
HDU	Home Defense Unit
KGB	Soviet Committee for State Security
MI1	Directorate of Military Intelligence
MI5	British Security Service
MI6	British Secret Intelligence Service
MI8	British Radio Security Service
MI9	British Escape and Evasion Service
NATO	North Atlantic Treaty Organization
NID	Naval Intelligence Division
NKVD	Soviet Intelligence Service
NSA	American National Security Agency

NZCSB	New Zealand Communications Security Bureau
PCO	Passport Control Officer
OSS	Office of Strategic Services
RSGB	Radio Society of Great Britain
RSS	Radio Security Service
SCU	Special Communications Unit
SD	Nazi Security Service
SIS	American Signal Intelligence Service
SLO	Security Liaison Officer
SLU	Special Liaison Unit
SOE	Special Operations Executive
SWG	Special Wireless Group
UKUSA	United Kingdom–United States of America Security Agreement
VI	Voluntary Interceptor
Y	Wireless Interception

Organizational Tables

DIRECTORS OF GCHQ

Alastair Denniston	1921–44
Sir Edward Travis	1944–52
Sir Eric Jones	1952–60
Sir Clive Loehnis	1960–64
Sir Leonard Hooper	1965–73
Sir Arthur Bonsall	1973–78
Sir Brian Tovey	1978–83
Sir Peter Marychurch	1983–

GCHQ

Director

Oakley   Palmer St
Benhall   Bletchley

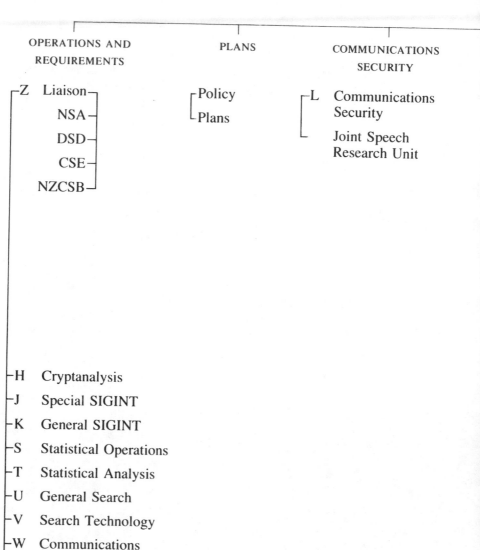

OPERATIONS AND   PLANS   COMMUNICATIONS
REQUIREMENTS   SECURITY

Z   Liaison   Policy   L   Communications
      NSA   Plans   Security
      DSD   Joint Speech
      CSE   Research Unit
      NZCSB

H   Cryptanalysis
J   Special SIGINT
K   General SIGINT
S   Statistical Operations
T   Statistical Analysis
U   General Search
V   Search Technology
W   Communications
X   Computer Science

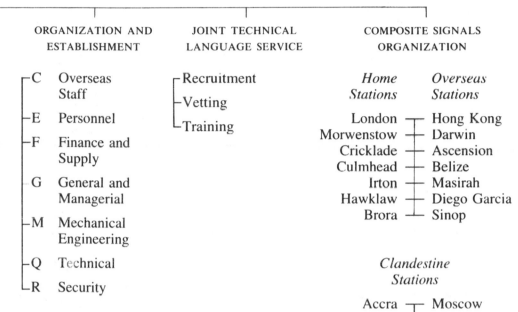

ORGANIZATION AND ESTABLISHMENT	JOINT TECHNICAL LANGUAGE SERVICE	COMPOSITE SIGNALS ORGANIZATION

ORGANIZATION AND ESTABLISHMENT

- C Overseas Staff
- E Personnel
- F Finance and Supply
- G General and Managerial
- M Mechanical Engineering
- Q Technical
- R Security

JOINT TECHNICAL LANGUAGE SERVICE

- Recruitment
- Vetting
- Training

COMPOSITE SIGNALS ORGANIZATION

Home Stations	*Overseas Stations*
London	Hong Kong
Morwenstow	Darwin
Cricklade	Ascension
Culmhead	Belize
Irton	Masirah
Hawklaw	Diego Garcia
Brora	Sinop

Clandestine Stations

Accra	Moscow
Nairobi	Prague
Lilongwe	Budapest
Freetown	Warsaw
Lusaka	Pretoria

National Security Agency
Fort George G. Meade
    Maryland
-Office of Administration

-Office of General Counsel

-Office of Plans and Policy

-Office of Programs and Resources

-Office of Installations and Logistics

-Office of Telecommunications and Computer Services

-National Cryptographic School

-Office of Research Engineering ┌ Intercept Equipment Division
                                └ Cryptographic Equipment Division

	┌ A Group	Soviet Traffic and Eastern Bloc
-Office of Signals	├ B Group	Asian Communist Traffic
Intelligence	├ C Group	Telecommunications
Operations	├ G Group	General Traffic
	└ W Group	Intercept Management

| Central Security Service |

U.S. Army Intelligence and Security Command	U.S. Naval Group	USAF Electronic Security Command
Arlington Hall Virginia	Nebraska Avenue Washington D.C.	Kelly AFB San Antonio Texas
Vint Hill Farm Warrenton Virginia	Sugar Grove West Virginia	Buckley AFB Aurora Colorado
Two Rock Ranch California	Winter Harbor Maine	

NSA Bases in the U.S.	NSA Bases Overseas	National Reconnaissance Office/CIA
Yakima Washington		Sunnyvale California
Kent Island Virginia		

Introduction

For the greater part of this century a secret war has been waged over the airwaves. It has been prosecuted in conditions of extraordinary secrecy, and has had a profound effect on world events. Indeed, the whole course of history has been altered by what might be termed the secret wireless war. Take, for example, an incident that occurred in 1938, following Prime Minister Neville Chamberlain's famous journey to Munich to negotiate a few extra months of peace from Hitler. Europe was on the brink of catastrophe, about to be engulfed by a Nazi regime bent on aggressive expansion. Appallingly ill-prepared for the coming conflict, Britain extracted the promise of a short breathing space in which to reequip and mobilize. Chamberlain returned to London certain only that the German Chancellor could not be trusted. Had hostilities really been averted, and had the Allies won sufficient time to rearm? Had Britain and France gained a few precious months to prepare for the onslaught, or had Hitler simply manipulated the talks to deceive his enemies and consolidate his enormous advantage? Was his undertaking genuine, or nothing more than a cynical ruse to conceal a massive impending offensive?

These key questions needed *immediate* answers. It is no exaggeration to say that the future of civilization hung in the balance. All the usual sources of secret intelligence failed to give the crucial answer. Neither the British Secret Intelligence Service nor the French Service de Renseignements possessed an agent in Berlin sufficiently well placed to discover the truth. And since espionage was unable to supply the necessary information, what was it that persuaded the Cabinet that, on this occasion at least, Hitler had kept his word and the imminent conflict had been delayed, albeit temporarily? It certainly was not any cryptographic source, for Britain's code-breaking agency had proved incapable of solving the German machine ciphers that might have betrayed a clue to the Chancellor's true intentions.

The government's confidence in the German promise turned out to be well founded. The blitzkrieg was postponed for a further year . . . just enough time for the Allies to put into action a desperate last-minute program to enhance their defenses. But what was it, that crucial piece of data that had persuaded the decision-makers there was to be respite, brief though it proved to be, but nonetheless just enough to prevent a complete collapse?

The critical item that marked a historic turning point, and gave such welcome relief to the Allies, was a brilliant analysis of signals sent and received by a Kriegsmarine warship in the Atlantic. The pocket battleship *Deutschland* was then on a courtesy visit to the Spanish port of Vigo, part of a cruise on which a disproportionate number of its complement, some eight hundred in total, were recently recruited cadets still undergoing basic training. The British Admiralty's Naval Intelligence Division reckoned that if war was about to be declared, the *Deutschland*'s captain would immediately return to Germany to replace the cadets with his regular, more experienced crew.

By scrutinizing the volume of wireless traffic sent to and from the ship, and determining its exact position by radio direction-finding, the British Admiralty was able to plot the *Deutschland*'s movements. The signals-intelligence analysts had concentrated on one vital clue in particular while the Munich crisis had been at its height. They had determined that if the *Deutschland* left its Spanish hosts and headed north, for her home port, Chamberlain would know that he had been duped, and war was about to be declared at any moment. If the battleship sailed south, out into the Atlantic, hostilities would have been averted. A fix had been taken on every signal transmitted by the warship as it steamed out of Spanish territorial waters . . . and the subsequent plot revealed the *Deutschland* to have taken up a southerly course. The news was conveyed instantly to the Prime Minister, who had promptly assured his French counterpart that all was well . . . for the time being.

Thus it was the art of signals intelligence, known as SIGINT, and not the more conventional methods of information gathering, that had helped Chamberlain ascertain Hitler's true intentions. This little-known episode remained a tightly held secret for years, but is a graphic illustration of how SIGINT achieves results when more recognized sources have been unable to rise to the task.

SIGINT is the field of battle on which the wireless war is fought. It embraces traffic analysis, direction finding, call-sign research, and a host of other highly specialized skills, quite apart from the more straightforward and obvious technique of cryptography or code breaking. Indeed, certain SIGINT organizations, particularly those with a record of success, have gone to extraordinary lengths to conceal the true nature of their calling and divert attention away from SIGINT to the more manageable area of cipher-busting.

It is now a common belief that "the Allies broke the Enigma codes" during the last war in an operation known as "Ultra." The revelation in 1974, principally by Group Captain F. W. Winterbotham in *The Ultra Secret*, that the war had been appreciably shortened by reading the enemy's Enigma-generated signals, led to a major revision of our historical perspective. Gradually the claims became more extravagant as the conduct of the war was reexamined in the light of the latest disclosures. The reputations of such supposed military giants as Eisenhower and Montgomery sustained sharp knocks as their strategies were looked at again, armed with the knowledge that an extra, unseen and unacknowledged assistance had been given to them by the cryptographic boffins based at Bletchley Park.

Slowly the impression developed that under cover of the code name Ultra, a magnificent team of brilliant minds, aided by the first generation of prototype computers, had enabled the Allies to break the Enigma code. Winterbotham talked of breaking the supposedly "unbreakable German machine cyphers . . . ," an "operation which was accomplished by a team of brilliant mathematicians and cryptographers," but other similar examples are legion. Thomas Parrish put it in these terms:

> The Western Allies possessed a remarkable secret weapon called Ultra
> that gave them the ability to look over the shoulder of Adolf Hitler
> and read the high-level radio communications of the German armed
> forces.

The distinguished British military historian Ronald Lewin said: "The operation called Ultra involved intercepting enemy signals that had been mechanically enciphered, rendering them intelligible, and then distributing their translated texts by secure means to appropriate headquarters."

Peter Calvocoressi, who had worked at Bletchley Park, recalled: "Enigma was the name given by the Germans to their machine. Ultra was the name given by us to the intelligence we got from breaking Enigma." The common denominator of all the books written on the subject, and the many revisionist histories prompted by the revelation of Ultra's existence, is the certainty that "the Enigma code was cracked."

What makes the truth all the more remarkable is the fact that the Enigma machine was never broken. Certainly much of the wireless traffic generated by the Enigma was read by the Allies, but that is not to say that the machine itself, when used properly, could be defeated. Quite simply, it could not.

The idea has been cultivated and deliberately propagated that clever men with ingenious machines managed to outwit the Enigma's flawed technology. In fact nothing could be further from the truth, and the various agencies charged with protecting the real story have gone to extraordinary lengths to create a myth. Their motive? To avoid the potentially damaging disclosure that the mere interception of signals can reveal significant intelligence. Put more simply, that men with pencils can extract useful information from listening to Morse. Analysis and interpretation of the intercepts may provide extremely useful data, even if the actual content resists decryption. In the classic case of the *Deutschland,* a straightforward direction-finding exercise had been enough to allow some very far-reaching conclusions to be drawn. In other circumstances, nothing more sophisticated than a statistical comparison of transmissions can highlight anomalies and concentrate attention on to recognizable patterns and procedures. Why has a regular schedule been altered? Is the operator using his normal frequency? Has the number of groups in a message increased? How many stations have acknowledged the transmission? Are they working from their usual locations? What significance should be attached to a perceptible increase in signal strength? When can a particular call sign be expected to change? These are questions for skilled analysts to answer, but once the fundamental principles involved are recognized, the necessary experience can be gained quite easily. In terms of cost-effectiveness, a SIGINT interception and analysis program can prove extremely valuable and yield far greater benefit, without the attendant risk, of any equivalent effort devoted to intelligence-gathering operations relying on other disciplines. A useful spy may be well placed, but he can also be manipulated. Indeed, he may not even be conscious of being under someone else's control. Perhaps quite unwittingly an agent may become a conduit for deception. Alternatively, he may succumb to coercion or blandishments and simply switch sides. Thus, under many circumstances, a radio signal may be more reliable as a source, and as we shall see, vast resources were dedicated to SIGINT collection by all sides during the Second World War.

For their part the Germans put heavy emphasis on tactical data, intercepting theater communications, particularly voice channels, and decrypting low-grade field ciphers. In complete contrast to the Allies, the Nazis opted against any concerted attack on strategic traffic because they recognized the invulnerability of the cipher machine employed. Having captured several examples of the TypeX device during the chaotic British retreat to Dunkirk in 1940, the German Signal Service, the Forschungsamt, recognized it as a close copy of its own Enigma. In fact, the TypeX was a blatant infringement of the Enigma's patent, and as such enjoyed most of its high security qualities. Accordingly, the Forschungsamt deployed only a handful of personnel to the task of studying TypeX intercepts. It was their mistaken belief that any prolonged examination of Allied strategic signals would be a waste of time and resources because of the Enigma's proven reliability.

The Allies, on the other hand, had reached the same conclusion about the intrinsic security of the Enigma, but had made an extraordinary discovery that worked to undermine it. Sloppy operating procedures, compounded by errors committed by lazy signal staff, occasionally allowed the ever-vigilant monitors to spot a compromised text. German operations were so imbued with the machine's complexity, and thus its basic invulnerability, that they often succumbed to the pressures imposed by combat conditions. They took unauthorized shortcuts, reverted to familiar sequences when supposedly choosing random variants, and abused the secure communication nets by indulging in that most attractive temptation, operator chatter. Isolated, perhaps on another continent, only the most disciplined could resist the opportunity to swop private messages with home bases. The illicit exchanges could vary from a short preamble to identify the individual operators working a particular circuit to a more leisurely interchange of lengthy texts to circumvent the strict censorship governing letters. This systematic rule breaking was endemic among enemy radio networks and negated many of the Enigma's specially developed security features.

Ironically, the machine's complicated nature sometimes worked against itself. Frustrated by the highly involved keying arrangements, operators working to a tight schedule occasionally resorted to asking for guidance from others on the same net in plain language. This served to compromise all the resulting traffic. The exception was the very high standard maintained by the U-boat crews. The submarine operators always displayed extreme caution, and it is therefore not surprising to learn that the Kriegsmarine cipher known as OYSTER was never read, even retrospectively, even for a single day.

Practically all the cryptographers who spent any time studying the Enigma concurred that, when used correctly, and without years of sustained attack, the cipher traffic generated was impregnable. The prospect of current solutions was a virtual impossibility. Yet lapses in procedure and the indiscretion of operators did allow the sharp-eyed interceptor to spot clues to the all-important key settings that formed the basis of the machine's method of encryption. Each time two correspondents engaged the mechanism to pass messages, they were obliged to agree about a "key," which amounted to the starting position of all the Enigma's three rotors. Unless they were identical, the resulting text would be meaningless gibberish. Thus the exchange of preambles, *en clair*, before the main signal was transmitted, held the essential information needed to produce an uncorrupted text at the other end. Careful analysis of the preambles and call signs, together with the interrogation of operators taken prisoner and the study of captured documents, revealed the procedures adopted by the Axis.

Variations from the norm stood out as nonstandard "free-lancing" by overtired or ill-disciplined operators. When these intercepts were scrutinized for clues to the construction of the "discriminator," or that part of the preamble used to convey the vital keying data, the experienced analyst could sometimes detect enough to enable him to duplicate the keying process. It was by this means that some Enigma keys were recovered . . . without recourse to any cryptographic technique. It was simply a matter of tracing flawed preambles so as to reconstruct a key. Even if a key could be only partially identified, it often proved enough of a guide or "crib," by reducing substantially the vast range of permutations available, to assist the decoders to find the remainder by mechanical means. This technique usually required a high-speed data-processing gadget to race through all the possible options in search of a key that could unlock a particular intercept.

In short, the successful breaks into Enigma-generated cipher traffic were due not to any malfunction of the machine itself but to the skillful exploitation of human error. It is this essential truth that lies at the heart of the wireless war prosecuted during World War II, and is the reason for the bizarre events that, as recently as 1985, led directly to the death of one of Bletchley's most respected backroom boys.

* * *

At the end of the war the Allies went to considerable lengths to preserve two vital aspects to their code-breaking operations. First, the sheer scale of the undertaking. Every one of the many thousands of individuals who had participated was warned of the dire consequences of breathing a word about the occupation known, euphemistically, as "special signals." Second, an even tighter embargo was imposed on any discussion of cipher machines, including the Enigma. Despite the very large number of people involved in all the different branches of the operation, the restriction was honored for nearly thirty years. One reason for its longevity was the relative handful of technicians who knew the full details. Of course, several thousand analysts had been employed to intercept and log all the Axis wireless traffic, and quite a sizable proportion must have been able to assess the profound consequences of their work. But while many realized Enigma keys were being recovered, and the resulting traffic read, really very few actually knew the secret of exactly *how* the miracle had been achieved. That knowledge required a detailed understanding of the Enigma machine itself, combined with a grasp of traffic analysis. The West's two principal cryptographic agencies, the U.S. National Security Agency and its British counterpart, the Government Communications Headquarters, jealously guarded the truth and actively promoted canards.

Even as recently as January 1978, when people were first permitted by the British government to discuss the decryption of wartime Enigma material, the ban on "any technical details of the work" was continued and enhanced. In other words, although it was officially admitted that wartime enemy signals had been decrypted, the exact methodology used was to remain classified. Retired personnel with Enigma experience were instructed that although they were now free to talk of the effect "breaking the Enigma" had on the overall war effort, they were to avoid all discussion on two vital subjects: "technical details of the structure, logic and operations of the Enigma machine, or similar machines" and "weaknesses of German or other communications systems and the methods of exploitation of such weaknesses."

The stricture to remain silent must have been hard to endure for the very few surviving veterans of the war who still possessed the kind of firsthand knowledge GCHQ and the NSA sought to discourage. Some must have been incensed at the distortion of historical fact they had witnessed since the original Ultra disclosures, but it was not until Gordon Welchman prepared his memoirs that any direct action was taken against anyone for giving his version of events.

Welchman was a Cambridge-trained mathematician who had played a crucial role in the early development of the Allied program for dealing with Nazi signals. Not only had he recognized the importance of devoting time and effort to the Enigma-generated wireless traffic, he had also gained the confidence of the traditionally skeptical intelligence bureaucrats who had not initially foreseen the possibilities. Welchman had been captivated by the opportunities offered by the frequent mistakes made by enemy signalers, and had been convinced that human error could be exploited to the Enigma's disadvantage. His other great achievement had been to galvanize the authorities into matching his commitment. After a refreshingly tonic-like pep talk from the enthusiastic academic, few had the gall to turn him down, especially when the rewards seemed so promising. Fortunately, most of Welchman's predictions were proved correct, and Whitehall responded positively to his demands to concentrate Bletchley's limited resources on certain kinds of intercepts.

After the war Welchman emigrated to the United States, where, having already learned the lessons of SIGINT attack, he turned his attention to defense, and evolved countermeasures to help protect Allied communications from hostile interception. His specialty was signal security, and having spent the war years supervising the devising of methods to circumvent the most sophisticated systems then in existence, he was better placed than most to advise on the subject. As he himself said, he knew "more than anyone else why the security of the German Enigma traffic broke down." This was no idle boast, but a genuine reflection of his own work at Bletchley. His choice of words should also be noted. He never once suggested or claimed that the Enigma machine itself had been broken. He knew that to be untrue. But he did have firsthand knowledge of how the Enigma's built-in security had been circumvented, and he also acknowledged that complacency and ill-founded confidence in crypto systems could be exploited. However technologically complex the cipher, it could still be jeopardized by poor procedure.

Throughout most of the 1960s and 1970s Welchman worked for a U.S. government contractor, the Mitre Corporation, devising improved cipher systems for the modern battlefield environment. Unlike most of his colleagues, Welchman had enjoyed initiating and running a hostile decryption program, so he was aware of all the pitfalls to be avoided. But toward the end of his career he came to the conclusion that too many of the lessons of the Second World War had *not* been learned properly. He became increasingly anxious about the West's ability to deploy and protect a communications net that would respond to the needs of a contemporary conflict. Accordingly, while in his retirement but still on contract in an advisory capacity to Mitre, he wrote a detailed account of his own experiences at Bletchley, together with a lengthy critique of modern trends in the field. His endeavor was greeted with alarm.

The announcement that Welchman had written *The Hut Six Story* sent shock waves throughout the West's cryptographic agencies. Until his intervention, GCHQ and the NSA had perpetuated the myth that code breaking had won the war and the Enigma machine had been solved. Very few knew this to be a distortion of what had really happened. In consequence public attention had focused on cryptography and been diverted away from the more sensitive matter of traffic analysis. No doubt those countries contemplating the creation of a latter-day Bletchley were deterred by the apparent complexity of recruiting suitable personnel and acquiring the appropriate equipment.

This explains the impact that Welchman had on the West's intelligence community when the news of his book circulated. His intention was interpreted as the first attempt to break ranks and compromise the carefully nurtured cover story of the Enigma's vulnerability. Worse than that, there seemed to be few sanctions that might be applied to him. He had told his publisher he had verbal permission to write and that he would not breach any security matters. He received no state pension, and his employment was on a part-time basis as a consultant to a private corporation. He had also acquired U.S. citizenship, thus removing him from the jurisdiction of the draconian penalties of Britain's Official Secrets Act, which, he claimed, he had never signed. After he had executed a contract with a major New York publisher, the Anglo-American authorities were in no doubt that Welchman, the one-time architect of the Allied attack on the Enigma traffic, was about to disclose the operation's well-protected secrets.

However, it was only after the release of his book that GCHQ and the NSA moved against him. In April 1982 he was visited by federal agents who took statements from him. He was warned that his action might lead to prosecution and a long sentence of imprisonment. In Britain preparations were made to ban the book and to bring criminal proceedings against him in the event of his return. But rather than adopt any of these tactics the NSA resorted to other measures. The terms of the NSA's wide-ranging embargo on what Welchman was allowed to mention, which included all ''methodologies which cryptanalysts use to successfully exploit code or cipher systems,'' were so constricting that he was unable to promote his book. Indeed, on one occasion he was inhibited from discussing an example of an Enigma machine that happened to be on display at a bookfair. But in spite of Welchman's compliance with the prohibition, his security clearance was rescinded. He could no longer work for Mitre, even as a consultant. He was then subjected to constant harassment, which, aggravated by his heart condition, led to his premature death in October 1985.

Welchman's consolation must have been the successful publication of his memoir, in the face of very determined opposition. GCHQ and the NSA were united in their view that any disclosure of exactly what measures had been taken to exploit human error in the context of the Enigma machine must be avoided, however dated the information. As the NSA warned, ''Public discussion of the technical details of any of these measures would not be in the national interest.'' Welchman argued the reverse. The lessons of the war years had still not been learned, he claimed. And unless Congress and the public were alerted to the dangers, there was a probability that history would repeat itself. His message, despite its laudably patriotic motive, failed to move the authorities, although after the release of *The Hut Six Story,* they were obliged to admit defeat.

Welchman's melancholy experience is an eloquent demonstration of the sensitivity with which the whole subject of SIGINT must be approached. While the exploits of spies may be more attractive, on a superficial level, to the public, the field of signals intelligence has profound implications for history. Nor is this a recent development. As will be seen in the pages that follow, the interception and analysis of wireless signals has been a preoccupation of governments throughout the world since an Italian inventor named Marconi first tried to peddle his apparatus in the last century.

1

The Empire Chain

Before money is spent on wireless stations, it is essential to ascertain precisely what advantages would be secured in return. What were the probabilities that they would be "jammed" in time of war; that they would be put out of gear by evilly disposed persons?

—R. F. WILKINS, Committee of Imperial Defense, June 29, 1914

Up to the middle of the last century, military and diplomatic information, orders and intelligence reports could be sent by couriers, by post or by diplomatic bag; they could also be sent by visual signals such as semaphore flags or heliograph mirrors. But ships out of sight of land, or of each other, were still unable to communicate except through scouting vessels.

By 1878, Alexander Graham Bell had brought his telephone to London and had set up London's first telephone exchange with just seven subscribers. Also by this time, messages were able to be sent considerable distances at speed in Morse code by electric telegraphy along specially laid landlines and under the sea by submarine cables. The General Post Office soon boasted of being able to tap out and transmit at a speed of four hundred words a minute along its monopoly-run telegraph cables which linked Great Britain with her far-flung empire, with her colonies and dominions. Such cables could only be interfered with by a lengthy trawling and cutting exercise; however, as the Royal Navy commanded the sea, such activity by an enemy power was thought to be unlikely. Providing those receiving and sending messages at each end were friendly to each other, cable transmission was remarkably secure. Commercial users coded their secrets to keep them from their rivals, but most messages were sent *en clair*. However, keeping in touch with scattered naval vessels at sea was still a problem until the development of wireless.

A wireless transmitter is an instrument that generates electromagnetic radiation. This radiation travels in the form of impulses. The frequency of the impulses is expressed in kilocycles per second, and are distributed equally, in every direction, by means of an aerial. The greater the power of the transmitter, which is measured in watts, the longer the distances traveled by the radiating signals. Alternating the electrical current of the signal in a recognizable form produces dots, dashes and spaces, which Samuel Morse developed into the telegraphic alphabet universally adopted by international convention.

The frequency of the waves generated by a transmitter differ considerably, from continuous waves, which carry voices or pictures (usually telephonic conversations and television pictures), through long and medium waves, down to short and very short waves. At the lowest end of the wave scale (corresponding to the highest frequencies) are ultraviolet and X rays.

Signals transmitted on the shortwave tend to travel the farthest because of an invisible layer in the atmosphere known as the ionosphere. This phenomenon acts as a mirror and returns the waves propagated back to the surface of the earth, which in turn bounces them back into the atmosphere. Thus, thanks to a freak of nature, a shortwave signal can often be heard perfectly at very long distances. The ionosphere is subject to seasonal change, but in theory at least, given sufficient transmitting power, the right frequency and a suitable aerial, a radio signal sent on one side of the earth can be bounced round the world to be intercepted and interpreted on the other side, with little more than an aerial, receiver and amplifier. A longer wave on a lower frequency will travel much less far and so will only be of local importance.

The first man to construct an apparatus capable of sending, amplifying and receiving wireless signals was Guglielmo Marconi. In 1895, this second son of an Italian landowner and the heiress to the Jameson Irish whiskey fortune was just twenty-one. He had offered to demonstrate his equipment, which was set up at his parents' home near Bologna, to the Italian government, but the invitation had been turned down. Marconi believed that his invention would revolutionize communications with shipping, which had hardly changed since the days of the Romans, but apparently no one in authority in Italy had been able to see any useful applications for his device. Exasperated, he had turned to his mother's family for help, and they had told him to travel to London without further delay for London was the center of the maritime world at that time. Most of the important merchant fleets had their headquarters located there. It was also the home of Lloyd's and the international marine insurance market. An added attraction was that it was at that time the headquarters of the world's largest navy.

However, Marconi's initial experience in England was hardly encouraging. The overenthusiastic customs official who examined his remarkable apparatus was suitably intrigued, and completely dismantled it in a futile attempt to learn its secrets. Unfortunately, he was not up to putting all the pieces back together, and Marconi was obliged to rebuild it before he could submit an application to register the first wireless telegraphy patent.

Undeterred, Marconi completed the necessary repairs in time for a series of major demonstrations in July and August 1896. His wealthy cousin, Jameson Davis, invited a number of influential friends to attend, and the young Marconi succeeded in transmitting a signal from the roof of the GPO's headquarters in St. Martin's-le-Grand to a wireless station erected on the roof of the GPO's Savings Bank Department in Queen Victoria Street, a distance of just over a mile. One of those who witnessed this historic event was (Sir) William Preece, then the General Post Office chief engineer and guardian of the GPO's monopoly on the transmission of signals along telegraph wires. Word of Marconi's impressive results spread quickly, and public interest in his technique grew. The British army, however, remained somewhat skeptical although the navy was interested, but the ranges needed to be covered for ship-to-ship signaling at sea were still beyond Marconi's apparatus.

However, on September 2, 1896, Marconi conducted a demonstration for the army and the Admiralty on Salisbury Plain, and achieved a faintly detectable signal over a distance of a mile and three quarters. The War Office observer, Major Carr, still remained unimpressed, but the navy saw that the invention might well have a potential for them. It also occurred to Captain Henry Jackson RN (later to become the First Sea Lord) that Marconi's wireless signals might possibly be used for the remote detonation of an underwater mine. Instead of depending on shore batteries, naval establishments might be protected by underwater minefields, which could be triggered by a wireless signal from some distance away. The proposal was attractive, but Marconi was unable to build a receiver that could operate at the required depth, so the scheme was shelved.

During the twelve months following the ill-fated Salisbury Plain demonstration, Marconi continued trying to increase the range of his equipment. The GPO was now sufficiently interested in his progress to assign one of its own technicians, G.S. Kemp, to work as Marconi's principal assistant. Kemp, who had been a chief instructor in the Royal Navy, specializing in torpedoes and electronics, was to remain with Marconi for the rest of his life. Meanwhile, the GPO constructed its own secret wireless station near Dover with apparatus borrowed from Marconi and adapted by its own technicians, but it was unable to increase its range.

The breakthrough that Marconi had been waiting for was eventually achieved in 1897, when his newly incorporated Wireless Telegraphy and Signal Company built a shore station in the Needles Hotel on the Isle of Wight. With the aid of a 120-foot aerial in the hotel grounds, Marconi sent a signal across to the *Mayflower,* a steamer plying between Swanage Pier on the mainland and Alum Bay in the Isle of Wight. Just two days before Christmas 1897, Marconi transmitted messages to the *Mayflower* at a rate of four words a minute . . . over a distance of eighteen and a half miles.

Marconi was so pleased with this development that he promptly built a second shore station at Madeira House in Bournemouth and proceeded to exchange signals with the Needles Hotel, a distance of about twenty miles. Coincidentally, Bournemouth was isolated from the rest of the country by a sudden snowstorm. This would not have been an event of any particular significance if the eighty-eight-year-old former Prime Minister William Gladstone had not been in the town on his deathbed, surrounded by dozens of press reporters anxious to keep in touch with Fleet Street. The Bournemouth telegraph lines were down, so Marconi offered to transmit the newspapermen's stories to the Isle of Wight and thence by intact telegraph lines to London. Marconi's timely offer was accepted, and each reporter filed his story successfully. It was a publicity coup which demonstrated the value of wireless and ensured a renewed interest from the military in the new year of 1898.

The Royal Engineer Committee now appointed Captain J.N.C. Kennedy to liaise with Marconi, and he attended a number of Marconi's early experiments on Three Mile Hill, Salisbury Plain. Initially he reported that the equipment was so cumbersome, and the range so uncertain, that he felt it had few immediate military applications. However, if the army hesitated, the Admiralty did not, and on March 27, 1899, naval officers witnessed an exchange of signals between a shore station at South Foreland and Wimereux, on the French coast, thirty-two miles away. Further experiments followed, with sets being installed in the cruiser HMS *Juno* and the battleship HMS *Alexandria.* On July 14, Marconi, aboard the *Juno*, received a signal from the Needles Hotel, over a distance of eighty-seven miles, and the following month both warships made contact with each other when they were seventy-four nautical miles apart. The Admiralty was delighted and purchased the exclusive rights to Marconi's equipment. Its contract, dated July 4, 1900, was the first major purchase of wireless equipment by Britain. The army responded by establishing an experimental unit at Aldershot, headed by Major Carr, to investigate the possibilities further, in spite of the fact that Marconi's license to the Admiralty excluded the War Office. By the end of the year, the unit had built its first field set.

The Boer War, which had begun the year before in October 1899, appeared to offer a unique opportunity to test the new sets, so Captain Kennedy was posted to South Africa with a group of volunteer operators from Marconi's company (now renamed Marconi's Wireless Telegraph Company), led by G.L. Bullocke. The expedition was not a success, although an initial exercise in Cape Town was well reported by foreign military observers. It had originally been planned to use the detachment to reinforce the existing railway telegraphs, and perhaps to experiment by communicating with merchant shipping at Durban, but a more ambitious scheme was proposed. A consignment of six Siemens sets, apparently destined for the Boers, had been discovered in a customs shed; these were cannibalized and their parts added to the existing Marconi sets. All were then loaded onto horse-drawn, springless wagons and sent to de Aar, Modder, Belmont, Eslin, Orange River and Enslin. However, this first field trial proved unsuccessful because none of the aerials would work after such a jolting journey. New aerials were made from thirty-foot lengths of jointed bamboo pole lashed together, but when these were eventually placed in position they proved unsatisfactory and disintegrated at the first sign of inclement weather. Various improvisations were tried, including some experiments with Baden-Powell box kite aerials made of linen and string, but it was never possible to ensure good kite-flying conditions at the appropriate times at both ends of the signal net; eventually, all the kites were torn adrift by cyclonic dust storms. Even when the original eighty-foot Marconi mast was brought up from Cape Town, it turned out to be less than ideal. In an attempt to earth it better, sheets of tin were buried in the sandy soil but the result was still unsatisfactory.

The army judged this land trial a failure, so in March 1900 the wireless sets were handed over to the Royal Navy, who established shore stations at Durban and Dalagoa Bay. Further sets were installed in the three British warships, HMS *Forte, Thetis* and *Magicienne*, deployed on blockade enforcement duties. Several fast blockade-runners were intercepted as a result. The navy's experience was rather more positive than the army's (not least because the wireless enabled certain officers to make advance arrangements for their leave, thus saving valuable time onshore), and in the following months the navy supplied sets, equipped with improved kite aerials, for several military operations, including some camelborne sets for the Somaliland expedition in 1903. Enthusiastic reports reaching London from South Africa endorsed the wireless, so the Admiralty ordered the construction of six Marconi shore stations in England and Ireland and the installation of wireless equipment aboard twenty-six warships. The coastal stations were to be sited at North Foreland, Holyhead, Rosslare, Caister, Withernsea and Crookhaven. While Marconi worked on this important contract, signals from his research station at Poldhu in Cornwall were received in Newfoundland.

Meanwhile, the War Office was more interested in the GPO's monopoly of telegraph cables. To make sure that strict security was maintained during the Boer War, a special unit designated Section H was established to coordinate inspection and censorship of mail and cables. Major James Edmonds was the head of the unit; two other members were Colonel H. Walker and Captain H.V. Kent. Section H was responsible for monitoring all traffic using the two main submarine cables connecting South Africa to Portugal and Aden, for maintaining strict control over the civil landline cables and for examining the mail of suspect foreigners in conjunction with the Special Branch of the Metropolitan Police. As a result, Section H became a clearinghouse of information about enemy agents and acquired a wealth of useful intelligence. Offices were opened at Cape Town, Durban, Zanzibar and Aden, although this blatant interference with nonmilitary traffic caused considerable local resentment. Merchants in German East Africa and Portugal complained that they were unable to conduct their businesses, and some questioned the legality of the British action. Soon demands for compensation began arriving in London and Edmonds, who had been posted to Cape Town, was required to relax the censorship of the cable traffic and even "to permit the use of certain selected codes and afford special facilities to foreign government messages."

Section H remained in existence until the end of the Boer War, when it was taken over by a single officer, Colonel J.F. Davies, who was charged with the preparation of contingency plans for any future conflicts. Davies's wide-ranging duties included: "Secret service (dossiers of individuals, accounts, shipment of warlike stores, organization), ciphers, government telegraph code, compensation claims, wireless telegraphy, cable, censorship, press correspondents, control of the press.''[1]

As well as being a member of the new Wireless Telegraphy Committee, Davies was also the principal military intelligence officer on the Royal Engineer Committee and the important Cable Landing Rights Committee. As such, he attended a conference for the revision of the Geneva Convention and first International Wireless Telegraphy Conference in Berlin in August 1903. It soon became clear to him that the German firm Telefunken, which was largely underwritten by the German government, was carrying out considerable research into long-distance wireless. The Kaiser had not liked being dependent on British-owned cables for communicating with his overseas possessions, nor did he care to rely on laying his own as he realized he could neither hide nor protect them from the Royal Navy in time of war. At the end of the conference all the delegates, apart from those from Britain and Italy, pledged themselves to the pooling of technical information and the universal exchange of signals between ship and shore. The door was now open for international wireless communications; the scene was also set for international wireless intrigue.

Wireless telegraphy was not a totally secure method of transmitting messages, as Professor Oliver Lodge confirmed to the GPO in 1903:

> Submarine cables will for a long time be preeminent for the purpose of long-distance telegraphy. It is manifest that wireless or open methods cannot compete in point of secrecy or certainty with closed or cable methods, and can only compete with them in point of speed and accuracy by aid of great improvements and new inventions involving little less than discoveries.[2]

Professor Lodge's view coincided exactly with that held by the army. Wireless communications were inherently insecure, for anyone with the right equipment could get in on the eavesdropping game and leave no trace. The experience of the Boer War had shown how useful it was to exercise complete control over such transmissions, and in 1904 Parliament passed the Wireless Telegraphy Act which prohibited the installation or use of any wireless equipment without a license from the Postmaster General. The army wanted little part in the new development and felt safer with the Empire's cable arrangements. Davies remained at Section H until the end of 1906, by which time he had done his best, against the odds, to establish wireless telegraphy in the War Office's intelligence bureaucracy. However, when Davies was eventually posted elsewhere, he was not replaced and Section H's records were consigned to the archives.

The army's prejudices were not shared by the Committee of Imperial Defense (CID). This body had been created by the Cabinet after the disasters of the Boer War to coordinate service strategy and advise the Prime Minister on matters of defense policy. The CID included the Chiefs of Staff and had the use of a small permanent secretariat. One of its principal roles was to review Britain's intelligence capability, and Colonel Edmonds, the original head of Section H, was selected to prepare a report on the subject. Edmonds quickly became preoccupied by tales of foreign spies, but it was not until the mayor of Canterbury warned Richard Haldane MP of a German espionage offensive that any precautions were taken. According to the mayor, two inebriated German dinner guests had claimed to be undertaking a reconnaissance mission for the German Foreign Office. Apparently, the Kaiser had planned to advance on London after beachheads had been established at Folkestone and other seaside resorts on the south coast.

Haldane, who was then the Liberal Secretary of State for War, ordered Edmonds to investigate these reports (which proved to be false) and later authorized him to draw up a War Book of measures to be implemented in the event of a major conflict. His main recommendations concerned the formation of a Secret Service Bureau, the Home Section of which was later to be headed by Captain Vernon Kell and acquire the familiar War Office military intelligence designation MO5 (later MI5), but Edmonds also prepared a highly secret annex to the War Book. His idea was to compile a list of experts in deciphering and a reserve of officers suitable for wartime intelligence duties. He found that the army boasted an impressive number of officers who had qualified as interpreters, but when he inquired further he discovered that very few would be available for interpretation work if war broke out. Almost all officers would then be asked to return to their respective regiments.

Confronted by opposition from the War Office, the CID approached the Board of Education in the hope that the Permanent Secretary, Sir Robert Morant, might be persuaded to collaborate in the compilation of lists of people who might become translators, interpreters or cryptographers in time of war. Morant proved unhelpful in the extreme. As well as saying that war with Germany was unthinkable, he insisted that "his subordinates did not like enquiries being made into their qualifications." Furthermore, Morant refused absolutely to antagonize his staff by ordering their cooperation.

Edmonds abandoned this idea and, instead, turned to the business world for help. Here he was marginally more successful. Sir John Pender, of the Eastern Telegraph Company, agreed to monitor all his company's commercial traffic with Germany in case there was any military information hidden in it, and senior officers in several shipping firms, such as the Union Castle Line, were recruited as informants. The Rothschilds agreed to alert the CID if Germany underwent any "financial mobilization," a necessary preliminary to war, and other City institutions were approached for similar help. Several companies responded favorably, although some with special German connections, such as wine shippers and those in the musical instrument trade, pointed out that their linguists had little grasp of the German military vocabulary. Accordingly, the War Office's Director of Special Intelligence, Major George Cockerill, was requested to compile a dictionary of German military terms.

Incredibly, the War Office obstinately refused to encourage officers to improve their foreign languages. The Deputy Director of Staff Duties, General (later Field-Marshal Sir) Henry Wilson, is reported to have said that he saw no reason for any officer to speak any language other than his own. He is also alleged to have claimed, furthermore, that no great commander had ever spoken another language.

In the face of this kind of ignorant opposition, it seems remarkable that the War Office ever sanctioned the development of the army's wireless capability, but the Royal Engineers continued with their experiments. Much of their work centered on the Army Signal School at Aldershot (which was headed by Colonel R.S. Curtis of the Royal Engineers) and the Telegraph School at the Royal Engineers' hometown of Chatham. In 1906, a War Office Committee chaired by Sir Evelyn Wood recommended the introduction of a centralized post of Director of Telegraphs and Signaling, and the formation of a new Signal Service to supervise communications between headquarters down to brigade level and all artillery messages down to individual batteries. Although it took nearly six years to implement the bulk of these changes, they were finally executed, with the Signal Service remaining a part of the Royal Engineers. The last transition of "telegraph" to "signals" took place in 1913, when the Telegraph School at Chatham was amalgamated with the Army Signal School at Aldershot under Colonel J.S. Fowler RE.

Marconi had been exasperated by Whitehall's infighting. He began to bombard Whitehall with reports of the progress made by the Germans and, in March 1910, submitted an ambitious plan for an Imperial Wireless

Chain. The scheme involved the construction of eighteen high-powered radio stations.

The 1910 plan was impressive. England was to be linked to Alexandria, Aden, Mombasa, Natal, Cape Colony, Bombay, Colombo, Singapore, Hong Kong, North Australia, Sydney, New Zealand, St. Helena, Sierra Leone, Bathurst, British Guiana and the West Indies. Additional sites were recommended at Mauritius, Nelson Island, Nairobi, Singapore and Poona. Official reluctance about the plan was eventually overcome when the British ambassador in Berlin reported, coincidentally, on a German scheme to link the main transmitter at Nauen to several German colonies. Apparently, Nauen had already established a permanent link with Atakepame in Togoland, and the British consul in German South West Africa claimed that Telefunken was in the process of erecting stations at Windhoek, Tabora and the Caroline Islands in the Pacific.

Marconi's proposal was considered by the Committee of Imperial Defense's Cable Landing Rights Committee, and they finally gave Marconi their qualified approval for a reduced Imperial Wireless Chain when it was learned that the French had built a station atop the Eiffel Tower to communicate with three sites in French West Africa. After considerable discussion, they recommended that Marconi be allowed, initially at least, to build six stations linking England to Australia. The full CID board approved this in December 1911. The plan was then considered by a Select Committee of the House of Commons, and the final contract received parliamentary confirmation on August 8, 1913. The grander eighteen-station Imperial Chain scheme was postponed.

While Marconi was still busy negotiating the construction of his six-station chain, several incidents occurred which heralded a universal appreciation of the opportunities presented by wireless intelligence. In July 1910, Doctor Crippen had achieved fame by being the first murderer to be arrested as a result of ship-to-shore wireless. The captain of the liner *Montrose*, bound for Canada, had spotted the fugitive among his passengers and had sent a description to Scotland Yard. The police had responded by having a detective travel by a faster boat to Quebec. Crippen had been arrested as he stepped ashore and subsequently had been executed for the murder of his wife in London. Although the case had proved the value of wireless communications, it had also demonstrated their intrinsic lack of security. Several Fleet Street newspapers had listened in to the messages exchanged between the *Montrose* and the police and had reported them. As it happened, no great harm had been done, but senior officials at Scotland Yard had noted the dangers.

The Crippen case had been followed by another example of wireless interception the following year. In July 1911, the owner of the *Los Angeles Express* had published the contents of a wireless message which had been sent to the editor of the main rival, the *Los Angeles Herald*. The editor of the *Express*, Edwin T. Earl, had been promptly arrested on a charge of theft, but the prosecution had failed when Judge Walter Bordwell ruled that the interception of what was termed "an aerogram" was not illegal in California. The case had highlighted a loophole in the law and, to Marconi's consternation, it was realized that such interceptions had become commonplace. Marconi's transatlantic station at Poldhu routinely transmitted news telegrams to Cape Cod at night, and wireless operators on board some liners often selected a few of the more interesting messages and distributed them among the passengers. In November 1911, Marconi had complained about the practice to the GPO, but the company had been advised that the Telegraphy Acts did not outlaw it. As Judge Bordwell had pointed out, "free as air" was a commonly used expression and an appropriate one when used in connection with wireless communications.

These two cases spelled out the need for wireless security. But the War Office, which had always been more cable conscious and hence more aware for the need to guard the centers from which the cable messages were sent and received than the texts of the messages themselves, did not see these cases as a reason for looking at the problems of coding and decoding; it was much more worried about the security of the wireless stations themselves. There were two stations in Marconi's chain which were located in England: the receiver at Devizes in Wiltshire and the transmitter at Whichwood, near Leafield in Oxfordshire. In December 1913, the War Office reviewed security at the sites and suggested that fences be erected around the stations. The GPO, who operated both stations, was advised to agree on contingency plans with local police forces so that they could "be suitably protected against the action of ill-disposed persons." It was observed by the War Office that the Admiralty had already encircled its medium-power stations with chain-link fencing. The CID was so anxious to protect all the wireless sites in England that it was suggested that Marconi's should only be granted the necessary GPO licenses if it built adequate fortifications around its transmitters and included bulletproof shutters in its designs. Predictably, the Marconi Company, which had been struggling against the GPO to maintain a commercially worthwhile service, was highly indignant and commented:

> . . . we cannot accept the responsibility of making, at our own expense, at least without its being defined, such provision of defensive purposes as may be regarded as necessary by the naval and military

authorities. In the first instance the condition is so general and so broad that it might put us under the obligation of building fortresses or supplying dreadnoughts; there would certainly seem to us to be no limitation whatsoever, under the clause, to the responsibility which we would assume. Secondly, it would seem to us that we pay our quota with all other of His Majesty's subjects toward the army and navy for such protection as Parliament from time to time deems necessary, and we fail to appreciate why, because our construction may be one for the transmission of telegrams, it should be subjected to any greater expense in the matter of defense than would be an iron foundry, business premises of any other description, or a private dwelling.[3]

As has been explained, the War Office had not, up until 1913, seen wireless in anything but a negative light. No serious thought had been given to wireless as a strategic weapon. The navy, however, had not been so fainthearted, but then wireless had from the beginning always been of much greater value to ship communications.

This was made clear at the first meeting of a secret subcommittee set up on the recommendation of the Prime Minister under the Committee of Imperial Defense to review the security arrangements at Leafield and Devizes and assess the vulnerability of the rest of the chain in war conditions. The first meeting took place on April 28, 1914, at the CID's offices at 2 Whitehall Gardens and was attended by eleven officials, including two senior admirals, Colonel George Macdonogh from the War Office, Sir Alexander King representing the GPO, and representatives from the Treasury and the Board of Trade.

At this meeting the Admiralty showed its determination not to suffer any interference with the Fleet's ship-to-shore operations. Moreover, it made clear that its Naval Intelligence Division (NID) had taken the lead, in conjunction with the Marconi Company, in researching the wireless assets of other countries and, indeed, other British government departments. The Admiralty now revealed that for analytical purposes it had divided all Britain's wireless stations into three distinct categories: low-power stations using commercial wavelengths; high-power stations which could only be used by shipping; and high-power stations which could not be used by shipping. Of the first group, the Admiralty identified four GPO links: Bolt Head to Guernsey, Loch Boisdale to Tobermory, Stonehaven to Cullercoats and the projected net between Scotland and the Orkneys. The admirals claimed that these GPO stations were "possible sources of leakage of information and communication with the enemy and should be used only if cables break down, but that if any interference is experienced from them they should be closed down."[4] Of the second, high-power group which could be used by ships, the Admiralty identified the Marconi transatlantic station at Clifden, in County Galway, which was linked to Glace Bay in Canada. The NID observed generously: "The Admiralty policy is to make use of it as an emergency station in case of need, but when not used by them to allow it to continue its ordinary duties under censorship."[5]

The third category of high-power stations which the NID listed and which could not be used for shipping were the GPO stations at Leafield and Stonehaven, the Marconi stations at Caernarvon and the southwest of England, and the new Poulsen commercial station at Ballybunion in County Kerry.

The NID's assessment of the wireless assets of other countries was extraordinarily detailed. Dated June 10, 1914, it listed the exact location, range, use and ownership of every long-distance station in the world. Of the United States Navy's stations the NID commented: "Arlington is built. Darien is being completed. The site has been selected for San Diego. Hawaii, Samoa, Guam and Philippine Islands have been decided on, but not yet commenced."[6] Other countries listed included France, Belgium, Holland, Portugal, Spain, Norway, Chile, Uruguay, Italy and Germany. It was the first such complete survey ever conducted and gave an insight into the exact stage of wireless development in the world. It also identified those stations that had a military purpose. Some of the countries listed boasted just one transmitter powerful enough to be received at any distance. This was certainly true of Norway, Holland, Belgium and Portugal, where the stations were all in private hands, but the Italian government had built four stations, of which those at Coltano and Taranto were believed to be "used by the navy for communication with war vessels." France had developed a circuit of four naval radio bases, at Toulon, Bizerta and Ain-el-Turck outside Oran in North Africa which centered on the Eiffel Tower. This contrasted with the comparatively limited extent of the German network, which consisted of Nauen ("privately owned, but under the control of the State") and the naval wireless station at Neumünster in Schleswig-Holstein. The NID noted the existence of a third, experimental, German station at Brunswick, which occasionally exchanged commercial traffic with an American station at Tuckerton, New Jersey. Once the NID had completed its secret survey, it was left to the Committee of Imperial Defense to decide what communications, if any, should be disrupted or intercepted in time of war.

The CID subcommittee met again on June 29, 1914, and, according to the secret minutes, the following exchange took place on the sensitive subject of the intentional interruption of wireless communication:

> John Robertson MP (Parliamentary Secretary to the Board of Trade) asked if any reliable information regarding the ''jamming'' of wireless signals could be given.
>
> Admiral Charlton (Assistant Director of Torpedoes) said that a case had occurred recently of a station, probably French, deliberately attempting to ''block'' our signals, but we had got them through in the end; it was only a question of changing the tune by prearrangement if one tune was found to be ''blocked.'' Signals could in this way be got through before the interfering station had discovered the new tune. It would be quite possible to make a machine to ''jam'' all wireless messages within its range, but it would be very expensive. No existing station could do this.
>
> Mr. Wilkins (Treasury) said that it was for consideration how far it was worth expending money on apparatus that might be rendered useless when wanted in wartime.
>
> Sir Alexander King (GPO) said that the whole question was one of risks and chances, which must, however, be taken, as with cables, which could be cut.
>
> Admiral Charlton said that the chances for cables being cut or of wireless telegraphy being interrupted were about even.[7]

This remarkable debate took place a few weeks before the outbreak of the Great War and illustrates the profound ignorance of many senior officials in matters concerned with wireless. Of the sixteen members of the subcommittee present, only Mr. F.J. Brown of the Post Office had any technical knowledge of wireless, and he is not recorded as having made any remarks at all on the subject. It would seem that the rest of the subcommittee relied on the Assistant Director of Torpedoes to supply guidance on technical details. Yet in spite of this apparent handicap, the subcommittee met again on July 14 to finalize arrangements for war.

In the month before the formal declaration of war, the Admiralty began to acknowledge the vulnerability of Britain's wireless stations and investigated ways of defending them. The three Marconi stations at Clifden, Poldhu and Caernarvon, which were engaged on commercial work but communicated with the outside world, were thought to be particularly susceptible to attack from "evil disposed persons and small raiding parties up to 200 landed from a ship." Both Clifden and Poldhu had been earmarked for takeover by the Royal Navy anyway, and the Admiralty concluded that Caernarvon's relative distance from the sea made the station there an unlikely target.

In a survey dated July 14, 1914, the Admiralty reviewed the GPO's fourteen wireless stations and assessed their vulnerability. Four, responsible for linking Guernsey and the Orkneys with the mainland, had been shut down but were being held in reserve in case of a break in the underwater cable. Seven scattered around the coast supplied an essential ship-to-shore service, and the Admiralty decided that because of their low power they could not be relocated inland. Of greatest interest were the three remaining stations at Caister, Niton and Fishguard, which were to be kept open "to check illicit correspondence." This was the first recognition by any government department that the wireless might be used for espionage.

At this late stage the authorities were alerted to two threats to their wireless communications. The first related to physical security and had been the subject of debate in secret since May 1914, when the superintending engineer at Leafield reported that some women, believed to be suffragettes, had been spotted entering the site. Marconi's responded by employing a night watchman, but pointed out that "it would be somewhat difficult to prevent malicious damage being done" because of the scattered nature of the installation.

The second threat concerned the possibility of illicit signals, although, when Lord Abinger raised the matter in Parliament in September 1914 after war had been declared, the *Sunday Chronicle* observed that "the matter is not felt to be one of much seriousness." In fact, the Defense Regulations introduced on the outbreak of war required all amateur sets to be surrendered to the police. This had provoked some opposition from the London Wireless Society, whose spokesman, Frank Hope Jones, complained that his members might have been mobilized to intercept illegal transmissions. There were a number of misunderstandings about the confiscation of experimental wireless apparatus during the first weeks of the war because several private radio masts merely had been disconnected by the police and not been completely dismantled. In some cases the GPO had declined to remove equipment from private homes and had settled on sealing up the aerial sockets, with the additional precaution of a fortnightly inspection. The explanation for this apparent complacency was a reluctance on the part of the GPO to take items of expensive and sensitive apparatus into custody. This view was neither shared nor understood by the police or the services, who themselves had only a vague grasp of the potential of wireless. On one memorable occasion, an overzealous officer from HMS *Vernon* caused a considerable fuss over a radio mast he had spotted on private land in a secluded part of Hampshire. He was only placated by an assurance that the aerial was unserviceable.

Curiously, dealers in wireless equipment were allowed to continue their business, and there was no restriction placed on the sale of radio components. The Admiralty noted on September 23, 1914, that there was little point in licensing these retailers or prohibiting the open sale of apparatus because any competent person could construct a wireless and conceal its aerial if they really wished to do so.

By the end of August 1914, 2,500 licensed experimental stations had been dealt with and a further 750 unlicensed sets had been discovered and dismantled by the GPO. The chief problem remaining was the matter of enforcement. Since the Post Office was virtually the only national organization which understood the principles of wireless telegraphy, it had been agreed that the GPO would be responsible for ensuring that the Defense Regulations were obeyed. The Admiralty was in a position to feel quite confident about such a division of responsibility because the chief of the Post Office's Wireless Branch was a former Royal Naval officer, Commander Loring. Inevitably, the police stumbled on a few private wireless sets, and sometimes these haphazard lines of demarcation became confused. In one celebrated incident a respected academic, Professor Schuster, was prosecuted by the police after the GPO had sealed his apparatus. Following several lengthy meetings at the Admiralty and the Post Office, it was formally agreed that GPO engineers engaged on wireless detection work should liaise more closely with their local police forces, and that Colonel Kell's Security service, MO5, would ensure the cooperation of the military authorities. In spite of these measures, isolated cases of overlapping authority continued to occur, prompting angry correspondence between MO5, the GPO and the police. One complication was Kell's lack of a nationwide organization. The local police or GPO had no idea whom to approach with information concerning a suspected illicit transmitter, so MO5 undertook to appoint a security officer in every home garrison and to distribute his particulars. This ambitious exercise took some months to complete and only became available in March 1915.

Actual surveillance of the airwaves remained in the GPO's jurisdiction, and by the end of September 1914 forty-four stations had been set up to monitor transmissions. Twenty-four were naval stations, with Marconi and the Post Office operating ten each. In the opinion of the Postmaster General, it was "almost impossible for an illicit sending station to escape detection." These forty stations fell under the supervision of the Admiralty's Intelligence Division, but as the summer wore on Whitehall came under increasing pressure to accept offers of help from radio amateurs. Offers were received from hundreds of self-styled experts, many of whom had succumbed to the spy-fever then prevalent. MO5 was perturbed that "the question was first raised by Mr. R.H. Klein, who is a naturalized British subject." Were there sinister implications? More serious approaches were made by Alan Campbell Swinton, president of the Wireless Society, Dr. J. Erskine-Murray, an eminent scientist who had written many of the standard textbooks on the subject, and William Duddell, the recently retired president of the Institute of Electrical Engineers. At first, all these approaches were turned down, with the comment that "the successful detection of illicit Wireless Telegraphy Stations depends on the careful collation of relevant observations; and it is obvious that a small and select body of observers can give much better results than a very large number who have not the necessary knowledge of the circumstances." Statements such as this merely served to alarm the radio amateurs, who were anyway convinced of the government's profound ignorance of wireless. Commander Loring, for the Post Office, argued that a wholesale, total ban on private apparatus was the best policy. He contended that the public knew that no one was allowed any equipment, and this enabled newly erected aerials to be spotted quickly. However, pressure continued to build, especially in journals like *The Electrician*, and eventually it was judged that to ignore offers of assistance from distinguished sources would be "impolitic." On October 29, 1914, the Admiralty informed the GPO that "public uneasiness may grow and pressure be put on the government to unseal certain private installations which it might be difficult to resist." Accordingly, Alan Campbell Swinton was admitted into the Admiralty's Intelligence Division. This enabled him to make a public statement reassuring the membership of the Wireless Society that "the authorities are taking all needful steps to prevent illicit wireless telegraphy being used to the detriment of this country."

Alan Campbell Swinton's reassurance did little to persuade Britain's patriotic amateurs that the government knew what it was doing, and by the end of November 1914 the GPO had become increasingly alarmed at the amount of newspaper space devoted to criticizing the apparent reluctance of the authorities to harness the abundant amateur radio talent available. On November 12, 1914, the *Daily Telegraph* printed an article headed "Wireless Spying":

> Wireless telegraphy conferred a boon upon mankind, but it is not without its dangers in times of international complications. A representative of the *Daily Telegraph* was yesterday shown messages originating in Germany, France and the North Sea, which some time ago were received at a private wireless station in the West-end. Like the telephone when it was in its infancy, the wireless system attracted many amateurs and experimentalists, and numbers of aerials were erected. In time of war these installations may be used against the public weal. They may also be brought to serve in the best interests of the Empire by "catching" stray messages intended for the enemy.

This was the first time that signals intelligence had been advocated in a public forum as a practical counterintelligence weapon. Certainly it contributed to the embarrassingly large clamor for a nationwide system of radio vigilantes. On the same day the *Daily Chronicle* observed, "Of the many forms of espionage adopted by Germany, the use of wireless telegraphy was one that, in the hands of competent operators, promised many profitable results to the enemy." Eventually, the scale of the protests proved impossible to ignore and a compromise was hit upon: a select group of amateurs known to the main wireless societies would be enrolled as special constables and be given radio duties. Each was obliged to swear a "wireless pledge," the first of its kind anywhere, to

> solemnly and sincerely declare that I will not improperly divulge to any person the purport of any message which I may transmit or receive by means of any wireless telegraphic apparatus operated by me or which may come to my knowledge in connection with the operation of the said telegraphic apparatus.

The scheme aimed to recruit two amateur experts in every large town in the country, and it was hoped that this would allay the fears of the amateur community and at the same time provide the police with some technical advice. The project was greeted with delight by the Wireless Society, which undertook to recommend suitable candidates for recruitment, but there were several unforeseen difficulties. A large number of the Wireless Society's members turned out to be in the police already, and when a circular was prepared for the sixteen or so other radio clubs, only seven bothered to reply; the secretaries of the rest had already joined up.

Although the plan to enroll radio amateurs seemed, on the face of it, attractive, the police raised plenty of objections. The chief constable of Leeds spoke for many of his colleagues when he stated in a confidential minute to the Home Office, in January 1915:

> It seems very undesirable that men of doubtful qualifications, under no Departmental control, and without proper standard ideas of the ranges of wireless apparatus, should cooperate directly with the Police and without the aid of any Post Office representative in the investigation of matters with which the Postmaster General is intimately concerned.

It was in answer to criticism like this that the political nature of the decision to recruit amateurs was revealed. In one note the GPO secretariat commented: "The period of great pressure in Wireless matters was when the thousands of stations were being dismantled at the beginning of the war. Several of the selected people had unauthorized stations at the beginning of the war!" These exchanges seem, in retrospect, to be fairly academic, bearing in mind that virtually all parties were entirely agreed that there was actually no real risk of illicit radio transmissions. The exercise appears now to have been nothing more than a demonstration of the political power wielded by the amateur fraternity, and the relative intransigence of the GPO and the police. Many of the lessons learned by the government during the first few months of the war, and in particular by Colonel Kell's Security Service, were well taken and later used to advantage by the Committee of Imperial Defense for its contingency plans. The initial confusion caused by poorly defined areas of responsibility among the various authorities was not to be repeated in the Second World War when, as shall be seen, much of the Radio Society of Great Britain was drafted into a highly secret branch of Kell's department, known as the Radio Security Service. Suffice it to say that, in spite of the precautions taken between August and December 1914, not a single case of espionage involving a wireless was reported in the United Kingdom while hostilities lasted.

There were, of course, plenty of false alarms. Sir Basil Thomson, who was then Assistant Commissioner (Crime) at Scotland Yard in charge of the Special Branch, later recalled one hilarious incident:

The authorities dispatched to the Eastern Counties a car equipped with a Marconi apparatus and two skilled operators to intercept any illicit messages that might be passing over the North Sea. They left London at noon; at 3 they were under lock and key in Essex. After an exchange of telegrams they were set free, but at 7 P.M. they telegraphed from the police cells in another part of the county, imploring help. When again liberated they refused to move without the escort of a Territorial officer in uniform, but on the following morning the police of another county had got hold of them and telegraphed, ''Three German spies arrested with car and complete wireless installation, one in uniform of British officer.''[8]

On another memorable occasion, a full-scale raid was launched by the GPO to detect the war's first wireless spy. The suspect, named Farager, was believed to be operating from military premises, namely a barracks in Dover, and the mistaken raid prompted the following curt rebuke from Kell on November 18, 1914:

A case has been reported to the Army Council where a man's premises were searched by Post Office officials for what was believed to be an unlicensed wireless station, without first informing the Fortress Commander of their intention to do so.

It is essential that the military authority concerned should know of any suspected person living within his command, and it would therefore appear desirable if in future the General Post Office officials would first communicate with the officer concerned before taking any active steps. Would you therefore take the matter up on these lines, with a view to this policy being adopted in future cases, if possible?[9]

In spite of the occasional internal disputes between the Security service, the police and the GPO over who should investigate breaches of the wartime ban on radio amateurs, the exact nature of the threat, and the secret measures taken to enforce the Defense Regulations, were never made public. Ferdinand Tuohy observed, in his postwar history of the Intelligence Corps, *The Secret Corps*:

Though at the beginning of the war the Allies possessed no effective system of policing unauthorized wireless, and messages of grave consequence may have actually been sent out by spies, on the other hand it should be borne in mind that the working of a wireless transmitting apparatus is in itself no light matter. Petrol and a motor are only two of the requisites necessary, and the difficulty in obtaining the former was as serious an obstacle as was the likelihood of the engine being overheard.[10]

In retrospect, the precautions taken in 1914 had a ludicrous flavor, but the history of wireless was moving apace. In a few short years, Guglielmo Marconi had offered his apparatus to Britain and seen the response. To a fellow countryman the interdepartmental wranglings might have been expected. Indeed, an English inventor or entrepreneur might have been disappointed if Whitehall had let him down and showed enthusiasm for his technological breakthrough; but for a foreigner, and a volatile Italian at that, to peddle his extraordinary apparatus and then have to watch the embattled services indulge in lengthy debates and refer difficult questions to a protracted committee system, that was itself beyond the understanding of the most sophisticated of men. The army seemed anxious only to protect its cable links with the Empire; the Admiralty determined only to cling to its superiority and to avoid falling behind the developments made in other countries.

Once war had become a reality, the bureaucrats responded in typical fashion: first banning the wireless amateurs; then prosecuting them; finally enrolling them and claiming all the credit. The key to the future of SIGINT lay with Colonel Edmonds and his recommendation that a list be compiled of those willing to be trained in the arcane arts of encryption, decryption, censorship, analysis and, most valued of all, interception.

2

The Great War

Science has certainly made war a strange thing.

—E.W.B. GILL in *War, Wireless and Wangles*

The reports written by Colonel Edmonds as head of Section H, now renamed MO5, for the Committee of Imperial Defense in the years before 1914 emphasized the advantages to be gained from combining censorship with intelligence. He pointed out that during the Boer War numerous opportunities had been lost because two vital functions had been dealt with separately. Apart from the regular mails, which could be handled by the GPO, external communications fell into two categories: those dependent upon landline and underwater cables, and those (relatively few in number) that were transmitted from station to station by means of wireless telegraphy. The War Office's MO5 dealt with them by drafting a paper entitled "Regulations for Censorship of Submarine Cable Communications and Certain Frontier Land Lines Throughout the British Empire and of Radio-Telegraphy in Overseas Possessions and Protectorates," which was followed by an addition to the CID's War Book entitled "Memoranda on the action to be taken by His Majesty's government."

The secret arrangements proposed by the War Book were comprehensive and were executed at exactly six o'clock in the evening on Sunday, August 2, 1914. All external cables were channeled through thirteen special centers administered by the GPO, but responsible to the War Office, where preselected clerks exercised total control over information leaving the United Kingdom. At the War Office the Chief Cable Censor designate was Colonel Arthur Churchill, a retired staff officer who had previously served as the British military attaché with the Japanese forces in China in 1900. The War Book allocated him a staff of twelve officers, twenty-five clerks and forty typists, forming four subsections: MI8(a), dealing with questions of policy including wireless traffic; MI8(b), based at the GPO and handling commercial and trade cables; MI8(c), which distributed the intelligence obtained from censorship; and MI8(d), responsible for liaising with the private cable companies. Churchill was also lent the services of two special advisers, R.J. Mackay from the GPO and Commander John Tyre RN from the Admiralty, each of whom would liaise with their own organizations. After war was declared, it became necessary to appoint Montagu Norman as a trade adviser from the Bank of England.

Because, over the preceding eight years, the Admiralty had developed close links with the Marconi organization, the censorship of wireless telegraphy was left to the navy and the Chief Censor of Radio-Telegraphy. The person nominated for this post was Commodore Sir Douglas Brownrigg, an officer who, before his retirement in 1913, had been the British naval attaché in Tokyo. The Admiralty's idea was that Brownrigg would sift through the messages submitted by Marconi's. After reading the few slim volumes available on the subject, Brownrigg set about privately recruiting his own staff. His first two assistants were Commander Thomas Crease RN and Lieutenant Cyprian Bridge RN, both retired officers who had gone into business.

While Colonel Churchill made the final preparations for his takeover of Britain's communications, Brownrigg dispatched Bridge and Crease to the Marconi transatlantic relay stations at Poldhu Point, overlooking Mullion in Cornwall, and at Clifden in County Galway, Ireland. They soon discovered that no suitable accommodation had been provided for them. They were required, initially at least, to be on duty for twenty-four hours a day, monitoring Marconi's traffic, so some flimsy tents were erected hastily beside the stations. An additional ten staff were recruited from various shipbuilding concerns, including Cammell Laird and the Fairfield Shipbuilding Company, and, after the first few uncomfortable weeks, Marconi's general manager, Mr. Bradfield, arranged more suitable housing for the censors and their stenographers.

By May 1915, Brownrigg had set up his main central organization at Room 37, Old Admiralty Building, where they were handling up to eight hundred cables a day. All were read either by the Chief Censor himself or his deputy, Commander the Honorable Gerald Digby. Specialized cables which seemed dubious were referred to Captain Richard Webb of the Admiralty's Trade Division, where he employed several liaison officers, each an expert in his own field. A suspicious insurance cable would be read by Mr. Bilborough (seconded from Lloyd's of London), while commodity imports were examined by Commander F. Leverton Harris RNVR.

Later in the war, both the stations at Poldhu and Clifden were brought under direct Admiralty control. Clifden was eventually closed down on August 4, 1917, so as to eliminate all commercial transatlantic traffic and reduce the risk of leaks concerning American troop movements.

Once the preliminary arrangements as described by the War Book had been carried out, it remained for Colonel Churchill to enforce the new Defense Regulations and prevent any leakages. His first unforeseen crisis concerned the use of private codes. At that time there was no government agency involved in the business of cryptanalysis, so Churchill demanded that all domestic and international cable traffic should be transmitted *en clair*. There was an immediate howl of protest from numerous commercial enterprises who routinely conducted their confidential business in some form of cipher in order to protect their trade secrets from their rivals. It is a measure of the British government's determination to protect international trade that both the GPO and the Board of Trade were persuaded to intercede with Churchill. A compromise was reached whereby certain reputable firms could lodge copies of their private ciphers with the Board of Trade and continue to code their messages.

The major flaw in the War Book's arrangements concerned postal censorship. The Committee of Imperial Defense had never contemplated a system of censoring private letters, except in those rare cases where the Home Secretary had signed an interception warrant. Churchill quickly pointed out that the scheme to cover the cable traffic would be entirely wasted if the mails were to go unchecked. The War Office and Admiralty agreed, so, somewhat belatedly, a small room in the War Office was found for a recently retired Foreign Office official, Mr. George Pearson, who was appointed the Chief Postal Censor. By the end of the year, Pearson had been commissioned with the rank of colonel and presided over a censorship staff of 60 women and 110 men, based at an office in Liverpool and Strand House in London. By the end of the war, Pearson's organization had grown to employ a total of 4,861 censors.

Although Colonel Edmonds had made a series of prewar recommendations concerning the control of cable traffic, he had effectively left all matters relating to wireless in the hands of the Admiralty. This was not entirely surprising, considering that up to 1914 the army had taken minimal interest in the subject, allocating its few Marconi sets to the cavalry on the grounds that only they would have need of them in any future conflict. Within three months of war breaking out, it had become painfully obvious that the textbooks would have to be rewritten. Instead of fighting a highly mobile war on limited fronts with cavalry supported by light field guns, there was a continuous, static front extending from Nieuwpoort on the Belgian coast southward to the Swiss frontier. Far from relying on mounted units, the cavalry were dismounted and had been redeployed in trenches, supported by concentrations of heavy artillery. For the British General Staff, the war showed no signs of going according to plan. Communications along the Western Front were so bad, with scarcely a telegraph line left intact after each enemy bombardment, that the Director of Army Signals was eventually forced to resort to the many hundreds of privately owned pigeons kept around St. Omer. By the end of the war, the Signal Service was employing more than 20,000 pigeons to carry messages.

Like the rest of the army, the Royal Engineers Signal Service was quite unprepared for modern war. The 2nd Divisional Signal Company, which went to France with the British Expeditionary Force (BEF), consisted of 5 officers and 170 other ranks in three field sections and one headquarters section. Each section was subdivided into three cable attachments, which consisted of one officer and twenty-six other ranks. Each was equipped with a horse-drawn cable layer, some ancient telephones and a backup visual system. A wireless section was not added until 1917.

The Royal Engineers were equally unprepared for the stream of experienced GPO volunteers who arrived at the RE recruiting centers at Birmingham and Bradford. A newly formed Reserve Signal Depot was set up at Aldershot and then, to ease the pressure still further, Colonel R.H.H. Boys, who had been wounded in France, formed a Signal Training Center at Ridgmont, near Woburn Abbey. Gradually the Signal Service began to expand and additional depots were later formed at Hitchin and Stevenage. Once recruits had been accepted at these holding depots, they were assigned to specialized training centers in Bedfordshire. The Army Signal School was now moved to Houghton Regis and a wireless school was set up at Fenny Stratford to train instructors. Moving with speed, the Royal Engineers increased their Signals Units from 17 to 110 in the first twelve months of the war.

As already mentioned, the only people with wireless equipment in France in 1914 were the cavalry. They had a cable troop, a visual and dispatch rider troop and a wireless troop, with three Marconi sets mounted on wagons, attached to each division and each brigade. It had been hoped that the cavalry would have been highly mobile and so been able to make use of their excellent communications setup. But they were dismounted, dug in and bogged down in static trench warfare like everyone else. Advances were counted in yards rather than miles and the front line was subject to endless heavy gunfire; under these conditions wireless sets were not a reliable means of relaying instructions to the front line from headquarters and back again. Standard telegraph landlines buried three feet deep carrying messages by buzzer or vibrator were much more effective.

However, some of the wireless sections closest to the German positions continued to keep their equipment in working order and they made the discovery that the enemy was generating a considerable volume of wireless traffic. When this was reported, it served to reinforce GHQ's reservations concerning the security of wireless signals and, as Major-General R.F. Nalder later commented in his history of the *Royal Corps of Signals*: "Wireless sections therefore turned their attention to other fields and before long were almost exclusively used for intercepting enemy transmissions, with appreciable success."[1]

At this early stage in the war the army had had absolutely no experience of signals intelligence, and reports of the German intercepts were channeled to GHQ in St. Omer which authorized the construction, in October 1914, of a wireless compass by two Marconi technicians who had been seconded to intelligence duties. H.C. Round and C.S. Franklin had both worked on frequency amplifiers before the outbreak of war, and Round, now commissioned with the rank of lieutenant, had been invited by the War Office to continue his direction-finding project in France, at Blendecques. Work on the system had been pioneered at a recently established station located on the Wiltshire Downs above Devizes. According to the results obtained with a group of six high masts, it was perfectly possible to determine the origin of a radio signal by comparing the receiving strengths on an array of aerials constructed in a circle. The aerial closest to the source would get the best reception and, if the result was compared with that obtained at another station, bearings could be taken which gave a reasonably accurate fix for the transmitter's location. Round took his seventy-foot masts to France in December 1914 and built a second station near Abbeville. This was elementary direction finding (DF), and when a Bellini Tosi, the first valve receiver, was incorporated, the compass betrayed the exact positions of the enemy's wireless. When DF results from Abbeville were compared with the content of the intercepted enemy messages in January 1915, it became clear that particular stations and call signs were associated with identifiable military formations. By analyzing the wireless traffic, the BEF was frequently able to identify certain German units and plot their movements, if not actually monitor their orders. Delighted by the preliminary results, Round moved his base line to Calais-Amiens and greatly increased the range and accuracy of the apparatus. The War Office rewarded him with a special landline to GHQ.

Further experiments were conducted during 1915 in the St. Pol area by Captain Rupert Stanley, formerly the Professor of Electrical Engineering at Belfast University who had published the standard *Textbook on Wireless Telegraphy* in 1914. In addition to being a wireless expert, he had also made a study of German developments in the field and, before the war, had actually visited Nauen, where he had sketched the 900-foot aerial and had examined the massive steel umbrella radiating from the top of the mast. Stanley was assisted in his experiments by a young Signals NCO, Ronald Nesbitt-Hawes (who was later knighted and appointed Director of Posts and Telegraphs in Burma). Their apparatus, which was known as the "I-Tock," was a combination of two V-shaped earth aerials connected to a three-valve receiver. During the first tests carried out by Stanley and Nesbitt-Hawes, enemy telephone conversations were heard at a range of 100 yards. The initial excitement was soon tempered with caution when it was learned that the Germans were also intercepting Allied buzzer signals by using a low-resistance telephone receiver connected to a good earth. The German telephone tappers had perfected a system which enabled them to overhear plans being discussed, without a physical attachment to the Allied cables. This discovery, which coincided with some unofficial monitoring of Allied conversations by the wireless experimenters, proved that the Germans had obtained vital intelligence concerning future engagements from the indiscretion of senior officers. When this lamentable state of affairs was reported to GHQ, all phone speech was banned within 3,000 yards of the front line. Major-General Nalder later commented:

> . . . step by step the countermeasures were tightened. But the main obstacle throughout the process was the frequent disregard by telephone users of the orders relating to forbidden subjects, the worst offenders being often the more senior officers who had most to give away. It is no exaggeration to say that thousands of casualties resulted from these indiscretions during the course of 1915 and 1916, and it

was not until 1917 that the countermeasures became reasonably effective.

This was the birth of modern signals intelligence, or SIGINT, and its potential was not lost on the War Office's intelligence establishment which, at that moment, was undergoing reorganization at the hands of the Secretary of State for War, Lord Kitchener.

Under Kitchener's new administration, the post of Director of Military Intelligence (DMI), which had been abandoned in 1904, was reintroduced and Colonel (Sir) George Macdonogh appointed. The BEF in France also acquired a Director of Intelligence, and this post fell to a Royal Engineers major, John Charteris. His organization was based at GHQ Montreuil and formed Britain's first military unit dedicated to SIGINT. The new department came under the supervision of Colonel Macdonogh and his deputy, George Cockerill, who, it will be remembered, had compiled a dictionary of military terms at the CID's request before the war. The day-to-day operations were in the hands of a Royal Marines colonel, Arthur French, who had won the DSO during the defense of Antwerp. His MI1 organization also contained a subdivision, MI1(e), which initially was composed of Colonel Adrian Simpson and two seconded officers who were German scholars. During the winter of 1916, the army had responded to the enemy's increasing use of landlines as an alternative to wireless signaling by developing a system of "listening sets." The first had been acquired from the French and had enabled intelligence officers at the front to eavesdrop on conversations conveyed by German telegraph lines up to 3,000 yards away. Eventually, the army built a service of thirty "IT" sets, presided over by an Inspector of Listening Sets who had responsibility for intercepting the enemy's signals and monitoring Allied communications. The resulting SIGINT was sent to a special GHQ cipher bureau at Le Touquet for analysis and action by Oswald Hitchings's staff. Elsewhere, the War Office had created an organization that often paralleled that of the Admiralty, although in England Colonel French's chief preoccupation was monitoring the enemy's airships. A small network of direction-finding stations located at Leiston in Suffolk, Devizes in Wiltshire and on the roof of the War Office, intercepted signals from zeppelins. All were linked to Room 417 at the War Office, where the DF bearings were plotted on four separate map tables. In the field of cryptanalysis there was further evidence of wasteful duplication. During the course of 1916, MI1(b) had acquired the services of Major Malcolm Hay, a recently repatriated prisoner of war (and a noted historian) who gathered a large number of academics into the Intelligence Corps at 5 Cork Street, Mayfair, and eventually accumulated a staff of fifty officers, supported by thirty female clerical assistants. Among them were J. St. Vincent Pletts from Marconi, Professors Arthur Hunt, David Margoliouth and John Fraser (from Oxford) and (Sir) Ellis Minns, Zachary Brooke and Professor Norman Jopson (from Cambridge).

Their task was to carry the Signal Service's achievements a stage further by studying its intercepts and developing the science of "traffic analysis." Meanwhile, another decryption unit, MI1(e), was set up in London with a view to breaking the enemy's codes.

At the War Office, Brigadier Anderson at MI1(b) soon began to receive useful information from his French Allies, for the French had been able to pick up German military wireless signals during the Marne offensive at the very beginning of the war. Both von Kluck and von Bülow had relied upon wireless telegraphy to communicate with the General Staff at Koblenz while conducting their invasion of Belgium, but they had encountered a number of unforeseen difficulties. One problem was the unsuitability of the German military cipher, which was based on a relatively simple substitution-transposition system ($a = k$, $b = j$, etc.). This was a proven method of encoding messages, but a single error tended to corrupt an entire text. Under battle conditions the system frequently broke down, causing German operators to repeat the same message, perhaps as many as ten times, and it was not unknown for German operators to resort to clear language in their frustration. This presented the Allies with a splendid opportunity, and the French Ministry of War in particular was swift to take advantage of the situation. A group of French cryptographers were gathered under the leadership of Colonel François Cartier, and included Major Marcel Givierge and the eminent criminologist Dr. Edmond Locard. By the end of August 1914, they were reading a sizable quantity of the German military traffic, and the Ministry of War had started work on the development of a chain of intercept stations based at existing fortresses along France's eastern frontier. As the confidence of the French grew, more information was pooled with Brigadier Anderson's MI1(b) at the War Office and Sir Alfred Ewing at the Admiralty.

The Admiralty had made some startling discoveries in the first few weeks of the war. During the summer of 1914, the Director of Naval Intelligence (DNI), Admiral Oliver, began receiving reports of what were believed to be German wireless signals from the Post Office's radio station at Stockton, near Lowestoft. Similar reports reached the Admiralty from

Colonel Richard Hippisley RE, formerly the Director of Telegraphs in South Africa. Hippisley had returned to England in 1902 and had been Chief Engineer, Scottish Command, until his retirement in 1910. He had retained an interest in wireless and held an amateur license to operate with the call sign HLX. He and another radio enthusiast, a barrister from Abergavenny named Russell Clarke (call sign THX), had isolated a number of regular signals from what they suspected were the German naval stations at Neumünster and Norddeich. Their report was passed to the Admiralty's Intelligence Division and considered by Oliver and Commanders William Kettlewell and Alldin Moore, the two officers who had represented the DNI on the CID subcommittee which had been set up to deal with illegal wireless stations.

As we have seen, the GPO and the military authorities had always resisted the idea of employing amateurs to police the airwaves. The forty-four government-controlled stations were considered more than adequate to cope with any hypothetical illicit signals. The GPO had insisted that the stations

> are organized in such a way that a constant watch is maintained over the whole practicable range of wavelengths. It is almost impossible that an illicit station could be worked without detection by one or other of these stations. Nevertheless in order to leave nothing to chance, it was agreed that the Engineer-in-Chief at the Post Office should establish special watching stations in addition in different parts of the country from time to time. As indicated on the annexed report on the results of this work, nothing has been observed up to the present to give rise to suspicion, and it seems virtually certain that no station has been engaged in illicit signaling since the war began. There remains the possibility that some secret stations may be in existence ready to establish communication with the enemy at some critical time; but it is considered that the present organization is adequate to ensure that the existence of such illicit communication would be quickly detected.[2]

In spite of this complacency, the influential radio amateurs had pressed their case and Alan Campbell Swinton had been taken on by the Admiralty in order to placate the wireless fraternity. But the GPO's Engineer-in-Chief had raised one valid criticism concerning the official use of amateurs: "It would be impossible, in view of the large amount of legitimate signaling constantly in progress, for amateur observers to render useful assistance unless their work was very carefully organized by some central authority."[3] Although the GPO did not realize it at the time, this conclusion was seized on by the NID which saw itself in the role of the suggested "central authority." The DNI already possessed two officers, Kettlewell and Moore, who had acquainted themselves with the problems of wireless. In addition, they had access to Hippisley and Clarke, who were anxious to obtain permission to continue their monitoring of the German signals. All that was needed was a coordinating body to interpret the intercepted signals traffic. Admiral Oliver had no hesitation in turning for help to Sir Alfred Ewing, a diminutive Scottish academic who then held the post of Director of Naval Education at Dartmouth.

Ewing himself was no stranger to wireless, having patented an "electromagnetic wave detector" some years earlier and having addressed the Royal Society in 1904 on the subject of identifying the electric oscillations that occur during wireless transmissions. Perhaps even more significantly, Ewing had recently been preoccupied with ciphers and had already been consulted by the Admiralty about the construction of secure codes for British naval vessels. The DNI suggested that Ewing's education duties should "lapse" for the duration of the war and, as Ewing was "a man of brains," he should turn his attention to the NID's existing collection of intercepts and determine whether any sense could be made of them. According to Ewing's son, who published his father's biography in 1939, a fruitless search was made at Lloyd's and the British Museum to trace any old German commercial code books which might shed light on current coding practices. Several were turned up, but it was not for some months that Ewing's work showed any signs of success.

Meanwhile, at Ewing's suggestion, Oliver authorized Hippisley and Clarke to set up their equipment in the coast guard hut at Hunstanton, on the Wash, the site of an existing but primitive Admiralty station, in the belief that this site would improve the quality of the intercepted signals, especially those originating from Flanders. In September 1914, they were joined by another radio amateur, Leslie Lambert, who was later to become well known as a BBC broadcaster under the pseudonym A.J. Allen. Together these three amateurs began a tradition, albeit a secret one: they were the first of those who were to become known in intelligence circles as "voluntary interceptors" (VIs), men whose work was to prove vital in two world wars.

Hippisley and Clarke found that interception conditions across the North Sea were good and that there was a remarkably large amount of German wireless traffic going on, both diplomatic and naval, for the

Admiralty had taken steps at the beginning of the war to isolate Germany's cable communications system, as the Kaiser had always feared would happen. Upon the outbreak of war, Admiral Sir Henry Jackson had formally refused German access to British cable systems. This had been followed by rather more aggressive action: the *Telconia*, one of Britain's fleet of thirty-seven cable layers, received orders to dredge for the five German transatlantic telegraph cables off Emden and sever them. Three days later HMS *Anstraea* bombarded the German wireless station at Dar-es-Salaam, and soon afterward HMS *Minotaur* destroyed the station at Yap in the Caroline Islands. HMAS *Melbourne* dealt with the station at Nauru and a force from New Zealand occupied the station on Samoa. In Africa two special missions, from Nigeria and the Gold Coast, invaded Togoland and blew up the German transmitter at Kamina; Rabaul and Augaur in the Pacific were also eliminated, and on September 27 a joint Anglo-French expedition knocked out the station at Duala in the Cameroons. By the end of the month, only two enemy stations remained intact: Windhoek in German Southwest Africa and Tsingtao on the Yellow Sea coast of China. Windhoek did not fall until May 1915, but the Japanese took Tsingtao on November 7, 1914. In a swift and well-coordinated series of operations, Germany's communications with her overseas possessions had been severely truncated. Apart from the telegraph landlines to neutral Sweden, Denmark and Holland (and so through their transatlantic cables), and her allies in Austro-Hungary and Turkey, Berlin was forced to communicate with the Kaiser's envoys abroad via the vulnerable surface mails and the chief long-distance radio station at Nauen, which had been taken over by the Foreign Ministry. Both these methods offered scope for obtaining an intelligence advantage, and the Committee of Imperial Defense opted to allow Nauen's transmissions to continue uninterrupted rather than order the German signals to be jammed.

Gradually, those working at Hunstanton mastered the German wireless techniques and call signs and began supplying Ewing in London with a growing volume of intercepted material. However, Ewing himself was unable to make much progress on the enciphered groups; he therefore obtained the services of three additional German-speaking volunteers, all masters from the naval training colleges of Dartmouth and Osborne. They were E.J.C. Green, G.L.N. Hope and A.G. Denniston, and they set to work studying British and German commercial ciphers. Two of these individuals, Hope and Denniston, were to exert a major influence on the development of Britain's SIGINT capability, and the latter, undoubtedly one of the most remarkable men of his generation, was eventually to become Britain's first official, peacetime cryptanalyst.

Although christened Alexander, Denniston used the name Alastair. At the time of his transfer from Osborne, on the Isle of Wight, to the Admiralty, he was just thirty-two years old. The son of a Glasgow general practitioner who had died of tuberculosis at the young age of forty-two, he had been educated at Bowden College in Cheshire, at Bonn University and at the Sorbonne. He had also helped his mother bring up his brother and sister, both of whom had become doctors. In 1909, he had been appointed an assistant master at Merchiston Castle School, having played hockey for Scotland in the Olympics. Three years later, he had gone to Osborne as a teacher of foreign languages. Denniston himself believed his posting was to be of a temporary nature, but events (and history) were to overtake him.

When Denniston joined Ewing, he had just moved into Room 40 of the Old Admiralty Buildings at the instigation of the new DNI, Admiral Reginald "Blinker" Hall, who had recently succeeded Admiral Oliver. Room 40 was very cramped, but a system of watches was introduced and the linguists set about studying the incoming intercepts and filing them on cards. Delivered by post and messenger and addressed simply "Ewing, Admiralty," the intercepts arrived in prodigious numbers, sometimes up to 2,000 a day. The watches became a shift system, which enabled the self-styled cryptologists to perform their duties under the supervision of Ewing or two other specially recruited "watchkeepers," a retired Foreign Office man, R.D. Norton, and the second Baron Herschell. Lord Herschell's appointment to such a sensitive position has long been a matter of speculation, considering his apparent lack of qualifications. The son of Gladstone's Lord Chancellor, he had succeeded to his father's title upon his death in 1899, at the age of twenty-one, and had served as Lord Aberdeen's private secretary during the latter's tenure as Lord Lieutenant of Ireland. In 1907, he had become a Lord in Waiting to King Edward VII, and then to King George V. The only clue to a reason for his move to the Admiralty is his London address, 3 Whitehall Court. His neighbor at 2 Whitehall Court happened to be Mansfield Smith-Cumming, the first chief of the Secret Intelligence service. It may well be that Dick Herschell was an SIS nominee. In any event, neither he nor any other member of Ewing's team was able to decode, translate or solve any of the intercepts until the first breakthrough occurred, which took place following an incident in the Baltic on September 6, 1914.

On that date the Russian naval attaché informed the Admiralty that a German naval code book, number 151 of the *Signalbuch der Kaiserlichen Marine* (SKM), had been recovered from the *Magdeburg*, a German light cruiser that had run aground in fog a week earlier while being engaged by two Russian warships, the *Pallada* and the *Bogatyr*. The Russians generously offered their prize to the British Admiralty, and on October 10 two Imperial Navy officers arrived at Scapa Flow on board HMS *Theseus* to deliver the SKM to the First Lord, Winston Churchill, who promptly passed it on to Ewing. Ewing and his staff took three weeks to trace the *Magdeburg*'s codes in the Hunstanton intercepts; having done this, they were able to gain access, albeit retrospectively, to a quantity of German naval messages bearing the call sign KAV. This station was identified as Norddeich. Once the texts had been traced and deciphered, they had to be translated into English and their technical terms made clear. Credit for doing this was due to Fleet-Paymaster Charles Rotter, whose father had been born in Germany but had become a naturalized British subject. In 1911, Charles Rotter had been transferred to intelligence duties and had become NID's resident expert on the Kaiser's navy. His excellent knowledge of German naval terms not only enabled him to decipher the KAV messages but also to solve the "reciphering key" which had hitherto eluded Ewing. Once translated the messages turned out to be of only minor importance, consisting in the main of weather reports, but they were the first complete decrypts made by Room 40 and offered an invaluable insight into German procedures. As a reward for his achievement, Rotter was made a Companion of the Bath.

A further, useful development which coincided with Rotter's work on the *SKM* was the delivery of a package of photographed enemy documents from the Australian Naval Board. These documents had been seized from the German steamer *Hobart* in Australia at the outbreak of hostilities and included copy number 369 of the *Handelsverkehrsbuch* (*HVB*), the code book used by German merchantmen and some units of the High Seas Fleet. Although the *HVB* had been confiscated early in August, it did not reach Room 40 from Melbourne until the end of October, but its arrival was warmly welcomed.

As soon as it had become clear that SIGINT from the *SKM* and *HVB* captured code books was likely to yield useful information, the Admiralty imposed the first restrictions on its dissemination. The First Lord of the Admiralty, Winston Churchill, and the First Sea Lord, Lord Fisher, directed that an officer

> be selected to study all the decoded intercepts, not only current but past, and to compare them continually with what actually took place in order to penetrate the German mind and movements and make reports. All these intercepts are to be written in a locked book with

their decodes and all other copies are to be collected and burned. All
new messages are to be entered in the book, and the book is only to
be handled under direction from COS [Chief of Staff]. The officer
selected is for the present to do no other work.[4]

The importance of SIGINT had at last been gathered, but not its
scope and range. It quickly became clear that the *Magdeburg*'s code book
was one of several currently in use and, fortuitously, a second book, the
Verkehrsbuch (*VB*), was acquired on November 30 and delivered to the
Admiralty. Apparently, the book was one of several important documents
found inside a lead-lined sea chest which had been scooped up by a
British trawler operating in the North Sea. The chest had been jettisoned
by the commander of the German destroyer S119, which had been engaged by British forces on October 17 and sunk. Possession of both code
books was a tremendous boon to Ewing's staff. Their increase in status
was further recognized by making Ewing and his men an official subsection of the Naval Intelligence Division, entitled NID 25.

Comparative analysis of the three captured documents, *SKM, HVB*
and *VB*, shed dramatic light on the German Admiralstab's coding procedures and revealed the basic principles employed by the enemy to
change their cipher keys. Commonly used naval words were listed against
a series of five-figure groups, each constructed in a column. The advantage
of the system was its adaptability: the choice of column could be switched
as often as required. The system's flaw lay in the fact that the correct
identification of a single five-figure group immediately betrayed the column from which it had been selected, and thus enabled the decrypter to
solve the remaining groups. Once this fundamental had been grasped by
Ewing's team, they were able to intercept and decrypt much of the enemy's naval signals traffic. The Admiralty was sufficiently impressed
with these developments, despite its comment that the first intercepts had
"lacked weight," for two additional stations, at Leafield and the original
Marconi wireless factory at Hall Street, Chelmsford, to be instructed to
concentrate on German naval signals. The enemy was clearly unaware
of the scale of British intercept operations, and the wireless operators of
the German fleet appeared to think that their low-power ship-to-ship and
ship-to-shore transmissions could not possibly reach a receiver more than
fifty miles away. Accordingly, there were no institutionalized security
procedures over long distances; instead, an ever-growing quantity of
operator "chatter" could be heard which proved highly revealing. It was
not until the battle of Jutland, two years later, that the Germans began

to realize that some of their most important communications had been compromised. As Alastair Denniston later remarked:

> Everything the Germans said was contained in one of the three books in 40 Old Buildings and in those days the Germans were by no means discreet or cryptic in their W/T. The exact dispositions of the High Seas Fleet, the submarines and airships were mentioned from time to time and duly read and circulated.[5]

In early November 1914, the German fleet under Admiral Hipper successfully attacked Yarmouth on the East Anglian coast and then returned across the North Sea to home waters long before the Royal Navy could steam south from its base at Scapa Flow in time to catch them. About a month later, Room 40 discovered a considerable increase in enemy wireless traffic, apparently in expectation of a major German fleet movement. It looked as if Admiral Hipper might be going to repeat his successful attack. Just before midnight on December 14, Room 40 informed Admiral Lord Jellicoe that he should anticipate an entry of a German battle-cruiser squadron into the North Sea. Two days later, the English east coast towns of Scarborough, Hartlepool and Whitby were bombarded by a force of German battle-cruisers.

Thanks to the warning he had received from Room 40, Jellicoe was given enough time to prepare a trap for Hipper. He deployed six battleships under the command of Sir George Warrender and a force of four battle-cruisers under Admiral Beatty. Both Royal Naval forces converged on Hipper's battle-cruisers, unaware that Germany's main High Seas Fleet had, without warning, emerged from Wilhelmshaven and looked set to take Beatty and Warrender by surprise.

Room 40 took just seventy minutes to ascertain the exact position of the German High Seas Fleet and reported it to Warrender and Beatty. By that time Warrender had briefly made contact with some German destroyers, which had promptly turned for home, and Beatty had attempted, and failed, to engage Hipper's raiders. A visual signal from Beatty's lamp to his battle-cruisers had been misinterpreted in the opening moments of what promised to be the war's most important sea battle, and they had all promptly broken off the engagement. The Germans had made good their escape in deteriorating weather, and no pursuit was given for fear of meeting the entire High Seas Fleet. Both sides had lost splendid opportunities, and the episode highlighted the considerable difficulties in conveying operational intelligence to ships at sea and persuading the officers on the scene to take account of advice from Room 40. The Admiralty's disappointment at having inadvertently let Hipper off the hook was tempered by the SIGINT postmortem, which analyzed in detail the moves made by both sides and demonstrated how Jellicoe's trap had nearly ended in catastrophe.

The immediate consequence of what had become known as the Scarborough Raid was an increase of staff for Room 40 so that the number of watches could be increased to four. The new recruits were Lord Monk Bretton, formerly Joseph Chamberlain's private secretary at the Colonial Office, Commander Charles Fremantle RN, DSO, Herbert Morrah, the author of *The Optimist* and former president of the Oxford Union, H.W. Lawrence, the furniture and art connoisseur, and W.H. Anstie, from Dartmouth.

The Germans now changed the key to their main naval cipher, but Room 40 was able to solve the new key in just twelve hours, much to the surprise of the Admiralty. It later turned out that this alteration, which consisted of moving a "slider," was merely the preliminary to a more fundamental change which was instituted some days later . . . and took six hours to solve. An unexpected bonus was the German Admiralstab's decision to contact every set in its High Seas Fleet to check that the necessary changes had been understood. By monitoring this traffic, Room 40 was able to build its first complete enemy naval order of battle.

Soon after this triumph, on the morning of January 23, 1915, Room 40 decrypted the following German message:

First and Second Scouting Groups, Senior Officers of Destroyers and two flotillas to be selected by the Senior Officer Scouting Forces are to reconnoiter the Dogger Bank. They are to leave harbor this evening after dark and return tomorrow evening after dark.[6]

According to the latest appreciation of the German order of battle, the enemy force would consist of four battle-cruisers and six light cruisers, a truly tempting target for the Grand Fleet. The scene was set for a really spectacular trap in which Jellicoe hoped to eliminate Hipper and his fleet once and for all. The plan called for strict radio silence and a surprise attack once the German warships reached the Dogger Bank.

Admiral Hipper's force entered the North Sea exactly on schedule, at 1745 hours on January 23, and the engagement began at 0800 the following morning when the *Blücher* was sunk by Admiral Beatty's squadron, although his own flagship, HMS *Lion*, was itself put out of action. Owing to yet another mixup over misinterpreted visual signals, Hipper's three remaining battle-cruisers, the *Moltke, Derfflinger* and *Seydlitz*, succeeded in extracting themselves from the conflict and escaped back to home waters. It subsequently turned out that Beatty had mistakenly thought that there were enemy submarines in the vicinity and had not pursued Hipper's three survivors. In fact, Room 40 was able to establish that there were no German submarines within forty miles of Beatty's position, but the news failed to reach him until it was too late. HMS *Lion* limped back to Rosyth, and the *Seydlitz*, badly damaged and with 159 dead on board, returned to Wilhelmshaven. The battle of the Dogger Bank was hailed as a momentous victory in London, but in reality it was just another lost opportunity. The German High Seas Fleet was to remain bottled up for the next eighteen months, and Room 40 had more time to analyze the three captured German codes and compare them to some of the other wireless traffic intercepted.

Soon there were fifty officers in Room 40, each specifically selected for his exceptionally fluent and detailed knowledge of German . . . and his discretion. Ewing's academic connections with the universities ensured him access to the country's best brains and his recruits were the most brilliant of their generation. The list of the Room 40 collaborators is impressive testimony to Ewing's determination to harness intellectual capacity long before the days of computers. Practically every discipline was represented in the Admiralty Old Building—historians, bankers, actors, archaeologists, authors, linguists, lawyers, artists, stockbrokers, and even a few naval officers: Claud Serocold, Lionel Fraser and Frank Tiarks from the City of London; Herbert Hope, one of the NID's few regular officers; Dillwyn Knox, the brilliant classicist from King's, Cambridge, and, briefly, his brother, the Catholic theologian Ronald Knox; (Sir) Frank Adcock, later Professor of Ancient History at Cambridge; John Beazley, later Professor of Classical Archaeology at Oxford; Edward Bullough, from Caius, Cambridge; Gilbert Waterhouse, the Professor of German at Queen's University, Belfast; Edward Molyneux, the couturier; William Clarke, the barrister; Gerald Lawrence, the actor; and G.P. Mackeson, the cartoonist. Later recruits included Francis Birch, from King's, Cambridge; Professor Leonard Willoughby, the Senior Taylorian Lecturer in German at Oxford; Walter Bruford from St. John's, Cambridge; Professor C.E. Gough, from Leeds; Dr. E.C. Quiggin, from Caius, Cambridge; Professor Douglas Savory, from Queen's University, Belfast; Professor F.E. Sandbach, from Birmingham University; and John Francis Toye, later the music critic of the *Morning Post*.

Admiral Hall's indoctrination into the Signal Service's progress included a visit to Captain Round's chain of radio compass direction-finding aerials still under construction in France. Hall was sufficiently impressed by what he saw to recommend the immediate construction of a network of these high-masted "directional" aerials along the east coast in a line from Lerwick in the Shetlands to Birchington, just outside Westgate-on-Sea. Others were sited at Aberdeen, York, Flamborough Head and Lowestoft, and an additional four stations were eventually completed in Ireland and linked to the naval base at Queenstown. By the end of the war, no less than nineteen had been put into operation and as many as possible had been linked to the Admiralty in London by a direct landline.

By taking cross bearings from among these nineteen centers, it was possible to pinpoint the location of German transmission stations, to assess the routing and volume of traffic emitted and to learn the enemy's call signs. By mid-1916, Room 40 had become thoroughly professional in its approach. Special landlines had been built to the wireless intercept stations at Hunstanton, Stockton, Leafield and Hall Street, and a never-ending stream of postmen were delivering intercepts from the other stations to the Admiralty Old Building. Once arrived at Room 40, the intercepted messages were decrypted and analyzed in order to learn from whom the messages had been sent and who was receiving them. The contents were then translated into English, assessed for technicalities and summarized. When all the different elements of signals intelligence were combined—direction finding, interception, traffic analysis and decryption—all those privy to the secrets of Room 40 began to discover just how powerful a weapon they had created.

One major problem was that German signal books included four additional Morse letters, known to the enemy as alpha, beta, gamma and delta, for which there was no equivalent in British Morse, so that the first landline transmissions from the coastal intercept stations created havoc. Eventually, Russell Clarke evolved a new Morse alphabet to overcome the difficulty, but this was never adopted by the War Office, nor for that matter by the French, who developed their own alternatives.

The newly recruited academic talent were also often stumped by proper naval usage. They knew nothing of the German fleet, little about the geography of the German coastline and their ignorance of German naval phraseology was profound. Admiral Lord Fisher pointed out that warships did not "run in" and begged the staff to adopt the word "proceed." In the end Herbert Hope, one of the early arrivals with Denniston from Dartmouth, who knew little of cryptanalysis and who, according to

Denniston, never did know why he had been assigned to the Intelligence Division, was asked to turn the translated decrypts into recognizable Royal Naval terminology.

As well as presiding over a growing team of academics who were trying to "solve" the German cipher codes, Ewing arranged for another team of analysts to make a detailed study of the German call signs and yet another group to plot the direction-finding reports. All desks in Room 40 were connected by an overhead system of pneumatic tubes, which passed the incoming flimsies from one desk to another. When all aspects of an intercept had been assessed, it was shot to the final recipient at the end of the room who was a former ADC to Queen Victoria, Admiral of the Fleet, Sir Arthur Wilson. He brought the various strands together, collated them and ensured that the results were correctly distributed to the staff of the Naval Operations division who were responsible for relaying the information to the fleet.

As the volume of intercepts gained momentum, the pressure on the Room 40 staff increased. Russell Clarke was obliged to turn his home into a photographic studio so that the original *SKM* from the *Magdeburg* could be copied, and he produced three facsimiles which were distributed among the watchkeepers. Unfortunately, he had had no access to any government photographic equipment, so his copies were rather smaller than the original, which caused considerable eyestrain among the cryptologists working by electric light. New developments also added to the burden borne by Ewing's staff. For example, it was discovered through painstaking analysis by Lord Lytton and a Foreign Office recruit, B.F. Talbot, that the *VB* code, which had provided much helpful information about the enemy's cruisers, was also used for communicating with German naval attachés around the world.

As Room 40's expertise grew, so did the technical skills of the interceptors. Operators were allotted particular call signs and wavelengths to monitor, and the more skilled staff could differentiate between the shortwave wireless circuits used by the Baltic and North Sea Fleets. Submarines formed quite different groups, and the smaller units in the German Bight produced yet another. All messages were relayed, sometimes in triplicate, to Room 40, where they were categorized and then tested against the known cipher keys. Those that failed to respond were filed for further examination, and those that succumbed were analyzed and then passed on for the appropriate action. Because, following the battle of the Dogger Bank, the German High Seas Fleet had been reluctant to commit its relatively small number of battleships to the North Sea, the chief results of the secret wireless war were achieved in the increasingly bitter submarine conflict.

The Royal Navy's supremacy of the seas was greatly assisted by a large number of minefields that had been sown around the German coast in an attempt to keep the enemy's fleets permanently bottled up. The Straits of Dover could only be navigated along certain cleared routes, which were constantly patrolled. Another minefield stretched from the Orkneys across the North Sea to Norway. These were designed to restrict the passage of the U-boats based in Germany and three captured ports in Belgium. A further field had been sown across the mouth of the Adriatic to restrict the U-boats operating from Pola and Cattaro.

In order to avoid Allied minefields, German submarines had to be escorted in and out of their ports by minesweepers and patrol craft. For those at sea this meant arranging a rendezvous by wireless; it also meant sending out endless radio progress reports to warn of new minefields or sightings of enemy shipping. In addition, there was a substantial volume of radio traffic exchanged with lightships and inshore vessels laying buoys to guide ships through local defenses. To enable individual submarine commanders to code their reports and conceal their own positions when transmitting, the Admiralstab equipped its U-boats with special charts, marked with grids. Their messages conformed to a predetermined formula, which usually consisted of a call sign followed by several groups of figures. One of the most common was that reporting a successful attack. The text "UCJ - 1 - 2 - 8 - 027A" would indicate that the *UC-72* had sunk one ship of 2,000 tons in quadrant 027 Alpha and had eight torpedoes left. Such a signal would have little value to the Allies unless sense could be made of the grid reference, and on March 16, 1916, the Admiralty scored its first success when the minelaying submarine *UC-12* was blown up in Taranto harbor by one of her own mines. The Italians wasted no time in raising the wreck and recovering her wireless equipment, navigation charts and code book. A month later, on April 14, 1916, the *UB-16* was forced to surrender after having become entangled in an underwater net outside Le Havre. Upon examination it was found to contain a complete set of German charts and instructions for operating in the English Channel. Later the same month another minelayer, the *UC-5*, went aground on Shipwash Shoal and was towed into Harwich by a destroyer. These valuable prizes enabled the Room 40 decrypters to review much of their filed intercepts and reconstruct the German navigation grid for the Western Approaches, the Channel and the North Sea.

When Admiral Hall's chain of nineteen "directionals" had been constructed, it was possible for information from these stations to be fed into a central plotting room at the Admiralty, where two NID officers, Commander Alfred Dewar and Paymaster-Captain Ernest Thring, checked the individual U-boat call signs against intelligence reports received from other sources (such as prisoners of war) and marked the updated location of each U-boat on a wall map. The system eventually became so sophisticated that the NID was able to build comprehensive card indices on many of the important personalities in the U-boat fleets and monitor the progress of each submarine as it was made ready for an operational patrol. Once it was clear of its escorts, the NID watched its every moment.

For their part the Germans built new naval wireless transmitters, at Nordholz, Borkum and Sylt, and established a special U-boat weather station in Bruges to broadcast regular coded weather reports. All messages were routinely intercepted in England and relayed to London for assessment. Whenever necessary, the Admiralty prepared to divert Allied shipping from the path of marauding enemy submarines. It was while Room 40 was completing its order of battle of the German submarine fleets in 1916 that the first indications were received that the German High Seas Fleet was about to mount a major sortie into the North Sea.

The first hints came from French direction-finding stations, which had plotted a series of Zeppelin reconnaissance flights originating from Wilhelmshaven and the Jade estuary. French direction-finding stations had become sufficiently sophisticated and accurate to be able to plot a wireless transmitter's movement of just one-and-a-half degrees. As the course of each Zeppelin was logged, it became clear that a major German fleet operation was soon to be undertaken. Evidence increased during the last week in May, and by midday on May 30, 1916, a warning had been passed to Admiral Jellicoe at Scapa Flow. Later the same day, his Grand Fleet of thirty-five Dreadnoughts put to sea with the intention of eliminating the entire German High Seas Fleet. Early the following day, a force of cruisers emerged from Wilhelmshaven, closely followed by Admiral von Scheer and a force of twenty-one battleships. In total, nearly 250 warships were on a collision course, and both sides expected a mighty sea battle that might decide the outcome of the war. The German plan called for one or two British squadrons to be lured into an ambush where a force of eighteen U-boats would pick off the most tempting targets. Jellicoe, on the other hand, simply intended to find the German fleet and bombard it into submission. Thanks to an inefficient system of exploiting SIGINT, and the reluctance of the individual commanders at sea to believe its advice, events turned out quite differently.

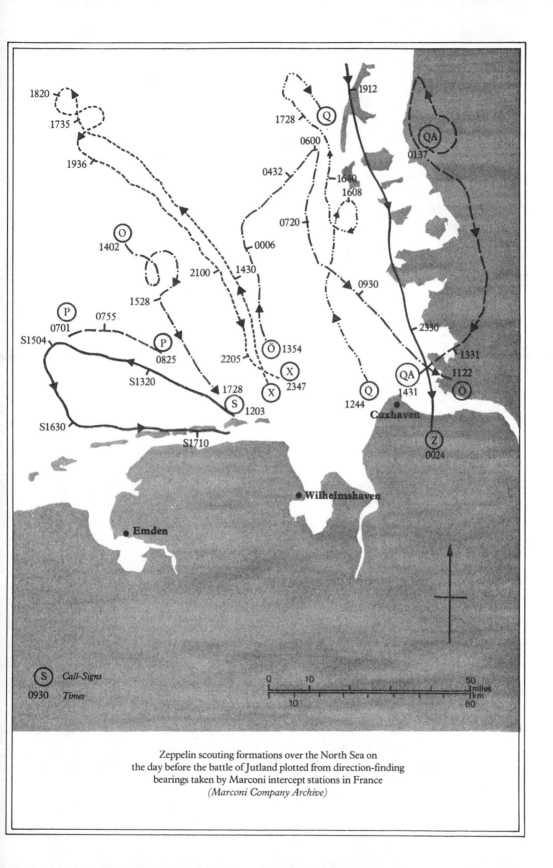

Zeppelin scouting formations over the North Sea on
the day before the battle of Jutland plotted from direction-finding
bearings taken by Marconi intercept stations in France
(Marconi Company Archive)

The controversy surrounding the battle of Jutland continues more than half a century later, with both sides claiming victory. The Germans succeeded in sinking three British battle-cruisers, three armored cruisers and eight destroyers, for the loss of one battleship, one battle-cruiser, four light cruisers and five destroyers, and severe damage to several other important warships. Certainly Jellicoe failed to achieve the full-scale battle he had planned, and Admiral Scheer had likewise been unable to spring his trap. The oft-told history of Jutland is one of mistakes, lost opportunities, misunderstandings and bad judgment, but above all else it is a demonstration of exactly how *not* to exploit good intelligence.

The first major blunder occured when the Royal Naval Grand Fleet was advised, in error, that the bulk of Scheer's fleet was still in the Jade estuary when, in fact, it was already at sea and closing on Admiral Beatty's battle squadron. This crucial signal from the Admiralty's Operations Division, timed at 1230 on May 31, 1916, read:

> No definite news of enemy. They made all preparations for sailing this morning. It was thought Fleet had sailed but Directionals place flagship in Jade at 11.10 A.M. GMT. Apparently they have been unable to carry out air reconnaissance which had delayed them.

This disastrous piece of advice was the result of some independent intelligence analysis by the Operations Division without reference to the SIGINT experts in Room 40. The direction-finding stations had indeed monitored Admiral Scheer's old call sign DK at Wilhelmshaven earlier that morning, but experience had taught Room 40 that the Germans issued new call signs when an operation was about to be initiated, including a new one for the German admiral commanding the High Seas Fleet. Since call sign recognition was but one facet of SIGINT, the ploy rarely fooled anyone. However, on this occasion the Admiralty's Operations Division had taken it upon themselves to interpret the bearings of call sign DK. The Room 40 staff later claimed to have been perfectly well aware that Admiral Scheer was at sea and heading for Beatty and Jellicoe in radio silence, when the Admiralty had assured the Grand Fleet that there was still plenty of time before the conflict.

When Beatty did make contact with the enemy, his battle squadron was mauled badly and lost two of his six cruisers. Scheer pressed home what he perceived as his advantage, only to be confronted by Jellicoe's massive force. Once he realized the scale of his opposition, he broke away and, in a series of maneuvers in the dusk, headed for home. However, his options were limited, for there were only four possible routes through the various minefields and other obstacles that lay between the High Seas Fleet and safety. Scheer chose the shortest course, and Jellicoe decided to cover another. By the time the Admiralty had identified Scheer's escape route and advised Jellicoe, it was too late, and the German fleet, though badly damaged, avoided annihilation. Incredibly, Room 40 had the correct information to hand at the critical moment, but the Operations Division had failed to pass it on. Indeed, between 2155 on May 31 and 0300 on June 1 some sixteen decrypts with a relevance to the battle had been prepared by Room 40, but of that number only three had been relayed to the Grand Fleet. Unfortunately, one of the three, identifying the position of the rear ship in the enemy's main fleet, the *Regensburg*, was entirely inaccurate, and Admiral Beatty knew it to be so from his own observation. The fault, however, lay with the *Regensburg*, which had signaled her position but had made an unintentional error of ten miles. The subsequent decrypt was promptly transmitted to Beatty, who became more disillusioned than ever with the reliability of Admiralty intelligence.

The subsequent London postmortem was conducted in conditions of great secrecy: very few were privy to all the details, or were allowed to learn the scale of the blunder. The commanders at sea were in no doubt about who was to blame, but nothing could be said publicly about signals intelligence. The DNI, on the other hand, was quite convinced that responsibility lay with the Naval Operations Division, which had effectively divided the single discipline of signals interception and signals analysis. Hall was sure that interception and interpretation were two sides of the same coin and that the Jutland fiasco had been caused by the Operations staff making their own assessment of SIGINT summaries.

In fact, there was rather more to the Jutland fiasco than an administrative breakdown in the assessment and timely distribution of SIGINT product. After the war, it became clear that the Germans had themselves participated in a secret operation to conceal their intentions and baffle their opponents. The wireless station at Neumünster, which had become very familiar to the British intercept operators, had a small cryptographic unit attached to it, and it had occasionally succeeded in breaking the Royal Navy's two-figure code which was used for communicating low-grade, routine traffic to coastal shipping. On Ewing's advice, the key to the code was altered every month, but this precaution failed to deter the Germans. One officer in particular, Commander H. Kraschutzki, became increasingly adept at interpreting the changing pattern of British signals, and in the spring of 1916 had written a memorandum to the Admiralstab recommending a change in German naval call signs. On the eve of Jutland, the call sign of the flagship of the High Seas Fleet, the *Friedrich der Grosse*, had been switched from DK to UW, which had previously been used by the Wilhelmshaven shore base. It was this simple maneuver which had led the Operations Division in London to advise Beatty that the enemy had not left port in the fatal message of May 31. Instead of issuing a new call sign to the *Friedrich der Grosse*, it had swopped with one already in operation and known to the enemy. The subterfuge had achieved exactly the desired effect, and Admiral Scheer was able to steam out of Wilhelmshaven knowing that, if bearings were taken on his old call sign, his true position would not be betrayed. The Room 40 staff, of course, later insisted that they would not have been taken in by a switch in call signs, but it has to be noted that their previous experience had been in the issue of new call signs, not the deliberate transfer of existing ones.

Another hard lesson which had yet to be learned centered on the *Regensburg*'s unintentional navigational error when signaling her position. When radio silence is broken after a long period of quiet, there is a tendency to give added weight to the intercepted message. In the case of the *Regensburg*, a navigational error had been made (as was subsequently admitted in the German official history of the battle) but was accepted in the heat of the moment at its face value. If the *Regensburg* had intended to mislead Room 40, she could hardly have succeeded better, a clear indication of SIGINT's deception possibilities.

At the outbreak of war the German army had boasted more than twenty airships, while the Admiralstab's Naval Airship Division had possessed just one, the *L3*. However, during 1914 most of the airships had been wrecked in accidents and no offensive missions had been flown against England. That situation had changed on the night of January 19, 1915, when two Zeppelins from an enlarged Naval Airship Division, the *L3* and *L4*, had crossed the East Anglian coast and dropped twenty-five bombs on the market town of King's Lynn. It was Britain's first experience of an air raid: four people had been killed and a further sixteen injured.

Adverse weather conditions had prevented the Germans from repeating the exercise until April 14, when a woman and child had been injured in Wallsend. During the following twelve months there were a further twenty-nine raids, concentrated along the east coast, in which 382 civilians were killed. The losses, however, were not entirely confined to one side. During the same period three Zeppelins were shot down by ground fire and crashed into the sea. Although the airships themselves sank, prisoners were recovered from the *L15* and the *L7*.

Most of the Zeppelins participating in these raids were under the control of the German Naval Airship Division and were, therefore, answerable to the Admiralstab. Accordingly, they were issued with naval call signs for all their wireless communications and were required to signal progress reports to the flagship of the admiral of the German High Seas Fleet every hour. This extraordinary procedure, which appeared to have no obvious purpose apart from satisfying naval protocol, gave the Allies an excellent opportunity to analyze their traffic.

Initially all the Naval Airship Division's craft were designated two-letter call signs, beginning LA, LB, etc. Thus the *L3* identified herself as LC. The Admiralstab later decreed that all the call signs should change, so with Teutonic consistency and logic the call sign LC was altered to MD, and then NE. Furthermore, these changes took place at regular (and therefore predictable) three-monthly intervals. It was also discovered that the Naval Airship Division relied on the compromised *Handelsverkehrsbuch* for encoding much of its traffic which, surprisingly, was not subjected to any form of recipherment.

Conditions on board the airships were frequently so bad that the wireless operators often abandoned such security procedures as they had been instructed to use and reverted to sending *en clair*. This was not entirely surprising, considering that only one operator was carried on each airship, and he generally sat alone in a tiny soundproofed cabin in the control car of the forward gondola. In addition, he frequently had to carry out his duties in complete darkness, especially when the door to the control car was left open. Many of the flights lasted for more than twenty hours, at a height of up to 19,000 feet, where he was obliged to strap on a primitive oxygen mask. There was never any relief because standing orders demanded that a constant wireless watch be maintained, whatever the duration of the mission. Navigation depended on a constant series of signals transmitted by three stations in Germany located at List, Tondern and Nordholz, and Bruges in occupied Belgium. Because the three German stations were uncomfortably close to each other for practical bearings to be taken on flights across the North Sea, everything depended on the signal from the Bruges station which was notoriously unreliable and often went off the air at vital moments, leaving airships effectively stranded over cloud or fog, maybe in bad weather conditions, high over enemy territory or the inhospitable North Sea. Sometimes the cross bearings transmitted by the four navigational stations appeared not to intersect, or their angle was too acute to be of any help. The only alternative was to lose height to make a visual observation and risk being caught by fighter aircraft which, of course, were only able to operate at relatively low altitudes.

There were plenty of other hazards for the Zeppelin crews to face. The craft were inflated with some two million cubic feet of inflammable hydrogen, so at the first sign of a thunderstorm the wireless antenna had to be wound in to avoid attracting atmospheric lightning. Without a wireless the airship was completely "blind." All of these factors contributed to the confusion and occasional panic of ill-disciplined radio operators, who had to cope with the cold, fatigue and altitude sickness, and bad-tempered commanders demanding bearings and weather reports. In these circumstances, it is understandable that German operators sometimes committed the most fundamental breaches of wireless security.

Through a combination of efficient direction finding and signal interception (with an element of cryptanalysis), the Admiralty in London was able to build up an elementary early warning system so that the somewhat embryonic English air defenses could be alerted in plenty of time before the appearance of an enemy air raid. During the course of 1916, no less than eight Zeppelins were shot down over England, of which five were dispatched by aircraft. The business of finding a hostile raider in the dark was by no means easy, with searchlights generally manned by untrained volunteers from the police and ground batteries lacking any effective quick-firing antiaircraft weapons. Nor, at first, was there any established method of vectoring aircraft toward the airships, especially when ground observers had no accurate system of judging height.

After the battle of Jutland, the Germans began to increase their Zeppelin fleet and, at the same time, the Admiralstab ordered the introduction of a new code which at first Room 40 could not decrypt. Work continued on the laborious reconstruction of this new code throughout the summer of 1916, until there was an unexpected breakthrough.

On September 24, 1916, Zeppelin *L32*, returning from an air raid on London, was shot down over Essex by Lieutenant Frederick Sowrey, one of the Royal Flying Corps's first air aces. The *L32* crashed in flames at Snail's Hall Farm, Great Burstead. All the crew of twenty-two perished in the fire, which burned furiously for more than an hour, but the following morning what was left of the wreckage was examined by experts from the Admiralty and the War Office.

Among those sifting through the *L32*'s remains was a special team from the Naval Intelligence Division. It was headed by Major Bernard

Trench RM, who was very well qualified for this particular work. Before the war, in May 1910, Trench had been arrested just outside a shore battery on the German island of Borkum while conducting an undercover hydrographic survey of the coastline with Captain Vivian Brandon RN, another officer attached to the NID. A much-publicized trial had followed in Leipzig, at which both men admitted their covert roles and had been sentenced to four years' "fortress detention." This disagreeable punishment was supposed to be a convenient peacetime device for officers caught spying so that they might avoid the stigma attached to the dishonor of a criminal conviction. Brandon had been turned over to the military at Wesel, but Trench had been sent to the fortress at Glatz, in Silesia, where he had later been joined by a Frenchman, Captain Lux. This French officer had been charged with engaging in espionage at Friedrichshafen, the home of the Zeppelin Airship Company, in December 1910 and had been sentenced to six years' imprisonment. Quite by chance he and Trench had been accommodated together. Then, in December 1911, Lux had succeeded in escaping and had made his way back to Paris. As a result, security at Glatz had been tightened up. Trench had also tried to escape and had even feigned a suicide attempt in order to get a transfer to a hospital, and so to a more relaxed regime, but his ploy had failed. Both Trench and Brandon were kept in custody for a total of twenty-nine months. In May 1913, they had both been pardoned on the occasion of King George V's visit to Berlin for the wedding of his niece, the Kaiser's only daughter. Brandon was subsequently given the command of HMS *Bramble*, but Trench had returned to the Admiralty where he had been assigned to Charles Rotter's German Section.

After a brief spell at Queenstown, where he had organized a submarine plotting room for the Western Approaches, Trench had returned to London and concentrated on using his fluent command of the language to interrogate German prisoners rescued from Zeppelins. Trench soon established a formidable reputation among the naval prisoners of war at Donnington Hall, the special prisoner-of-war camp which housed captured enemy officers undergoing interrogation. After his own experiences at Glatz, Trench had become bitterly anti-German and was not above coercing his subjects into cooperating. Alois Bocker, the *L15*'s commander, later described undergoing a ruthless interrogation at Trench's hands and recalled being threatened with a civil trial for the murder of civilians unless he cooperated by identifying all the Zeppelin call signs he knew. According to Bocker, he had refused to be intimidated, and eventually Trench had demonstrated the depth of the NID's knowledge by showing him a complete schedule of the Naval Airship Division's current call signs. As well as questioning newly captured prisoners of war, Trench specialized in Zeppelin intelligence and so was quickly on the scene to salvage anything of value from the *L32*.

Two items of interest were recovered: a long gray coat, which had belonged to the *L32*'s commander, Oberleutnant Werner Peterson, and a slightly charred copy of the *Allgemeinefunkspruchbuch* (*AFB*), the Naval Airship Division's new code book. In spite of the burn marks, the *L32*'s *AFB* was more than enough to fill in the gaps left in Room 40's reconstructed version. It also enabled the Admiralty to predict accurately all future hostile airship raids several hours before they crossed the coastline.

Room 40 was now thriving: interception techniques were improving and the monitoring stations had been assigned particular wavelengths to watch; the decipherment of the *AFB* codes enabled Zeppelins to be tracked and shot down and the reading of other ciphers led to more and more U-boats being sunk. There were still a few administrative problems to be ironed out over the analysis and distribution of the final message material, but the whole concept of SIGINT had been put together and brought to positive fruition. There was, therefore, little reason to retain Sir Alfred Ewing, who was now well over the navy's official retirement age. He had fulfilled his primary task, that of recruiting suitable number-crunchers for Room 40, and had watched the unit he had created expand and prosper.

As a Director of Naval Education, Ewing was entitled to a pension, but his days in the Admiralty were effectively over so he was asked if he would like to be principal and vice-chancellor of his old university, Edinburgh, as from October 1, 1916, on the understanding that he would still be available to Room 40 as a consultant when required. As his son later commented:

> In the discovery of enemy ciphers Ewing took little direct part, except during the first year, for, as the staff of assistants grew from a zero beginning, it came to comprise members whose faculty for that kind of inspired guessing and quick inference was far greater than his own; and it must be remembered that the problems themselves had, by this time, grown much harder.[7]

Ewing had obtained the services of a brilliant collection of brains and had given the Admiralty's entire SIGINT program plausible cover through his Naval Education department. Now he had outlived his usefulness, and Admiral Hall was anxious to absorb Room 40 into his own Naval Intelligence Division. In 1916, Ewing moved to Scotland and gradually his visits to London became fewer and fewer. What remains surprising is that apart from one or two appreciative letters, his achievements received no official recognition. In later years, this led to some bitterness and prompted him in December 1927 to give a much-criticized lecture to the Edinburgh Philosophical Institution on the subject of his "Special War Work," in which he described the activities of Room 40. He had not sought permission from the Admiralty before delivering his address, and there were to be serious consequences.

In the meantime, in Ewing's absence, Room 40 continued to digest its daily intake of wireless intercepts and proffer advice in its special bright red envelopes to the Operations Division of the Admiralty and the War Office. The New Year of 1917 proved to be the turning point of the Great War. It was the year that saw more U-boats sunk than in any of the previous years, the Zeppelin losses higher than ever, and the entry into the conflict of the United States. All three developments were directly attributable to the Allied acquisition and evaluation of SIGINT.

During 1915, just eighteen U-boats were sunk, with mines being the principal cause. This rate of attrition was considered entirely unsatisfactory as it enabled the enemy to maintain its stranglehold blockade on Britain's supplies. During the following year, this figure rose to twenty-two, but it was not until 1917 that the statistics really jumped, with sixty-three enemy craft being sent to the bottom. Approximately half this number were eliminated after they had been engaged by Allied forces around the British Isles. The method varied from ramming and gunfire to torpedoes, but the result was the same: the U-boat fleet was suffering an appalling rate of losses because the location of virtually every German submarine was known to the Admiralty in London, and naval forces in the area were being supplied with enough information to close in.

Having obtained a copy of the *AFB* from the site of the *L32*, the NID extended its inspection of enemy wrecks to the sea. A diving instructor, Shipwright E.C. Miller RN, was selected to head a team of divers, and the first U-boat to undergo a thorough inspection by divers on an intelligence-gathering mission was the *UC-32*, which sank following a massive underwater explosion off Sunderland on the evening of February 23, 1917. A patrol vessel later picked up just three survivors, including the commander, Kapitanleutnant Breyer. A team of volunteers dived down to the submarine on February 26 and recovered some valuable equipment and a complete torpedo. The U-boat had been sunk by one of her own newly laid mines, a familiar hazard for the underwater mine-layers.

By June 1917, the NID had assembled an experienced group of divers and had introduced a system of bounties to encourage the recovery of interesting material. Following the success of the *UC-32* operation, exploratory dives were made on two known wrecks, the *UC-2*, a small minelayer which had been accidentally rammed by a steamer in Yarmouth Roads in July 1915, and the *UC-39*, which had surrendered to HMS *Thrasher* on February 8, 1917. The *UC-2* had already been visited by Admiralty divers several times, and there were no documents to be found.

The *UC-39* had been shelling a coastal steamer off Flamborough Head when *Thrasher* had appeared on the scene and had engaged the submarine. The U-boat made an emergency dive, but the destroyer soon brought her to the surface with a pattern of depth charges. A short exchange of gunfire followed until the German commander, Kapitanleutnant Ehrentraut, had hoisted a white flag. Fifteen Germans and two British seamen prisoners had been taken off, but the submarine had sunk after the *Thrasher* had attempted to take it in tow. Once in custody, Ehrentraut had produced the U-boat's log.

In 1938, the head of the diving team, Shipwright Miller, gave an American journalist, Richard Rowan, an account of his Great War underwater adventures for the Intelligence Division and recalled how "huge salt-water eels and other voracious specimens of the deep were feasting upon the bodies of the German crew" in a submarine he had dived to in 1915. It is not possible to identify the submarine that he referred to, as no U-boat was sunk in the exact circumstances he outlined (sunk by gunfire off the Kentish coast in 1915), but he gave a graphic description of his experience which no doubt enabled Rowan to capture the flavor of Miller's work inside "the foully choked and hazardous compartments" of a sunken U-boat:

> Still carefully protecting his air line, he forced his way aft and finally into the officers' quarters, into the captain's cabin. There, in a kind of strong room, he discovered a stout metal box, dragged it out of the hull and attached it to a line to be hauled to the surface. Miller himself ascended at once to help open this prize. He could describe all the up-to-date innovations aboard the U-boat; but from the captured strongbox came such unexpected treasures as the latest plans of the enemy's minefields, two new code books of the German Navy, and another, a very precious code, used only to communicate with the Imperial High Seas Fleet.[8]

It is not known if Miller did indeed find any such code books on the *UC-39* or whether Rowan's description is mere poetic license, but it is known that the next submarine to be examined, the *UC-61*, was captured intact with all the latest Channel charts and code books, which were seized before they could be destroyed. The *UC-61* was stranded off Cap Griz Nez on July 26 after grounding accidentally and the crew were taken off. When interrogated, the wireless operator gave a detailed account of his own procedures and described how the Admiralstab broadcast new orders to the U-boat fleet. The transmitter at Bruges came on the air five times a day, at 0100, 0500, 1000, 1500 and 2000 GMT, and was backed up by two further signals, one from Nauen at 2300 and one at 1800 from the battle-cruiser *Arkona*, then based at Emden. The rest of the crew also gave some valuable information, which helped the Intelligence Division to confirm the accuracy of its assessment of the current order of battle of the U-boat fleet based at Zeebrugge and Ostend.

Early the following month, the *UC-44* was blown up while laying mines off Waterford Harbor. The commander and his two companions in the conning tower managed to escape, but only Kapitanleutnant Teben-Johanns survived in the water until being rescued by a local rowboat. On August 6, a team of NID divers found the *UC-44* in ninety feet of water and salvaged the log, a code book and a sheaf of orders relating to the conduct of submarine operations in the Channel. The divers continued to work on the wreck, repairing the damage to the hull, until September 26 when it was brought to the surface and towed on to a beach. There SIGINT experts examined the radio on board in an effort to confirm its transmission frequencies. Comfortingly, they discovered that it had nine preset wavelengths on a range from 300 meters to 820, exactly the range monitored by the Admiralty intercept stations.

Success in the battle against the U-boats in 1917 was matched by the heavy losses inflicted on the enemy's airship fleet. Four Zeppelins were brought down during the year by British forces, of which one, the *L48*, yielded many secrets. The *L48* was intercepted during her thirteenth mission to England by Lieutenant L.P. Watkins of No. 37 Squadron shortly after a bombing raid on Harwich on the night of June 17, 1917. The Zeppelin's compass had frozen solid, and instead of turning for home the commander, Franz Eichler, set a course due north which only brought him further inland over hostile territory. Desperately he sought guidance from the wireless stations on the German Bight, but by the time they had responded with his bearings Lieutenant Watkins had attacked and set the airship's tail on fire. The entire craft slowly fell to the ground in flames, landing at Holly Tree Farm, Theberton, only a short distance from the

Admiralty intercept station at Leiston. All but three of the crew perished, but the front portion of the craft survived and a number of useful documents were recovered from the wireless cabin inside the forward gondola. Contrary to the Admiralstab's standing orders, the Zeppelin was found to be carrying a general cipher table for the current naval signal book, the *AFB*, and three lists of recently introduced code words. Unfortunately, the fate of the *L48* had been watched at a distance by the *L42*, and the Naval Airship Division was alerted to the fact that the *L48* had not been completely destroyed. This led Admiral Scheer, on June 22, 1917, to ask the Chief of the Naval Staff to change the cipher tables then in use as a precaution.

This setback was offset, four months later in France, when two airships, the *L49* and *L50*, drifted hopelessly off course following an abortive air raid on Norwich. Crippled by engine failures and the breakdown of its wireless, the *L49* was attacked by a flight of five French Nieuports. The fighters inflicted no damage on the airship, but they succeeded in thoroughly demoralizing the German crew who had mistakenly believed themselves to be over neutral Holland. Most were suffering from exhaustion and altitude sickness, and when the dawn came the commander, Hans-Karl Gayer, decided to abandon his mission. He landed his Zeppelin safely in a wood near Bourbonne-les-Bains, to the northeast of Dijon, and then tried, without success, to set the ship on fire. Gayer's Very pistol misfired and the self-destruct mechanism refused to function. Before he could improvise, a French pensioner out on a boar hunt, armed with an ancient shotgun, suddenly appeared and disarmed him and his bedraggled crew of nineteen. Meanwhile, the crew of the *L50* were suffering a rather more disagreeable fate: two of their engines had failed. The commander, Kapitanleutnant Roderich Schwonder, had decided to abandon his mission and limp home but, like his crew, he succumbed to altitude sickness and became increasingly disorientated. The craft literally bumped across France before losing its forward control gondola in a tree near Dammartin. Sixteen men leaped clear and survived, but four were trapped aboard as the airship bounced into the air and, with its lightened payload, drifted southward. Later in the day, it crossed the Mediterranean coast near Fréjus and is presumed to have crashed into the sea.

French and American military intelligence officers were swiftly on the scene of the *L49*'s crash to take control, but there were no useful documents to be found. They also visited the *L50*'s control gondola, but that too was devoid of anything with an intelligence value. A search was made of the *L50*'s flight path by Colonel Richard Williams, from General Pershing's intelligence staff, and two map fragments were recovered, one from a tree and the other from a swamp. Subsequent examination proved the maps to be the Admiralstab's latest grids for the whole of the North Sea, the Irish Sea, the Skaggerak and the Kattegat. Further inquiries at the American headquarters at Chaumont revealed that the site of the *L49*'s crash had been visited by two American officers shortly before the arrival of the intelligence search party, and that the Zeppelin's code book had been removed from the wreck as a souvenir. This booty was subsequently recovered from the officers concerned and driven straight to London by Captain Samuel Hubbard. These treasures were of immense value and compensated for the code changes recommended by Scheer following the loss of the *L48*. On October 25, 1917, Admiral Hall wrote a letter of thanks to Pershing's staff congratulating them on their prompt action:

> I hasten to express to you my most grateful thanks for your kindness and promptitude in sending me this most valuable document, which I assure you will be of the greatest value. You may rely that any information therein which will be of value to the United States forces will be at once communicated to them.[9]

In retrospect, it is evident that Allied knowledge of German naval procedures, concerning both Zeppelin and U-boat operations, stemmed in the main from avoidable breaches in security. Airships were routinely deployed over hostile territory equipped with documents that were not essential to their missions. Furthermore, some of these documents, such as the ocean grids, had a special relevance to other branches of the Admiralstab.

Impressive though the achievements of the Admiralty SIGINT analysts were in the war against the zeppelins and the U-boat packs, they tend to pale in comparison to Room 40's triumph in the field of diplomatic communications.

In April 1915, the German consul at Bushire in the Persian Gulf, Herr Helmuth Listemann, had abandoned his consulate and, in so doing, had left behind a copy of his diplomatic code, known as 13040. This code book was eventually delivered, via a circuitous route, to Room 40, where it proved invaluable.

Various versions of how the Admiralty came to acquire 13040 have been published; indeed, speculation has been so rampant that an alleged master spy named Alexander Szek has even emerged. It therefore seems essential to pause for a moment here and explain the variations in some detail in order to set the record straight. Alexander Szek first materialized in print in 1930 when a French author, Robert Boucard, described an interesting and novel version of Room 40's cryptographic affairs in *Revelations from the Secret Service*. Boucard had apparently been a military intelligence officer attached to MI6 at a joint Anglo-French office in Folkestone, where he had learned of the circumstances in which the German "Secret Diplomatic Code" had been acquired. Boucard's credentials were confirmed by his translator, Raglan Somerset, himself a barrister, journalist and former wartime MI6 officer. According to Boucard, the enemy's code had been delivered to the British military attaché in Holland, Colonel Laurie Oppenheim, by a volunteer, "a young and talented" radio engineer called Szek employed by the German headquarters in Brussels. Szek supposedly had been born in Forest Hill, just outside London, of Austrian parents and had spent months copying the diplomatic code before smuggling it out of Belgium in August 1915. Having completed his mission, he apparently disappeared and "may have been the victim of the machinations of the German Secret Police or of the British Intelligence Service."

Boucard's extraordinary story seems to contradict the accepted one about the capture of a German diplomatic cipher book in Persia, although both events appear to have occurred during 1915. Boucard dated Szek's disappearance in Holland as August 15, 1915, while the alternative story suggests that Room 40 discovered the code book which had been left behind by the former German consul at Bushire in April 1915.

Boucard's reliability is difficult to assess, as many of the other stories contained in *Revelations from the Secret Service* are a little inaccurate. One chapter describes the SIS chief, Mansfield Smith-Cumming, as having been Admiral Hall's second in command, and gives a colorful account of how he came to lose his hand in a motor accident. In fact, Smith-Cumming had had his left foot amputated. Boucard also suggests that Smith-Cumming had vanished during a wartime mission to Romania and had suddenly turned up, years later, in March 1922. This at least was complete fiction, but other authors have lent some credence to the Szek affair. Henry Landau, another former MI6 officer, refers to the case in the last two of his four books on the subject of Great War espionage, *The Enemy Within* (1937) and *Spreading the Spy Net* (1938). Landau claims to have investigated the whereabouts of Szek after the conclusion of hostilities, but inexplicably identifies Szek as "Alexander Soll" in his later book. His account of the cipher coup differs considerably from Boucard, who portrays Szek as a patriotic volunteer. Landau describes him as a reluctant collaborator who was urged to cooperate by a mysterious agent, code-named "H.523," who had visited Soll in Brussels, equipped with a persuasive letter from Soll's sister. Landau asserts that "what happened to Soll will ever remain one of the mysteries of the war," but suggests that, according to an unnamed prison warder in Namur, Soll had been court-martialed by the Germans for desertion and shot.

The story of Szek (or Soll) would probably never have gained any credence if Boucard and Landau had been the only people to peddle the tale, but in 1980 Captain Stephen Roskill, the noted naval historian, revealed that the former Director of Naval Intelligence, Admiral Sir Henry Oliver, had once claimed to have "paid £1,000 to have that man shot." During 1915, Oliver had been chief of the Admiralty War Staff, and it is difficult to ascertain quite how someone who had long since left the Naval Intelligence Division could have ordered a murder in a foreign country. Oliver apparently made the remark to Roskill at some undetermined date "in the fifties," when Oliver was in his nineties. Roskill repeated it in his biography of Admiral of the Fleet Lord Beatty in 1980.

That Alexander Gerard Heinrich Szek actually existed is beyond doubt. There is a record of his birth on September 3, 1894 at 168 Stanstead Road, Forest Hill, to Joseph and Elizabeth Szek. How much more of the story is true is difficult to judge. It has been repeated in numerous histories, but none can quote any authority for the story apart from Boucard and Landau's two strangely divergent versions. In the absence of any independent corroboration, and bearing in mind the original author's poor record on his other verifiable statements, it is fair to assume that Boucard invented the tale (or embroidered a similar one) and Landau subsequently confirmed it, having mistaken a similar case (possibly one named Soll) for Szek's. It is certainly very strange that Landau's two books, published within twelve months of each other (albeit by different publishers), should repeat, word for word, the same episode, but give the central character two different surnames. In almost every other respect chapter eighteen of *Spreading the Spy Net* is identical to chapter sixteen of *The Enemy Within*. There is no obvious explanation for this; nor can one be found for Admiral Oliver's incredible admission nearly twenty years later, except to put it down to further confusion. In any event, Boucard's original account fails every possible test that can be applied after so many years have elapsed, but perhaps one can detect the plausible elements that go to make up a really enduring cover story. Obviously, GC&CS was not overanxious to publicize the wartime triumphs of Room 40 in case hostile powers acquired similar skills or took measures to secure its codes. In those circumstances, one can well understand the authorities wishing to promote (or at least not deny) the part played by a secret agent who betrayed a cipher, as opposed to a team of cryptanalysts applying easily available scientific procedures to solve particularly resistant cipher systems. Clearly the former explanation is credible and offers the loser some reassurance that an improvement in physical security will preserve the integrity of a code that has already been compromised. If such a ploy works, the cryptographers might easily achieve that most exalted of goals, a second bite at the cherry.

Alastair Denniston, who was not privy to all Room 40's secrets at that time, recalled the Bushire episode and remarked that the "treasure trove" had been "obtained by sandbagging said one, by payment said another." Whatever the source, Room 40 was delighted to get a copy of the 13040 code in 1915 as this held out the prospect of getting access to Germany's most sensitive diplomatic communications.

It was now decided to create two new rooms, 40A and 40B, specifically to deal with the diplomatic traffic, under the leadership of George Young, in conditions of even greater secrecy than those that had pervaded the rest of the Intelligence Division.

Young was then forty-three and had been educated at Eton and universities in France, Germany and Russia. An accomplished linguist, he had joined the staff of the British Embassy in Washington in 1896 and had subsequently served in Athens, Constantinople (where he had learned Turkish and become an expert in Ottoman law), Madrid and Belgrade. Various senior diplomatic posts had followed, ending with his appointment in 1914 as First Secretary in Lisbon. (In March 1918 he was to leave Room 40 to become Professor of Portuguese at London University, inherit his father's baronetcy and be adopted as a Labour parliamentary candidate.) His chief assistant, Desmond MacCarthy, a fellow Etonian, was six years younger, with a rather less colorful career behind him. He had graduated from Trinity College, Cambridge, and had been a literary critic as well as the editor of *Life and Letters*. Young's other helpers in the Diplomatic Section included Nigel de Grey, a relatively youthful but brilliant linguist from the William Heinemann publishing house, Benjamin Faudel-Phillips and the Reverend William Montgomery, from the Westminster Presbyterian College, Cambridge, who had translated Albert Schweitzer's *Quest of the Historical Jesus*. All were to make brilliant contributions to Young's team and, indeed, to its postwar peacetime successors. Certainly the work in Rooms 40A and 40B was intellectually stimulating, challenging . . . and demanding. In August 1915, Charles Rotter was the first victim of the intense pressure of work and succumbed to a breakdown. He had been applying some of his solved *SKM* codes to a series of intercepted letters and the strain proved too great. Accordingly, a special research room was organized to spread the load, and a separate Political Section was created to cope with the more stressful (not to say illegal) examinations of the coded transatlantic traffic, neutral, American and enemy.

Initially, the staff of the Political Section was limited to Faudel-Phillips, de Grey, Montgomery and an officer named Cox. The raw material they concentrated on consisted of a huge tin box of enemy intercepts that were clearly neither military nor naval. Much of it proved to be correspondence between Berlin and German naval attachés abroad, especially in Madrid, in a reciphered code based on the original *Verkehrsbuch*. In addition, they also drew on a quantity of current traffic tapped from the only transatlantic cable circuits left available for German use. After the *Telconia* had cut and wound up the five German transatlantic cables in the English Channel, Berlin switched most of its long-distance traffic to the Nauen wireless station, only occasionally using a cable between West Africa and Brazil for communication with America. The cable was American-owned, but some discreet pressure on Eastern Telegraph eventually closed this route to the Germans. Increasing isolation then forced Berlin to use the only two remaining transatlantic cables: the Swedish one from Stockholm to Buenos Aires and the American State Department line, which ran underwater from Copenhagen. Both the Swedish proprietors and the U.S. State Department had neglected to inform Berlin that the two latter routes were inherently insecure for they both went through a relay station at Porthcurno, near Land's End in Cornwall. From here, copies of all Berlin's telegrams on the Swedish and American cable routes were sent automatically to the Admiralty in London.

The German ambassador in Washington, Count Bernstorff, invariably duplicated his messages to Berlin and sent a copy through a different channel, so as to ensure that at least one reached its destination. He frequently used the Swedish cable route as his alternative, for it was considered so secure that one intercepted message from von Eckhardt, the German minister in Mexico, even recommended to Berlin that the Swedish ambassador be decorated in recognition of all the help he had given in connection with the transmission of German Foreign Ministry telegrams. All the German texts were enciphered but, as von Eckhardt later admitted: "The cipher was not changed as often as would have been the case under normal conditions . . . to the extent that it was possible to do so, we operated the existing ciphers by means of keys, but I learned later that the British decoded all our telegrams."

It should be stressed that in dealing with German diplomatic codes and ciphers, the Room 40A experts were given invaluable assistance by the War Office. For example, on one occasion the chief engineer of the German wireless station in Constantinople gave a dinner to mark his return to Turkey after a leave in Germany. At the end of the celebrations, the engineer repaired to the transmitter and sent identical messages to six of his colleagues around the world, but each in the appropriate consular cipher. The signals were intercepted by British stations at Salonika, Alexandria, Cairo, Cyprus and Lemnos. Because Room 40 already knew code 13040, it was able to decrypt the message and then compare the text to the remaining five signals and reconstruct the separate ciphering tables of each. Such a security lapse was a godsend to Room 40A.

After the war, the Germans preferred to believe in the existence of a powerful network of spies rather than accept that their own ineptitude had been responsible for most of the security breaches. Alastair Denniston later remarked that the Germans' "folly was greater than our stupidity."

Once the German diplomatic telegrams succumbed to Room 40A's treatment, there was an extraordinary flow of political intelligence available for the Cabinet, but Admiral Hall was reluctant to share his secret source with anyone for fear of losing it altogether. Indeed, it seems that he was not even prepared to tell the Admiralty's First Sea Lord, Arthur Balfour. Nor was he keen to reveal that his secret Political Section had gained access to President Wilson's private correspondence with his special emissary in Europe, Colonel E.M. House. On January 27, 1916, Maurice Hankey, the secretary of the War Cabinet, recorded: "I had a very interesting conversation with Hall re Col. House. Hall has succeeded in discovering his private cipher to President Wilson and has deciphered his telegrams." A few days later, on February 1, Hankey reported: "Saw Captain Hall again first thing in the morning. He showed me more of Col. House's telegrams, sent from Berlin. . . . I found that Hall had not shown the telegrams to the First Lord. This information is of course priceless."[10] Perhaps the most priceless item of all the German diplomatic traffic was a partial decrypt achieved by Nigel de Grey on Wednesday, January 17, 1917. The full text had been sent the previous day by the German Foreign Minister, Arthur Zimmermann, to Bernstorff in Washington by three different routes, all using the same code. One was transmitted from Nauen to the receiving station at Sayville, Long Island; the second went via the Swedish cable from Stockholm, and the last was delivered to the U.S. Embassy in Berlin for transmission along the Copenhagen cable. The American ambassador in Berlin, James Watson Gerard, had been instructed to let the Germans use the State Department cable for plaintext messages only, but on this occasion a specious excuse had been given to avoid handing in a plain-language version, and the message had been accepted for transmission by the very country it was designed to hurt. It was a piece of supreme cheek, and one that did not fail to have its impact on the DNI and others. All three messages were delivered to the Political Section at Room 40. They read:

BERLIN TO WASHINGTON   W.158   16 JANUARY 1917

MOST SECRET FOR YOUR EXCELLENCY'S PERSONAL INFORMATION AND
TO BE HANDED TO THE IMPERIAL MINISTER IN [?] MEXICO WITH . . .
BY A SAFE ROUTE.

WE PROPOSE TO BEGIN ON 1 FEBRUARY UNRESTRICTED SUBMARINE
WARFARE. IN DOING SO, HOWEVER, WE SHALL ENDEAVOUR TO KEEP
AMERICA NEUTRAL . . . [?] IF WE SHOULD NOT [succeed in doing so]
WE PROPOSE TO [?Mexico] AN ALLIANCE UPON THE FOLLOWING BASIS:
[Joint] CONDUCT OF WAR
[Joint] CONCLUSION OF PEACE
[. . . . . .]
YOUR EXCELLENCY SHOULD FOR THE PRESENT INFORM THE PRESIDENT
[of Mexico] SECRETLY [that we expect] WAR WITH THE USA [possibly]
[. . . Japan] AND AT THE SAME TIME TO NEGOTIATE BETWEEN US AND
JAPAN . . . [Corrupted sentence meaning "Please tell the President"]
THAT . . . OUR SUBMARINES . . . WILL COMPEL ENGLAND TO PEACE
WITHIN A FEW MONTHS. ACKNOWLEDGE RECEIPT. ZIMMERMANN.

This historic partial decrypt was obviously a propaganda weapon of unprecedented proportions, but Hall knew that any public disclosure, or even a controlled leak, would instantly compromise Room 40's activities. If the Americans were informed of the contents of the message, the Germans would inevitably hear of it and reach the inescapable conclusion that at least one of their transatlantic communication channels was insecure and that their diplomatic code had been broken. While Hall wrestled with his dilemma, American relations with Berlin deteriorated and, on February 3, 1917, President Wilson broke off diplomatic relations following Germany's announcement two days earlier, as predicted by Zimmermann's text, of the decision to commence unrestricted submarine warfare, a politically explosive issue in the United States since the sinking of the *Lusitania* in May 1915.

Hall did not actually approach the Foreign Office until February 5, 1917, by which time de Grey and Montgomery had managed to fill in some of the more stubborn gaps in the original decrypt. Hall handed a copy of the infamous document to the Permanent Under-Secretary, Lord Hardinge of Penshurst, and warned him of the consequences if the text was released. The pressure to make some kind of disclosure was greater than ever, for President Wilson was still talking in terms of an armed neutrality, in spite of the German declaration of February 1. Furthermore, de Grey had solved the difficult groups missing from his first draft which detailed Germany's terms for a pact with Mexico:

GENEROUS FINANCIAL SUPPORT AND AN UNDERTAKING ON OUR PART THAT MEXICO IS TO RECONQUER THE LOST TERRITORY IN TEXAS, NEW MEXICO AND ARIZONA. THE SETTLEMENT IN DETAIL IS LEFT TO YOU.

No single proposal could be more calculated to enrage the Americans, and Hall was convinced that they should be given a copy of the translated telegram. Accordingly, the secretary at the American Embassy in London, Edward Bell, was handed the full, complete text on February 19, on condition that he kept the secret to himself for the time being, until the Foreign Office had weighed up all its options. Bell was stunned, then angry, and then sure that the message was a fabrication. Finally, he was persuaded of its authenticity and assured the DNI that it was more than enough to bring America into the war. On February 20, Hall received permission to exploit the decrypt in any way he saw fit and promptly gave a copy to Dr. Walter Page, the American ambassador in London, at an unofficial briefing. After four days of discussion concerning the preparation of a cover story to protect the source, Dr. Page called at the Foreign Office and received an original of the Zimmermann telegram from the Foreign Secretary. He was also provided with an English translation and a cover story explaining how,

Early in the war the British government obtained possession of a copy of the German cypher code used in the above message and have made it their business to obtain copies of Bernstorff's cypher messages to Mexico, among others, which are sent back to London and decyphered here. This accounts for their being able to decypher this message from the German government to their representative in Mexico and also for the delay from January 19 until now in their receiving the information.[11]

All this was, of course, an elaborate fiction, but Room 40 could not allow the Americans to suspect that the State Department landline had also been subject to covert interception. The suggestion that the telegram had come from the Mexican end was also designed to divert the enemy's attention away from its compromised channels of communication in Europe.

The ploy worked, for Room 40 subsequently had the pleasure of intercepting and decrypting Page's report to President Wilson, in which he broke the news of the Zimmermann telegram for the first time:

> You can probably obtain a copy of the text relayed by Bernstorff from the cable office in Washington. The first group is the number of the telegram, 130, and the second is 13042, indicating the number of the code used. The last but two is 97556, which is Zimmermann's signature.[12]

Page ended his own message with Hall's cover story: "The copies of this, and other telegrams, were not obtained in Washington, but were bought in Mexico." On February 28, the State Department responded by asking Hall to decrypt three telegrams that had been intercepted between Bernstorff and certain German diplomatic missions in South America. Evidently, the Americans were anxious to prove beyond any doubt that the British Admiralty had indeed broken the diplomatic code used by the German Foreign Ministry. Hall duly obliged, and the full text of the Zimmermann telegram was released to the press and published on March 1, 1917. Astonishingly, instead of denouncing the telegram as a forgery, Zimmermann admitted that it was genuine, thereby ensuring America's entry into the war.

It was inevitable, as a consequence of the Zimmermann telegram and the Foreign Minister's admission of its authenticity, that President Wilson would end the United States neutrality, and this announcement was made to Congress on April 2, 1917.

Perhaps the most remarkable aspect of the entire episode was the extraordinary reluctance of the Germans to accept that their diplomatic code had been compromised. Demonstrating its continued faith in the integrity of its communications, Berlin assumed that the Americans had got hold of a translated version of the telegram, after it had been decrypted, at either their embassy in Washington or in Mexico. This flawed process of elimination did not impress Ambassador Eckhardt, who appeared to have guessed the truth and reported to Zimmermann: "Treachery or indiscretion here out of the question; therefore apparently it happened in USA, or cipher 13040 is compromised." Berlin was thoroughly unconvinced by Eckhardt's explanation and, on March 21, pursued the matter further by demanding: "Most secret. Decipher personally. Please cable in same cipher who deciphered Nos. I and II, how the originals and decodes were kept and in particular whether both dispatches were kept in the same place."[13] All this correspondence was exchanged in the same diplomatic code as the original telegram and must have caused some amusement to the Room 40 staff, who were, of course, routinely monitoring it. Eckhardt became increasingly indignant that his own security procedures should be questioned, especially when he was sure the leak had come from Washington. The Foreign Ministry in Berlin was less certain and advised that "Various indications suggest that treachery was committed in Mexico. The greatest caution is indicated. Burn all compromising material." This was the last straw for the innocent ambassador, who demanded that both he and his secretary, Magnus, receive an apology or formal clearance from a board of inquiry. This clearly did not suit the Foreign Ministry, which ended the increasingly acrimonious exchanges on a conciliatory note: "Hardly conceivable that betrayal took place in Mexico. No blame rests on either you or Magnus." Incredibly, no further attempt was made to identify the source of the Zimmermann disclosure, and the same diplomatic code continued to be used for Berlin's most sensitive cables.

America's entry into the war was to have a conclusive strategic impact on hostilities; this is, therefore, an appropriate moment to review the American SIGINT effort up to April 1917. The most significant American contribution to SIGINT had been made early in 1916 by an infantry officer, Captain Parker Hitt, who had written a *Manual for the Solution of Military Ciphers* for a course at the U.S. Signal Corps School, Fort Leavenworth, Kansas. This slim volume, of just one hundred pages, remains one of the great unclassified SIGINT classics. Hitt outlined the two basic methods of encipherment—transposition and substitution—and described how ciphers could be solved by the construction of alphabetic frequency tables. This was the system that had been developed in Room 40 and was founded on the belief that in any text of a particular language certain letters will appear in a reasonably predictable ratio to other letters. Once this principle has been grasped, Hitt asserted, "no message should be considered indecipherable.'' On the matter of interception, Hitt observed:

> All radio messages sent out can be copied at hostile stations within radio range. If the enemy can get a fine wire within one hundred feet of a buzzer line or within thirty feet of a telegraph line, the message can be copied by induction.[14]

Hitt also gave some excellent advice for future SIGINT analysts:

> The preamble, ''place from,'' date, address and signature give most important clues as to the language of the cipher, the cipher method probably used, and even the subject matter of the message. If the whole of a telegraphic or radio message is in cipher, it is highly probable that the preamble, ''place from'' etc. are in an operator's cipher and are distinct from the body of the message. As these operator's ciphers are necessarily simple, an attempt should always be made to discover, by means of analysis to be set forth later, the exact extent of the operator's cipher and then to decipher the parts of the message enciphered with it.[15]

Using Hitt's *Manual* as a guide, a young State Department telegraph operator named Herbert Yardley began examining many of the messages that routinely passed through his hands. On one occasion, he overheard a cable office in New York informing the White House operator that a telegram of five hundred coded groups was about to be transmitted from Colonel House to the President. Yardley copied the telegram and solved the message within two hours. This achievement led Yardley to write a lengthy *Exposition on the Solution of American Diplomatic Codes*, which caused the State Department to introduce a new code, but Yardley broke that too. Although the British had gone to some lengths to conceal Room 40's activities, the State Department was perfectly aware that ''England maintains a large bureau for solving diplomatic correspondence'' and assumed that U.S. cables were routinely intercepted. Like the Germans, the Americans had complete faith in the integrity of their cipher arrangements, or at least until Yardley demonstrated his prowess. For the first time the State Department acknowledged that its most sensitive communications had probably been read by the British; its response was to appoint Yardley to a secret unit, which subsequently became the War Department Cipher Bureau. By 1918, Yardley had 150 people under him and an annual budget of $100,000.

Ironically, as soon as the United States entered the war, the British government informed the President that it "considered the War Department's method of coding cablegrams entirely unsafe and a serious menace to secrecy." The news was also conveyed that the Germans were probably intercepting all of America's cable traffic. There is no evidence to support that claim, but no doubt the British Admiralty was anxious to persuade its new allies to exercise all possible caution. Washington was spun a yarn that enemy submarines often tapped underwater cables. Apparently by "stretching other wires alongside for a distance of several hundred feet telegraph operators stationed in the submarines can copy the passing messages by induction."[16] Yardley seems to have accepted this tall tale, for both the State and War departments quickly altered their coding practices and became more security conscious. The American Cipher Bureau, which was eventually to become notorious as the "Black Chamber," had considerable success, particularly with Spanish traffic, and even solved some British codes, including one used in a message from the British Embassy in Washington alerting the War Office to Yardley's imminent arrival in London on an official visit in August 1918. Yardley recalled later that he had

> consumed a great deal of tea and drank quantities of whisky and soda with various officers in the War Office. They were affable enough and invited me to their clubs. But I received no information. I was at a distinct disadvantage for I did not dare communicate with Washington, since the British would decode every word I sent.[17]

During the last twelve months of the war, the Admiralty's SIGINT experts completed their mastery of the airwaves. A further four Zeppelins were shot down over England and, during the first four months of 1918, no less than twenty-four U-boats were sunk, more than the total sunk during the whole of 1916.

The year 1918 also brought some other welcome developments. On April 11, the *UB-33* was sunk by a mine in the Channel. A fortnight later, the wreck was found by a minesweeper and, on May 6, divers started a search. On May 21, they recovered the body of the commander, Leutnant Gregor, and a steel case containing the latest signals. Evidently, the *UB-33* had been at sea for less than a week when she had strayed into a minefield. At the end of the following month, the *UC-11* was sunk by one of her own mines in the Shipwash and was promptly dived on by the NID team with good results.

On July 19, 1918, the *UB-110* was depth charged just off the coast of Yorkshire and sunk. Thirteen survivors were picked up, and after a visit from divers who succeeded in finding various significant documents, including the commander's log, it was decided to launch a salvage operation. The *UB-110* was brought to the surface and towed into Newcastle, where she went into a dry dock.

Finally, the last U-boat to yield SIGINT secrets was the *UB-109*, which was mined off the Azores on August 29 after a thirty-two-day patrol from Ostend. An NID team was on the scene the same afternoon and two divers, Leading Seaman E. Blackford and Able Seaman T. Clear, managed to swim inside through an open hatch. The supervising officer, Commander Guybon Damant, who was also the Royal Navy's Inspector of Diving (and, incidentally, the man who brought up five million pounds worth of gold bullion from the *Laurentic*), later reported:

> P.M. on day of sinking fore hatch was cleared of bodies, bedding, etc., and some personal material sent the Admiralty. On 30th and 31st much important material was recovered though weather only allowed work on one tide. Diver had by now got as far as the control room. On 1st September again only one tide could be worked but the control room was passed, the W/T [wireless telegraphy] cabinet entered and much valuable material found.[18]

Among the interesting items recovered were the most recently issued series of Channel charts. One remarkable entry in the submarine's log illustrated the Admiralstab's increasing concern about a link between the heavy reliance of U-boats on wireless and the escalating rate of losses. During August and September 1918, sixteen U-boats were lost, and the crew of the *UB-109* had used a carrier pigeon to report the submarine's intended return to base. Soon after the bird had been released, the *UB-109* had struck a mine and had sunk in fourteen fathoms of water.

In 1914, the British army had expected an old-fashioned war of movement in which cavalry might have been expected to find wireless useful; instead, it had been faced with a deadlocked war of attrition filled with static battles. The Royal Navy had thought itself invincible, but had underestimated the subtleties and destructive abilities of U-boats and Zeppelins. Germany's initial technical innovation at sea and in the air had placed England in difficulties which had only been overcome by British SIGINT ingenuity at making use of German human error.

3

GC&CS

When a long argument took place as to what the new department should be called I suggested "Public Benefactors." Considering the fact that the immediate task was bound to be mostly diplomatic ciphers, the obvious choice should have been the Foreign Office but as they had little faith in our work they turned down the idea and the Admiralty was left in charge.

—WILLIAM F. CLARKE in "The Years Between," *History of Room 40*

After the Armistice had been signed, the British government was confronted with the prospect of having to dismantle the highly sophisticated intelligence-gathering organizations which had, time and again, proved themselves to be invaluable sources of information. Neither the army nor the Admiralty wished to get rid of their special units. Even the most overt side of SIGINT, postal censorship, remained in operation until June 21, 1919. After this date, a skeleton staff was retained to make preparations for the swift reintroduction of censorship, if required. By July 1919, the staff had been reduced to fifteen, and by September there were just six censors left.

Although the civilian censors were being released, Colonel Arthur French was determined not to lose MI1(b), under Colonel Simpson, and Brigadier Anderson's army cryptographic unit, MI1(e). Admiral Hall did not want to lose NID 25 either, although it was clear that the artificial boundaries between the War Office and Admiralty bureaucracies had led to much unnecessary muddle. For example, when a Zeppelin was located over the countryside, the War Office alerted the Royal Flying Corps. As soon as the raider changed course for home, across the North Sea, the Royal Naval Air Service was sent into action by the Admiralty.

It was in part as a result of the duplication of effort, both in the SIGINT field and in the more general area of espionage, that the War Cabinet created a Secret Service Committee in 1919 to review the existing arrangements and offer advice for the future. The committee, whose existence was a closely guarded secret, was chaired by Sir Warren Fisher, the then Permanent Under-Secretary at the Treasury, and included Sir Eyre Crowe, the Assistant Under-Secretary of State at the Foreign Office, and Maurice Hankey, the Cabinet Secretary. Together they took evidence from a bewildering range of British intelligence officers from the Foreign Office, the Colonial Office, the India Office and the Home Office, who all made an equally wide range of proposals. Among those who offered opinions on the future of the postwar British intelligence establishment was the Director of Military Intelligence, Brigadier-General Sir George Cockerill, Sir Cecil Kaye, Director of India's Home Intelligence Department, Admiral Hall's successor as DNI, Admiral Hugh Sinclair, and the recently knighted Director-Generals of MI5 and SIS, Sir Vernon Kell and Sir Mansfield Smith-Cumming. All admitted that their respective services had been recruiting agents, and Fisher's committee concluded that there seemed to be no logical division of labor or effort. Eventually, it was decided to regularize the position in peacetime. Henceforth Kell's Imperial Security Service, MI5, would be responsible for intelligence and security matters within the Empire and would liaise closely with the colonial authorities and the Home Office, which would administer a separate Directorate of Intelligence (under the leadership of the Assistant Commissioner of the Metropolitan Police, Sir Basil Thomson). Sir Mansfield Smith-Cumming's Secret Intelligence Service would stay under the departmental control of the Foreign Office, but would take over all other overseas intelligence-gathering operations and provide the Admiralty and other services with information.

Just as there had been a multiplicity of organizations engaging in espionage during the Great War, there had also been a variety of specialist service units dealing with SIGINT. The War Cabinet had sought to eliminate the expensive, wasteful duplication by combining NID 25, better known as Room 40, and Colonel French's MI1(b), the War Office's cryptographic section, in a new body to be established under the civil administration of the Admiralty. It was the idea of an official from the Communications Department of the Foreign Office, (Sir) Courtenay Forbes, to conceal the unit under the disingenuous title of the Government Code and Cypher School.

That there was a need for such an organization was clear. Room 40's own achievements were, of course, only known to a small circle, but they had exerted a disproportionate influence on the conduct of the war and the Allied victory. Certainly Sinclair was anxious to retain the invaluable cryptographic expertise that had been built up and wanted to expand into such areas as the French diplomatic traffic which had, until the Armistice, remained untouched. He was also keen to pursue the work that had already begun on Greek, Italian, Spanish, Scandinavian and Balkan telegrams.

After a debate that had lasted throughout the spring and summer, a secret War Cabinet minute outlining the formation of the Government Code and Cypher School dated October 24, 1919, was circulated, in which it was announced that the new organization would come into formal existence on November 1, 1919, under the leadership of Alastair Denniston and the control of the DNI. The duties of the new organization were set out as follows:

(a) To compile and be responsible for printing all codes and cyphers used by British Government Departments, with the sole exception of those mentioned in paragraph 5 below.

(b) To examine all the British Government codes and cyphers now in force and the purpose for which they are used, mainly with a view to ascertaining and, where necessary, increasing their degree of security; but also so as to ensure that messages shall be free from ambiguity and undue delay ensuing from mutilation in transit, and that they shall be coded in the most economical manner possible.

(c) To maintain the closest liaison with all British Government Departments using codes and cyphers, and to advise them generally in matters relating thereto.

(d) To instruct as large a proportion of officers as possible who may be employed at any time in coding and cyphering.

(e) To assist in the preparation of any handbooks or instructions relating to coding or cyphering, or of those concerning the handling of code and cypher messages in general.

In addition, the Admiralty suggested the attachment of a liaison officer from the War Office, the Air Ministry, Foreign Office, India Office, Colonial Office, Ministry of Munitions, Ministry of Food, Ministry of Transport and the GPO. Their function would be:

(i) To keep in touch with the requirements of his Department as regards codes and cyphers and all matters in connection therewith, and to ensure that these requirements are met by the Government Code and Cypher School.

(ii) To be responsible for the suitability of the "Dictionary" (or

Vocabulary) of the codes and cyphers compiled for his Department.
(iii) To advise the Head of his Department on:-

(a) The institution of additional books to meet new developments.

(b) "Departmental Codes" before and during their construction.
(iv) To maintain a watch over his Departmental messages for faults in coding or cyphering, or any other defects, which might prejudice the security of the code or cypher used in this connection: he will work in close cooperation with the Head of the Coding and Cyphering Section of his Department.
(v) To assist in the instruction of the Officers of his own Service who may be employed at any time in coding and cyphering.
5. The preparation, etc., of the "Signal Books" and purely "Departmental Codes" of the three fighting Services will remain in the hands of the Services concerned. The Government Code and Cypher School, however, will advise on the general principles of their construction and the limitation of their "life." The decision as to what books are to be classed as "Departmental Codes" will be made by the Government Code and Cypher School after consultation with the Departments concerned.[1]

Although the Admiralty recommended that the preparation of signal books and departmental codes for the three fighting services should remain in its hands, it was suggested that GC&CS should advise on general principles, such as their construction and "life." What makes the War Cabinet's charter so extraordinary is the omission of any mention of SIGINT or the interception of extraneous, alien wireless signals. The "policing" functions of MI1(b) and Room 40 were insignificant when compared to their intelligence gathering, yet there is no mention of such a role in the document.

GC&CS was to be accommodated in Marconi's old headquarters at Watergate House, Adelphi (just a few yards from the Savoy Hotel), and the staff, under Denniston, was to consist of the school's deputy head, Edward Travis, four senior assistants: Lieutenant Fryer from MI1(b), Dillwyn Knox, Oliver Strachey, William Clarke from Room 40, and twenty-one junior assistants, including Ernest Hobart-Hampden, Felix Fetterlein, G.L.N. Hope, J. Hooper, Lieutenant W.P. Mayo, Captain E.D. Hanley, Captain R.N.C. Hunt, Lieutenants A.G.R. Rees, R. Aitken, W.C.S. Maine, E.H. McGrath, Mr. N.B. Jopson, Mr. E. Barnshaw-Smith, Leslie Lambert, the Reverend William Montgomery and Mr. J.

Turner. In addition, authorization was given for the employment (without benefit of pension) of four lady translators, one wireless expert, thirty-three women clerks, three typists and one junior administrative assistant. It was calculated that the total cost of twenty-five staff and their forty-six juniors would not exceed £21,217 during the first year of operation.

This establishment was approved by the Admiralty on January 26, 1919, and by the Treasury on March 18, 1920, although their Lordships expressed surprise that such senior figures as the Russian linguist, Felix Fetterlein, and the Japanese expert, Ernest Hobart-Hampden, should be categorized as junior assistants and paid on the civil service scale for assistant principals. They also had some reservations about the choice of Watergate House and suggested that as soon as "the present abnormal situation in the political world" had stabilized the School move to "some less expensive quarter."

As well as supporting the creation of GC&CS, the Cabinet also approved the insertion, at Sinclair's request, of a special clause into the 1920 Official Secrets Act. This remarkable piece of legislation, which escaped unnoticed at the time, required all international cable companies operating on British territory to submit copies of all their traffic (both dispatched and received) within ten days of transmission. This measure, which was similar to the emergency wartime censorship rules, relieved the pressure on the remaining intercept stations and reduced administration costs.

There had been many, particularly their Lordships in the Admiralty, who had said in 1919 that, in order to preserve the peace, the Treaty of Versailles should have included a clause forbidding countries to use any code for international messages that was not known and recognized, but this had not been done. After the war, most nations returned to their secretive ways. The German diplomatic traffic reverted to the use of impregnable one-time pads. In the absence of any useful German signals to intercept, GC&CS concentrated its efforts on Soviet traffic, which was monitored by the military, and Japanese signals, which were handled by the Royal Navy.

With the amalgamation of Room 40 and MI1(b), the War Office set about reorganizing its SIGINT capacity. On August 5, 1920, the King authorized the creation of a new Royal Corps of Signals which was to absorb the old Royal Engineers Signal Service. The Corps was based at the Signal Service Training Center at Bedford, commanded by Brigadier-General Godfrey-Faussett, and the Army Signal School at Dunstable. In addition, there were two hutted camps in Sussex, at Maresfield and Crowborough, which accommodated two training battalions. Overseas the Royal Corps maintained a network of stations known as the Army Chain, which linked Aldershot with Rhine Army Signals, Egypt Signals, No. 2 Wireless Company at Sarafand in Palestine, and Jubbulpore in India. There were also sections attached to British garrisons in Ireland, Gibraltar, Malta, Hong Kong, Malaya, Shanghai, Ceylon, Mauritius, Sierra Leone, Bermuda and Jamaica. In addition, some smaller, mobile intercept posts were established in a few mountain fortresses on India's Northwest Frontier, which were to prove extremely useful.

Traffic intercepted by these stations, and others in the Far East operated by the Admiralty, was relayed to GC&CS in London, where it was categorized with the aid of DF reports and traffic analysis. Once sorted (or "discriminated"), the raw material was examined by Fetterlein, the eccentric Russian émigré who had joined GC&CS from Room 40, and his three lady assistants who were also Russian refugees. Additional, temporary help was obtained from British consuls who had recently returned from the Soviet Union. Before the October Revolution, Fetterlein had been employed by General Jilinski's Russian cipher service, but had been obliged to flee to London where he had been hired by Admiral Hall in June 1918. The Soviets had scrapped the complex Tsarist codes which they inherited, which was just as well for them as Fetterlein had actually devised several of them himself. Instead, the new Soviet government resorted to relatively low-grade, manual ciphers for its diplomatic telegrams and these proved all too easy for Fetterlein. As a consequence, from November 1919 onward the British Cabinet was kept supplied with an impressive volume of Soviet decrypts. The intercepted traffic was highly regarded by the Prime Minister and the Foreign Secretary, and gave them an invaluable insight into Soviet foreign policy.

Of particular interest were decrypts of messages sent between Moscow and the Middle East, which eloquently betrayed Comintern's intention to subvert India. Moscow's public pronouncements were so completely contradicted by the intercepts that Lloyd George's government concluded that publication of the Soviets' secret diplomatic telegrams would have the desired effects of altering opinion at home and encouraging the Russians to cease funding subversion in the Empire. There was also plenty of evidence to suggest that the Soviet Trade Delegation (at that time the only official Soviet presence in Britain) was providing money to socialist extremists in England. A large part of that evidence was contained in Soviet diplomatic wireless messages passing between the Soviet headquarters in London, at Chesham Place, and Moscow. All this traffic had been intercepted at a discreet Home Office radio station located at 113 Grove Park, Camberwell, and relayed to GC&CS. Certainly the political climate appeared to be deteriorating rapidly and major civil unrest in London and the Midlands was predicted daily. Finally, and reluctantly, the Prime Minister conceded that there was no alternative but to publish some of the more incriminating decrypts. On August 17, 1920, various Fleet Street newspapers were issued with copies of Soviet telegrams, which revealed that the *Daily Herald* had been receiving a secret subsidy from Russia. *The Times* prefaced its report with the frank comment: "The following wireless messages have been intercepted by the British government." This was an astonishing disclosure, for very few people had any inkling of SIGINT or the secret work of GC&CS. Indeed, even the most historic SIGINT success, the Zimmermann telegram, was generally believed to have been obtained by espionage rather than wireless interception. The Cabinet had gambled on the Soviets assuming that a penetration agent had copied the texts after they had been deciphered, in much the same way that the German Foreign Ministry had suspected everyone and everything . . . except its precious diplomatic code. In spite of the indiscretion of *The Times*, the Soviets appeared to ignore the matter, and pressure grew for further disclosures. Even some professionals like Thomson and Sinclair believed the increasingly desperate situation justified the use of the decrypts, even if the source was to be compromised, ". . . we think that the publication of the decyphered cables has become so imperative that we must take the risks that will be entailed."[2] Others did not share this opinion. Maurice Hankey, the Cabinet Secretary, preferred not to risk losing such a "valuable and trustworthy source of secret information." On September 8, 1920, he sent the following memorandum to the Prime Minister:

> This particular cypher is a very ingenious one which was discovered by great cleverness and hard work. The key is changed daily and sometimes as often as three times in one message. Hence if it becomes known that we decoded the messages all the governments of the world will probably soon discover that no messages are safe.[3]

Denniston too was appalled by the way the politicians behaved. He became obsessively secretive and almost paranoid about security after these disclosures.

The newspaper stories that followed the government's statement were sensational and certainly appeared to have had the desired impact on British public opinion. The newspaper stories linking the Russian Trade Delegation with the *Daily Herald* continued into September, when further details of secret subsidies were made public and Lev Kamenev was expelled for smuggling stolen jewelry and using the proceeds to finance pro-Soviet propaganda. The leaders of the Trade Delegation offered a weak defense, but it must have been obvious to them that their own correspondence had been intercepted and read. In any event, by the end of December 1920, the Soviet wireless traffic had come to an abrupt halt all over the world and a system of couriers had been introduced. However, in March the following year the Director of Naval Intelligence reported to the Cabinet that the Soviet transmitters had resumed operations again, albeit with a more secure cipher. In that same month Lloyd George signed the Anglo-Soviet Trade Agreement, giving the West's first recognition to the legitimacy of Lenin's regime. One clause in the treaty bound the two countries to

> refrain from hostile actions or undertakings against the other and from conducting outside its own borders any official propaganda direct or indirect against the institutions of the British Empire or the Russian Soviet Republic respectively.

Within a matter of weeks of the signing, Felix Fetterlein had mastered the new Soviet ciphers and established that the Russians had no intention of honoring the new treaty.

As soon as GC&CS had broken into the new Soviet codes, summaries of the decrypts were circulated to the Cabinet. Fetterlein's extraordinary (and unexpected) breakthrough led the DNI to urge greater discretion in its exploitation. As he pointed out at the end of March 1921, "If intelligence is used for publicity it will be lost to us."

In spite of Sinclair's plea and the concerns voiced by other officials, including Sir Basil Thomson (then Assistant Commissioner [Crime] at Scotland Yard as well as Director of Intelligence at the Home Office), the politicians ignored the advice and prepared to deliver Moscow a broadside of evidence detailing the Soviet failure to keep to the 1921 Trade Agreement. The agreement had required Moscow to desist from actively supporting subversive elements within the British Empire, but the telegrams decrypted during the following two years showed clearly that the Russians had continued to finance Indian Nationalists and the Communist party of Great Britain.

The Cabinet's plan was to "rely exclusively upon communications which have passed in the last few months between the Russian government and its agents'' and to deliver a list of intercepts which were undeniably authentic. After much debate in Cabinet in April and May 1923, the Foreign Secretary, Lord Curzon, sent an ultimatum to Georgi Chicherin, the Soviet Commissar for Foreign Affairs, and in reply got a claim that his Note had been manufactured from ''decyphered parts of telegrams tendentiously manipulated and arbitrarily extended.'' In other words, the telegrams were authentic, but GC&CS's treatment of them had distorted their real meaning. Subsequent decrypts made it clear that Chicherin had been taken completely by surprise and had ordered an immediate suspension of contact with secret agents and anti-British extremists. This news was welcomed in Whitehall, and was some compensation for the inevitable change in Soviet coding procedures and the gradual introduction of the one-time pad which occurred later in the year. Certainly the Soviets could have had little doubt about the source of Lord Curzon's information. He quoted numerous Soviet communications and actually admitted in a public statement that none had been sent *en clair*.

GC&CS's long-awaited change of location eventually took place in April 1922 when the Foreign Office took over responsibility for GC&CS from the Admiralty, following the acceptance of the Cabinet's Secret Service Committee's recommendation on the subject. Denniston and his staff moved out of Watergate House to new offices in Queen's Gate. In practical terms, this was merely an administrative maneuver to reflect the Foreign Office's funding of GC&CS. In fact, overall responsibility for GC&CS remained with Admiral Sinclair, because in June 1923, following the unexpected death of Sir Mansfield Smith-Cumming, the DNI was appointed the new chief of the Secret Intelligence Service, and Sinclair took the titles CSS and Director of GC&CS.

The Secret Service Committee's decision to move GC&CS from the Admiralty was in response to two important conclusions which had been reached after a lengthy examination of SIGINT's contribution during the Great War. The first finding concerned the unsatisfactory nature of having different services involved in supplying Room 40 with its raw material. The intercept stations had been operated by both the Royal Navy and the military, while the equally important direction-finding stations were run almost exclusively by the Admiralty, apart from the small War Office network at Devizes and Leiston. Once the traffic had been analyzed, and perhaps decrypted, the resulting appreciations had been forwarded to various ''clients,'' including the Foreign Office. By moving GC&CS into the jurisdiction of the Foreign Office, the four vital processes of interception, direction finding, traffic analysis and decryption were placed under one roof. The fact that the CSS was also appointed Director of GC&CS was an acknowledgment of the unpalatable reality that SIGINT had proved consistently more reliable than the Secret Service's agents. The second finding stemmed from the belief that in peacetime the Diplomatic Section would become dominant, and that the Foreign Office would be its principal client. The government's preoccupation with Soviet Russia during the immediate postwar years seemed to prove this case conclusively, and led the services to complain jointly of their treatment under the new regime.

In January 1923, the three service directors of intelligence

arrived at the conclusion that the sole control of the government Code and Cypher School by the Foreign Office has inevitably affected the Fighting service as follows:

(a) They only receive a small proportion of the messages translated.

(b) They have no voice in the distribution of the messages.

(c) They have no means of ensuring that all messages which they may consider of interest to them are received by them.

(d) They have no voice in what cyphers are to be attacked, or what special "Subjects" are to receive attention.

(e) No provision is made for attacking or even systematically watching purely naval and military cyphers, nor for scrutinizing cyphers of local interest to various departments. Although information gained from them would be of little value at the time, a knowledge of the methods and systems as well as the vocabularies would be invaluable on the outbreak of war even though the actual cyphers were changed.

(f) In certain cases in the past, cyphers, which have been broken by the Government Code and Cypher School, have been arbitrarily withheld from the military organizations to whom they would have been of considerable value, on the grounds that the Foreign Office were not satisfied with the security of the organizations.[4]

The service objections to the Foreign Office's effective control over Britain's SIGINT program were to simmer on for some years in private. The secrets of the Great War were intended to remain secret, even though it was accepted that the regime in Moscow had obviously been alerted to GC&CS's cryptographic skills by the government's public disclosures. The eventual realization by the Soviet Union that many of its diplomatic ciphers had been compromised and read over a long period was an in-

THE COMPLETE ROLL OF GC&CS STAFF AT
QUEEN'S GATE[5]

1. Adams, Mrs. A.
2. Aitken, Miss M. M. A.
3. Aitken, Mr. R.
4. Anderson, Miss E.
5. Baker, Mrs. A.
6. Bostridge, Miss W. M.
7. Bowder, Mr. C. H.
8. Bremner, Miss K. J.
9. Buncher, Mrs. E. C.
10. Caw, Mrs. D.
11. Chesterman, Miss D.
12. Clarke, Mr. W. F.
13. Connor, Miss M. A.
14. Denniston, Mr. A. G.
15. Fetterlein, Mr. E. C.
16. Ford, Mr. H. R.
17. Fryer, Mr. S. E.
18. Gambril, Mr. O.
19. Gannell, Miss G. C.
20. Godfrey, Miss G. C.
21. Hanley, Captain E. D.
22. Harper, Miss C.
23. Harris, Miss M. M.
24. Harris, Miss N.
25. Hobart-Hampden, Mr. E.
26. Hooper, Mr. J.
27. Hope, Mr. G. L. N.
28. Hunt, Mr. R. N. C.
29. Jandrell, Miss E. K.
30. Jenkins, Miss F. M.
31. Jopson, Mr. N. B.
32. Joyce, Miss I. M.
33. Kennell, Miss E. M.
34. Knox, Mr. A. D.
35. Lambert, Mr. L. H.
36. Lawrence, Miss A.
37. Lilly, Mr. G. S.
38. Lunn, Miss H. C.
39. Lunn, Miss M. N.
40. Maine, Mr. H. C. S.
41. Martin, Miss K. A.
42. Mayhew, Miss E. J. C.
43. Mayo, Mr. M. P.
44. Mayo, Miss U.
45. McGrath, Mr. E. H.
46. Middows, Mrs. A. D.
47. Montgomery, Mr. W.
48. Mortimer, Miss E. M. N.
49. Muncey, Mrs. L. M.
50. Nicol, Miss O. M. L.
51. Nuttall, Miss A. M.
52. Oakes, Mrs. E. M.
53. O'Hea, Miss K.
54. Oxenford, Mrs. M.
55. Peile, Mr. M. J.
56. Pollard, Miss C. E.
57. Power, Mrs. C. J.
58. Prior, Miss M.
59. Pugh, Miss S. M.
60. Ramsay, Miss J. S.
61. Rees, Mr. A. G. R.
62. Rolfe, Mrs. M.
63. Rose, Miss W. V.
64. Saunders, Mr. A. E.
65. Seaward, Mrs. E. A.
66. Senyard, Miss P. G.
67. Sherwin, Miss C. E.
68. Slack, Miss S. V.
69. Smith, Mr. A. N.
70. Smith, Miss K. A.
71. Smith, Miss M.
72. Smith, Miss W. A.
73. Southwell, Miss M.
74. Spencer, Miss M. C.
75. Stevens, Miss A.
76. Stevenson, Miss C. A.
77. Strachey, Mr. O.
78. Stradling, Mr. S. A.
79. Swanston, Mrs. L.
80. Tanqueray, Miss G. E. C.
81. Travis, Mr. E. W. H.
82. Turner, Mr. J.
83. Varmen, Mrs. B. E.
84. Waker, Mrs. M. M.
85. Weatherill, Miss F.
86. Whinyates, Mr. G.
87. White, Miss W.
88. Whittingham, Mrs. J.
89. Williams, Miss T.
90. Wilson, Miss K. W.
91. Woods, Mr. G. S.

evitable consequence of the Cabinet's decision to expose Soviet duplicity, but there had never been any other breach of security in England to indicate to the general public the scale of the country's SIGINT program or, for that matter, the actual existence of GC&CS. The only book to have speculated on the subject was Ferdinand Tuohy's *The Secret Corps*, published in 1920, which elaborated on the principles of interception and direction finding, chiefly in the context of the Zeppelin raids and the monitoring of the enemy's naval movements, with the final comment that "the profound bearing of Marconi's patent on naval operations left one, at times, aghast." Tuohy claimed:

> Never once did Capelle or Tirpitz or Scheer engage on an operation, however insignificant, without some hint of it coming to the ears of our ever listening wireless operators. Hundreds of ships were located yearly, and thousands of code groups intercepted—all to be classified and studied and restudied day after day as each fresh wireless development arose. . . . Our operators, after years of listening, were able to recognize the principal German operators by their method of transmitting, no matter what call signs they used.[6]

Tuohy evidently knew much more about the secret wireless war that had been conducted by the Allies, but he was deliberately vague when citing examples of SIGINT operations. The true scale of the war's SIGINT conflict was to remain a closely guarded secret, at least for the time being.

Much of this changed, on October 31, 1925, when Admiral Sir Reginald Hall, now the Conservative Member of Parliament for Eastbourne, was invited to comment on the publication in America of Ambassador Page's letter of 1917 to President Wilson, in which he revealed the origins of the decrypted version of the Zimmermann telegram and credited Hall with having provided him with it. Hall was clearly very embarrassed by this development and said as little as poss.ble, beyond confirming the substance of Page's sensational claim:

> It can easily be understood that our aim was to prevent the Germans from attaching too much importance to the service which provided us with our information. When President Wilson published the famous telegram of Zimmermann, containing the overtures made to Mexico by Germany, I took great care to ensure that the Germans should never suspect our own part in the matter. . . . It is a tradition in our service never to talk of our work, and but for the recent publication

of the letter of Dr. Walter Hines Page, United States Ambassador in London, I should have continued to hold my peace.

There the matter ended, at least for the time being. Certainly GC&CS must have been anxious to suppress any further comment, for its work was being hampered by the introduction in Europe of a new phenomenon: automatic wireless transmitters linked to machine ciphers. The speed of signaling was considerably faster than the average achieved by tapping Morse messages by hand, and the machine ciphers appeared impregnable. Denniston's view was, understandably, that the less said on the subject in public the better. This opinion was not shared by Sir Alfred Ewing, who was still smarting from the lack of any recognition, private or public, of his contribution to Room 40's work. He may also have been more than a little piqued by Hall's modest remarks, for officially Room 40 had not come under the Intelligence Division's jurisdiction until 1917. Ewing proceeded to rectify the injustice of this by making a public statement which would clarify his own role, and an opportunity presented itself on December 13, 1927, when he gave a lecture to the Edinburgh Philosophical Institution on what he referred to as his "special war work." It was attended by an audience of nearly fifteen hundred and was reported in the press, which caused great consternation at the Admiralty. Ewing recalled many of his own experiences in Room 40, and among the other bombshells he dropped, which included the very first account of the recovery of the *Magdeburg*'s code book in 1914, was his statement that,

> besides intercepting naval signals, the cryptographers dealt successfully with much cipher to Germany's agents in Madrid, North and South America, Constantinople, Athens, Sofia and other places. One group of deciphered messages threw useful light in advance on the Easter Rebellion in Ireland, and another on the German intrigues in Persia. Among the many political messages read by the staff was the notorious Zimmermann Telegram. . . .

These were astonishing revelations, especially since Ewing himself had remarked, by way of a preface, "The fact that such work was going on was known to very few persons, even in official circles or in the Fleet. It remained a secret to the end, and was probably the best-kept secret of the war." As soon as news of this unprecedented breach of security reached London, the Admiralty immediately sought, and obtained, an undertaking from Sir Alfred not to discuss Room 40's activities any further. He was also obliged to scrap plans for his autobiography. He kept his word and said nothing more on the subject until his death in 1935, although he altered his entry in *Who's Who* from "Director of Naval Education 1909–16" to "was in charge of a department of the Admiralty dealing with enemy cipher, 1914–17." The Admiralty seriously considered prosecuting Ewing, but was eventually dissuaded, no doubt by those who were keen not to attract further attention to the incident. The damage, however, was already done, and two years later, in *The World Crisis*, Winston Churchill referred obliquely to Ewing's work tracking the German High Seas Fleet with the aid of the "cipher and signal books of the German navy" from the *Magdeburg*. Twelve years later, in 1939, Ewing's son wrote *The Man of Room 40*, in which he devoted a chapter of just thirty noncontentious pages to his late father's war work at the Admiralty. No doubt he wished to say more, but Sir Alfred's narrow escape from prosecution and the uncertain political climate counseled prudence and discretion.

No further comment was made about wartime SIGINT until June 1931, and the simultaneous publication in London and Indianapolis of Herbert Yardley's autobiography, *The American Black Chamber*, and its serialization in the *Saturday Evening Post*. Two years earlier, the newly elected President Hoover had appointed Henry Stimson his Secretary of State, and Yardley, who had been employed as a cryptographer by the State Department since 1919, had begun to channel summaries of decrypts to Stimson. Stimson had demanded to know the source of the summaries, and as soon as he had been informed that the State Department maintained a secret cipher bureau in New York, he had ordered its immediate closure and the dismissal of the staff. Even if the War Department had wished to keep Yardley's office open, as seemed possible at one stage, no one had been prepared to ignore Stimson's policy. Stimson was later to recall that he ordered the Black Chamber to be disbanded with the comment, since much quoted: "Gentlemen do not read each other's mail."

By this date, Yardley had spent some sixteen years decrypting foreign codes and had been brilliantly successful. He was convinced that if it were generally realized that most other nations had similar organizations for deciphering signals, the government would be less inclined to take such a moral view of the affair. Perhaps he also felt that if the American public appreciated the many SIGINT triumphs of the Black Chamber, it might be restored. But as he himself stated, "Now that the Black Chamber has been destroyed there is no valid reason for withholding its secrets." His autobiography caused instant controversy. One of the first secrets he "blew" was the true origins of the Zimmermann note: "This telegram was deciphered by the British Cryptographic Bureau early in 1917, just before we entered the war." And there was also plenty more. Quite apart from describing in detail many of the cases that had passed over his desk, Yardley's memoirs were liberally illustrated with photographs of various code books, including a part reconstruction of a British Foreign Office code. In chapter ten, entitled "The British Cipher Bureau," Yardley gave an account of his visit to Europe in 1918 when he had liaised with Colonel French at MI1(b) and attended the Peace Conference at Versailles as the American delegation's cryptographer. Yardley also gave a version of Room 40's work, although it was a trifle exaggerated:

> Though I discovered that the British decoder was no cleverer than our own, those in power in England considered a Cipher Bureau of such tremendous importance that they placed an Admiral at its head. This man, Admiral Hall, because of the information he obtained from the messages that his enormous bureau deciphered, stood next to Lloyd George in power. The Foreign Office was extremely jealous of his position for it was almost wholly dependent on him for information revealing the secret political intrigues of enemy and neutral governments.[7]

Yardley recalled how he had been introduced to Admiral Hall, who had refused to cooperate with the American government on an official level, but had been perfectly prepared to supply him with certain items of information on an informal, personal basis. He had apparently "remained firm in his refusal to give me any information about the German diplomatic codes used for wireless messages between Berlin and Madrid," but had eventually agreed to hand over "several copies of a certain neutral government's diplomatic codes and a copy of a German naval code in two volumes."

These disclosures were not, in the aftermath of Ewing's indiscretion, the first public statements concerning the interception and decryption of wireless signals, but none the less they caused a furor. Some of his stories were particularly awkward for the British government and obviously still embarrassingly relevant:

> As late as 1921, Clarence H. Mackay, President of the Postal Telegraph Company, testifying before a Senate Committee on cable landing licenses, said, "Since censorship ceased the British government have required us to turn over all messages 10 days after they had

been sent or received. This is a right which they claim under the landing licenses they issue to all cable companies.''[8]

Yardley concluded that he "did not wonder that England was a great power, for she read practically every code telegram that passed over her cables." He also mentioned the names of several British SIGINT experts, among them Colonel French and Captain Brooke-Hunt, both of MI1(b), and Captain Hitchings, "who, according to his superiors, was worth four divisions to the British army." The effect of the best seller on the authorities in Whitehall cannot be gauged now, but the American government responded by passing a law to prevent unauthorized disclosure of official codes or the information in them. Known as the Yardley Act "For the Protection of Government Records," it included penalties of fines up to $10,000 or imprisonment up to ten years, or both, upon conviction. Fortunately for Yardley, the law was not retroactive.

While Washington was coping with Yardley's unwelcome revelations, a book was published in London which reproduced some of Ewing's notorious lecture in Scotland and seemed to confirm many of his claims. *Strange Intelligence: Memoirs of Naval Secret Service*, written by two journalists, Hector Bywater, from the *Daily Telegraph* (who had been employed by Admiral Hall during the war), and H. C. Ferraby, the naval correspondent of the *Daily Express*, contained a chapter entitled "The Men Who Heard the U-Boats Talk," in which the authors stated that most of Germany's submarines had been tracked by the Admiralty's wartime Intelligence Division. The authors observed, "The sources of information were many and varied. The most valuable of all were the wireless directional stations round our coast." But they were not prepared to give away any secrets: "How was the decoding done? There were dozens of different ways, of course, some of them still too confidential to be divulged even after this lapse of time."[9]

A large part of the book is now considered to be unreliable and overdramatized, but it was obvious that both authors had received help from Admiral Hall, who had recently been refused permission to write his own autobiography. As already mentioned, Hall had been elected a Conservative Member of Parliament in 1919 and, on his retirement ten years later, had sought to publish his memoirs and expand on the remarks made in 1925 in response to the Page disclosures. Instead, he had to content himself with writing the foreword to the second edition of *Strange Intelligence* and commenting that the book's revelations "can now do no harm either to the public service or individuals."

A year later Hector Bywater returned to the subject with the publication of *Their Secret Purposes: Dramas and Mysteries of the Naval War*. Evidently this second book, and in particular the chapter entitled "Listening-In: Intelligence by Wireless," had been inspired by Yardley's revelations, but its most interesting feature was its assertion that the Black Chamber's "counterpart at the British Admiralty" had not "continued to function well into the postwar period." This denial was, of course, completely untrue, for GC&CS had remained under the supervision of the Director of Naval Intelligence until 1923, when it had come under the control of the Foreign Office. One is tempted to conclude that Bywater had been nobbled by one of his former colleagues from Room 40 so that Yardley's disclosures would be put into a wartime context, with the intention of avoiding any discussion of current British SIGINT activities. Certainly GC&CS must have been extremely concerned about Clarence Mackay's admission that the British government routinely required copies of all overseas telegrams to be delivered to the Foreign Office. Incredibly, this information was suppressed until February 1967, when the *Daily Express* was tipped off to the practice by a former employee of Commercial Cables & Western Union. A major political row ensued and became known as the D-Notice Affair (see page 281–83).

The publication of Bywater's *Their Secret Purposes* coincided with the release of a third book covering much the same ground, *40 O.B.*, written by Hugh Cleland Hoy, formerly a member of Admiral Hall's secretariat at the Admiralty's Intelligence Division. Hoy's foreword was contributed by Sir Basil Thomson, the former Director of Intelligence at the Home Office, who disingenuously referred to the author as "a private secretary to the Director of Naval Intelligence." Hoy freely admitted:

> I have also been obliged to omit many startling and exciting matters. The Official Secrets Act is far-reaching and I am also bound by personal loyalty to the service, and to the promptings of humanity and the demands of social obligation. So in making this compilation I have had to remember—and also to forget.[10]

His book gave a much criticized, but comprehensive, study of naval intelligence during the Great War, but made no mention of Yardley or, for that matter, of any of Room 40's personalities. According to one critic, Hoy had merely been a confidential typist and had never been allowed access to Room 40. With this in mind, it is clear that the book received some official sanction because the author included the first detailed version of how the Zimmermann telegram had been "picked up in the ordinary way in code by the listening stations on the east coast and flashed immediately to the Admiralty along with other messages to be deciphered.''

Possibly because Hoy's book had not been prosecuted or suppressed, others followed. Since the Royal Navy had taken much of the credit for SIGINT achievements during the Great War, it is perhaps not surprising that a military intelligence officer should have gone into print. In 1934, Walter Gill published *War, Wireless and Wangles*, the most candid account to date on the subject. Gill had been educated at Christ Church, Oxford, and had later become a Fellow at Merton, where he had specialized in electrical research. In 1914, he had joined the Hampshire Regiment as a private soldier, but had soon been commissioned into what he referred to as "Royal Engineers Wireless Intelligence" and had been responsible for the construction of intercept stations at Alexandria and the Near East. He had served with a Royal Engineers wireless company consisting of two sections trained in intercept procedures (but described, somewhat coyly, in regimental histories and elsewhere only as "special duties") that had been posted to Turkey and Iraq. In his entertaining memoirs he remarked:

> Even now the Official Secrets Act looms darkly over writers, and much that is of enthralling interest will never be told. For my part I propose to safeguard myself by disclosing nothing more than has already been revealed by Cabinet ministers, admirals, generals and other exalted writers of war books, and in addition no harm can come of referring to such things as direction-finding, which is now an everyday practice with ships and aircraft. Further, no secret is being given away in stating that it is possible to intercept a wireless message, and in some cases to decipher it.[11]

Gill had been indoctrinated into the secrets of SIGINT at the Marconi-built War Office station at Bishops Cannings, near Devizes, and in early 1916 had been sent to Egypt where he had built a 160-foot mast on top of the Great Pyramid. It was later discovered that German troops in Palestine had only been equipped with the most rudimentary of military ciphers, so a small cryptographic unit had been created in Cairo to solve locally intercepted messages. These were of considerable value and had also provided Admiral Hall's experts with additional clues, especially when texts received from Europe had been reciphered for onward transmission.

Gill's remarkable book, which he illustrated himself with cartoons, gave a unique insight into the work of the War Office's SIGINT organization. His unit remained in existence at the end of the war, although Gill himself returned to Oxford to become curator of the University Chest. His wireless company continued to intercept wireless traffic in the Middle East until 1923, when the section dealing with Turkish signals was absorbed into the No. 2 Wireless Company, based at Sarafand in Palestine and commanded by Major J.P.G. Worlledge. The Iraq-based section was not disbanded until 1930, by which time Sarafand had taken responsibility for feeding MI1(b), then under the leadership of Captain W.D. McGregor, with raw intelligence. At the outbreak of the Second World War, both Gill and Worlledge were to play important roles in Britain's SIGINT organization.

The end of 1923 marked an important moment in the development of the Government Code and Cypher School. The former DNI, Admiral Sinclair, had been appointed the new chief of the Secret Intelligence Service in June and had assumed the title of Director of GC&CS, although Alastair Denniston had retained day-to-day control of the organization's work. To date, that work had concentrated on the Soviet diplomatic messages intercepted by Grove Park, but the new CSS was anxious to expand Britain's SIGINT capacity and, together with Denniston, created a Cryptography and Interception Committee in 1924 to liaise between GC&CS and the services.

Compared to the wartime cryptographic establishments of the War Office and Admiralty, GC&CS during the 1920s and 1930s was relatively small, but still very secret. Only a handful of officials in Whitehall were aware of the existence of GC&CS, and any external communications were handled at a very senior level, usually by the Deputy Under-Secretary of State at the Foreign Office, (Sir C.) Hubert Montgomery. Officially, the organization's address was simply "Room 14, Foreign Office," but in reality Denniston and his team worked from the large town house in Queen's Gate, South Kensington, to which they had moved in 1922. Denniston, with his six senior assistants, all of whom were former members of Admiral Hall's staff at Room 40, was responsible for both the administrative running of "the School," as it was always referred to in official correspondence, and its operational activities. For more than twenty years Denniston essentially was GC&CS. From the moment Ewing had invited him to the Admiralty in August 1914, Denniston had become a quiet, reserved individual, who would discuss his work with no one except, occasionally, his wife, Dorothy Gilliat, whom he met working in Room 40. His modest entry in *Who's Who* simply mentioned "Admiralty NID 1914–21, Foreign Office, 1921–45." His name was not publicly linked to cryptography until 1955, when Admiral Hall's biography, *The Eyes of the Navy*, by Admiral Sir William James was published. James had taken over the running of Room 40, as Hall's subordinate, after the departure of Sir Alfred Ewing in 1917 and had an intimate knowledge of SIGINT during the Great War. Nevertheless, James made only one brief reference to Denniston who, after his retirement in 1945, had become very bitter about his treatment, much as Sir Alfred Ewing had thirty years earlier.

Denniston was not a first-rate cryptographer, as he himself was prepared to admit, and he could never suffer fools gladly. Nevertheless, he was an able administrator and managed to cope with the varying demands of the Treasury, Foreign Office and armed services during the difficult interwar period. He never wrote an autobiography, but he did leave several batches of manuscript notes which shed fascinating light on his own experiences. At the end of the Great War, Admiral Hall sent him to Scotland to interpret for the Commander in Chief at the surrender of the German Fleet, and Denniston recalled:

> For the last four years I had considered myself and the department in which I worked a very important cog in the machine; now, for the first time, I ran across the "business end" of the weapon and I realized most strongly what a tiny little cog we were. Practically no one I met had any idea of the existence of such a cog, which was satisfactory to know, as we had tried to conceal our identity. I had to keep a straight face and lie right well to many an old friend from Osborne days whom I met up there, who wanted to know what my job was. On the whole I fancy I gave myself and my department a highly sensational appearance, such as would rejoice the readers of William LeQueux.[12]

Denniston's deputy, seven years his junior, was Commander Edward Travis, a signals officer who had served on Lord Jellicoe's staff until 1916, when he transferred to the Signal Division at the Admiralty. Two years later he joined Room 40 and, in 1924, became Denniston's deputy and head of a newly introduced Naval Section. He eventually succeeded Denniston in 1944.

Denniston's other senior assistants, who formed the nucleus of the

School's cryptographic work, were Oliver Strachey, Dillwyn Knox and William Clarke, with John Turner and Lieutenant Sydney Fryer (who died in 1924) being the "master linguists." Strachey had been born in 1874 and, like his brother Lytton, had been educated at Eton. In his short entry in *Who's Who*, he described his employment simply as "Has been engaged in work on East Indian Railway, on Historical Research, and in the Foreign Office."

Alfred Dillwyn Knox, known to everyone as "Dilly," was the second of four very accomplished sons born to the daughter of the Bishop of Lahore and the Bishop of Manchester. All his brothers were to distinguish themselves: his eldest brother, Edmund, was a successful writer and, under the name Evoe, the editor of *Punch* for seventeen years; Wilfred was an Honorary Canon of Ely and the author of many theological works, including *The Catholic Movement in the Church of England*; and Ronald, the youngest, became a Catholic convert and was eventually Chaplain to Oxford University, where all but Dilly had been educated (he went to Cambridge). Dilly Knox had joined Room 40 in 1915, having tried tutoring a youthful Harold Macmillan for a scholarship to Balliol. As a talented, if unorthodox, mathematician, Dilly had immersed himself in the cryptological puzzles of the German Admiralstab's three-letter Flag Code and, by 1917, had succeeded in reconstructing a substantial part of it. He virtually lived in his Admiralty office, Room 53, although he also shared a house in Chelsea with his fellow code breaker Frank Birch. In 1920, Dilly married Olive Roddam, his former secretary, and agreed to continue working for Denniston instead of taking up the Librarianship of King's College, Cambridge. From then until his premature death from cancer in February 1943, he devoted himself to the mysteries of Soviet one-time pads and German machine ciphers.

William Clarke, a barrister by training, had joined Room 40 in 1916 and, after the war, had been commissioned to write the *Contribution to the History of German Naval Warfare 1914–1918* with Frank Birch. Among Denniston's "junior assistants" were several personalities from Room 40: G.L.N. Hope, William Montgomery, Felix Fetterlein and Leslie Lambert. This, then, was the vital nucleus of GC&CS, which had supplied Lord Curzon with the Soviet decrypts released by the government in 1923.

In 1925, with an agreed establishment of six senior and eighteen juniors, Denniston obtained approval for an increase to ten seniors and twenty juniors. This enabled him to recruit, for the first time, direct from the universities, although all the candidates were required to sit the Civil

Service Commission Examination and pass at the administrative level. This presented few difficulties for the individuals concerned, such as Joshua Cooper, but Denniston was unable to give his interviewees even the remotest idea of the kind of work they might be engaged in.

In the ten-year period between 1926 and 1936, GC&CS maintained its establishment total but, with increasing length of service and no prospects of promotion, was obliged to alter the personnel balance to fifteen juniors and fifteen assistants. Thanks to the prevailing economic climate few other changes took place, apart from a move in June 1926 from Queen's Gate into the third and fourth floors of Broadway Buildings, which also happened to accommodate the headquarters of Sinclair's Secret Intelligence Service. Fetterlein had succeeded in mastering the new Soviet ciphers again at the end of 1925 and, with the help of his two assistants, Miss Anderson and Miss Hayller, continued to provide important decrypts until his retirement in April 1938. Latterly, Fetterlein's output of Soviet decrypts became so great that Arthur Allen, a Russian linguist at the War Office, was added to the strength. While GC&CS retained responsibility for cryptanalysis, the army and Admiralty kept their respective responsibilities for traffic analysis, albeit on a very small scale, and interception was shared between the two, loosely organized by the GC&CS Cryptography and Interception Committee. This committee had not met since its introduction four years earlier, so in 1928 a new coordinating body, the Y Committee, was formed to bring some order into the work of the various service intercept stations. Another critical development at this time was the introduction of service sections in Broadway staffed by regular officers on "temporary" secondment. An Army Section was introduced in 1930 under Major John Tiltman, from the King's Own Scottish Borderers, consisting of Dick Pritchard, a German specialist (who also liaised with the French), Frederick Jacob and Tony Dangerfield, who concentrated on Japanese military ciphers.

Before Tiltman's arrival at Broadway, there was an informal arrangement in existence separating the intercept responsibilities between the services which were best able to offer facilities in particular geographical areas. In practice, interception was neatly shared by the Admiralty and the War Office. The Admiralty had long taken an interest in Japanese ciphers and had a GC&CS resident expert in Ernest Hobart-Hampden. He knew that the Japanese felt they need only employ low-grade ciphers because of the complexity of their language. The Naval Section came to an agreement with the Admiralty to transfer a number of its interpreters to GC&CS on a temporary basis and post at least one officer on active service permanently. In addition, Japanese linguists were routinely assigned to GC&CS before they joined the Royal Navy's China Station, which, incidentally, was responsible for all the Japanese interception work (apart, of course, for such diplomatic traffic as could be monitored from England). It was not until 1934 that the Admiralty, acting on a report by the Deputy DNI, Admiral William Tait, seconded Paymaster Captain Arthur Shaw RN to Hong Kong to supervise a Far East Bureau.

The War Office contribution to the SIGINT program was the No. 2 Wireless Company at Sarafand in Palestine (now renamed Zrifin), the remnant of the wartime MI1(b), which had monitored traffic in the Middle East from a small base in Constantinople. Sarafand was to develop into a major interception and analysis center, with its own cryptographic facility using personnel who had undergone training by GC&CS. In virtually every respect Sarafand was to mirror GC&CS, although the intercept operators naturally concentrated on the locally generated Arab, French and Italian signals. After the creation of the Army Section in GC&CS, further War Office intercept stations were established in China at Shanghai and on the Northwest Frontier of India under the supervision of Colonel (later Major-General Sir) Leslie Nicholls, who headed an Indian bureau, similar to Sarafand, which studied Persian, Afghan and Soviet signals. This division of labor between GC&CS, Sarafand, India and the China Station worked well, but throughout the period there was a perceptible increase in wireless traffic, and before long the Admiralty reported that approximately half of its home stations were listening to nonnaval business. In 1932, the Director of Naval Intelligence, Admiral Sir James Troup, created a special section, designated NID 9, to run all the Admiralty's stations and to begin research on whatever foreign naval ciphers could be extracted. The officer selected to supervise this work was Commander Humphrey Sandwith RN, of whom more will be heard later. The NID liaison officer posted to GC&CS to undertake the research was an inspired choice, (Vice-Admiral Sir) Norman Denning.

The decade between 1926 and 1936 is now best remembered in the history books for the tumultuous events in Germany that led to the Nazi party's climb to power, but GC&CS was preoccupied with monitoring the airwaves, and Hitler's illicit armed forces were, initially at least, suitably cautious in their wireless communications. There was no Luftwaffe traffic of any significance yet, and the first German naval signals of any consequence did not appear until the summer of 1936 when an exercise was held in the Mediterranean. In the absence of any raw material, the Naval Section contented itself with reconstructing the main Italian naval cipher. But up until this date, the GC&CS's chief concern was illicit signaling from the Soviet Union.

This subject remains extremely sensitive, even today, and it is unlikely that John Tiltman's comprehensive study of 1932 will ever be declassified. The question of exactly how successful the cryptographers were with the Soviet traffic is a matter of pure speculation, but there are certain clues to be found. It is generally acknowledged that after the government had executed its propaganda coup in 1923, and thereby alerted Moscow to the insecurity of its codes, the Comintern and diplomatic communications were routinely enciphered on one-time pads. Such systems are virtually impregnable, provided of course that there are no breakdowns in discipline and that the one-time pad really is used only once. If, as was to happen later, administrative errors lead to several identical pads being issued simultaneously, or the same pad is used over and over again, hostile cryptographers can profit. "Cribs" can also be developed if access can be gained to the decrypted versions of old signals. Such occasions are about as rare as that other opportunity to study encryption systems: the defection of a knowledgeable source. Just such an event seems to have taken place in May 1927, when the City of London headquarters of the All-Russian Cooperative Society was raided by the Metropolitan Police Special Branch.

The Arcos office was believed to be little more than a commercial front for a large-scale Soviet espionage organization, and the raid gave the Security Service an unprecedented chance to examine many thousands of Soviet documents which were recovered from a vault in the basement of the building, which also happened to be the premises of the Soviet Trade Delegation. The police burst into the building and carried out a thorough search lasting several days. The only mystery surrounding the event is the fate of Anton Miller, a Soviet coding clerk who was found to be pushing documents into a blazing fire in the sealed vault when the police burst in. Nine days later, when most of the Soviet staff had been withdrawn to Moscow, a parliamentary question to the Home Secretary was tabled by George Lansbury MP seeking information about Miller. The Parliamentary Under-Secretary, Douglas Hacking, replied for the Home Secretary and asserted that "it would not be in the public interest to say anything more about his activities."

Whether Miller decided to remain in Britain and to cooperate with the authorities or not is unknown, but such a reticent answer to a straightforward question in the House of Commons, from the left-wing proprietor of the *Daily Herald*, is certainly out of character. If Miller did defect, his value would have been inestimable, for he could easily have provided the clues needed to find cribs into the Soviet cipher system. In any event, the Soviet wireless traffic continued to be monitored in India, Sarafand and London, and it is known that in 1930 Commander Kenworthy, the controller of the Home Office intercept station at Grove Park, Camberwell, reported an illicit Comintern circuit operating between a site just outside Moscow and a terraced house in a suburb of London.

Denniston later commented that this extraordinary episode, which did not result in any prosecutions, was an example of a "cryptography attack which met with complete success." Evidently, Kenworthy and Leslie Lambert combined their resources to trace the exact location of the clandestine transmitter, while Tiltman solved the cipher. The only explanation for the apparent lack of overt police action in the case is presumably that it suited the Security Service (and, indeed, GC&CS) to allow transmission to continue uninterrupted. Their motives can only be guessed at.

In 1934, the Director of Air Intelligence at the Air Ministry, Sir Charles Blount, also began taking an interest in foreign wireless signals; he created a small unit, designated AI4, to monitor traffic from RAF Waddington, near Lincoln. AI4 accumulated so much raw material that the following year another section, AI1(e), was created under an existing GC&CS senior official, Joshua Cooper, who was transferred on the Air Ministry's strength to analyze it. Cooper, who had graduated from Brasenose College, Oxford, and King's College, London, was then just thirty-three years old, but he was to be an important figure in the British SIGINT establishment for the next quarter of a century. In 1936, he was appointed head of a new Air Section at GC&CS, thus completing representation of the three services at Broadway.

The major preoccupation of GC&CS at this time was the Soviet traffic, with Japanese signals in the Far East coming a close second, but late in 1937 the situation changed dramatically with a substantial increase in wireless traffic from the Iberian peninsula. The Spanish Civil War had erupted, and both the Italians and Germans were heavily involved. As well as the internal Nationalist signals which were watched closely, there was a great deal of naval cipher traffic originating from a pack of four Italian submarines which were attempting to enforce a blockade on the Republican-held ports. Instead of responding to Treasury demands for economies, GC&CS increased the Naval Section to eighteen, and an extra two linguists were drafted in to cope with the military traffic: Kenneth MacFarlan, an intercept expert on secondment from Sarafand, and Eric

Vincent, Professor of Italian at Cambridge University. Interception was conducted chiefly from two secret sites: by the War Office at Fort Bridgewoods, outside Chatham, and Flowerdown, the Admiralty station near Winchester.

Fort Bridgewoods was one of a series of hexagonal forts protected by deep moats and completed in 1883 to guard the naval town of Chatham. Commander Ellingworth was placed in charge of the station, which was largely accommodated underground in well-protected ammunition bunkers and even had a direct landline established with Broadway. Today Fort Bridgewoods is abandoned and vandalized, although several of the original aerial supports are still in position. Flowerdown, located just outside the village of Littleton, was then a small radio installation, but the entire site has recently been bulldozed to make way for a new, modern army depot. All that remains of the intercept station are the fifteen dwellings built for the operators near the gates and the concrete foundations of the wireless masts.

The Y Committee also arranged for further intercept facilities to concentrate on Italian and German diplomatic wireless traffic, and work began in 1937 on three new GPO stations, located at Sandridge, near St. Albans in Hertfordshire, Cupar in Fife and Brora in Sutherland, which were to be manned by Foreign Office personnel.

This expansion was undertaken at what appears now to be a rather relaxed pace, given the uneasy political climate in Europe during 1937, but there was considerable caution exercised at Broadway because both Denniston and Sinclair were acutely aware of a significant problem which threatened the future of GC&CS. This was the prospect of the wider use of automatic, electromagnetic ciphering machines.

The first introduction of ciphering machines had taken place shortly before the Armistice in 1918 when the German army had begun some experiments, but on a very limited scale. Fortunately for Room 40, which had no experience of such devices, the program had been abandoned when Germany was defeated. No further interest in the machines was expressed until 1926 when the German Admiralstab, perhaps in response to the disclosures made about Allied wartime SIGINT operations, such as the Zimmermann telegram, began equipping the navy with a version of a commercially available machine known as the "Enigma." This was widely used by banks on the Continent to protect their confidential messages. Two years later, the post-Versailles Reichswehr also started to use a military model of the same machine.

Contrary to much that has been written about the provenance of the

Enigma, there was no mystery about it at GC&CS. Two of the commercial versions had been purchased through the Admiralty in 1928, and active consideration had been given to the introduction of such a coding machine for encrypting the British government's most sensitive communications since 1926, when an interdepartmental Whitehall committee had investigated the options available. The committee pursued its enquiries for eight years before recommending, in January 1935, that the Air Ministry should supervise the construction and distribution of a cipher machine based on the Enigma which boasted an additional "Type X" attachment. This version, manufactured by the Creed Teleprinter Co., became known as the TypeX machine and was gradually made available to the Royal Air Force and the War Office. It was the opinion of all the experts that the ciphers generated by both the Enigma and the TypeX machines were impenetrable to hostile cryptanalytical attack, *if used correctly*.

Alistair Denniston and others at GC&CS were well aware that the number of possible cipher permutations that could be created by the Enigma and the TypeX machines, if correctly handled, were so great that no human being could isolate the right ones without months—or even years—of trying. Nor was there any machine known in those days which could run through the variables to find the right key to the code used. As a result, Denniston and others thought in the 1920s that the GC&CS might be made redundant if and when war broke out. The Germans too thought initially that it would be a waste of time trying to break into British machine ciphers. Both sides were correct in their assumptions, for indeed many Enigma codes were never broken. It was only by finding and making use of cribs and by exploiting human error that any Enigma codes proved fallible.

The first Enigma machines resembled large, self-contained, battery-operated cash registers, with three rows of typewriter-style letter keys and a further set of matching windows, each with a letter printed on it. When one of the twenty-six alphabetical keys was pressed down, another letter would light up instantly in one of the windows on the lampboard. The enciphered letter was chosen by the machine automatically, after an electrical current, discharged by the keying process, had followed a complex path through the interior, round a series of three moving, interchangeable, metal wheels with letters of the alphabet on them, called rotors, before finally lighting up a particular window on the lampboard section. The huge advantage of the machine lay in the three moving rotors and their gears, which thoroughly scrambled the electrical current before selecting the corresponding window. There was no regular or discernible

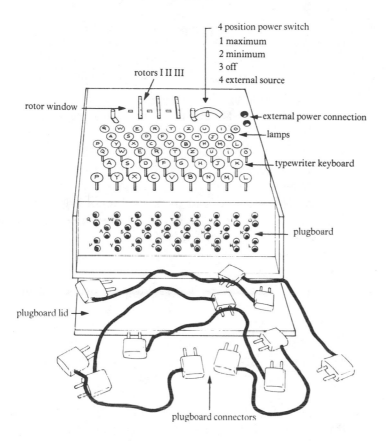

4 position power switch
1 maximum
2 minimum
3 off
4 external source

rotors I II III

rotor window

external power connection

lamps

typewriter keyboard

plugboard

plugboard lid

plugboard connectors

The Enigma machine with its classic three-rotor configuration.
To increase its security, additional devices such as an extra
plugboard and rotor were introduced during the war, but its
supposedly impregnable ciphers were compromised by poor
operating procedures.

pattern to be followed, so all the letter frequency tables and complicated statistics that had been developed during the Great War by the Allied cryptographers were useless. There were, however, some disadvantages to the machine. Firstly, it only had twenty-six letter keys, so individual numbers had to be spelled out in full. It was also labor-intensive. To encode and transmit a text at speed, four people were required: one to call out the message, letter by letter, one to key it into the Enigma by using the typewriter keys, another to read each letter as it lit up on the lampboard and a fourth to transmit the encoded text.

At the other end of a wireless net the process was reversed and, provided the Enigma operator had chosen the correct order for his three rotors and set them to exactly the right starting position, the text would be decoded. This was achieved by putting the three rotors into the correct sequence (rotor one into the third slot, etc.) and by adjusting the three rotors by moving the rotor flanges, which protruded through the machine's casing, above the lampboard. The rotor circumferences were marked with the twenty-six letters of the alphabet, one of which appeared in three small windows alongside the flanges, so that the position of each rotor could be identified individually. Once an operator had chosen the rotor positions, which came to be known as the "key," he was ready to receive. The encoded text could only be read by another operator with an identically set Enigma machine. In other words, possession of the machine alone was of little value if you wished to read someone's Enigma message, unless you knew exactly how to set each rotor. The security offered by the system seemed infallible.

In 1930, this impressive security was further enhanced by the introduction of a plugboard at the front of the machine which contained twenty-six pairs of plugs and sockets. By rewiring just six letters, the possible permutations was vastly increased by a factor of 100,391,791,500, thereby reducing the chances of anyone attempting to reproduce a text. The new Wehrmacht Enigma machine, therefore, boasted three basic features which assured its security: the three rotors, which were interchangeable; the vast range of keys available; and the choice of wiring on the plugboard. Unless all three were correctly set, the encoded message would remain exactly what it appeared, a scrambled collection of randomly chosen letters. In short, the German machine cipher system was impervious to the cryptologists. Each intercept was a meaningless jumble of letters which defied any statistical or mathematical analysis. Even the letter frequencies, which had provided clues to the Great War codes, appeared uniform and, therefore, avoided the usual giveaways. And even if some out of character repetition was isolated, it was only of use until the key was changed. The Enigma offered a mathematical choice of 5×10 (to the power of 92) cipher combinations (or 500 million, with the word million being repeated fifteen times) and thus threatened to put GC&CS out of business, at least so far as Germany was concerned.

By the end of 1935, the Germans had built more than 20,000 Enigma machines and had equipped the army, the navy, and Goering's new Luftwaffe. They were also standard issue to virtually every other government agency in the Reich, including the Abwehr, the military intelligence service, and the Sicherheitsdienst (SD), the Nazi party's security service. Each was equipped with its own particular version of the Enigma, using a different plugboard arrangement and a different selection of rotors. The choice of a key was simply a matter of logistical organization with different military units or government departments changing their keys according to a prearranged routine. The Wehrmacht, for example, started off by changing its plugboard connections every month, and eventually reduced this to every eight hours. New transmitting procedures were also introduced to defeat any eavesdroppers, including a rule that each message should contain at least ten cipher groups of five letters each. Shorter messages, like those that had been interpreted so easily in 1915 and 1916, were to be padded out to a minimum of fifty letters with nonsense texts. German Enigma-encoded wireless traffic was intercepted in the 1930s at Fort Bridgewoods, Flowerdown and numerous other stations on the Continent by Germany's anxious neighbors, but none could actually read any of the traffic, or so GC&CS thought.

For their part, the French had watched the development of the German Enigma traffic with increasing concern from three intercept stations located close to the frontier at Strasbourg, Metz and Mulhouse. The section of the French intelligence structure supervising these operations was the Service de Renseignements, of which the "Décryptement" department was run by Captain Gustave Bertrand, who took the closest possible interest in German communications. Bertrand was particularly well informed about the Enigma machine, thanks to the help of a young German named Hans-Thilo Schmidt who volunteered to sell many of the Enigma's secrets. Code-named ASCHE, Schmidt worked for the German Chiffrierstelle, or Cryptographic Agency, and was unable to support his gambling and exotic lifestyle on his insubstantial pay. Bertrand agreed to finance him and, between the autumn of 1931 and June 1939, held some nineteen clandestine meetings with ASCHE, who supplied a total of 303 separate secret documents concerning German codes and ciphers, such as several Enigma operating manuals (*Gebrauchsanweisung*) and copies of the Wehrmacht keying instructions (*Schlüsselanleitung*). The latter proved to be of exceptional importance and covered the period from December 1931 to the first half of 1934, when ASCHE was transferred to intercept duties. While all this material was of consuming importance to Bertrand, it did not really advance the prospects of actually reading any Enigma-based wireless traffic. If anything, ASCHE's documents merely served to confirm the very tight German security imposed around the Enigma and the machine's intrinsic security advantages.

On December 7, 1932, Bertrand visited Warsaw to exchange information with his Polish counterparts, the Cipher Bureau of the General Staff's Radio Intelligence Office, and agreed to combine forces with the Poles for a concerted attack on the German Enigma traffic. He also handed them a selection of ASCHE's secret documents, the operating instructions, the keying instructions and an out-of-date list of some daily key settings, without, of course, disclosing their source. By January 1933, the Poles had succeeded in rebuilding, in mathematical theory anyway, the complex wiring diagram of the Wehrmacht Enigma, and, in February 1933, they commissioned the AVA Radio Manufacturing Company to build their own version of the military Enigma, using an openly purchased commerical model as a base and ASCHE's material to reconstruct the wiring of the plugboard. By the middle of the following year AVA had almost completed its contract for fifteen versions of it for the Cipher Bureau in Warsaw.

As soon as the Poles had taken delivery of their first AVA Enigma, they began, by a lengthy process of elimination, to identify some of the keys used in past traffic. Three Polish intercept stations, located in a suburb of Poznan, Starogard, south of Danzig, and Krzeslowice, outside Krakow, provided a regular supply of intercepts, so that there was no shortage of material to work on. On busy days, they were able to monitor some really long messages, all sent on the same key, which increased the Cipher Bureau's chances of success. Unfortunately, the 17,576 possible combinations of the three rotor settings made the elimination exercise excruciatingly tedious. This calculation ($26 \times 26 \times 26$), incidentally, assumes that the three rotors have been placed in the duplicate Enigma in the correct order. The figure jumps to 105,456 possible combinations if the rotor selection is unknown. However, once the basic principles of the machine had been mastered, there was plenty of scope for progress. One interesting discovery made by the electrical engineers at AVA was that the Enigma, in fact, offered only a choice of twenty-five letters for substitution and not the full twenty-six in the alphabet; the machine was incapable of enciphering a letter with the same letter: if you pressed B, it would never come up with a B. Polish SIGINT analysts were also able to make a vital contribution. German wireless operators sending Enigma-based texts had to convey certain information to the receiver before the main text could be transmitted. Characteristically, the preambles conformed to a standard pattern: an exchange of call signs, thereby establishing the circuit; then a series of items together: the time, the number of letters in the text (which, as we know, was never less than fifty), and an indication whether the message was complete, or just part of another.

This was then followed by the really crucial clues: a three-letter group, known as the discriminant, which identified the type of Enigma machine (i.e., a Wehrmacht version or a Luftwaffe model, with their differing rotor and plugboard arrangements); and, finally, a second three-letter group, which gave the rotor setting used for the remainder of the message. Unless this information was received correctly by the other end of the wireless net, the text itself would remain gibberish. Once the cryptanalysts had grasped the full significance of the preamble, their task was much easier, because the German operators often made mistakes or lost their patience and sometimes even sent a preamble in plaintext. The first results achieved by the Poles seemed promising. Then, in 1934, the Wehrmacht began changing the plugboard configuration every month instead of every quarter.

The Cipher Bureau in Warsaw responded by taking two sets of the AVA rotors and improvising an electrical device, which became known as the cyclometer, to move the rotors through every possible sequence automatically. Another invention, involving a series of arithmetical grids marked on perforated paper, helped to deal with the varying connections in the plugboard and worked on the principle that if the Wehrmacht only linked six pairs of plugs, thirteen letters must remain unaltered. The trick was to identify the thirteen by trial and error. Gradually the Cipher Bureau achieved what was believed to be the impossible: the occasional discovery of an Enigma key. And among those solved were some employed by the Wehrmacht and the Sicherheitsdienst, and two used by the German navy. This was huge progress, and the Poles were certainly much further advanced than either the French or the British. Both had virtually abandoned the German machine ciphers as impossible, although the very early, unmodified Enigmas (without the plugboard) used by Franco and the Italian forces in Spain had been the subject of a concentrated effort by GC&CS. The Spanish traffic was the first opportunity to intercept and analyze a worthwhile volume of Enigma-based wireless traffic. Furthermore, the signals were transmitted under wartime operational conditions, so there were opportunities to exploit the kind of procedural mistakes that give traffic analysts and cryptographers their clues and cribs. A team consisting of Peter Twinn, Tony Kendrick and Wilfred Bodsworth, led by Dilly Knox, set to work on the machine ciphers, which eventually succumbed toward the end of 1937. This was a major achievement, but it also confirmed Knox's fears about the Enigma's principles. If used correctly, the cipher was to be considered impregnable. Nevertheless, the exercise had been extremely valuable, especially as it acted as a dress

rehearsal and gave at least a handful of intercept operators and cryptanalysts the chance to study some Enigma traffic under conditions that were
to be repeated four years later.

In the absence of any major effort against the more sophisticated
Enigma used inside the Reich, GC&CS had concentrated on trying to
break various low- and medium-grade manual ciphers. GC&CS was still
reading the Soviet military traffic (for there were as yet no cipher machines
in Moscow), which escalated during the Spanish Civil War. Similarly,
following German intervention in Spain, Knox had solved the Spanish
military code, and there was a program of collaboration with the French
on the Italian naval codes. Italian intervention in Abyssinia in 1935 had
also led to the establishment of a jointly run intercept station located in
the Mediterranean off the Riviera to monitor Italian naval and air-force
traffic. Between 1934 and 1937, Professor Vincent's Italian subsection
of the Naval Section at Broadway increased from five to fourteen officers
and the code used by Rome to communicate to Italy's colonies eventually
yielded, as did some fragments of the Italian diplomatic cipher. Another
GC&CS success was the breaking of both the main Japanese army and
naval ciphers by a team which included two brilliant Japanese linguists,
Sir Harold Parlett and Ernest Hobart-Hampden, working with the cryptographer who had solved the Comintern's traffic, John Tiltman. Both
linguists were retired diplomats who between them had spent a total of
sixty-seven years in Japan. Hobart-Hampden was a veteran who had
joined GC&CS after a long career in Japan. After leaving Brasenose he
had joined the Consular Service in China and, in 1904, had been appointed
a vice-consul in Yokohama. Five years later, he was transferred to the
British Embassy in Tokyo, where he remained until his retirement in
1919. He had been joined by Parlett in 1928, and together they had
compiled the first *English-Japanese Dictionary of the Spoken Word*. Parlett had first gone to Japan as a student interpreter in 1890, and his first
job had been as assistant registrar in a Yokohama court in 1898. Twelve
months later, he joined the British Embassy in Tokyo and, during the
course of the next twenty-eight years, held various consular posts around
the country. In 1927, he had returned to England and written *A Brief
Account of Diplomatic Events in Manchuria*, which was published shortly
after his recruitment to Broadway. Parlett retired for the second time in
1935, but was brought back, this time to Bletchley, in 1941.

According to Schmidt, the young German code-named ASCHE, the
British, French and Poles were not the only participants in the new secret
wireless war. In mid-1934, Schmidt himself had been moved from the

Reich Chiffrierstelle to the Forschungsamt, the Gestapo's intercept organization, and at his clandestine meetings with Bertrand he revealed just how much the Germans had learned from the Great War. The Forschungsamt employed some 2,000 personnel, and it was believed that the total number of people dedicated to signals intelligence duties in Germany was probably three times this number. The navy itself ran a network of seven intercept stations on the Baltic, and an additional four on the North Sea, with one secret station at Langenargen on the shores of Lake Constance, listening in to the Italians. The Wehrmacht also ran its own intercept stations, which supplied seven radio intelligence centers at Breslau, Dresden, Munich, Munster, Stuttgart and in the two army training areas at Jüterbog and Königsberg. Thanks to ASCHE, Britain was warned that the manual NIC 1 (Naval Intelligence Code 1), the French BGD 30 naval code and the French mobilization code, the Code d'Alerte, had all been compromised.

The crisis which proved to be the SIGINT watershed for both the French and the British was the Anschluss, Hitler's sudden annexation of Austria on March 12, 1938. With hardly any political notice, and certainly without any SIGINT warning, 100,000 German troops invaded Austria. The occupation was completed within two days, leaving the Allied governments almost too stunned to react. The speed of the operation had been breathtaking, and it had highlighted the ease with which Germany could transmit unprecedented volumes of military radio traffic without any apparent concern. Neither the French nor the British had the means to tap into it, and the Poles were unwilling to disclose the very limited progress they had achieved. GC&CS's existence was regarded as so secret that there was no direct communication between the School and any foreign cryptographic agency. By established convention, all overseas intelligence liaison with Britain was channeled through the Secret Intelligence Service or MI5. Dick Pritchard, of John Tiltman's Army Section, was primarily responsible for maintaining a very limited contact with the French, but collaboration against the German traffic had been limited to the diplomatic area because of the supposed impregnability of the machine ciphers. Nevertheless, a few meager joint traffic analysis and direction-finding experiments did get some results, including the identification of some sixty Luftwaffe ground stations. In the aftermath of the Anschluss the atmosphere changed, and Denniston was authorized by Admiral Sinclair to invite Bertrand to Broadway for a council of war. It was to prove a historic meeting.

Bertrand came to the meeting equipped with some of the ASCHE documents that he had traded with the Poles, and he now agreed to pool resources with Britain to combat the Nazis. There had already been active and fruitful collaboration over the Italian wireless traffic, and in the counterintelligence field both England and France had worked together to identify an Abwehr agent in the French navy, a certain Lieutenant Aubert, who had been "turned" and run successfully as a double agent. Aubert had originally been spotted as a result of a British source in the Abwehr's office in Hamburg, and he was used as a conduit to supply the Germans with some bogus French naval codes, which ASCHE had obligingly confirmed as compromised, along with several others that, as has been seen, had been solved by German cryptanalysis.

As well as offering some of ASCHE's documents, Bertrand suggested, perhaps a little disingenuously, that the Polish Cipher Bureau might prove a valuable ally in a triple alliance. The British demurred, apparently for fear of having to disclose their mastery of the Soviet military ciphers (which, in fact, the Poles had already solved without any external help). Whatever the motive, no formal contact was made between GC&CS and the Poles until January the following year.

In the meantime, Admiral Sinclair, the SIS chief, and Denniston began preparing for the conflict they believed inevitable, and in May 1938 a German Section was created at Broadway. A brief battle with the Treasury was fought, and sanction was given to increase the establishment with an extra eight civilian graduates. The Treasury also gave its consent to the admiral's contingency war plan, which authorized an emergency establishment of fifty-six seniors and thirty female graduate linguists. A series of elementary cryptographic courses for potential GC&CS recruits was held at Broadway, and an emergency list of sixty "professor types" was drawn up, with part-time personnel like Professor Vincent and old Room 40 hands like (Sir) Frank Adcock and Frank Birch recommending suitable candidates. And, on the assumption that the administrative center of London would be an immediate target for an enemy air attack, Sinclair arranged for the purchase of alternative headquarters for both SIS and GC&CS.

The property selected by Sinclair was Bletchley Park, a large country estate on the outskirts of the Buckinghamshire market town owned by Sir George Leon, an immensely wealthy Old Etonian barrister who had succeeded to the title in 1926. His father, the first baronet Sir Herbert Leon, had bought the Park in 1883, had subsequently been elected the Liberal Member of Parliament for North Buckinghamshire, and had then built the Victorian monstrosity. Sinclair, of course, was more interested in its secluded position and its strategic location (served by a mainline railway station and midway between Oxford and Cambridge) than its architectural shortcomings. During the Munich crisis in September 1938, a dress rehearsal was staged and the entire GC&CS staff at Broadway was evacuated to Bletchley and accommodated in the mansion and a group of hastily constructed wooden huts until October 8 when the panic ended. The landlines to Fort Bridgewoods and Flowerdown were relayed from Broadway, and the special German Section was increased to coordinate the work of the three service sections. That no such effort had been possible before this date seems extraordinary and remains an indictment of the Treasury's parsimony. Even the authors of the official history of *British Intelligence in the Second World War* seem a little incredulous at the lack of attention given to Germany at this late date:

> The naval subsection of the German Section, which was started with one officer and a clerk as late as May 1938, still had no cryptanalysts. Since virtually no military traffic was intercepted except during summer exercises, the only regular work by cryptanalysts in the army subsection was on police traffic. In the air subsection the communications of the German Air Force were being studied by only a handful of people.[13]

The excuse usually given for this apparent unwillingness to devote any serious attention to the German machine ciphers is that in the event of war complete radio silence was expected. Why waste precious resources on a particular type of wireless traffic that was bound to dry up? In fact, the volume did exactly the reverse and escalated enormously. Furthermore, it did so with some extra security from two Enigma modifications. Just two weeks before the Munich crisis, on September 15, 1938, the Germans introduced a new system for selecting the Enigma's key. Instead of notifying all the operators on a particular circuit which three letters to use, they were all told to choose their own. Thus the initial preamble used by operators would remain the same, with the originator inserting the required three-letter group, but instead of conforming to a prearranged table, a key would be selected at random for each separate message. For the Polish Cipher Bureau, the only organization with any experience of solving the German Enigma traffic, the changeover threatened to wreck all the work done to date, as did the second German modification: the introduction of two extra Enigma rotors on December 15, 1938. Both events added greater urgency to the meeting called by Bertrand in Paris on January 9, 1939.

The conference in Paris was held at the Service de Renseignements head-quarters, in the rue Tourville, and was attended by Denniston, Knox and the head of the local SIS Station, Wilfred Dunderdale. Dunderdale had transferred to Paris from Constantinople in 1926 and, since that date, had been the sole intelligence liaison officer with the French authorities. Although he had no knowledge of cryptography, he had developed an excellent relationship with numerous figures of the French intelligence establishment, including Gustave Bertrand, the Enigma expert, and Cap-tain Henri Bracquenie, of the French air-force intelligence. The latter pair represented the French at the meeting, while the Polish contingent consisted of Colonel Gwido Langer, director of the Cipher Bureau, and Major Maksymilian Ciezki, head of the Cipher Bureau's German section. It is perhaps interesting to note that Dick Pritchard, the Army Section member and German linguist responsible for handling queries from the French, did not participate in these talks, possibly because of his knowl-edge of GC&CS's complete coverage of the French coding procedures before 1935 (when a new, more complicated system had been introduced).

According to the minutes of the meetings, all three parties gave an account of their research work to date and agreed to exchange further information at two more conferences, which were to be held in Warsaw and London over the coming months.

> Although the methods used show some differences and the exchange of views was useful to all, the work seems to have arrived at an impasse, out of which only information from an agent can provide a way: to that end, a technical questionnaire has been drawn up, as simple as possible, to be given to such an agent as may be judged capable of carrying out the assignment.[14]

In the meantime, it was decided that each of the three participants would tackle a particular aspect of the Enigma machine. A secure landline teleprinter link would also be established between the three Allies to improve communications. In retrospect, it would appear that the British and French gave a true account of their lack of progress (although Bertrand neglected to mention his continued contact with ASCHE), but the Poles seem to have omitted to mention their various successes up to September 15 or, for that matter, their development of the Bombe.

The Bombe was an electromechanical device, an improvement on the cyclometer incorporating no less than six AVA Enigmas. In a period of two hours the Bombe—so named, allegedly, because the two inventors were eating an ice-cream bombe when they first discussed the idea—could move the three rotors through all 17,576 possible permutations to find a particular key. The first of fifteen Bombes had been built by AVA in November 1938 and installed at a heavily protected cryptographic center at Mokotov-Pyry, deep in the Kabackic woods, south of Warsaw. The Bombes worked well on the old, pre-September 1938 intercepts and also achieved results with Sicherheitsdienst traffic, which had stuck to the old keying procedures and continued to do so until July 1939. The modification of two extra, alternative rotors (making a total of five possible rotors in all, of which any three might be fitted into the Enigma) proved to be less disastrous than everyone had anticipated, because the German operators succumbed to human weakness when given the opportunity to select their own three-figure keys. The lazier signals personnel simply opted for AAA or ABC, or even the same letters of the first three-letter group in the preamble, which actually made the cryptographic problem much easier.

Another useful Polish improvisation was the construction of a series of perforated sheets of paper, worked out by a Cipher Bureau engineer, Henryk Zygalski. The Zygalski perforated sheets, in a stack of twenty-six and each marked with up to fifty-one holes at a time, were designed to exploit any detectable cipher patterns and identify a Wehrmacht key, whatever the plugboard connections. The perforated sheets worked brilliantly with just three rotors, and plenty of intercepts were read in full retrospectively, but the addition of two further rotors threw the Polish calculations into confusion. In order to break one key, the new system required no fewer than sixty sets of the Zygalski sheets to be used. To date, only two sets had been prepared, which left a shortfall of fifty-eight, just to cope with a single key. Considering the deepening political crisis in Europe, the Poles had neither the time nor the facilities to manufacture the required sheets, so in June 1939 a second emergency conference was arranged by Bertrand and Langer in Warsaw. On this occasion the British were to be represented by Denniston, Knox and a third officer, who was probably either Stewart Menzies, then Sinclair's deputy at SIS headquarters, or Humphrey Sandwith, the Naval Intelligence officer in charge of the Admiralty's network of intercept stations. The meeting was scheduled for the end of July, and the suggested date was more than a little inconvenient to Denniston because the Admiralty and the Air Ministry had chosen the period July 18–24 for a full-scale exercise to test their communications "under war conditions." A letter dated June 12, 1939, sent by Denniston to Gladwyn Jebb, then Private Secretary to Sir Alexander Cadogan, Permanent Under-Secretary at the Foreign Office, is a measure of just how strapped for cash GC&CS was at the time:

> I should like to carry out a test of our War Station at the same time, but as this will involve an expenditure of some £4,000 for the rent of the necessary telephone lines, etc., which the Post Office insist on, before taking any further steps in the matter, I should be glad to know if the expenses in connection with such a test would be paid for out of public funds.[15]

The necessary sanction was granted, and Bletchley Park was connected, temporarily, to the Admiralty and Air Ministry war rooms. But the day before the conclusion of the exercise, Denniston and Knox flew to Warsaw and checked into the Hotel Bristol.

The party from England was met by Colonel Langer, and the following day he accompanied them to his secret base at Mokotov-Pyry. There Langer disclosed to his visitors, for the first time, that the Cipher Bureau had reconstructed an unspecified number of duplicate Enigmas with the new plugboard wiring and was prepared to send one each to London and Paris. These were dispatched to Paris and delivered, on August 16, 1939, to Bertrand and Dunderdale. Dunderdale promptly passed his valuable delivery on to Broadway, where it was received by Denniston on behalf of GC&CS. Now his organization had an opportunity to see what advances the Poles had made, how they had wired up their version of the Enigma and whether anything new could be learned from tinkering with their machine. This Polish replica was to allow GC&CS to emerge from the realm of mathematical theory which had proved so depressing to Denniston.

Suddenly, in the remaining fortnight of peace in Europe, there was major activity at GC&CS, with the Treasury authorizing the recruitment of ninety-one "temporary clerks" from the emergency list, who were contacted quietly and instructed to report either to Room 47 of the Foreign Office or to the gates of Bletchley Park itself, which were now adorned with a discreet plaque bearing the name "Government Communications Bureau."

In such a very short space of time, GC&CS had been transformed

1939.

_____

£

Numbers.

1938.	1939.			
		Code and Cypher School.		
1	1	Head	..(1,150l.–50l.–1,450l.)	1,450
1	1	Deputy Head	..(1,150l.–50l.–1,450l.)	1,328
3	3	Chief Assistants	(847l.–30l.–1,150l. personal)	3,385
13	14	Senior „	(847l.–30l.–1,058l. „)	13,846
17	16†	Junior „	Men (275l.–25l.–635l.) Women (275l.–25l.–515l.) (5 with 100l. allowances)	8,082
1	1	Wireless Expert	(634l.–25l.–750l. personal)	750
11	12	Clerks	Women (85l. to 280l.) (3 with 60l. allowances)	2,341
1	1	Superintendent of Typists	(215l.–10l.–280l.)	267
2	2	Shorthand Typists	(40s. to 72s. a week)	315
15	15	Typists	(31s. to 60s. „)	1,860
13	13	Clerical Assistants, Grade I	(28s. to 72s. „)	1,994
1	1	Temporary Technical Assistant..		300
35	38 §	Temporary Clerks		5,462
7	8	Temporary Typists		959
—	1	Executive Engineer	(650l.–25l.–750l.)	650
—	2	Inspectors ..	(250l.–10l.–350l.)	500
1	1	Assistant Superintendent of Telegraphists (personal)		500
			Allowances	26
12	12	Telegraphists (25s. to 105s. a week) (with allowances varying from 5s. to 20s. „)		3,682
—	—	Overtime and Sunday Duty		850
12	12	Telegraphists 7 (53s. 9d.–2s. 6d.–67s. „) 5 (55s. 6d.–2s. 6d.–63s. „)		1,918
1	1	Doorkeeper and Head Officekeeper (145l.–7l. 10s.–190l.)		158
3	4	Unestablished Officekeepers or Messengers (47s. 6d.–1s. 6d.–55s. 6d. a week)		548
8	10	Women Cleaners (1 at 32s. and 9 at 29s. 6d. „)		777
—	—	National Insurance Schemes—Employer's contributions		244
—	—	Provision for additional staff		3,000
				325,903
		Adjustment of salaries consequent upon interchange of First, Second and Third Secretaries between the Foreign Office and posts abroad—*add* 975l. *Deduct* for vacancies 2,000l. } *deduct*		1,025
904	937	TOTAL FOR SALARIES, &c. ..		£324,878

The authorized GC&CS budget for the financial year 1939

from a tiny, under-funded backwater of the Foreign Office, employing just a handful of skilled (but ancient) cryptanalysts, into a concentrated unit of nearly two hundred boffins who were coordinating the SIGINT resources of all three services.

Admittedly, these resources were somewhat slender at this time. The Foreign Office relied solely on the dozen or so constables at the secret Metropolitan Police radio station in Grove Park, Camberwell, for wireless intercepts, although plans had been put in hand for another at Sandridge, just outside St. Albans, which was to be manned by Post Office engineers. This latter site was not to become operational until September 11, 1939. The Air Ministry depended upon the small section attached to RAF Waddington, but had prepared an alternative base at RAF Cheadle. The War Office controlled the antiquated Army Chain, which linked Britain's numerous garrisons across the globe, and maintained two intercept facilities: the Sarafand complex, masquerading as No. 2 Wireless Company, which had established several semipermanent satellite stations in the Middle East, including one on Malta; and No. 4 Wireless Company, based at Aldershot. This latter unit had been renamed No. 2 Company, General Headquarters Signals, in 1938.

By far the most sophisticated of the service SIGINT organizations was that run by the Royal Navy. During the previous decade, a separate wireless net had been created so that all His Majesty's ships could communicate, either directly or indirectly, with the Admiralty in London. Twelve high-frequency stations had been built in strategic locations around the world: Esquimalt and Halifax in Canada, Bermuda, Gibraltar, Malta, Simonstown, Aden, Ceylon, Singapore, Hong Kong, Melbourne and Wellington. These communicated with three transmitters in England (at Horsea Island in Portsmouth Harbour and Cleethorpes) and a receiver on the War Office site at Flowerdown. In addition, the Submarine Service was experimenting with a very low-frequency system, based at Rugby and Criggian, near Welshpool, which could send signals capable of being picked up underwater.

GC&CS itself, which went on to an official war footing on August 1, 1939, kept its long-standing responsibility for coordinating the intercept program via the interdepartmental Y Committee, which had been chaired by Admiral Sinclair since General Sir Cecil Romer's retirement in 1925. Accordingly, on August 1 most of the individual sections formally took up permanent residence in their new premises at Bletchley Park, leaving only the Diplomatic and Commercial sections to follow a fortnight later.

The general transfer to Bletchley gives a good opportunity to review

GC&CS's initial wartime structure. As can be gathered from this narrative, very little time had been expended on the organization's overt *raison d'être*, the security of Britain's own codes, and virtually the only person who devoted any time to this activity was the deputy director, Edward Travis, who also headed the Communications Security Section. The remainder of GC&CS's personnel was entirely concerned with the clandestine collection, analysis and decryption of foreign signals, which was prosecuted by a number of self-contained sections. By far the largest, and arguably the most important, was the Diplomatic Section, which consisted of a series of small geographically orientated subsections, each concentrating on particular target traffic. Greek, Portuguese, Spanish, Italian, United States and Persian diplomatic codes had been attacked with considerable success, and the resulting decrypts had been translated and circulated to the small number of indoctrinated officials in the form of daily summaries known as Black Jumbos or simply "B-Js." The Foreign Office had scrapped the effort against the Swedish, Danish and Norwegian codes, and from time to time attention had been given to various Balkan and South American codes, although the intercepted traffic rarely justified the exercise. Once a cryptographer in the Diplomatic Section had solved a particular problem, such as Knox's work on the Hungarian diplomatic cipher, he would move on to the next country subsection and begin anew. This methodical approach resulted in the diplomatic code books of many nations being reconstructed, and as the Diplomatic Section's expertise grew, it marked up successes against the more difficult challenges of certain reciphering tables and bigrammatic grids. Most, like the Quai d'Orsay's complex "hatted" reciphering systems, succumbed sooner or later, leaving only the one-time pads and the machine ciphers to be tackled.

Of the three service sections, the most recent addition had been Josh Cooper's Air Section, created in 1936 to advise the Air Ministry. The Army Section, now headed by John Tiltman with Fred Jacob, Dick Pritchard and Tony Dangerfield, had been operating since 1930 and, in the absence of any useful military traffic from the Continent, had pursued and solved various Japanese naval ciphers. The rest of the Japanese traffic was handled, from 1935 onward, by Captain Shaw's Far East Combined Bureau (FECB), based on Stonecutter's Island, Hong Kong, although Ernest Hobart-Hampden remained at GC&CS in his capacity as the resident Japanese Section. In September 1939, the FECB was obliged to retreat to Singapore, before being evacuated to Ceylon.

Clarke's Naval Section had been in existence since 1924, although successive DNIs had always expressed reservations about the section's continued incorporation into GC&CS. In fact, the Admiralty used the poor communications experienced during the temporary transfer to Bletchley during the Munich crisis as an excuse to demand that Clarke return to the Admiralty on the outbreak of war. A compromise was eventually reached which enabled Clarke and his team of twenty-eight to stay at Bletchley, and the recently formed German naval subsection (which only consisted of a handful of linguists, analysts and clerks) to go to London.

The most recent addition to the GC&CS establishment was the Commercial Section, which had been started by G.L.N. Hope in 1938. The demand for this section had arisen after the formation of Major Desmond Morton's Industrial Intelligence Center, which was subsequently absorbed into the Ministry of Economic Warfare. Hope began work by collecting copies of internationally available codes, and progressed into the cryptographic field by solving a number of encrypted commercial telegrams sent by some of Japan's largest trading companies. The results were sufficiently impressive to ensure the section's survival throughout the war.

During the second half of August 1939, the first group of GC&CS's new civilian "temporary clerks" made their way to Bletchley Park; among them were Nigel de Grey and two professors of German who had served in Room 40, Gilbert Waterhouse (from Queen's University, Belfast) and Walter Bruford (from Edinburgh University). This first intake was quickly followed by Leonard Forster from Selwyn College, Cambridge, who was later appointed professor of German at London University, with Professor Thomas Boase arriving from the Courtauld Institute on Saturday, September 2. Within twenty-four hours, Britain and France were at war with Nazi Germany. At some indeterminate moment in the following months, the Government Code and Cypher School adopted a new cover name of Government Communications Headquarters, GCHQ. Many of the prewar staff continued to refer to it as GC&CS, but most of the newcomers adopted the abbreviation GCHQ, so this is a convenient moment to make the necessary switch in this narrative.

4

The Radio Security Service

At the basis of the whole Ultra achievement was interception. This was the first stage. Without interception, nothing.

—PETER CALVOCORESSI in *Top Secret Ultra*

While Bletchley Park was absorbing its newly recruited academics, the rest of Britain's secret intelligence structure tried to cope with the results of years of financial neglect. Certainly the Secret Intelligence Service's preparations were woefully inadequate to deal with a world war in Europe or the threat, as carried out in Poland on September 1, of blitzkrieg, "lightning war" in which the Wehrmacht and the Luftwaffe cooperated together to bypass defended strongpoints and move directly to preselected targets. SIS was especially vulnerable to such an innovation because, until 1938, no work had been done to place any "stay-behind" networks on the Continent; the clandestine organizations that did exist had been established soon after the Great War and were largely moribund. SIS officers in foreign countries were also very susceptible to hostile penetration because they had all been given the same cover, the post of British Passport Control Officer (PCO). Because none of SIS's prewar networks were equipped with wireless, each case officer was obliged to rely on that most traditional method of communication, the letter written in secret ink to a post office box or cover address in a neutral territory. The Nazis countered by monitoring all the international mail to and from Germany, and were later to eliminate the neutral facilities in Belgium and Holland, the two countries which traditionally received most of SIS's covert post. The absence of any comprehensive wireless network also meant that SIS stations abroad could only keep in touch with headquarters via the King's Messenger service operated by the Foreign Office or the regular post.

Accordingly, SIS developed a system of codes based on a booklet containing frequently used words, and a "super-encipherment" procedure which involved altering the code groups by subtracting a particular key number. Thus the word submarine might be transformed into 87291 in the SIS code book, but would be written as 34238 after the key number, 53053, had been subtracted. Each SIS officer was issued with his own personal key so, in theory at least, his messages to headquarters were constructed in a unique code. The Royal Navy employed a similar arrangement and issued its ships with long subtractor tables which were changed periodically. Since the war, there has been little evidence that the Abwehr or the Sicherheitsdienst ever cracked SIS's system, but it might well be argued that the organization's communications at this period rarely contained information of any great consequence.

The first warning of what SIS could expect from the Nazis had occurred in August 1938, five months after the German takeover of Austria. The local SIS Head of Station in Vienna, Captain Thomas Kendrick, had been taken into custody by the Gestapo and interrogated for three days. Kendrick eventually had been released and deported to Hungary, but only after the intervention of the British ambassador in Berlin, Sir Nevile Henderson, who had delivered the strongest of protests. The incident highlighted two flaws in particular: SIS's dependence on a network of easily identifiable Passport Control Offices, and its lack of any independent means of communication. Both weaknesses were due to the Foreign Office's reluctance to confer diplomatic status on Secret Service officers, so only a selected minority of SIS personnel enjoyed immunity from local police forces. Furthermore, only a few embassies abroad were equipped with shortwave radios with which to exchange messages with London, so most diplomatic missions depended on sending coded telegrams by commercial telegraph companies or the local post office. In addition, many senior, more traditional foreign service diplomats disapproved strongly of Admiral Sinclair's organization and methods, and often declined to cooperate with the resident PCO, or at least wished to have nothing to do with him. In Kendrick's case, lack of diplomatic representation in Vienna had meant that the news of his arrest by the Gestapo had failed to reach Sinclair for forty-eight hours. The Nazis, of course, had been aware of the dual role of British Passport Control for years (as, indeed, had most of the world's hostile security authorities), and their decision to arrest Kendrick demonstrated the vulnerability of Sinclair's men in the field. Once isolated from their ambassadors' protection, the intelligence men were transformed into positive liabilities.

Each had an extensive grasp of Britain's overseas intelligence-gathering setup and could probably identify dozens of local agents. Unless steps were taken to establish a means of direct communication with SIS headquarters in London, the Gestapo might be tempted to detain and question many more PCO personnel within its jurisdiction. Without a readily available wireless link, SIS could have no way of knowing if one of its men had been picked up for interrogation.

Admiral Sinclair must have recognized the dangers of relying wholly on such a transparent system as the PCOs because he authorized one of his senior lieutenants, Claude Dansey, to build a second, parallel structure on the Continent. He also made arrangements to create his own self-contained communications unit, designated Section VIII, which would function without any Foreign Office interference. His choice to run the section was Richard Gambier-Parry, formerly a BBC public relations officer who had moved to the Pye electronics firm in 1931. An Old Etonian, Gambier-Parry had served with the Royal Welch Fusiliers and the Royal Flying Corps during the Great War, and in 1938 was given the task of modernizing SIS's links with its overseas stations.

Before Gambier-Parry's arrival, the Foreign Office had only a tiny Communications Department which had been run, since 1925, by Harold Eastwood, an Old Etonian and graduate of Trinity College, Cambridge. (In March 1940, Eastwood was to be ignominiously moved sideways to the post of "Senior King's Foreign Service Messenger.") Coinciding with Gambier-Parry's appointment was Eastwood's decision to purchase Hanslope Park, a large country house set deep in the Buckinghamshire countryside a few miles north of Bletchley, which was promptly transformed into the Foreign Office's first major wireless station. The officer selected to establish Hanslope was a SIS nominee, Major Ted Maltby, who had been recruited from the radio receiver industry by Gambier-Parry. Meanwhile, SIS acquired another, smaller, country property, Whaddon Manor, located on the edge of Whaddon village, approximately four miles east of Bletchley on the Buckingham road. Here, discreetly hidden by woodland from prying eyes, SIS built its first clandestine transmitter, known as the Mark XV, from openly available radio components. Eventually, the manor's stable buildings were converted into a factory for assembling wireless sets for the use of agents. Having organized the foundations of a covert wireless network, Gambier-Parry began to recruit suitable radio operators from the Merchant Navy and distribute shortwave transceivers to a few selected SIS stations overseas.

The deteriorating political climate post-Munich made northwestern Europe Gambier-Parry's priority, but unfortunately one of his first prototype transmitters was delivered straight to the Nazis. Soon after the outbreak of war, the Passport Control Officer in neutral Holland, Major Richard Stevens, reported that he had made contact with a group of high-ranking but disaffected German officers who were plotting a *coup d'état* in Berlin. Stevens was instructed to proceed with caution, so he took care to meet his contacts only in the company of another SIS officer and only on Dutch territory. Late in October 1939, these meetings became more difficult to organize and Stevens received permission to give his German contact, Hauptman Schaemmel, a Mark XV wireless transceiver and a code to facilitate communications between the SIS station in The Hague and Schaemmel's billet in Düsseldorf. The set fitted neatly into two varnished wood boxes, which weighed a hefty forty-five pounds but could be fitted into a pair of suitcases. Between October 30 and November 9, the German was in constant touch with SIS, using the call sign ON4, to make arrangements for a special delegation of senior staff officers to travel to London for secret negotiations with Lord Halifax, the British Foreign Secretary. The German signals were received in The Hague and then relayed to Hanslope, where they were decoded and sent by a secure teleprinter to London. A pair of SIS operators, Inman and Walsh, maintained a twenty-four-hour radio watch in case of any last-minute alterations to the plan, but on the appointed day Stevens and his two companions, Captain Sigismund Best and Lieutenant Dirk Klop, kept their appointment close to the frontier at Venlo.

The events that followed at Venlo are now well documented. Hauptman Schaemmel turned out to be a Sicherheitsdienst officer, Walter Schellenberg, and the entire charade was nothing more than an elaborate trap designed to kidnap Stevens and Best. When the two SIS officers arrived at the border crossing point, they were ambushed by armed SD men who shot Lieutenant Klop, their Dutch liaison officer, and drove them into German territory. News of the incident took some time to reach The Hague, where the local SIS staff waited anxiously for news of Stevens and Best. A week later, ON4 resumed contact with The Hague in a message transmitted shortly after midnight. The text acknowledged the Venlo episode, but it seemed that Schaemmel was still willing to work with SIS:

We are prepared now as before to continue negotiations along lines previous agreed upon. Next meeting must await results of consultation with President Daladier of France. In view of what happened, must proceed henceforth with utmost caution.[1]

Quite what reaction this prompted in London can only be guessed at. SIS headquarters was in turmoil, partly because of the seizure of its two senior officers and partly because of the death, on November 4, 1939, of Admiral Sinclair. In the absence of any instructions to the contrary, The Hague station maintained the contact, at least until Schacmmcl's final signal had been decoded by Walsh:

> Negotiations for any length of time with conceited and silly people are tedious. You will understand, therefore, that we are giving them up. You are hereby bidden a hearty farewell by your affectionate German opposition. Signed: The Gestapo.[2]

If any confirmation was needed of the fate of Best and Stevens, this was it. The first major Allied intelligence operation of the war had been a disaster, and the enemy had profited by two senior SIS operatives and the very latest in SIS's radio technology. Best and Stevens spent the rest of the war in captivity. To add insult to injury, the Sicherheitsdienst had continued to exploit SIS for more than a week after the abduction. It was the first successful German radio game or *funkspiel* of the war, and it was not to be the last.

Unfortunately, most of SIS's early experiences with radio ended in disappointment. Ted Maltby flew to Riga to equip the local SIS station with wireless equipment, and even gave a short operating course to a few selected agents who were also entrusted with sets. Only one, code-named SACK, ever made contact with Hanslope, and his messages were unintelligible. Maltby had taught him to transmit his signals well enough, but insufficient time had been spent tutoring him in SIS cipher procedures. SACK eventually went off the air after the Soviet occupation of the Baltic states, when the SIS station was forced to withdraw. Rather more successful was the stay-behind organization created by the long-serving SIS Head of Station in Helsinki, Harry Carr, who continued to operate his net behind the Russian lines long after the Soviet invasion during the winter of 1940. He eventually escaped to Stockholm in 1941, but many of his agents continued to maintain their schedules with Hanslope for some months longer. Remarkably, Carr's Finnish network and its very modest achievements was the only example of SIS keeping up a sustained contact with any of its overseas rings during the first twelve months of the war. The inevitable consequence of the appalling neglect of SIS's prewar lines of communication was the reduction of its intelligence product. This information starvation did not go unnoticed in Whitehall, where the service chiefs complained bitterly of the quality of SIS's advice. When the Nazis eventually swept into France, Belgium and Holland in May 1940, the very limited trickle of intelligence was cut off overnight.

SIS was by no means the only part of Britain's intelligence-gathering apparatus that was caught ill-prepared by the war. Illicit signals had not played a major role in the Great War, but by the mid-1930s there was every indication that the Germans had planted a number of radio spies in England. Even if SIS had been unable to equip its agents with transmitters, it seemed that the Abwehr had succeeded with theirs. The Security Service knew this for certain, because one of its case officers had been running an Abwehr spy as a double agent for nearly three years, and in January 1939 he had been given a Telefunken transmitter.

When Arthur Owens began working for the Abwehr in 1936, he was just thirty-seven years old and a successful businessman. He habitually posed as a fanatical Welsh nationalist and at the time of his recruitment by the Germans had been supplying both SIS and the Naval Intelligence Division with useful information that he had picked up while selling his company's electronic products on the Continent. When, in January 1939, he had taken delivery of a miniaturized German wireless set, known as an *agentfunkgerate*, which had been deposited for him at Victoria Station, Owens had reported the event to his Special Branch handler, Inspector Gagen, who had offered the set to MI5 for examination. At that time MI5 had no technical facilities, so the set was passed on to Gambier-Parry, who succeeded in dismantling it, but failed to reassemble it correctly. It was therefore given back to Owens, who, not surprisingly, was unable to raise his Abwehr contact. Fortunately, the set was for use only in the event of war, and in the meantime he was obliged to rely on a post office box number in Hamburg. Without his knowledge, all his communications were routinely monitored by MI5's Letter Interception Unit. As an added precaution, Owens's name was placed on the Suspects Index, which resulted in his being served with a detention order on September 4, 1939, and dumped in Wandsworth Prison.

Owens's incarceration proved to be short, because he volunteered to bring his radio from his home in Kingston and begin transmitting to the Germans, under MI5's control, from prison. His offer was accepted, but John Burton, a prison warder who had previously been a Royal Signals operator at an intercept station on the Northwest Frontier, took over

Owens's role with a British set tuned to the frequency selected on his defunct Telefunken. A circuit was established, and later in the month Owens, now code-named SNOW by his Security Service case officer, Major T.A. (Tar) Robertson, traveled to neutral Antwerp for the first of several important rendezvous with the Abwehr.

When SNOW returned from these covert meetings, he invariably did so equipped with codes and instructions describing the wireless procedures he should adopt. These were to prove of historic importance in the secret wireless war and eventually led to the breaking of the Abwehr's hand ciphers, which in turn gave Bletchley a crib which helped them reconstruct some of the Abwehr's Enigma keys.

As well as rounding up all the names on the Suspects Index on the outbreak of hostilities, MI5 introduced one of its contingency plans to deal with the anticipated problem of illicit signals. SNOW was firmly under MI5's control, but what of the other spies planted in England by the enemy? To cope with what was perceived to be a major headache, MI5 created an entirely new body, the Radio Security Service, under the leadership of Major J.P.G. Worlledge, the veteran interceptor who, up until 1927, had commanded the No. 2 Wireless Company in Palestine. He was given a brief to "intercept, locate and close down illicit wireless stations operated either by enemy agents in Great Britain or by other persons not being licensed to do so under Defense Regulations, 1939." Lacking both permanent stations and staff, the newly created RSS was obliged to build an entire organization on the outbreak of war. Worlledge selected Majors Sclater and Cole-Adams as his aides and placed Walter Gill, of *War, Wireless and Wangles* fame, as his chief traffic analyst. It only remained to find some suitable illicit signals, and Worlledge opted to rely on a network of radio amateurs working in their spare time. Many had volunteered the previous year to join the RAF's Civilian Wireless Reserve, a shadowy group of Radio Society of Great Britain (RSGB) operators which paralleled the Royal Navy's Wireless Volunteer Reserve. As a security precaution, the RSS was granted the military intelligence cover designation MI8c. The task of developing a comprehensive organization was given to Lord Sandhurst, then managing director of Hatch Mansfield & Company, the wine shippers. An enthusiastic amateur license holder, Jimmy Sandhurst had served with the Royal Engineers' Signal Service in France during the Great War, where he had led a group of owner-rider dispatch riders. He had joined up in August 1914 as a lance-corporal and had been commissioned soon afterward. Educated at Winchester and Trinity, Cambridge, he had succeeded to his father's baronetcy in 1933. In September 1939, he had been commissioned into the Royal Corps of Signals with the rank of major, given an office in the Security Service's temporary headquarters in Wormwood Scrubs Prison and instructed to liaise with R.L. Hughes, a wartime recruit into MI5. Sandhurst's first act was to approach the president of the Radio Society of Great Britain for assistance. The then RSGB president was Arthur Watts, a veteran of the Great War who had lost a leg at Gallipoli and had subsequently become a traffic analyst in Room 40. Watts recommended the recruitment of the entire RSGB Council and, after routine security clearance, all were indoctrinated into RSS.

Because nothing has ever been officially disclosed concerning the work of the RSS, this is an appropriate moment to describe its activities in some detail. It will then become evident that it was largely thanks to the RSS that the cryptographers at Bletchley Park were able to continue their work.

In many ways the RSS was a classic example of time-honored British improvisation, with voluntary workers making considerable personal sacrifices to rescue the ill-prepared Whitehall establishment. During the first months of the war, domestic wireless interception in Britain was limited to the two War Office stations at Fort Bridgewoods and Flowerdown, with some additional work being carried out by the new GPO stations at Sandridge, St. Albans, Cupar and Brora. The latter three concentrated on a futile search for navigational aids, known as meacons, which the Luftwaffe was believed to have constructed in secret locations across the country. In fact, none ever existed, but while the GPO was otherwise occupied, the business of monitoring illicit radio transmissions fell to the RSS. In addition, direction-finding stations were built at Thurso and Forfar in Scotland, Bridgwater in Somerset, Gilnahirk in Northern Ireland, St. Erth (which was largely underground, just outside the village of Leedstown) in Cornwall, Wymondham in Norfolk, and Hanslope Park; seven in all.

Mobilizing a volunteer force was by no means easy, especially in conditions of the greatest secrecy and without any special equipment. Sandhurst once warned: "The VI [voluntary interceptor] is under obligation. He has written his good name to that effect. If he does talk too much he may find himself in jug. In almost any other country in Europe he would be shot."[3]

The operators had to be skilled, discreet and dedicated, so the recruitment process was necessarily slow. By Christmas 1939, the Home South region boasted only seven VIs on its roll. Their task was particularly arduous, with several hundred enemy stations to monitor. Furthermore, intercepting the enemy's signals was no easy matter. For example, the BBC was accustomed to broadcast its entertainment programs at a strength of 100 millivolts per meter. The loudest German signal was 10,000 times weaker, and the weakest were a million times below the BBC. Nevertheless, in spite of these difficulties, Sandhurst proved to be a popular, inspired leader and introduced an element of humor into his personal messages of encouragement to his volunteers.

He also produced a fortnightly newsletter, entitled *The Hunt*, in which he referred to himself as "Dogsbody" or "T.W. Earp," the enemy as "Foxes" and "Skunks" with friendly Service stations labeled as "Rabbits." Sandhurst even composed a poem to explain the procedure to new VIs:

> If you can find a fox on your RX
> And copy him whatever be his fist,
> If you can dig him out of the schedule BERTIE,
> And get his traffic daily, nothing missed,
> If you can find his QSU's and answers,
> Or supply Group 13's missing link;
> If you can copy SHL's fast bug-key
> And send the log in neatly done in ink,
> If you can dodge the blinking German Army,
> Or copy AOR through thick and thin
> And you can copy VIOLET's QRX's,
> You're a better bloke than me so
> BUNG IT IN!

The first task of the VI was to distinguish between the various different types of five-letter ciphers being transmitted in Europe. They fell broadly into three separate categories: the commercial traffic, which generally used the international Q-code and could easily be spotted by its automatic transmissions at a uniform pace. If there were no texts to be sent, the circuit would be kept open by the continuous signaling of "ABC." Commercial messages invariably concluded with a time or date. The only two exceptions were the Russian and Spanish inland telegraph services, which were still largely manual, but their procedures were equally easy to distinguish. The second category was the British armed services, which all used the same call sign format of three letters, with mixed figure and letter. There were other easy clues in the Rabbit traffic, such as the inclusion of a five-figure group of "QQQQQ" which British operators with prewar amateur experience habitually transmitted, given the opportunity. Each country had its own characteristic procedures, and the patient interceptor would gradually learn them all. The Italians, for example, used a five-figure cipher in which every tenth group was numbered; the Russians invariably inserted the letter "R" between their groups, and the Spaniards used groups beginning with the letter "P." Thus, P2371 was sure to come from Spain and, therefore, to be of no interest, and the German army often finished its messages with a six-figure group, which also told the interceptor to scan another frequency.

The third category, which was supposed to be left to the army and Admiralty interceptors, was the German army and naval traffic. The Wehrmacht signals always opened with their distinctive preambles, and the naval transmissions were usually sent in four-letter ciphers by very steady operators using exceptionally good Morse. They were also trained to repeat the first two groups of the preamble as the last two on the end of the message.

Once the VI had eliminated this traffic, he was left with the more interesting, and secret, foxes. These were enemy point-to-point messages which were quite unlike anything else and contained very high-grade intelligence information, either between an Abwehr agent and his base, or two Abwehr stations. Sometimes the call and reply would occur on different frequencies and employed a variety of such maneuvers to avoid interception. By doing so, they actually attracted attention to themselves and thus aided the RSS interceptors, who became very adept at spotting unusual preambles or operating procedures. It was these out-of-the-ordinary intercepted signals which were to give the Bletchley cryptographers some of the breakthroughs for which they had been waiting. Some of the more crafty enemy operators quickly established themselves as "dar-diddley-dar merchants" by first signing off and then starting to transmit a few moments later. The really clever opposition stood out from the usual routine of poor security and the exchange of private messages or initials, and proved very popular with the interceptors. One game, known as "finding the lady," involved checking the previous schedules to work out which outstation a particular fox would operate to next.

One of the first circulars issued to the VIs included a description of a few notorious foxes:

> ANNA is a very delicate lily, the flower of them all, our beautiful
> heroine. Oft may you see her flitting gracefully through the bluebells,
> or in and out of the kilocycles. She is demure; she speaks not often,

but when she does it is clear and sweet, and her utterances pearls of priceless worth. Anna dresses well, and thirty times a month you will find her in fresh apparel. She is tall and slender, and her long arms may reach across the ocean. You will always know her by her simple preamble: CT ANNA PURE AND SHY BT

BRUNO is a young gentleman who lives mostly in the north of France. Like Anna, he does not say much, but he is easily recognized by his clear Group 6 voice. Sometimes his hand is a little uncertain, but he always tries to be smart, and changes his suit daily.

CAESAR is the village idiot. He spends most of his time talking to himself, but even then he has to repeat everything many times before he gets it right, with his rough ICW voice and his Group 7 accent with the dreadful sss-stammer.

DORA is the elusive witch. We don't see much of her, she is always hiding on skunk or commercial frequencies. Her preamble varies. Sometimes she tries to pass as Anna, but spends too much time with the skunks to make the illusion a success.

Emil and his wife Ada are the old folks of the Group 3 family. They are dull and stupid, and MOST prolific. Their family is so large that they have been entirely unable to rear and discipline them. Ada's Group 2 chromosomes have come out strong in many of her offspring, but the old man's Group 3 have contributed a very unruly element. Their children include Gun de Sie, the only ones not always wanted by the police, the elusive OLM and ADF, the ugly great leering Fritz, and those dreadful BUM boys.

FRITZ a great fat ugly good for nothing lout struts all around six bands sowing his filthy oats all the time. Wherever you look among the kilocycles (bluebells wilt) you will find his illegitimates grinning at you. They talk all day, their fat mouths giving away everybody's secrets, trying to dodge the police, for they are all very much wanted.

The BUM boys. These highly disreputable nancies, sorry, Nazis, have never even learned to use a preamble when they speak. They use wicked words, they can't spell, and, not satisfied with that, they can't always send Morse. They have got a way of vanishing round the corner just when you think they are going to give you something, and then come up behind you, round another kilocycle to shout their ruderies. . . . There is a price on their heads.[4]

Fox preambles were a little different from the Enigma messages because, with a manual cipher, there was no "discriminant" rotor setting to be chosen. Instead, they consisted of date, time, serial number, the

The Crest of the
Radio Security Service

Post receptif rampant on field electromagnetic,
key telegraphic stagnant, bar sinister poignant, quarter
censored. Surmounted helmet armor civilian duty.

"indicator" (to identify which code was to be used), followed by two
figures: the total number of letters in the message and the total of groups.
The more a VI concentrated on a particular fox, the more skilled he
became. The RSS management reckoned that the minimum product for
a reasonable VI was eight logs a month; most started with an average of
ten, but forty-eight a month was the minimum to ensure exemption from
other duties, such as fire watching.

Within three months of starting work, RSS had recruited fifty VIs
and identified approximately six hundred foxes, but they were all firmly
on the other side of the English Channel. In December 1939, the number
of logs submitted by the Home South section produced a total of 1,932
logs. By March the following year, the figure had jumped to 3,052.

These logs of Morse messages collected by the VIs on their own private sets were sent into RSS headquarters at Wormwood Scrubs via their regional officers. Sandhurst had appointed twenty regional officers to supervise the work of the VIs and to allocate particular frequencies on a routine of watches. The country was divided into RSS regions, which were identified by letters denoting geographical areas. Those closest to London became Home North and Home South, and individual VIs were allocated special code numbers, based on their geographical region. Logs signed by SW/127 immediately identified the operator as J.W. Clayton of Fowey in Cornwall, and NW/185 as Gerry Openshaw of Bolton in Lancashire. The VIs would return from their regular work in the evening and listen for three or four hours to a predetermined wavelength. As the organization grew, the country was further divided into subgroups, each headed by a group leader who was identified by a group number. In correspondence with headquarters, group leaders would head their logs "V. HS/120, Sub Group HNS 4." Initially, the VIs concentrated on evening and night work, with hardly anyone available to work their sets during the day. With further recruitment, Sandhurst was able to fill the gaps with enthusiastic volunteers.

Before a code could be subjected to cryptanalytical attack, it was first necessary to intercept a series of examples of radio messages. The more texts available for study, the better the chances of cracking a code. However, the intercepts had to be copied with absolute accuracy. There was no point in attempting to solve a code with corrupted texts. The responsibility for getting the intercept 100 percent accurate rested with the interceptor, and if more than one could take down a message the opportunity for error was reduced. If the analysts could compare the handiwork of several different VIs, they would quickly spot the odd mistake.

Once received at headquarters, the VI's log was examined by discriminators who decided if the raw material was a hand cipher or machine code. Comparison with direction-finding reports often gave additional information. These would identify the bearings of the sending station and be marked with the exact time of the message, its length and its frequency. Thus, by the time the intercept reached the cryptanalysts, they already knew a considerable amount about the text's background. They knew, for example, the location of the sending station and, if the receiving end acknowledged it, the recipient. If the location was a familiar one, it might identify whether the traffic was Abwehr, Wehrmacht or Luftwaffe. The length of the message and the style of the sender might also reveal important details. If the intercept's distinctive preamble showed that an

Enigma machine had been employed, the analysts endeavored to work out which key had been used. If the key was recognized, it was examined for any mistakes that might give a clue to the content. When the discriminators had completed their task, the intercept would be passed to the specialist units staffed by officers who concentrated on particular kinds of enemy traffic. A message intercepted from the Abwehr in Hamburg, for example, would go to the RSS substation which dealt with that material alone, and was equipped with a card index listing all the past intercepts and cross-referring those with similar characteristics. The process of traffic analysis thus gave RSS a wealth of information, even if the exact content of a message might be elusive.

The rapid expansion of the VI network created so much raw material to be processed at Wormwood Scrubs that, early in 1940, arrangements were made for the entire headquarters to move out of London to the small village of Arkley, near Barnet in Middlesex. Arkley View, a large house on the outskirts of the village, was requisitioned and a staff of traffic analysts installed, led by Walter Gill. Among them were Denys Page (later Regius Professor of Greek at Cambridge) and Hugh Trevor-Roper (later Lord Dacre, and Regius Professor of History at Oxford). Eventually, their numbers were to be swelled by three further Oxford academics: Charles Stuart, Gilbert Ryle and (Sir) Stuart Hampshire (now Warden of Wadham College).

Kenneth Morton-Evans received the VI logs mailed to "Box 25, Barnet" and divided them into a series of numbered groups, which sorted the logs into known and unknown stations, roughly identifying the origin of the intercepted signals. The groups ranged from GROUP 1 to GROUP 15 and were further subdivided into actual wireless stations. Thus BERTIE on GROUP 1 was Berlin, HARRY was Hamburg and WILLIE was Wiesbaden. If too many VIs duplicated each other, their logs would be returned with remarks such as: "German Army, covered, thank you." Or a VI might be told: "Suspect, more please."

On a good day "Box 25, Barnet" was receiving around three hundred logs a day, with some of the logs covering up to fifty separate sheets. Analysis of this huge volume revealed that RSS was concentrating solely on the interception of enemy signals from the Continent and not on the stalking of illicit signals from home, the job that the War Office had at first envisaged for them. This, of course, is not to suggest that the War Office was at all dissatisfied with RSS's performance. On the contrary, it was quickly accepted that the RSS amateurs were far more skilled SIGINT interceptors than the so-called professionals of the GPO. The licensed amateurs were extremely practiced at exchanging very weak signals from other hams around the world, often operating substandard equipment. In contrast, the GPO staff had experienced only very high-quality standards in signaling and were, therefore, ill-prepared for catching the faintest transmissions. Worlledge once commented on RSS's impressive ability to spot and monitor even the weakest of enemy signals: "We have continually wiped the eye of the Post Office over it, and I am very anxious that we should wipe it cleaner."

By March 1940, it was realized (not without some disbelief) that the RSS had actually completed its original mission. Incredible as it may have seemed at the time, there simply were no illicit signals for the VIs to monitor. According to the analysts at Arkley, all the intercepts were German in origin and consisted of station to station nets on the Continent. However, instead of disbanding the VI network, RSS prepared a handbook of German Morse techniques and issued it to the VIs later the same month. This book was to prove of enormous benefit when, some eight weeks later, the Germans launched their offensive into Belgium, Holland and France. To the amazement of everyone at Arkley, the Abstelle at Wiesbaden was monitored sending special messages to its agents in those countries, alerting them to the imminent attack.

The Abwehr's increase in signal activity during the summer of 1940 was final confirmation that, contrary to all expectations, the Germans intended to rely more heavily on wireless communications. Evidently, they believed their hand and machine ciphers to be unbreakable, but there was a mass of other valuable intelligence to be gleaned from the ether. Gossipy German operators were comparatively undisciplined by British standards and tended to engage in radio chatter while establishing contact with another operator. The purpose of the exchanges was apparently to identify the particular operator at the other end of the net and proved very useful to RSS. By the end of the war, a special index of "personality cards" had been opened on several hundred German operators, and analysis of their geographical locations often helped to confirm the movement of certain military units. Sometimes the operators would discuss details of new codes, or agree the updated settings of their cipher machines or even debate the merits of a manual code. Another important advantage gained from these indiscretions was the opportunity to keep pace with the frequent changes in the call signs of enemy stations. When an operator kept to a routine signal plan and transmitted at the same time each day, it was fairly straightforward for the monitoring VI to recognize his opponent's fist. Furthermore, if two Germans indulged in some chat, it enabled the VI to find the enemy's operating frequencies, because they did not, as a rule, net on the same frequency.

RSS's extraordinary success at harnessing the radio amateurs was to cause political problems for the organization. By eliminating the possibility of illegal transmissions, RSS had, in one sense, worked itself out of a job. RSS had been created under MI5's wing, in the belief that its role was a defensive one. But thanks to MI5's comprehensive action in rounding up all those on its Suspects Index, there was little hope of any Abwehr agent remaining at liberty. The one that had been detected, SNOW, had been turned at an early stage and this had enabled MI5 to appear uncharacteristically aggressive. The SNOW case had yielded dividends at an unexpectedly early stage, leading Guy Liddell, the director of MI5's counterespionage branch, B Division, to risk poaching on an area that had previously been SIS's preserve: offensive counterintelligence operations. Since RSS had little to monitor in terms of homegrown signals, it too had inevitably strayed into what had previously been regarded as SIS's territory.

If matters had rested there it is likely that interservice conflict might have been avoided, given that everyone was committed to fighting a common enemy, but there were other ingredients in the mixture which ensured that it was a volatile one. Not least of these was SIS's own position in the intercept game. Bletchley's first, limited successes against the Enigma did not occur until January 1940, yet RSS had broken into the Abwehr's hand ciphers the previous December, thanks to SNOW's cooperation. He had promptly surrendered to MI5 the Abwehr's manual cipher that he had been entrusted with in Antwerp in September 1939. This had then been handed on to Oliver Strachey at Bletchley, who had used it to break some other Abwehr traffic.

Direction finding on SNOW's messages (which, of course, were actually being transmitted by John Burton) showed that his signals were being acknowledged from a position close to Norway. This was a development of some interest to MI5 because SNOW had been told that his transmissions would be received at a secret Abwehr station located at Wohldorf, a suburb to the north of Hamburg. However, RSS and the GPO traced the Abwehr's replies to a point in the North Sea off the Norwegian coast. Early in 1940, the Royal Navy investigated the mysterious source and found a German spy ship cruising slowly in international waters. At the request of RSS no further action was taken, thus enabling all the ship's considerable output to be monitored and, in some cases, actually decrypted. The ship served as a slave relay for SNOW, receiving his hand-coded messages and then reciphering them on an

Enigma machine for immediate onward transmission to Hamburg-Wohldorf. Knowledge of SNOW's complete texts, which were specially prepared by MI5, enabled Knox to follow SNOW's messages as they were routed from him to the ship and then reciphered on an Enigma to their final destination in Germany. At last, Strachey had achieved a long-awaited breakthrough.

Strachey's treatment of SNOW's material during the latter part of 1939 coincided with some excellent progress achieved by his colleagues on the Enigma team. The full team consisted of three distinguished mathematicians from Cambridge, Gordon Welchman from Sidney Sussex College, Alan Turing from King's and John Jeffreys from Downing College, who had all attended prewar GC&CS indoctrination courses. To this formidable collection of brainpower were added the talents of Peter Twinn, an Oxford physicist, Patrick Wilkinson, a Classics don from King's, and two assistants, Mavis Lever and Margaret Lock.

While Dilly Knox, who was fighting a losing battle against cancer, was collaborating with Strachey on SNOW's hand ciphers and consequent machine traffic with some success, the Enigma team had been establishing themselves in the stables at Bletchley Park, with Gordon Welchman in the old Schoolhouse accompanied by his two assistants, Patricia Newman and Peggy Taylor. Jeffries and Turing now planned new Zygalski-type perforated sheets in order to discover the rotor keys. Meanwhile, Welchman analyzed the intercept traffic from Fort Bridgewoods and divided it into three distinct categories which he marked with colored pencils. The first were RED, BLUE and GREEN, and they were later followed by ORANGE and BROWN. Each was a clearly identified type of traffic, with its keys changing on a daily basis. Beyond that, the cryptologists were in the dark. Even the SIGINT analysts could offer little advice because many of these first intercepts were weak, and the Service operators were still relatively inexperienced at catching complete texts without corrupting a message, or distinguishing between the telltale preambles and the text proper on their log sheets.

In order to make clear what stage English Enigma research had reached at this time, it is necessary to go back for a moment and show how the Bletchley team had been greatly assisted in its initial researches by both the French and what remained of the Polish Cipher Bureau during the early part of 1939.

The Polish Bureau had been evacuated from Warsaw via neutral Romania and had taken up residence with Bertrand's organization at the Château de Vignolles, a country house near Gretl-Armainvillers, some thirty miles northeast of Paris. Code-named Poste de Commandement BRUNO, the château had been linked to Bletchley by a direct teleprinter line, operated by a British liaison officer, Kenneth MacFarlan. An accomplished linguist, MacFarlan had been recruited into SIGINT from the No. 2 Wireless Company at Sarafand back in April 1935 and, apart from a few spells at Broadway assisting John Tiltman with Japanese cryptological problems, he had spent much of his service overseas. In 1938, he had built a direction-finding station at Chartres with Commander Ellingworth and three civilian operators, followed by a similar establishment at Arras.

The Poles, still under the leadership of Colonel Gwido Langer, had lost much of their equipment and files during their long journey across Europe, but their expertise was such that, with a set of sixty perforated Zygalski-type sheets provided by Alan Turing, they had been able to assist the French to break one of the keys for October 28, 1939. This news had been imparted to Bletchley by Colonel Langer and Captain Branquenie during the first week of December 1939 and had given Welchman his first insight into the GREEN intercepts which, according to the French, was a Wehrmacht key, used for administrative messages within Germany's twenty military districts. The content of the resulting decrypts had not been of enormous value, but it was believed that applying the sixty perforated sheets to other intercepts might yield other detectable cipher patterns.

This is indeed what happened, and the GREEN key for October 25 succumbed early in the New Year. This was followed by a RED key for January 6, 1940, which turned out to be Luftwaffe traffic. This was the first occasion that Denniston's organization had broken a wartime Enigma key without direct assistance. Suddenly the prospects of reading the German machine cipher signals seemed brighter, and an agreement was reached with BRUNO, leaving all basic decryption research to the French and the Poles in the future, while Bletchley worked on a technical improvement of the Polish Bombe.

There was, however, a slight complication which threatened to jeopardize these latest achievements. During the first six months of the war, the Secret Intelligence Service had been roundly condemned by the intelligence divisions of the armed services for having provided little or no information of any strategic relevance. Morale within SIS had suffered a severe blow in November 1939, a few days after the death of Admiral Sinclair, when Best and Stevens, officers with a considerable knowledge of British clandestine networks in Europe, had been kidnapped by the Nazis in broad daylight. Some weeks earlier, in a related incident, SIS had also lost its best German agent, a homosexual diplomat named Wolfgang zu Putlitz, who had been recruited by MI5 before the war when the anti-Nazi had been press attaché at the German Embassy in London. He had subsequently been transferred to The Hague, where he had continued to supply his British case officer with valuable information. Soon after the outbreak of war, he had demanded to be rescued because he believed his identity had been compromised by a breach of SIS's security. A rescue mission had been launched, and Putlitz had been brought to London where, of course, he was of comparatively little use to anyone. With virtually nothing else left to rely on, Stewart Menzies, Sinclair's successor as CSS, found that GC&CS, or rather its new wartime cover of GCHQ, had exceeded all expectations and had actually solved an impregnable German machine cipher. SIS was at a low ebb, but now all that was needed was the necessary financial support to complete the development of an English version of the Bombe. Such a commitment was essential if Bletchley's work was to continue, and Denniston's organization looked more likely to produce promising results than SIS, especially after the *U-33* coup in February 1940.

Before describing this episode in detail, it is necessary briefly to examine the Naval Intelligence Division's dilemma during the opening months of the phony war. At the outbreak of hostilities, the Royal Navy enjoyed an overwhelming numerical superiority over Admiral Raeder's comparatively tiny German fleet. However, the experience of the U-boat blockade of the Great War had demonstrated the vulnerability of the Empire's merchantmen to submarine attack. Unknown to the British, Germany in fact possessed only a relatively small naval force (just three pocket battleships, two battle-cruisers and eight light cruisers in September 1939), which was completely outnumbered and outgunned by the Royal Navy's strength of twelve battleships, three battle-cruisers and sixty-two cruisers. However, supremacy in surface vessels was no guarantee of safe passage for Allied convoys. Given enough submarines, Admiral Raeder could isolate the British Isles because of insufficient Allied destroyers and escort vessels. In contrast, Germany could import its raw materials overland, in complete safety. Britian's industries required constant replenishment at a prodigious rate.

It was in this atmosphere of near paranoia that the NID analysts tried to calculate the exact size of the U-boat fleet. Thanks largely to exaggerated reports from SIS agents, they got their arithmetic dramatically wrong, by a factor of 12 percent, and estimated a total of sixty-six enemy submarines, all thought to have been built since 1933. In fact, in September 1939, Germany possessed just fifty-seven U-boats (the exact figure the Reich was entitled to build under the 1935 Anglo-German Naval

Agreement) of which only twenty-six were modern oceangoing craft.

Admiralty uncertainty about the enemy's most potent naval weapon inevitably led to much speculation on the subject, but GCHQ's Naval Section, formed in May 1938 under William Clarke, could offer no comfort. Traffic analysis and direction finding proved to be of little help in establishing the German naval order of battle, and wartime crytanalysis merely confirmed the existence of a mass of incomprehensible signal traffic exchanged at high speed with enviable wireless discipline.

If Britain was to defeat the U-boat, a breach would have to be made in the wall of secrecy surrounding its operations. The first such opportunity was offered by the *U-33*, an oceangoing Type VIIA submarine, launched in 1936 and attached to the 2nd U-boat flotilla (known as the Flotilla Salzwedel) based at Wilhelmshaven. Commanded by Hans-Wilhelm von Dresky, with four officers and forty-one men on board, the *U-33* had been on patrol in the waters off the west of Scotland late in 1939. On Christmas Day, it had laid a minefield in the path of the *Stanholme*, a steamer which had sunk soon after hitting a mine. A fortnight later, on January 16, von Dresky had laid another mine which was struck by the *Inverdargle*, a small tanker. That too had sunk in much the same area as the *Stanholme*, so the Royal Navy responded by deploying several ships from the Anti-Submarine Striking Force in the approaches to the Firth of Clyde. Among them was HMS *Gleaner*, a converted sloop armed with some forty depth charges, the very latest Asdic equipment and two four-inch guns. The *Gleaner* had been a hydrographic survey vessel, and her captain, Lieutenant-Commander Hugh Price RN, was a distinguished hydrographer who had spent the past fifteen years making charts for the Admiralty's Survey Service. Suddenly, very early in the morning of February 12, the *Gleaner*'s Asdic operator reported a surface contact one and a half miles away. The officer of the watch, Sub-Lieutenant E.P. Reade, altered course to intercept the intruder, and soon afterward the searchlight spotted the wash of a periscope in the calm sea. During the following two hours Commander Price dropped ten depth charges in the area, but the only damage caused was actually sustained by the *Gleaner*. The underwater explosions knocked out the sensitive Asdic gear, blew the ship's dynamo and even broke the carbon elements in the searchlight. In spite of these handicaps the *Gleaner* continued its patrol, using two Aldis signaling lamps to scour the surface for clues to the fate of the submarine. Eventually, at exactly 5:22 in the morning, the *U-33* was seen stationary in the water, about a mile away. Five rounds were fired from the four-inch guns, and Price prepared to ram. As the *Gleaner* approached, it became clear that the U-boat was willing to surrender. The German crew swarmed onto the casing, waving their arms over their heads. Moments later sparks were seen flying out of the conning tower, and the crew abandoned ship. Evidently, the captain had scuttled his submarine and had gone down with it. Only four officers and seventeen ratings survived the icy water to be taken prisoner. All the rest died of exposure, even though they were wearing lifebelts and emergency breathing apparatus.

Price carefully marked where the *U-33* had sunk, and soon afterward, in conditions of great secrecy, HMS *Tedworth* arrived on the scene with a team of divers to locate the wreck, which was discovered in just thirty fathoms of water. On their first dive, they succeeded in recovering various items from the interior, including no less than three intact Enigma rotors. This was the first incident of its kind in the war and proved to be Bletchley's earliest opportunity to examine an original enemy rotor. The interrogation of the crew yielded more valuable information. Apparently, von Dresky was very unpopular with his men and had mistakenly identified the *Gleaner* as a British cruiser. He had shadowed the *Gleaner* for several hours before deciding to slip past her and, in the opinion of his engineering officer, his U-boat had not sustained much damage from the depth charges. Only the lighting and the auxiliary machinery had been put out of action, and most of the crew were convinced that the *U-33* could have made the journey back to Germany. The captain had thought otherwise; nor had he ordered the submarine's gun to be manned when he finally brought his submarine to the surface. These shortcomings were skillfully exploited by the NID 1/PW interrogators at the London District Cage in Kensington Gardens before the *U-33*'s resentful crew were finally delivered to their prisoner-of-war camps in Canada.

Further interrogation established that the Enigma rotors retrieved by the divers were just three of a total of eight carried aboard all German submarines. It seemed that although the U-boats were equipped with the same Enigma machines as the Wehrmacht and Luftwaffe, the Kriegsmarine had a greater choice of rotors and, therefore, boasted substantially better security. The chances of tackling the German naval traffic appeared to recede, but there was still plenty of scope offered by the many other Enigma users. Commander Price was decorated with the DSO for his feat, although the exact circumstances of the *U-33*'s loss, and the recovery of the three Enigma rotors, was to be a closely guarded secret for many years to follow.

Although the *U-33* incident gave no direct assistance to the Naval

Section cryptanalysts at Bletchley, it did provide an invaluable insight into the enemy's operating procedures. The Kriegsmarine apparently employed no less than three separate Enigma keys: the Home Waters key (*Heimisch*), which was promptly code-named DOLPHIN by GCHQ; the Distant Waters key (*Ausserheimisch*), designated PIKE (which was always to resist decryption); and the Officers Only key for high-grade transmissions, known as OYSTER. Later BARRACUDA, a fourth naval key, referred to by the Kriegsmarine as *Neptun*, was identified as carrying top-level fleet messages between Berlin and Raeder's coastal bases. Within these ciphers was a special "short signaling" code designed to allow routine texts to be exchanged in the minimum of time. So in other words, a solution to a particular DOLPHIN key would yield only limited information unless Bletchley found, or reconstructed, the short code book. Insofar as the enemy's naval traffic was concerned, the prospects looked bleak.

Between January and March 1940, no less than fifty GREEN and BLUE Enigma keys were broken, the latter being used by the Luftwaffe for exercises. On April 10, the first YELLOW traffic was intercepted, and five days later it too succumbed. It turned out to be operational messages dealing with the new Nazi campaign in Norway, and chiefly concerned the Luftwaffe, although all three fighting arms used it for interservice communications. Bletchley tapped the intercepts for the next month, gaining its first detailed view of the Nazi reliance on the machine cipher, and the many abbreviations and conventions used to reduce the volume of signals. If the Enigma decrypts were to be exploited to the full, GCHQ would require three items as a matter of urgency: a sophisticated device to find the keys; a massive team of translators to master the linguistic intricacies; and a secure method of distributing the decrypts. As yet, neither Denniston nor Menzies could offer any of these. This, then, was the background to a remarkable letter, dated April 18, 1940, sent by Sir Frederick Butler, the Foreign Office's finance officer, on behalf of GCHQ, to the Treasury:

> Sir,
>   I am directed by Viscount Halifax to request you to inform the Lords Commissioners of His Majesty's Treasury that certain investigations in the Code and Cypher School developed rapidly at the end of January last and that in the intervening period it has been found necessary to engage temporary staff in excess of the authorized establishment.

2. The circumstances in which the additional staff was engaged, and the nature of the work on which they are employed, have been explained verbally to officers of Their Lordships' department and it is understood that they will be prepared to give their covering sanction for the extra staff engaged.

3. Authorities now in force cover an establishment of 91 temporary clerks, 3 shorthand typists and 62 typists and it was found that an increase to 160 temporary clerks, 4 shorthand typists and 72 typists was necessary.

4. The return of the Commercial Section of the School to London and the increased accommodation necessitated by the developments at Oxford and Bletchley also involved the engagement of 2 additional officekeepers and one charwoman.

5. It was also explained that approximately 30 Grade III clerks are now employed on duties which necessitate a good working knowledge of at least one foreign language and while this need not be of so high a standard as that of the linguist class, it is essential for the proper and successful performance of their particular work. It is understood that Their Lordships would be prepared to authorize the provision of the Grade II posts for these officers in addition to the three authorized by Treasury letter E 4278/7 of the 24th February last.

6. I am, therefore, to request that Their Lordships may be moved to give their covering sanction for an addition of:-

60 temporary clerks of whom 30 should be Grade II.

1 temporary shorthand typist

10 temporary typists

2 temporary officekeepers

1 charwoman

as from the several dates on which the officers concerned were first employed.

7. I am further to state that in consequence of the necessity to employ a certain part of the Mechanical Section of the School on a twenty-four-hour-day instead of an eight-hour-day basis, it will be necessary to triplicate the staff of this section.

8. Approximately twenty Grade III clerks are required for each eight-hour shift and I am, therefore, to request that Their Lordships may be moved to sanction a further addition of 40 Grade III temporary clerks to provide the two additional shifts.[5]

Forty years later it seems difficult to believe that with Poland occupied, Britain about to fight for her existence and the rest of the world on the brink of catastrophe, the Foreign Office should be submitting polite requests for the services of an extra charlady to assist in an operation that was ultimately to ensure the defeat of the Nazis. It is, perhaps more than any other document, an indication of the attitudes prevailing in Chamberlain's administration and of the unexpected nature of GCHQ's breakthrough.

As soon as Stewart Menzies grasped the significance of the breakdown of the Luftwaffe BLUE, GREEN and YELLOW keys at Bletchley and recognized the value of this knowledge, which became easier to discern after the fall of Denmark and Norway, he instinctively sought measures both to protect and to exploit his source. Up until the very unexpected Norwegian campaign, there had lurked the possibility that Bletchley's efforts might prove to have been wasted. There was the possibility (indeed, in the minds of many experienced old hands, a probability) that the enemy's wireless traffic would diminish, not increase, as hostilities continued. Other pessimists took the view that the Germans might momentarily switch the bulk of their operational orders on to another cipher system, leaving relatively unprofitable administrative matters to the Enigma. Now, for the first time, there was clear evidence that the familiar Enigma machine was to be employed in a major way during an important new military campaign. Overnight Menzies was in control of a crucial and reliable fount, which promised to restore his organization's sinking reputation. His first consideration, of course, was security. Obviously, special procedures had to be introduced to avoid compromising the fact that the newly acquired intelligence was actually SIGINT in origin, or the enemy would switch off the tap by tightening their own security; but what of distribution? Intelligence is invariably worthless unless it can be disseminated to those in a position to act upon it. The tactical advantages to be gained from the material were perfectly clear. It did not require a genius of strategy to work out the implications of Bletchley's product, but how was it to be distributed in the theater of operations without alerting the enemy? Menzies's initial solution proved entirely unsatisfactory. The SIGINT was offered to the Air Ministry and the War Office as though the information had been acquired from a well-placed agent, possibly a senior officer in Berlin. This fictitious master spy was even given the code name BONIFACE, and Bletchley's material was circulated on sheets of flimsy paper headed with the word. The Admiralty, predictably, was not to be fooled, and the DNI wasted no time in demanding a direct teleprinter link between "Station X" or "BP," as Bletchley Park was referred to in correspondence, and the huge new reinforced concrete fortress beside Horse Guards Parade which housed the Royal Navy's Operational Intelligence Center. For the next eighteen months, the Admiralty made its own assessments after the SIGINT had been processed by the Navy Section at GCHQ, and distributed it itself under the code name HYDRO. Fortunately, HYDRO was transmitted to those indoctrinated commanders at sea in a special cipher based on a one-time pad. Just as well, for the Germans had broken the main British naval cipher in 1938 and continued to read a substantial part of the Admiralty's communications until September 1941, when the extent of the damage to the Royal Navy was learned from a decrypted enemy signal.

At this stage, during the spring of 1940, the HYDRO summaries were necessarily based on the RED and YELLOW decrypts, but in May the Naval Section at Bletchley was able retrospectively to examine the enemy's naval signals for a period of just six days in the previous month. This was no breakthrough on the scale of RED or YELLOW, because the information had come from a batch of old messages found on board a German patrol vessel captured in the North Sea, but it did enable the cryptanalysts to confirm an important conclusion: all the German U-boat and surface fleets were issued with the same improved Enigma machines with the extra rotors, but used only two keys: one for home waters and one for ships venturing further afield. The latter key was never mastered but, as will be seen, the home key was eventually dealt with after some particularly ingenious operations had been executed by the Naval Intelligence Division.

Once the BONIFACE system had been instituted, two problems quickly manifested themselves. Firstly, the wretched fictitious spy was disbelieved. The Secret Intelligence Service was generally held in such low regard in Whitehall, where only about thirty officials had been told the full story, that few were willing to believe that Menzies had, at long last, really found a worthwhile agent. Most of SIS's military appreciations had been proved completely worthless and the Venlo business had shown how easily SIS could be taken in. Because Menzies was not willing to tell the truth (and thereby increase the circle of those in the know), the BONIFACE cover persisted and the skeptical authorities were inclined to disregard the advice. The second difficulty concerned the make-up of BONIFACE's summaries. There was insufficient GCHQ staff of a military background able to understand the military and strategic consequences of the decrypts they were suddenly inundated with. Nor were they able to translate or interpret the decrypts. The YELLOW Luftwaffe operational traffic was so entirely unexpected that GCHQ was unable to concentrate the required analytical resources in time to take the best advantage of it. To date, the only important success had been in the RED Luftwaffe material, so GCHQ was ill-prepared for the new development which naturally demanded a different kind of analysis. As a result, many of the first BONIFACE summaries were poorly constructed. This only served to undermine further the confidence of the uninitiated in the dubious BONIFACE, and it was some weeks before GCHQ could mobilize the much-needed staff who were qualified to assess the wide military implications of the YELLOW decrypts.

There were also plenty of other administrative considerations for Menzies to cope with. When Sinclair had purchased Bletchley Park, he had done so with the intention of moving all SIS's departments there. His contingency plan had taken account of the possibility of a massed enemy air attack on the seat of government, and most of the specialist sections that had no reason to stay in the capital had completed the transfer. However, no one had envisaged the recent tremendous expansion of GCHQ, and there was insufficient space for both SIS and Denniston's men. To solve the accommodation problem, a hasty building program was embarked upon, and a trustworthy local contractor, a certain Captain Hubert Faulkner, was instructed to erect a series of Nissen huts in the grounds of the park. In addition, the RAF regiment was prevailed upon to send a detachment for perimeter security duties, which was placed under the temporary command of Captain Ridley's administration unit based in the mansion itself. As well as taking responsibility for physical security, it was Ridley's task to find enough billets in the surrounding countryside for the ever-increasing number of civilians reporting for work.

To everyone's delight, the YELLOW and RED traffic continued throughout April 1940, and more arrangements were made to distribute BONIFACE to a wider list of recipients, and in particular to the British Expeditionary Force in France. No such plans were contemplated for the Allied forces in the Norwegian theater which, unlike GHQ staff at Arras, were not equipped with any field SIGINT equipment. There were no Royal Signals or RAF field units in Norway to conduct any local wireless interception, nor were there any suitable facilities for the transmission of BONIFACE. SIS had never had many agents in Scandinavia and the Passport Control Office in Oslo had only been opened late in 1939. In contrast, the BEF had a well-established line of communication to London, and SIS also enjoyed a secret channel to General Templer, Lord Gort's Director of Military Intelligence. According to Wing Commander Fred Winterbotham, then head of SIS's Air Section located in Hut 6 at

Bletchley, it was his idea to introduce an entirely new organization to distribute the decrypts, which would operate under a plausible but ambiguous cover. The raw SIGINT would be transformed into summaries and then delivered to the field along a completely secure channel, which would be separated from the regular flow of military and intelligence communications. Thus a Special Liaison Unit (SLU) was to be attached to the BEF's headquarters at GHQ and granted a direct wireless link to Gambier-Parry's section at Whaddon. The processed SIGINT would pass by teleprinter from Bletchley to Whaddon, where it would be transmitted to Wachines in France using a one-time pad cipher. There the SLU could show the text to Lord Gort and then ensure that it was destroyed. This responsibility fell to two MI6 officers, Robert Gore-Browne and Humphrey Plowden, who became the first two Special Liaison Officers. Soon afterward a third SLU, headed by Squadron-Leader F.W. (Tubby) Long, was attached to Air Vice-Marshal Barratt's Advanced Air Striking Force headquarters at Meaux. But almost as soon as the two SLUs were in position, disaster struck. On May 1, 1940, the RED material failed to respond to the GCHQ decryption process, and it became clear that the Germans had introduced a new procedure for selecting the Enigma machine's key. The traffic to France simply dried up, although the YELLOW operational traffic seemed unaffected.

The first clues to the massive German offensive of May 10, 1940, were spotted by the Radio Security Service, thanks to the sudden increase in wireless traffic from the regular transmitters, which had been identified by Arkley as Abwehr stations, to their covert correspondents in France, Belgium and Luxembourg. It was also noted that traffic from Wiesbaden, which usually serviced a Gestapo radio circuit, had switched to matters concerning local defenses. Why the sudden interest in military affairs, which would probably only have a short intelligence "shelf life"? While RSS puzzled over the significance of the escalation, the analysts at Bletchley were alarmed to note a reduction in the enemy's volume of Enigma signals and continued to try to work out the change in German procedures. The decrypts seemed to be drying up, at the most inconvenient moment possible, when the phony war was drawing to a close.

Most of the British intelligence hierarchy was caught entirely unprepared by the German onslaught of May 10. SIS had no useful assets within the Reich, and the only advance warning came from well-disposed anti-Nazi elements in Berlin who, of course, were either disbelieved or regarded as *agents provocateurs*. SIS had virtually nothing to offer and GCHQ was too inexperienced to interpret the signs correctly. The consequence was an appalling shambles in which a substantial part of the

British Expeditionary Force was immobilized and captured on the French coast.

The French were no better off. BRUNO itself was threatened by the enemy advance, and all the personnel, including the Polish exiles who had achieved so much against the Enigma, were moved to the headquarters of the Deuxième Bureau in the rue Tourville in Paris. Within a fortnight they were obliged to flee again (see page 187).

The brief French campaign had been a fiasco, insofar as SIGINT was concerned. The forward direction-finding stations were hastily abandoned and vital equipment destroyed. But ironically, the short-lived campaign was to have one lasting benefit. The blitzkrieg tactics used by the Germans involved the deployment of fast motorized units coordinated with the Luftwaffe's ground-attack wings. Both branches of the enemy's armed forces were, therefore, heavily reliant on wireless communications, and from dawn on the morning of May 10 the volume of German radio traffic escalated to unprecedented proportions. After twelve days of battle, and continuous interception, GCHQ retrospectively broke into the new RED traffic for May 20. As soon as that success was achieved, the RED key was decrypted continuously and Bletchley was soon averaging one thousand decrypts a day. Although most of the RED intercepts were concerned with the Luftwaffe, they proved to be of great importance because the Luftwaffe was working so closely with the Wehrmacht. Yet even this remarkable scale of access to the enemy's current operational orders was unable to help the military situation on the ground. The Allies were in full retreat, and even though the SLU was able to get a mass of decrypts passed to Lord Gort, the Commander in Chief was in no position to take advantage of them. The prevailing chaotic conditions eventually forced the breakup of Templer's organization and the field units, which Bletchley relied on for the interception of the enemy's low-power transmissions, were ordered to the coast before they were overwhelmed. Numerous histories have related how the German tanks stopped short of Dunkirk and Operation DYNAMO, the rescue of what remained of the BEF from Dunkirk, was hurriedly enacted. Certainly none of the returning soldiers realized that, even before they had completed their journey across the Channel, GCHQ had already discerned the next phase of the war. The Japanese Section at Bletchley had successfully decrypted a signal sent by the Japanese ambassador in Budapest to the Foreign Ministry in Tokyo, in which he reported a recent conversation with Admiral Miklos Horthy, the Hungarian Prime Minister. In brief, Horthy had apparently confirmed that Hitler definitely intended to launch an invasion of Britain.

Top: Fort Bridgewoods, on the outskirts of Chatham, was Britain's first intercept station. Built largely underground in 1883, the site was occupied by the War Office in 1933 and monitored the first of the German signals enciphered with the Enigma cipher machine. Now it is vandalized and derelict. Nevertheless, many of the fortified bunkers survive, as do some of the original aerial emplacements.

Above: Hanslope Park, Buckinghamshire, was the pre-war headquarters of the Foreign Office's embryonic Communications Department and intercepted many of the first German radio signals. Today the estate is still surrounded by strict security and houses the Diplomatic Wireless Service's receiving station.

Left: A standard three-rotor Wehrmacht Enigma machine of the kind issued to most enemy units during the Second World War. If used correctly, the ciphered text was virtually unbreakable, but poor operating procedures enabled GCHQ to retrieve many of the individual 'keys' or rotor settings used to encrypt German messages. This particular machine was looted after the war and is now in the author's collection.

Left: Alastair Denniston, the first Director of GC & CS who was recruited into the Naval Intelligence Division from Osborne in 1914. In 1923 he was appointed Britain's cryptographic chief, a post he held until 1943.

Below: Bletchley Park, Buckinghamshire. This secluded country estate was purchased in 1938 by Admiral Sinclair, the Chief of the Secret Intelligence Service. By 1941 GCHQ had taken possession of the mansion and scores of huts had been built in the grounds to accommodate the 10,000 staff who were eventually to work on the organization's secret task.

Left: One of the many Bombes constructed by the British Tabulating Machine Company of Letchworth which, in the hands of Wren volunteers, enabled GCHQ to identify the keys to some of the enemy's Enigma cipher machines.

Below: Adstock Manor, Buckinghamshire, where the stable block was converted to house the first Enigma Bombes.

Middle and bottom: Gayhurst, the magnificent Elizabethan home near Newport Pagnell of the late Sir Walter Carlile MP. During the war hundreds of Wren Bombe operators were billeted here, and a secret Bombe annexe was built in a wood close to the house, where it remains today.

Left: A typical voluntary interceptor's apparatus. This one, pictured in 1941, was in the home of the local RSS Group Leader in Bolton.

Below: Lord Sandhurst (centre) with members of his Special Communications Unit at Whaddon, the SCU's secret headquarters near Bletchley.

Bottom: Lord Sandhurst's War Office pass. 'Box 25 Barnet' was the cover address of the RSS headquarters at Arkley.

OFFICIAL PASS and IDENTITY CARD

(GOVERNMENT OFFICIAL)

Great Britain and Northern Ireland

This is to Certify that

Lieut Col Lord Sandhurst

is a British Subject who is serving His Majesty in the Official Capacity of

Officer – Radio Security Service

and should be afforded all facilities necessary for the discharge of his Official Duties.

Given at *Barnet*

the *25th* day of *July* 1945

Block Signature of Head of Department

LT. Colonel

Issued and Registered by

Gen. Serial No. 21735

Departmental No. 1870

Signature of Bearer: *Sandhurst*

Postal Address of Bearer:
*P.O. Box 25,
Barnet, Herts.*

Left: Each RSS direction-finding station was calibrated with great accuracy. Here the Thurso station is being checked against a compass in 1944.

Below: In cramped conditions underground, an RSS operator takes the bearing of a suspect signal.

Bottom and overleaf: Three of the main wireless stations set up by Special Operations Executive: Grendon Underwood House (now a prison); Thame Park and Fawley Court, near Henley. All kept up regular communications schedules with SOE's agents operating from enemy-occupied territory.

Below: Block B at Stanmore, one of GCHQ's principal wartime bases on the outskirts of London. Today only a small part of the estate is retained by the Ministry of Defence.

Above: Code-named VICTOR, this American wireless station at Ladye Place, in the picturesque village of Hurley, in Berkshire, was responsible for co-ordinating most of the Allied special forces during 1944.

Left: One of the intercept positions at RSS headquarters at Arkley, shortly before the organization was absorbed into GCHQ in 1946.

Above: At the end of the war, GCHQ transferred most of its code-breaking operations to a new, secret site at Eastcote in Middlesex. Amid tight security, cryptographic experts examined intercepted Soviet signals. Meanwhile, less than a mile away, Peter and Helen Kroger set up their own secret radio station which continued in use until their arrest in January 1961.

Top: One of GCHQ's principal intercept stations, located on the site of an old airfield at Blakehill, just outside the Wiltshire market town of Cricklade.

Above left: The transmitting station at Signal Hill, Buckinghamshire, which operates in conjunction with Hanslope Park. During the war, it was part of one of SOE's first wireless stations at Poundon House nearby.

Above right: Sandridge, St Albans. Originally built by the Foreign Office to intercept Nazi diplomatic wireless traffic, it now monitors illicit signals under the jurisdiction of the Home Office's Radio Technology Directorate.

Below left: Culmhead, south of Taunton in Somerset, is one of GCHQ's largest radio-teletype intercept stations, operating under 'Composite Signals Organization' cover.

Below right: One of the six large satellite dish receivers located at GCHQ's most advanced listening post at Morwenstow, on the north Cornwall coast.

5

War

Cryptographers were for a long time regarded as mere cross-word puzzle solvers and not as the experienced intelligence officers which years of training and experience had made them.

—WILLIAM F. CLARKE in "War and Rumours of War," *History of Room 40*

The swift success of the blitzkrieg left Germany occupying Belgium, Denmark, Holland and much of France, and throughout the "invasion summer" of 1940 the War Cabinet prepared the country for the coming Nazi offensive. Britain was never more isolated, in terms of geography, politics and communications.

At the outbreak of war, the Cable & Wireless Company had operated 155,000 of the 350,000 miles of cable spanning the globe. It also ran approximately 130 permanent radio circuits. These were the practical means by which Britain kept in touch with the Empire and the rest of the world. Since 1928, Cable & Wireless had appeared to enjoy an independent existence, with the British government owning much of the capital and nominating the chairman, Sir Edward Wilshaw, and one other director. In reality, Cable & Wireless was another clandestine method of acquiring raw intelligence for GCHQ. The Official Secrets Act of 1920 had required all cable operators to supply copies of their traffic to the British government, and all this material had been delivered to Room 47 of the Foreign Office for GC&CS's scrutiny. Most were returned for onward transmission, but a quantity of those believed to be of interest were duplicated and circulated to MI5, SIS or any other indoctrinated party. This elaborate arrangement had been the brainchild of Henry Maine, a colorful Etonian and graduate of Trinity Hall, Cambridge, who had served in the King's Private Secretary's office at Buckingham Palace for four years before joining the Grenadiers in 1916. The following year he had transferred to MI1(b), and from there had progressed into GC&CS.

Maine's principal occupation at GC&CS was liaison with Cable & Wireless, for as well as supplying the telegrams sent to and from Britain, the company routinely copied foreign traffic passing through its relay stations at Bermuda, Malta and Hong Kong and shipped carbon flimsies back by diplomatic bag to London, where they were examined by teams of "slip readers." Denniston later boasted:

> Between us and the companies there has never been any question as to why we wanted the traffic and what we did with it. . . . I have no doubt that the managers and the senior officials must have guessed the true answer but I have never heard of any indiscretions through all these years with so many people involved.[1]

Maine had also kept on close terms with the GPO's chief engineer at the Central Telegraph Exchange (CTE) at Moorgate and had devised a system of tapping the telephone lines of virtually every foreign mission in London. Even the special, so-called secure lines, installed by the GPO at the request of powers negotiating peace treaties and alliances in London, were not overlooked. All were routed through the CTE and the resulting "P/L" or plain-language conversations transcribed for the benefit of the secret eavesdroppers.

On September 3, 1939, the company had placed itself at the disposal of the government and well-prepared contingency plans were put into operation. But unlike the confused first days of the Great War, there were only a handful of civilian stations to be taken under control within the British Isles. Although Cable & Wireless ran some two hundred overseas bases, there were just five in England: two receiving stations (at Brentwood and Somerton) and two transmitters (at Ongar and Dorchester) and Bodmin, which was promptly taken over by the Air Ministry. All were linked to the Central Telegraph Exchange, but secret conduits had been laid so that Electra House, Cable & Wireless's specially strengthened headquarters in London on the Victoria Embankment, could take over operations in the event of Moorgate, which, in effect, was the center of the Empire, being knocked out by sabotage or an air raid. Supposedly bomb- and gas-proof, Electra House also accommodated a staff of one hundred cable censors and the Foreign Office's Political Intelligence Department (which subsequently became the Political Warfare Executive). Electra House was also the alternative terminal for the country's main overseas cable system, which was routed underground to the heavily protected relay station at Porthcurno, Land's End, where the cables went into the ocean. As a further precaution, an unassuming detached house at 12 Hamilton Road, near Ealing Broadway station, was quietly taken over and equipped as a secret standby cablehead and radio station. It came into operation only on one occasion, on August 16, 1940, when the Porthcurno to Moorgate cable was hit by a bomb which fell near Hammersmith.

The military authorities, of course, maintained their own wireless links quite independently of the Cable & Wireless network; these consisted of the Army Chain, linking Aldershot to Cairo, Jubbulpore and Hong Kong, which the Treasury had consistently refused to allow the War Office to expand and modernize, and an internal security network. This latter circuit was similar to those established in Egypt, India, China and Northern Ireland, but had an unusual "civil powers" capacity which enabled the various regional commissioners up and down the country to take control in the event of an emergency preventing the central government from functioning. Actually the entire system, which sounded a practical proposition on paper, was equipped with obsolete radio sets and would never have been able to cope if London had been occupied or knocked out after an invasion. The shortcomings of the domestic system were so obvious that the government was forced to divert resources to speed up the Defense Telecommunications Network, which had been started at the time of the Munich crisis. Surprisingly, the international Army Chain remained largely unaltered throughout the war, with the exception of the two extra stations which were established later at Catterick and Singapore.

In contrast to the somewhat limited Army Chain, Cable & Wireless operated on a truly worldwide basis, incorporating the huge relays of the old Empire Chain pioneered by Marconi. Big underground bunkers were built at Gibraltar, Malta, Alexandria, Suez, Penang, Singapore and Hong Kong to protect the cableheads from sabotage, but Germany made little effort to interfere with Britain's lines of communications. In fact, there were only two attempts of any consequence. When Mussolini joined the war in June 1940, a team of Italian saboteurs tried to dredge up the main Mediterranean cables which happened to be routed close to Pantellaria, the tiny Italian possession between Sicily and Tunisia. Through sheer incompetence, the Italians only succeeded in cutting the same cable in five different places, leaving the others intact. On another occasion, in the Great War, the German cruiser *Emden* landed a raiding party on the Cocos Islands in the Indian Ocean (approximately halfway between Colombo and Perth) to destroy a cable relay but, once again, the wrong cables were severed. As soon as the *Emden* had left, the station resumed operations and signaled the enemy's position to HMAS *Sydney*, which chased and sank the *Emden*.

Although Britain's isolation was to increase with Italy's entry into the war, her ability to communicate via overseas cables was actually rather better than Germany's, which owned just three cables, to Lisbon, the Azores and Dublin. Both Germany's long Channel cables had been cut on September 3, 1939, in a repeat performance of the *Telconia*'s operation in August 1914, but, rather conveniently, the Dublin cable turned out to be routed through Moorgate. As it was the German ambassador to Eire's principal means of communicating with Berlin, the line was left intact so that the traffic could be monitored. The arrangement continued for three years before it was eventually decided, for security reasons, to disconnect the ambassador. Apart from this minor exception, the Reich was, once again, obliged to make heavy use of its long-distance wireless transmitters. From Bletchley's viewpoint this could hardly be more helpful. It was almost as though none of the lessons of the Zimmermann telegram had been learned.

In the weeks following the evacuation from Dunkirk, GCHQ experienced a reduction in the number of profitable Enigma intercepts. This was due in part to the loss of the BEF's capability and the destruction of many valuable logs and records, which had been burned in order to prevent them from falling into the enemy's hands. In fact, security concerning the BEF's SIGINT program had been so good that it seemed, against the odds, that the Germans still had no inkling of the Allied effort. Indeed, it later became known that at least two of the BEF's TypeX cipher machines, without their all-important wheels, had fallen into enemy hands at Dunkirk. Because only a relative handful of Whitehall officials knew the truth of the source known as BONIFACE, confidence in the TypeX's invulnerability was unaffected. The only cause for concern was, apparently, the irretrievable loss of intercept material that Bletchley desperately needed if further progress was to be made against the new Enigma procedures. The changes that had been introduced by the Germans so suddenly on May 1 were still in force, and much work had to be done before the RED key could be exploited again in significant quantities. Indeed, as the Nazis gradually established themselves as permanent occupiers in northwestern Europe, they reduced their volume of wireless signals and reverted to the use of landlines which, of course, were virtually impossible to monitor. And as the prospects of an invasion grew, measures were taken to improve and expand all three services' interception programs and move the more vulnerable stations away from the south of England. Fort Bridgewoods was a particularly easy target for the Luftwaffe, so a new War Office intercept station headed by John Tishart was built at Beaumanor Hall, at Woodhouse near Quorn in Leicestershire. For its part, the RAF constructed two intercept stations—at Montrose on the east coast of Scotland, and Chicksands Priory, at Shefford in Bedfordshire—and improved facilities at the two older bases at Waddington and "No. 61 RAF Wireless Unit" at Cheadle.

Given the shortcomings of the more traditional sources of intelligence, and the perilous situation at home, those in authority were now prepared to authorize expenditure on GCHQ, which at least held out the hope of better Enigma analysis and further interpretation of RED and YELLOW. At the end of May 1940, the first electromechanical Bombe to be made in Britain, which had been built in conditions of great secrecy by the British Tabulating Machinery factory at Letchworth, was delivered to the Machine Room at Bletchley. Nicknamed *Agnes*, the prototype was designed to race through all the possible Enigma key combinations to find a particular key, a method not dissimilar to the earlier Polish invention. Eventually, Bletchley was to employ up to one hundred Bombes, operated by nearly two thousand Wrens and dispersed to some of the neighboring country estates and to two secret sites on the outskirts of London. The management at GCHQ was determined to recover its pre–May 1 position, and it was clear that unless Bletchley achieved some results there was little chance of anything of importance coming from its parent organization. Certainly, SIS's position in the intelligence hierarchy was extraordinarily weak and was to be made rather more awkward by its poor performance elsewhere. A series of unfortunate incidents during the phony war, such as the Venlo incident, had left SIS wholly unprepared for the Nazi invasion of France, Belgium, Denmark and Holland. Once the blitzkrieg was over, SIS had been left devoid of useful sources. After Dunkirk, the situation was so poor that Whaddon had not a single agent in enemy-occupied territory to exchange messages with. One consequence of SIS's perceived impotence was the Prime Minister's decision in mid-July 1940 to create a new organization to foment resistance in Europe. The resulting political negotiations for the establishment of what was to become known as Special Operations Executive (SOE) were to undermine SIS's previously unchallenged and unique authority to engage in irregular operations overseas. Quite apart from the shortage of suitable transport, SIS's chronic lack of wireless sets and operating personnel had prevented any such undertakings, and these deficiencies had served to sharpen Menzies's sensitivity to what he interpreted as poaching by the Radio Security Service. More will be heard of this antagonism later.

Whatever the optimistic hopes and intentions of the War Cabinet, SOE was bound to be regarded as something of a sideshow while the threat of a full-scale invasion persisted. Certainly, there was no hope of preventing or diverting the Luftwaffe's air offensive by means of alternative warfare. Nor, for that matter, was GCHQ able to make much contribution. While the Battle of Britain was fought in the skies of the southern counties, GCHQ could offer little assistance. Neither the RED nor YELLOW keys shed any light on Luftwaffe losses or other information that might help Fighter Command. The Germans had wisely opted to transmit the Luftwaffe's strategic intelligence (targets, dates, times and numbers of aircraft) via the French landlines. Nevertheless, as the battle continued, some of the RED traffic offered clues to the targets selected for individual raids. This was sometimes very timely and useful, but more often than not the necessary decrypts failed to reach the appropriate authorities in time to be acted upon. On occasions when a specific warning could be issued in time, it often turned out to be useless. The Luftwaffe frequently made last-minute alterations to its plans, resulting in much frustration on the British side and giving rise to an element of skepticism in the reactions of some Air Ministry officials.

Although Bletchley was unable to give much in the way of operational intelligence, the RAF had discovered the advantages of SIGINT and had trained several teams of German linguists to eavesdrop on the Luftwaffe's non-Morse chatter. Most German aircrews were appallingly insecure in their radio conversations, and a special Air Intelligence Section, designated AI1(e), was created under the leadership of Air Commodore Lyster Blandy to intercept and exploit the traffic. Blandy was then sixty-seven years old, a Great War veteran who had retired in 1928 as Controller of Ministry Communications. He started an embryonic intercept organization at RAF Hawkinge, just inland from Folkestone, and then, after some initial success, acquired a disused toy factory at West Kingsdown, high on the downs of north Kent. Gradually, AI1(e) was to expand and take in nine very-high-frequency intercept stations, which operated under the innocuous-sounding name of RAF Home Defense Units (HDU), and covered the coast from Scarborough to Strete. The German-speaking HDU operators soon mastered the enemy's jargon and became adept at distinguishing between diversionary maneuvers and genuine raids. When this intelligence was coordinated with the radar plots,

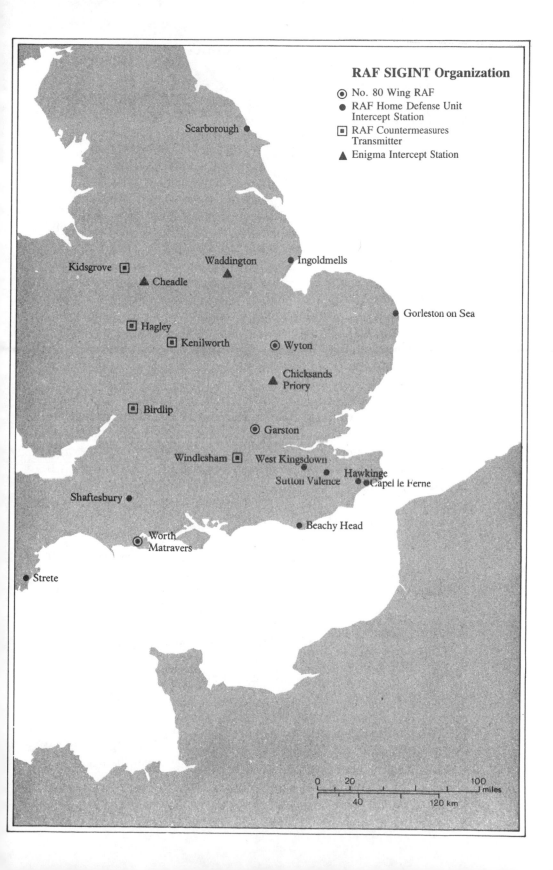

RAF SIGINT Organization

◎ No. 80 Wing RAF
● RAF Home Defense Unit
  Intercept Station
▣ RAF Countermeasures
  Transmitter
▲ Enigma Intercept Station

Scarborough ●

Kidsgrove ▣   Waddington ▲   ● Ingoldmells
        ▲ Cheadle

                                    ● Gorleston on Sea

▣ Hagley
   ▣ Kenilworth   ◎ Wyton

                    ▲ Chicksands
                      Priory

▣ Birdlip

        ◎ Garston

Windlesham ▣   West Kingsdown ●
                              ● Hawkinge
              Sutton Valence ● ● Capel le Ferne

Shaftesbury ●

                ● Beachy Head

   ◎ Worth
     Matravers

● Strete

0   20   100
                      miles
      40
           120 km

it enabled the hard-pressed RAF to judge exactly where and when to deploy its aircraft to maximum effect. Analysis of the intercepts from West Kingsdown during the early part of 1940 revealed that German aircrews received very little navigational training, and that the Luftwaffe had been experimenting with a well-known prewar blind landing device, known as the Lorenz, to develop a Morse-code flight path. Instead of pilots homing on to a signal radiating from one of the elusive beacons which had so excited the Radio Security Service in 1939, the enemy had developed a more sophisticated system of directing two beams of dots and dashes from transmitters on the Continent which, according to some indiscreet RED Enigma decrypts, were code-named *Knickebein* (literally, "crooked leg"). With the right equipment, the German pilots simply followed the route of the *Knickebein* signals to their appointed targets and dropped their cargo of bombs when the two beams crossed. Evidence from the HDUs, together with additional clues from the Air Intelligence interrogators of AI1(k) at the prisoner-of-war cage at Trent Park, Cockfosters, suggested that it might be possible to interfere with the enemy's signals, and the task was given to No. 80 Wing RAF, which had already undertaken some research into night-landing navigational aids. Hopes were boosted in June 1940 when a Heinkel 111, returning from a raid on south Wales, landed at Honiton. The pilot had crossed the Bristol Channel on his return journey and had mistaken Devon for the north coast of France. He had only realized the enormity of his error after he had taxied right up to the control tower. In the confusion that followed, he had neglected to destroy some valuable documents which disclosed the operating frequencies of the *Knickebein*.

As soon as this information was received by No. 80 Wing, a flight of three specially equipped Ansons was dispatched from the recently formed Wireless Intelligence and Development Unit at RAF Wyton, and they succeeded in tracing a beam over Spalding. This, incidentally, was the first time an enemy signal had been intercepted by an aircraft. The task of preparing suitable countermeasures was given to No. 80 Wing's research branch, then located at the Mildmay Institute at Garston, near Watford, and the Telecommunications Research Establishment at Worth Matravers, near Swanage in Dorset. During the next few months, two *Knickebein* transmitters were found in France, at Cherbourg and Calais, and a further three identified in Germany, at Bredstedt, Cleve and Stollberg. Once isolated, the directional beams from the enemy's stations were jammed by more powerful signals transmitted from a group of five transmitters strategically placed in the Midlands, which had the effect of bending the beams. The idea, code-named COLD WATER, was to divert the Luftwaffe away from important industrial targets to the empty countryside. During the course of 1940, *Knickebein* was improved by two further versions, the *X-Gerat* (literally, X-Apparatus) and *Y-Gerat*, but nevertheless No. 80 Wing achieved considerable success. However, on one now notorious occasion, on November 14, 1940, the COLD WATER jamming transmitters were tuned to the wrong frequency and the enemy bombers managed to reach Coventry, with devastating consequences. In spite of this disaster, the RAF's beam countermeasures proved highly effective, and it can be said that while SIGINT played a relatively small role in the Battle of Britain, intelligence as a whole ensured success.

The long invasion summer of 1940 continued until September 15, when what appeared to be exactly the same text was transmitted on every German naval frequency. As the long-overdue invasion did not materialize during the following forty-eight hours, it was guessed that the signal had been an announcement of the cancellation or postponement of the armada. Six days later the code word SEALION appeared in a RED decrypt, and further references over the next few days confirmed its significance: SEALION was the code word for the amphibious landings, and the operation had been called off.

The eventual arrival of the winter of 1940 ended the chances of an invasion attempt across the Channel and offered Bletchley a breathing space, in which the cryptologists could concentrate on the elusive RED key. Once again, it was sloppy signaling by the enemy which gave the clue that enabled the RED traffic to be broken.

Analysis of the pre- and post-May 1940 RED traffic showed a distinct change in the construction of the Enigma preambles. The information contained in these texts was essential if the receiving operator was to have a chance of deciphering the full message. It will be recalled that whoever originated a transmission first had to identify the relevant key (i.e., which three Enigma rotors were to be used out of the set of five, and the sequence in which they were to be placed in the cipher machine, together with the change to the plugboard wiring) and then the three letters showing on the top of the rotors. Once a correspondent had set up his Enigma to the same key and moved his three rotors to the same starting point, he could decode the text. Before May 1, the procedure had been relatively straightforward. The sender would check that he had the correct key, and then make contact with his correspondent by transmitting his call sign and waiting for an acknowledgment *en clair*. Once this was obtained, he would move the rotors to three letters of his own choice, say "HTC," which would be the starting point of his message. However, in order to convey this crucial information in code, the rules required the operator to select a second, random group of three letters, say "BLG." Using BLG as a rotor position, he would tap out HTC twice, thus transforming it into RWSANW. In order to tell the receiver that the letters HTC had been chosen as the rotor positions, the operator would transmit a preamble *en clair* which included BLG and was then followed by RWSANW. The receiver simply spotted the BLG in the preamble and made the adjustment to BLG on his rotors. Once he had selected BLG, he could unscramble the RWSANW and find HTCHTC. Once that had been completed, the receiver and transmitter were able to exchange messages using the same setting. Although depressingly complicated for the uninitiated, the procedure enabled two operators to transmit the chosen setting in enciphered form, thus supposedly eliminating the possibility of illicit decryption. As we have seen, detailed analysis of the preambles, combined with careless chatter, had betrayed the arrangement and had allowed Bletchley to exploit it.

The May 1 alteration introduced a subtlety that made the procedure even more complex and, therefore, secure. Instead of tapping out the main setting twice (HTCHTC) and obtaining an encoded version (RWSANW), the HTC part was done only once and was included in the beginning of the preamble along with the BLG setting. Thus, what might have originally been transmitted in the customary five-figure groups as BLGRW SANW, after May 1 became BLGRW S. The loss of the three extra letters was, in proportional terms, catastrophically high. Long before the three individual settings of an Enigma machine could be established, it was Bletchley's task to determine the exact key in use. The only clues to the key had been the vital nine letters of the preamble, which were then tested mathematically against every possible permutation. The plugboard alone boasted a possible 200 trillion combinations, but the prototype Bombe had been designed to try them all in a matter of seconds. But the reduction to six letters made the task even more difficult and seemed to threaten the expensive Bombe plan. Astonishingly, once the cryptographers had discovered the exact change that had taken place, they were able to overcome the new preambles.

By November 1940, GCHQ was back on track in pursuit of some interesting keys, and this is a convenient moment to describe the organization's internal structure. The raw intercepts were received via a teleprinter link from the satellite stations and from the RSS in Hut 6, where they were processed in the Registration Room. Work there was monitored by John Colman in the Intercept Control Room who also kept an eye on the next stage, the Machine Room, where the cryptographic work was centered. If a particular series of intercepts looked promising, they might be passed to the Sheet Stacking Room for testing, and if successful the remainder of the series would be passed to the Decoding Room where specially adapted British TypeX cipher machines completed the decryption process. Once deciphered, the intercept went for translation and was then forwarded to the appropriate hut for analysis and interpretation by intelligence officers. Since the content of the RED traffic was primarily (but not exclusively) to do with the Luftwaffe, it was dealt with in Hut 3; Hut 4 concentrated on naval processing, while Hut 8 specialized in naval cryptanalysis. Hut 6 handled most of the original Wehrmacht material and was staffed by some 250 people, including translators, typists and filing clerks, all working a shift system to give twenty-four-hour coverage. For those wishing to find some logic to the system of huts, it should be remembered that, although the hut numbers remained the same, their location within the sprawling complex in the park itself often changed. Thus, Hut 6 actually comprised several different buildings.

Once the decrypted material had been processed, it was entered in a massive organ card index supervised by the author and biographer Hector Bolitho, and a team of girls led by Celia Knowles. It then underwent translation, was compared to the traffic analysis reports accompanying the raw intercepts (and disclosed details of the preambles and the likely location of the transmitter) and was then transformed into BONIFACE summaries bearing the prefix CX, one of the SIS Chief's personal reference numbers. Up until September 27, 1940, these highly secret flimsies were delivered to Stewart Menzies for his consideration; if he deemed the information sufficiently promising, he personally conveyed a selection to the Prime Minister, thereby building up an unprecedented personal relationship. This selection usually contained one or two RED summaries, a couple of Abwehr messages (thanks to Oliver Strachey's work on the Abwehr's hand ciphers) and the odd Axis diplomatic telegram. After September 27, 1940, Churchill insisted on receiving all the decrypts, together with the SIGINT appreciations of the traffic that had been intercepted but not solved, on a daily basis. Accordingly, a special box was prepared by Menzies, who brought it to the Cabinet War Room where the Prime Minister pored over it. The reason for this change in attitude was twofold. Firstly, the BONIFACE source had really proved its worth by revealing the German code word Seelöwe

for Operation SEALION, the planned invasion of Britain. The RED key
had enabled GCHQ to reconstruct a graphic account of the role intended
for the Luftwaffe. It was so detailed that it was circulated in Whitehall
under the cover name SMITH and gave a unique glimpse into Hitler's
future intentions. Churchill's enthusiasm was also fired by the idea of
reading the authentic decrypts for himself, before they had been processed
and paraphrased or shown to the rest of his advisers. Only Stewart Menzies
knew the full truth. None of Churchill's ministers realized the scope of
GCHQ's operations, or the extent of the SIGINT program, although
several were aware of some aspects of it. Certainly, the Prime Minister's
apparent inside knowledge gave him the edge whenever he was challenged, and he could easily silence opposition to his schemes by citing
his extraordinary "most secret source." Even the Permanent Under-
Secretary at the Foreign Office, Sir Alexander Cadogan, was sometimes
floored by how well informed Churchill appeared to be on rather obscure
areas of German policy. Churchill also believed that his own instincts
and political judgment gave him a far better grasp of BONIFACE's
significance than the GCHQ bureaucrats, who were obliged to conceal
the source of the summaries. In fact, the Prime Minister was later to
complain that GCHQ's treatment of particular decrypts tended to obscure
their significance. On one occasion, he criticized GCHQ for failing to
emphasize Hitler's stated personal interest in a particular enemy undertaking. If GCHQ was too conscientious in covering its sources, there was
a danger of misleading the BONIFACE recipients or reducing the impact
of individual texts.

The two principal British intelligence services, MI5 and MI6, were
so concerned about GCHQ's advice that, during the latter part of 1940,
each introduced a specialist section to handle and distribute the BONI-
FACE product. At the Security Service, which was then undergoing a
long-overdue internal reorganization, a "Special Research" unit, designated B1(b), was started under the leadership of a recent recruit from
New College, Herbert Hart (a future Professor of Jurisprudence at Oxford). His panel of experts was to include Helenus Milmo, E.B. Stamp,
Anthony Blunt and Patrick Day. Their chief occupation was the examination of GCHQ's decrypts for clues to the identities and locations of
Abwehr agents.

At MI6 the recently expanded counterintelligence unit, Section V,
was doing much the same kind of work at a group of country houses on
Lord Verulam's estate at St. Albans, which was conveniently close to
Station X, as Bletchley Park was referred to in Secret Intelligence Service

documents. The Abwehr decrypts were circulated to a series of subsections organized on a geographical basis so that representatives abroad could be advised of forthcoming hostile activities. During the course of the war, B1(b) and Section V were to become by far the most important (not to say reliable) regular sources of intelligence for their respective services.

Meanwhile, at the production end at Bletchley, Denniston and Travis had prevailed upon C.P. Snow, who was then pursuing a scientific career at Christ's College, Cambridge, to act as a recruiter for the best university brains available to confront the challenge of Enigma. Classics dons, mathematicians and linguists like Frederick Norman, the Professor of German at London University, were brought together to cope with the complexities of the enemy's cipher traffic. Also invited were chess players such as the British chess champion, Hugh Alexander, and (Sir) Stuart Milner-Barry, the former British boy champion of 1923 who had been appointed *The Times*'s chess correspondent in 1938. Both had been earmarked for Bletchley before the war, but the outbreak of hostilities had found them stranded in Argentina, at the 1939 Chess Olympiad.

This is a convenient moment to list some of the distinguished figures, apart from those already mentioned, who were instructed to present themselves at Bletchley Station during the first twelve months of the war: Alexander Aitken, Professor of Mathematics at Edinburgh University; Patrick (now Viscount) Barrington, then a barrister at the Inner Temple; (Sir) James Blair-Cunynghame, from St. Catharine's College; Peter Calvocoressi, later chairman of Penguin Books; I. (Jack) Good, the Cambridge mathematician; Thomas Higham, senior tutor of Trinity College, Oxford; Professor Harry Hinsley, from St. John's College, Cambridge; Frank Lucas, from King's College, Cambridge, and a veteran of the Intelligence Corps during the Great War; (Sir) Herbert Marchant, who had been teaching at Harrow; Charles Morgan, the *Times* drama critic; E. James Passant, the historian from Sidney Sussex College, Cambridge; Arthur Halto, from Queen Mary College; Hugh Last from Oxford; Alan Pryce-Jones, later editor of *The Times Literary Supplement*; E.J.B. (Jim) Rose, later literary editor of the *Observer*; (Sir) Howard Smith, from Sidney Sussex College, and a future Director-General of MI5; and Thomas Webster, Professor of Greek at Manchester University.

While these "temporary clerks" were delving into the mysteries of the Enigma decryption program, a similar undercover operation was taking place in France. Some of the French veterans from the Château de Vignolles had slipped away from Paris shortly before its collapse and had taken temporary refuge in Oran. Soon afterward, they resumed their activities in the Vichy zone; new accommodation had been found in a secluded country estate in Provence near Uzes, some twenty-five kilometers north of Nîmes, and code-named Poste de Commande CADIX. Here, in an ancient fortified château known as Les Fouzes, Bertrand's men regrouped.

In spite of the German occupation of Paris and northern France, CADIX became the center of a joint French-Polish cryptographic effort to recover the ground that had been lost on the Enigma. The two teams led by Bertrand and Langer cooperated with a small group of Spanish exiles, who concentrated on Franco's wireless traffic. In theory, CADIX was under the sponsorship of the Vichy Deuxième Bureau, and was assisting Captain Paul Paillole's undercover military counterespionage department to identify Allied agents. In reality, SIS was unable to establish contact by radio with any stay-behind networks in France until December 1940, so there was no illicit traffic for CADIX to monitor. Instead, Bertrand intercepted German signals and resumed his prewar role, signaling his progress to a Polish station at Stanmore. Furthermore, he made independent contact with SIS and arranged to receive ten of Gambier-Parry's latest wireless transmitters, with which he maintained a regular net with Whaddon until October 1942, when the Germans eventually closed in.

By February 1941, GCHQ's organization was in a position to handle a large number of intercepts, but the success rate was still very low. The decrypts consisted in the main of RED traffic with a sprinkling of Wehrmacht and other Luftwaffe keys, which served to whet the appetite of the cryptographers. Very little had been achieved by the Naval Section so, perhaps in response to the Royal Navy's disappointing performance to date, the Naval Intelligence Division mounted a scheme against an isolated group of Norwegian islands designed to improve GCHQ's fortunes.

On the face of it Operation CLAYMORE had little justification, apart from a propaganda exercise to boost morale. The Lofoten Islands, just off the Norwegian coast and inside the Arctic Circle, did possess a token German garrison but they were of insignificant military or strategic value. The local cod and herring industry produced a limited quantity of oil, which could be used by the enemy for the manufacture of munitions, but there was no obvious reason for the commitment of such a substantial force, which consisted of Nos. 3 and 4 Commando, with a group of

Sappers and fifty-five Norwegian volunteers, backed by five destroyers, a submarine and two converted cross-Channel ferries. Critics of the plan pointed out that the exercise would destroy the livelihood of the indigenous Norwegians and leave them vulnerable to appalling German reprisals. Only a handful of officers were told of the mission's real motive: the capture of an enemy Enigma machine. It was assumed, wrongly, that there might be up to three available: a Luftwaffe machine at the local airfield, a Wehrmacht unit for the garrison, and a prized naval variation on one of the German vessels in harbor.

In spite of the criticisms, CLAYMORE was executed on March 3, 1941. The amphibious landing was largely unopposed, the only shots being fired from an armed trawler, the *Krebs*, which engaged the destroyers with her own relatively puny armament. Fourteen German sailors were killed in the brief, one-sided battle that followed, and eventually the crew took to their boats. A boarding party seized control of the badly damaged *Krebs*, but it was soon discovered that the commander, Leutnant Hans Kupfinger, had thrown his Enigma machine overboard. However, he had been killed before he could destroy his coding documents or the Enigma rotors, and within a week this material had enabled the Naval Section to break retrospectively the German Home Waters naval traffic for the whole of February. Cryptographic clues in the captured booty also betrayed most of the April traffic, although GCHQ took some three weeks to work it out. The subsequent decrypts were code-named DOLPHIN. Altogether, the *Krebs* find opened up the enemy's naval signals, to a greater or lesser extent, from March 1 to May 10, which was no mean achievement. Apart from the capture of twenty-five German combatants, and the destruction of the local oil stocks, the operation was a failure. No Enigma machines were recovered intact, and the commando unit led by Lord Lovat which raided the Luftwaffe airfield found nothing worthwhile.

Once the DOLPHIN traffic succumbed to the Naval Section, it was noticed that the enemy was extraordinarily well informed about the Royal Navy's movements. The reason was simple: the Admiralty's two main codes had been broken by the Beobachtungs-Dienst, known as the B-Dienst.

Unlike the Air Ministry and the War Office, their Lordships had resisted the introduction of the TypeX cipher machine. Instead, they had relied upon a five-figure administrative code for routine communications, and a four-figure naval cipher for the use of officers. Both consisted of frequently used terms, which were altered by means of super-encipherment subtraction tables which were themselves subject to frequent change. The B-Dienst had been monitoring the navy's traffic since its reestablishment in 1934, and was eventually to boast some five thousand staff and more than forty intercept and direction-finding stations spread from the Crimea to Brest and the northernmost point of Norway. The organization had achieved considerable success in reconstructing the navy's administrative code by the expedient of comparing the known movements of particular, named merchantmen with the routes of the ships as published in the *Lloyd's Weekly Shipping Report*. The navy's habit of signaling the details of every merchant vessel sighted at sea enabled the B-Dienst to guess the likely content of many messages, which in turn led to the discovery of up to half of the relevant subtraction systems currently in use.

The real breakthrough for the B-Dienst was the depth-charging, on January 6, 7 and 9, 1940, of three British submarines, the *Undine*, *Seahorse* and *Starfish*, in the Heligoland Bight by German patrol craft. All three sank in shallow waters and were promptly visited by divers, who extracted the invaluable subtraction tables for the Admiralty's codes. A further catastrophe was to follow soon afterward, during the course of the Norwegian campaign, in April 1940. Another set of tables was recovered from HMS *Hardy*, one of the two British destroyers lost at Narvik on April 10. The *Hardy*'s commander, Captain Warburton-Lee, was killed by overwhelming enemy gunfire during his third attack on the harbor, and his ship ran aground on the beach of the Ofot Fjord. Warburton-Lee was later awarded a posthumous Victoria Cross. The survivors pulled his body from the wreck, but in the confusion the coding material was left behind for the German garrison to find.

A month later the Merchant Navy's code book fell into the enemy's hands during the evacuation of Bergen, together with a copy of the Foreign Office's interdepartmental cipher. Overnight the B-Dienst's position had been transformed, and there was little the Admiralty could do about it because reissuing a code book or table is altogether a more complex affair than simply signaling the introduction of a new key for a cipher machine. The navy had no TypeX machines on any ships, and new instructions could hardly be transmitted to ships at sea by wireless in a code known to be intercepted and read by the enemy. The Admiralty acknowledged that physical compromise had taken place and, somewhat belatedly, changed some of the encryption procedures and issued restrictions on the number of subtraction tables that could be taken on board submarines and other ships likely to be engaged in combat, but by that time the damage had been done. One of these changes, which introduced the super-encipherment of the naval cipher, actually assisted the B-Dienst. Because of the logistical problems of sending new subtraction tables all over the world and manufacturing the necessary quantities of one-time pads, the Admiralty simply ordered the naval cipher, which had hitherto resisted decryption by the enemy, to be subjected to the same subtraction method as the administrative code. As soon as the B-Dienst discovered the new procedure, it was able to read the greater part of the navy's two separate signal systems.

Eventually, on August 20, 1940, the Admiralty was able to replace the compromised administrative code with a four-figure Naval Code No. 1, and the naval cipher with Naval Cipher No. 2. Because the five-figure version had been scrapped, the two had identical characteristics, so that the German cryptanalysts experienced great difficulty in telling one from the other. In fact, they resisted decryption by the enemy until September 1941. Quite by coincidence, the B-Dienst code-named the two new ciphers BLUE and BROWN.

Meanwhile, the Allies were struggling by comparison. GCHQ realized that the Admiralty's signals were probably being read, and Commander Travis spent much of the spring urging a general overhaul of Britain's cipher systems. His arguments were accepted in principle, but it was more than a year before all the necessary changes could be made. However, GCHQ was also on the offensive and was now in possession of the rotors from the U-33 and the *Krebs*, even though it still lacked a complete Enigma machine. There were few opportunities to acquire one, and still less chance of finding one undetected. However, some of the traffic compromised by the *Krebs* episode itself suggested a method. A few of the intercepts which had been decrypted successfully had been traced to an unarmed intelligence gatherer, the *München*. This 306-ton trawler, one of half a dozen based at Drontheim, was primarily a weather ship, making regular reports in the German Home Waters key, but, in addition, it routinely reported any movements of shipping. On May 7, 1941, HMS *Manchester*, one of three Royal Navy cruisers, and four destroyers sent to the *München*'s operating area north of Iceland closed in on the trawler. Captain Caslon, on HMS *Somali*, fired a few warning shots and then watched the crew abandon ship. The *München*'s Enigma machine was promptly jettisoned over the side, but a specially briefed NID officer, Captain Jasper Haines, secured some useful coding documents including a list of the following month's Enigma keys. These were dispatched to Scapa Flow immediately aboard HMS *Nestor* and enabled

GCHQ to read most of the DOLPHIN Home Waters naval key for June
on a concurrent basis, the first time any German naval traffic had been
broken without a delay. Once the *München* had been searched thoroughly,
it was used for target practice and sunk in the hope that the Germans
would not realize exactly what had occurred until the Red Cross notified
Berlin of the crew's capture.

Just two days after this incident, the Allied convoy designated OB
318 was attacked by a pair of U-boats in the Atlantic, south of Greenland.
Shortly before midday on May 9, two steamers, the *Esmond* and the
Bengore Head, were hit by torpedoes, but a lookout on HMS *Aubretia*,
one of the 3rd Escort Group's destroyers, spotted a periscope and a pattern
of depth charges was dropped in the vicinity. HMS *Broadway* and *Bulldog*
joined in, and thirty minutes later a Type IXB, long-distance, oceangoing
submarine was forced to the surface. HMS *Bulldog*'s commander, Captain
A.D. Baker-Cresswell, prepared to ram the stricken vessel, but at the
last moment he decided to turn away and open fire. The U-boat's commander, Korvetleutnant Fritz-Julius Lemp, promptly ordered his crew of
forty-seven into the water and then primed the scuttling charges. HMS
Aubretia and *Bulldog* picked up the survivors, but much to the surprise
of everyone the *U-110* lay still in the water. Her detonators had failed,
and Lemp apparently drowned while attempting to return to his stricken
submarine. The sight of the empty, drifting U-boat was irresistible, so
Lieutenant David Balme took a prize crew of five ratings over to the
enemy vessel and managed to board her, no easy feat without help from
aboard. For the next three hours, at considerable risk to himself, Balme
ferried everything that could be carried across to the *Bulldog*, including
an Enigma which he found in the radio cubicle. Since the explosive
charges had still not gone off, Baker-Cresswell decided to tow the
U-110 back to Iceland. Unfortunately, none of the *Bulldog*'s crew had
any knowledge of submarines, and the following day the U-boat lost its
buoyancy and had to be cut loose. After a brief stop in Iceland, the
Bulldog headed for Scapa Flow where an Admiralty liaison officer from
GCHQ's Naval Section, Lieutenant Allan Bacon, took receipt of the
U-110's Enigma, its complete set of rotors, a list of "officer only" keys
(code-named OYSTER), and a special code book used for the construction
of short signals dealing with the sighting of enemy ships. There was also
a list of the Home Waters keys for April and June (the May list having
been destroyed) and a series of naval grid charts. Neither of the Home
Waters keys were of much consequence since most of the April Home
Waters traffic had been decrypted by Hut 8, thanks to the *Krebs* material,

and the June list had simply duplicated the haul from the *München*. Nonetheless, the naval Enigma machine was priceless and was to be of tremendous importance when Bletchley came to build a Bombe to cope with the enemy's naval traffic.

The prospects were now judged to be so promising that it was decided to repeat the *München* exercise on another unarmed weather ship. This time it was the *Lauenburg*, and the plan called for her capture toward the end of June, when the radio operator would have the new Enigma key settings for July close to hand. The operation was completed on June 28, and as anticipated she was rather overstocked with cipher material for her long patrol.

One interesting and useful crib for the Home Waters DOLPHIN traffic centered on a relatively simple German procedure which, when discovered, made the Naval Section's task a little easier, even though the Kriegsmarine's version of the Enigma machine was the most complex of them all. Instead of changing all the Enigma rotors together, only the starting positions of the two outer rotors were moved every day; the inner pair were altered every other day.

By mid-1941, Bletchley Park had demonstrated its potential and the number of staff had increased to nearly nine hundred. The first tentative steps had also been taken to expand into the Middle East. In May 1941, Freddie Jacob, John Tiltman's deputy in GCHQ's Army Section, traveled to Egypt to open a local branch. He went as a "Fort Control Officer" to preserve secrecy, but in fact he was laying the foundations for a Combined Bureau Middle East. CBME was intended to duplicate some of Bletchley's cryptographic work and carry out intercept and traffic analysis work as well. Unsolved material was to be relayed back to Whaddon on TypeX machines, with any decrypts returning on one-time pads. All three services were supposed to cooperate, but in practice the CBME base, located in a partially built museum on the Suez road just outside the Heliopolis airfield north of Cairo, was an air-force establishment. Designated "RAF Wireless Unit Numbers 50 and 53," it was staffed by military personnel (posted to "General Staff, Intelligence (Signals) B"), with a liaison representative from the Naval Intelligence Division. Interception was in the hands of the RAF (under the command of Squadron Leader J.R. Jeudwine), with the Royal Navy's monitoring program continuing to operate from its prewar station at Alexandria. In addition, Jacob's secret organization was to supply the local MI5 and MI6 offices ("Security Intelligence Middle East" [SIME] and the "Inter-Services Liaison Department" [ISLD], respectively) with interesting decrypts. As has been seen, the Abwehr's hand ciphers, code-named ISOS by GCHQ, had been broken by Oliver Strachey some eighteen months earlier, and almost as soon as SIME and ISLD began receiving the summaries, the performance of their counterintelligence branches improved. Later in the war, the CBME was to deploy more than a dozen field units throughout the Mediterranean, under RAF Special Wireless cover, to increase the daily "take" of enemy signals. Although never publicized, or even mentioned in the official histories of the war, Jacob's CBME was to play a vital part in the Allied victory in the region.

Before developing the story further, the considerable progress made at Bletchley should be reviewed. In fact, dozens of different keys had been intercepted, but only a handful had actually been decrypted. In order to distinguish the various separate categories, a classification of code words was introduced: the Naval Section would stick to seafood (such as DOLPHIN and OYSTER); vegetables (ONION and MUSTARD) would be the Luftwaffe's weather and navigational keys, and the original colors would continue to indicate the first, general keys to be broken. Later on insects, birds and flowers were added to the system. Because successful decryption sometimes depended on having very large quantities of intercepts, it was inevitable that the performance of the cryptanalysts would improve with the expansion of the intercept program. More eavesdropping meant larger samples, and better results reduced service resistance to the deployment of valuable radio operators.

The GREEN and YELLOW keys had succumbed in January and April, but they had proved to be of little operational or strategic value. GREEN had dealt with administrative matters, while YELLOW was limited to the Norwegian theater. On June 27, VULTURE was broken for the first time, albeit briefly, and proved to be traffic dealing with Hitler's newly established eastern front. KESTREL followed, which turned out to be air reconnaissance reports from the eastern front. Another useful source was CHAFFINCH, which exposed the signals exchanged between three supply units at Rome, Salonika and North Africa, and occasionally provided insights into the routine daily supply assessments which were relayed back to Berlin. The CHAFFINCH material was later to develop after a series of documents betraying future CHAFFINCH keys were captured during Operation CRUSADER, the recapture of Cyrenaica, in November 1941. This, in turn, provided some clues for PHOENIX, an Afrika Korps key assigned to several Panzer formations. Of shorter life was SCORPION, a special key used to coordinate the Afrika Korps and the Luftwaffe. No other Wehrmacht traffic was to be solved until 1943.

The Luftwaffe material was altogether more impressive. The solution of RED and BLUE, of course, dated back to January 1940, but several other keys followed during 1941. LIGHT BLUE was cracked in February and was revealed as a RED derivative assigned to a Luftwaffe supply unit. BROWN and ONION followed in May, and were found to convey navigational information for the beam receivers that had been installed in the Luftwaffe's bombers so as to guide them to their targets (and home again) during night raids on England. It seemed that the Luftwaffe's boffins experienced considerable technical problems with their gadgets, and in their frustration the German scientists used to take over the radio nets to sort out the hitches. The experts rarely mastered the intricacies of the Enigma machine and, to Bletchley's delight, frequently exchanged messages in clear language to describe their Enigma settings before en- crypting a signal. The next month MUSTARD yielded, which caused great excitement. It was the key used by the Luftwaffe's interception service, known to the enemy as the Horchdienst, to report its progress.

The Horchdienst's chief occupation was the surveillance of the RAF's radio channels and it provided indisputable evidence of the insecurity of Allied aircrews. RAF equipment was always tested before a sortie and, however brief the transmission, the signal was spotted by the Luftwaffe. A certain Hauptman Kuhlmann had become so adept at recognizing and interpreting this traffic that he was regarded by the enemy as a one-man early-warning system. Indeed, the Horchdienst was eventually to be re- ferred to as the "Kuhlmannmeldungen." After appropriate advice from GCHQ, the RAF took the necessary countermeasures to stem the indis- cretions. Finally, in July 1941, LEEK was demonstrated to be a weather reporting service.

Not all GCHQ's successes were based on cryptanalysis. Traffic anal- ysis played a crucial role, and the detailed recording and examination of all the enemy's call signs began to pay off during the summer of 1941 following a decision to establish a joint GCHQ/MI8 team of experts. The team, which included Hamish Blair-Cunynghame, Rodney Bax, Ivor Dundas and Christopher Wells, had logged all the intercepted preambles under the supervision of Colonel Arthur Sayer, a retired former president of the Royal Engineers and Signals Board, the body which had overseen Britain's prewar military intercept program. After eighteen months of tedium, the exercise showed dividends and GCHQ finally mastered the intricacies of the Wehrmacht's system of allocating radio call signs to individual units. Having gained the means of deciding who was com- municating with whom on the German army's wireless net, attention could now be focused on the message contents.

By June 1941, Bletchley had truly established itself and had gained the Prime Minister's confidence, but one further obstacle remained before the "most secret source" could be exploited fully. Although BONIFACE had acquired a very exalted status within the privileged circle of the indoctrinated, many slightly lower down the scale automatically distrusted advice from SIS. Experience had taught the professional intelligence analysts, who were not privy to BONIFACE's real nature, to be skeptical of anything claimed by SIS on behalf of some well-placed agent. Between January 1940 and June 1941, Bletchley had turned in some veritable gems of intelligence, but Menzies realized that only Churchill was taking the decrypt summaries seriously. One major breakthrough which seemed likely to be ignored was GCHQ's solution of the Italian navy's Mediterranean cipher. The Italians depended upon the C38m version of the popular, commercially available, Hagelin cipher machine manufactured in Sweden. For reasons that are unclear, the Germans had urged their Axis partners to switch from their reliance on an early Enigma and adopt the Hagelin C38m. This entirely suited Bletchley, which discovered the changeover through the interception of some indiscreet operator chatter. Most of the Hagelin traffic, which yielded vital information concerning naval movements in the Mediterranean, particularly between Genoa and North Africa, continued to be solved from May 1941 onward. In order to boost the already heavy C38m traffic, the Royal Navy severed the underwater cable linking Malaga to Genoa. Suddenly, GCHQ began acquiring trump cards in the secret wireless war and, accordingly, it was agreed that the BONIFACE charade should be phased out and that a wider group of specialist planners should be allowed to learn GCHQ's secrets. A new series of security classifications was introduced, although the prefix CX was retained for internal use at Broadway. Elsewhere the term ULTRA SECRET was employed, with the "most secret source" initials, MSS, being used as a reference prefix. Characteristically, Churchill ignored the new arrangements and continued to talk of BONIFACE.

As an aid to the recipients, a starring system was also created, so as to give a rating to the relative importance of the information in the style of a *Michelin Guide*. A single letter Z was the lowest on the scale; a document bearing five Zs demanded instant action.

During the second half of 1941, following Hitler's invasion of the Soviet Union, progress on the Enigma seemed to stall, and there were increasing indications that GCHQ's peacetime management was unable to cope with the vastly expanded size and complexity of the organization, and the commensurate pressures. The new Russian dimension offered the possibility of a useful ally with territory close to the Reich, which would

Lord Sandhurst's idea of the Radio Security Service's insignia

facilitate interception but might also jeopardize security. In fact, Moscow quickly authorized the creation of a station manned by British personnel in Murmansk, but Commander Travis cautioned against the sharing of any SIGINT secrets. He argued that most of the Soviet procedures and ciphers were thoroughly insecure (a clue to GCHQ's prewar success in the field), so a plausible way of explaining the decrypts was dreamed up for Russian consumption: all the information had allegedly been disclosed by a sympathetic Austrian prisoner of war. Since the NKVD had already penetrated GCHQ, Section V of SIS and B1(b) of MI5, this charade is not thought to have fooled many intelligence officers in Moscow, although they went through the pretense out of politeness and discretion.

Back on the domestic front, GCHQ's successes had increased the pressure on its main suppliers of wireless intercepts, the three services and the Radio Security Service. The more raw material the Bletchley number-crunchers could study, the greater the chances of breaking into some new Enigma keys. Unfortunately, none of the three services could meet the demand, and a major political row loomed ahead.

The root of the problem was the grave shortage of skilled radio operators, and the role that the Radio Security Service had obtained for itself. In a relatively short period, Jimmy Sandhurst had turned RSS from an amateur listening group into the most professional of organizations. The work of the voluntary interceptors had been divided into "rota" (a system that subsequently became known as General Search) and "free-lancing," which either allocated certain frequencies to named watches or gave the VIs a chance to initiate their own search schedules. Sandhurst later recalled:

> When we started out on this job at the end of 1939 all we had to do was to cover the bands and wait for the local pirates to appear, and log anything suspicious. Well, the locals have never turned up but "suspicious" has produced a vast network of stations of great interest. As we got to know them we found that they were highly organized but not ordinary service stations, and as slippery as eels, trying to dodge all the time. It needs a vast army of experts to keep track of them, and their output is very valuable. We are the experts. The job has grown so that we can hardly do this and the rota watches as well. The chaps who do lots of rota don't have much chance; they have to keep on the move and find 'em. Having found 'em it is best to follow up daily and get to know them. Or maybe, take a slice of the ether, live on it, get to know its inhabitants. A lot of the wanted stations mess for a week and then shoot a message over quickly. The man who knows him gets it, the other more often doesn't.[2]

The VIs recruited by Sandhurst's regional officers were dedicated to their craft and spent many hours a week hunched over their receivers, unable to tell even their families exactly what their duties were. As cover, a "Special Branch" of the Royal Observer Corps was invented, and the secrecy surrounding the RSS was breached only once—by the *Daily Mirror* on February 14, 1941, in a feature which inexplicably slipped past the censor and was headlined SPIES TAP NAZI CODE. "Britain's radio spies are at work every night," reported the *Mirror* Special Correspondent:

> . . . they sit, headphones on ears, taking down the Morse code messages which fill the air. To the layman these would be just a meaningless jumble of letters. But in the hands of code experts they might produce a message of vital importance to our Intelligence service.

Although the article had begun, "Their job isn't one to be talked about . . . ," it contained a quote from an unidentified RSS operator: "Naturally we have no idea of the codes used by German agents. But it is a great thrill to feel you might be getting down a message which, decoded, might prove of supreme importance." This remarkable lapse caused tremendous agitation at Bletchley, but either the enemy ignored it or they missed it. Either way, there was no deterioration perceptible in the quality or the volume of traffic intercepted.

At RSS's secret headquarters at Arkley View, where the preliminary discrimination was carried out, some 23,000 complete logs were being received a month by August 1941, comprising up to 10,000 sheets a day. Most were Abwehr hand ciphers, although there was also some duplication of the machine cipher traffic monitored at the five big service stations: at Cheadle, Waddington, Montrose, Beaumanor Hall and Chicksands Priory. The VIs had proved themselves to be totally committed to their tasks, but the growth in their numbers had created difficulties for the services, which were unable to find enough qualified people to man their own intercept equipment at their bases. The first signs of a crisis had been spotted late in 1940, when the Prime Minister had asked Lord Hankey, then Chancellor of the Duchy of Lancaster, to investigate. At his recommendation, a number of RSS operators had been transferred into the services, a solution that had been bitterly resented by Worlledge.

The RSS rightly regarded itself as an elite, recognizing only that most rigid of disciplines, the self-imposed, which was based on respect for Lord Sandhurst and a genuine willingness and enthusiasm for the job. The VIs were all volunteers and drove themselves to extraordinary lengths to cover their allotted wavebands. One VI, a bedridden Great War veteran, wrote in response to a "Box 25" letter of thanks for some masterly radio work: "You may not know that owing too close acquaintanceship with a land mine in the last war, I am completely paralysed from the arms down, and in my arms have not even the strength to roll a bandage!"

The official RSS invasion instruction gives an idea of the bizarre conditions under which the VIs worked:

(a) General watch over the 24 hours, covering from 0600 to 1700 5½ to 9 Mc, and 1700 to 0800 hours 3 to 6½ Mc.
(b) Special group watching.
(c) Find out from your employer if he will release you in the event of an invasion, so that as long as you are in unoccupied territory you can put in full-time watch.

y Sought a Life of —Now He's Got It

een - year - old John Evans the
's boy, but John's secret dream
adventure, so he suddenly threw
lgan, South Wales, to join a ship.
me a storm blew his ship away
le tasted his first dose of really
ked it.

's sixteenth birthday. All the
celebrate it when Nazi bombs
Then a plane swooped down
chine-gunning the crew as they

of the crew
several hours
awler.
gest birthday
ve.
ure and I've
waiting for

SPIES TAP NAZI CODE

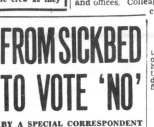

BY A SPECIAL CORRESPONDENT

BRITAIN'S radio spies are at work every night.
During the day they work in factories, shops
and offices. Colleagues wonder why they never go to
cinemas or dances.

But questions are parried with a
smile—and silence. Their job isn't
one to be talked about.

Home from work, a quick meal, and
the hush-hush men unlock the door
of a room usually at the top of the
house. There, until the small hours,
they sit, head-phones on ears, taking
down the Morse code messages which
fill the air.

To the layman these would be
just a meaningless jumble of
letters.

But in the hands of code experts
they might produce a message of
vital importance to our Intelligence Service.

No pay is given to the men who
tap the air for these messages.

Their Reward

They are drawn from the radio
enthusiasts who operated their own
short-wave transmitters before the
war.

" We are glad to serve the country
in this way," one of them told me
"A letter of thanks from headquarters telling us that we have
been able to supply some useful information is all the reward we ask.
'Naturally we have no idea of the
codes used by German agents.
'But it is a great thrill to feel you
might be getting down a message
which, decoded, might prove of
supreme importance."

NAME FASCISTS IN KEY JOBS

To eliminate danger to the State
in case of invasion, will you send to
the heads of departments a list of
people in key positions who were in
the British Union of Fascists when
war began ?

Mr. Josiah Wedgwood (Soc., New-
castle-under-Lyme) put this question
to the Home Secretary in the House
of Commons yesterday.

The Under-Secretary replied that
all necessary steps were taken to
guard against such risks, but it
would not be in the public interest to
give details.

Mr. Wedgwood: I want to know
whether those who were Fascists
are known in the departments in
which they are employed ?

The Under-Secretary: Once I begin
telling what steps are taken by the
security services I should be creating
a precedent which might have very
awkward repercussions

Works Won for Wavell

BY A SPECIAL CORRESPONDENT

HUNDREDS of men and women
worked day and night, gave
up their holidays, to enable the
Army of the Nile to advance to
the capture of Cyrenaica.

Their unceasing toil, backing the
inventive genius of Mr. Cecil Gordon
Vokes, an engineer who has never
failed to solve any problem of filtra-
tion set before him, enabled British
tanks and aeroplanes to be fitted
with filters to beat a more persistent
and dangerous enemy than the
Italians—sand.

Sand very quickly choked the
engines of tanks and aeroplanes
operating in the desert. It got into
the bearings, rapidly wearing out
good engines, shortening the life of
valuable mechanised vehicles.

Cure in 10 Days

Some time ago it was realised that
something would have to be done if
our forces were to advance across the
desert with any chance of success.

In ten days Mr. Vokes designed
and made a filter that would
enable our tanks and other
vehicles to travel 150 miles a day
without the least trouble from
sand.

Tests on machines in this count
occupied another fortnight. The
factories buckled to, working day and
night so that the filters could be
flown out to Egypt in time for
General Wavell to launch his great
attack

And everybody knows the wonder-
ful sweeps and drives our armoured
vehicles have made out there, and
the vitally essential part they have
played in the victory.

Refused Time Off

At one factory engaged on filters
after it had been decided to give the
workers two hours off just before
Christmas to do their shopping, a
deputation said: " We don't want the
time off. We'll shop later on. We've
a job of work to do."

Mr. Vokes not only designs the
filters which have contributed so
much to our victories, he is the driv-
ing force behind the workers. He
gives them talks on their job and the
part they play in making victory
secure.

Last week he arranged for an air
man to tell them how the filters he
enabled him and his comrades to
sweep the Italians from the skies.

FROM SICKBED TO VOTE 'NO'

BY A SPECIAL CORRESPONDENT

MR. JOE BATEY, M.P. for
Spennymoor, who has been
ill for months, travelled to Westminster yesterday to vote against
the Government on the second
reading of the Household Means
Test Bill.

" Old Joe," as he is known to his
colleagues, feels passionately about
abolishing the test.

" We Labour M.P.s," he declared,
" owe our election to promises we
made to our electors, the most important of which was that we would
vote against the Means Test.
" I am here to keep my promise,
and no Party Whip or any threat
that can be made against me, will
prevent me doing so."

The seventeen Socialist M.P.s
who voted against the Bill are to
be officially censured.

The Parliamentary Labour Party
is to hold a special meeting next week
to discuss their action, which was
contrary to the official policy of the
party.

173 Votes to 19

When the House divided after
listening to the winding-up speech of
the Minister of Labour, the second
reading of the Bill was passed by 173
votes to nineteen.

Every M.P. agreed that the Bill is
an improvement on the present
position, but the critics, led by Mr.
Ness Edwards, a Welsh miner, bombarded the Chancellor and the Minister of Labour with alleged in-
justices.

The Minister of Labour said the
Bill substituted a personal means test
for the household test.

He promised that overtime and
Sunday labour would not be taken
into account in assessing the income
of a household for means test purposes.

Also, up to £375 of war savings will
be excluded from the reckoning of
the income of those applying for
supplementary old age pensions.

GAVE GERMAN SALUTE: GAOL

A man who did the goosestep and
gave the Nazi salute was sent to prison for a month at Sheffield yesterday.

He was Oswald Skidmore, aged
forty-eight, of Rural-lane, Sheffield,
who was accused of making statements about the war likely to cause

LANDLORDS NEED NOT REPAIR WAR DAMAGE

To a tenant who had left his home
following damage by blast, Judge
Earengey at Clerkenwell County Court
said yesterday:

" Tenants come before me and complain about damage done by the
enemy. They seem to think it is the
landlord's obligation to put the
premises in condition.

" Perhaps the main provision of
the Landlord and Tenant (War
Damage) Act is that even if there

HOLD ...S

...OSEVELT in-
...e an order
...ign funds in
... soon as Con-
...nd-and-Lease
...able informa-
...hington.

...ch as Britain,
... the Latin-
...ould be issued
...making it pos-
...ithdraw funds
...ates at will.—

E SONG

...ote " Waltzing
... to music which
...le song of the
... died in Sydney
...le was A. B.
...ustralia's best

... was the song
...s sang as they
...and Benghazi

...ittee, formally
... using an oxy-
... railings which
...bout 200 years
...ey take all this
... cut these rail-
... yield a paltry
...hen half a mile
...London, there
...of tons of iron
...ldings—in fact,
...n iron and steel

...he problem of
...netal cannot be
...In these scenes
...normous wealth
...rders that no
...hing. By all
...s when we need
...nd neglect this
...plain lunacy

...the German
...w to Bulgaria
...on Dr. Filov—
...Minister—are
...ng.

...t they are to
...nce of the two
...nterests " and

INCREASE IN CHEAP SWEETS

The proportion of cheaper sweets
produced is being further increased
at the expense of the dearer, states
the Parliamentary Secretary to the
Ministry of Food, in a written reply.

The industry is trying to distribute
reduced supplies equitably on the basis
of pre-war purchases adjusted in the
light of present distribution of popu-
lation.

Now the last one is difficult. I have already heard of the results of attempts elsewhere to do this. If you work for a big organization like the GPO or EMI it is not likely to come off because of the difficulty of approach to the right quarter, and your employer may in any case have other plans for you.

Those of you employed by small firms will probably be asked for how long it goes on. If it is for a day or two, that will probably be alright, but if it is for longer, then they will say they obviously can't be expected to pay any wages. I am afraid that HQ have not shed any light on the answer. But will you please see what can be done, and let me know as soon as possible whether you would be free for (a) a short period of a few days, or (b) indefinitely, and then I will see what can be done about arranging things.

HQ will arrange to collect logs from convenient centers, and we can possibly arrange to centralize receiving points.[3]

As well as the monitoring duties carried out by the VIs, RSS undertook additional work from the granary in the garden of Arkley View, which was transformed, with the help of five seventy-five-foot aerial masts, into a primitive but effective intercept station. An indication of its range is to be found in one bulletin which instructed VIs that "Garda cars and their control in Dublin are to be ignored." Once copied and discriminated, the resulting logs were passed by courier to Bletchley Park, where most landed on Oliver Strachey's desk to be turned into summaries, code-named ISOS. RSS's prodigious rate of supply, relative to the services, was largely due to having cornered the market in experienced amateurs. VIs frequently recommended other hams for recruitment, and those under thirty-five years of age were able to resist their call-up. Instead of joining up and then being channeled to the right quarters, the hams were being concealed by RSS's cloak of secrecy.

The alarm voiced by the services coincided with a growing sense of unease at Broadway over the way the Allies were coping with the secret wireless war. In the virtual absence of any stay-behind networks on the Continent, the Secret Intelligence Service had only SIGINT to rely on. The major expansion in SIS's manpower since the outbreak of war had been confined largely to Section V, which, in effect, was a body designed to exploit the enemy's intelligence traffic. Other responsibilities, such as the prosecution of irregular warfare and the promotion of resistance networks in occupied territory, had been transferred, somewhat ignominiously, to the newly formed Special Operations Executive. Stewart Menzies had failed to prevent SOE's creation (indeed, he was not even consulted on the matter, or on the transfer of one of his own paramilitary wings, Section D, to the rival organization), but he had at least succeeded in retaining control over its communications. In April 1941, after just eight months in existence, SOE petitioned to be freed from Section VIII's domination, but again Menzies managed to get the request overruled, albeit temporarily. SIS was under sustained attack in Whitehall, and with RSS poaching on its SIGINT preserves, Menzies struck back to reestablish his control. After some intensive lobbying, which probably took place at the Prime Minister's weakest moment, when he was studying Menzies's daily offering of decrypts, Churchill consented to a plan which moved RSS away from the Security Service and into SIS's administrative control. A further proposal to establish a single SIS representative from Section V as a liaison officer inside MI5's B Division was also approved, and in May 1941 Ian Coghill took up residence in St. James's Street. In other circumstances MI5 might have been expected to resist such a scheme, but Menzies made his move while the newly appointed Director-General, Sir David Petrie, was in the throes of restructuring his entire organization.

With MI5 demoted to client status within SIS's SIGINT empire, Menzies could be said to have regained control overall and fought off a challenge that had threatened his future. Certainly SIS had few weapons left in its depleted armory. There were only a handful of productive SIS stations left around the world; those in neutral capitals in Europe resembled refugee assembly points, providing hospitality to dispossessed former agents, more than centers of espionage. Menzies was starved of routes into occupied territory and, because of the chronic shortage of suitable aircraft and ships, could offer only limited clandestine transport facilities to the exiled resistance leaders. In brief, Station X (Bletchley Park) and the exploitation of its product by Section V were his only viable assets. Menzies consolidated his position on Saturday, September 6, 1941, by escorting the Prime Minister around Bletchley Park, the occasion on which Churchill is supposed to have remarked on what was later to be referred to as its "condition of creative anarchy": "I know I told you to leave no stone unturned to find the necessary staff, but I didn't mean you to take me so literally." Churchill toured several of the huts and was introduced to some of the senior staff. Professor Vincent provided a small cryptographic demonstration by showing how an Italian submarine code had been solved by a member of his section named Wall. Suitably impressed, Churchill delivered a morale-boosting address to the staff, who gathered around him on the front lawn, and then swept off with his entourage in a fleet of cars with flags flying. Later the same day, Denniston issued an order that the visit should remain a secret, but by that time word had spread throughout the town.

Soon after this visit, there occurred what amounted to a palace revolution at Bletchley. On October 21, Alan Turing, Gordon Welchman, Hugh Alexander and Stuart Milner-Barry sent a "Secret and Confidential" letter to Churchill cataloguing their complaints about Bletchley Park's administration, although they were careful to preface their remarks with some words of praise for Travis's "energy and foresight." Three items were singled out for criticism: a shortage of at least twenty women clerks in Hut 8, which had prevented the section working a recently acquired Hollerith punch-card sorter from operating at night (the result was an estimated twelve-hour delay in tracing the daily change in the DOLPHIN key); a shortage of typists and decryption staff in Hut 6, which was holding up study of LIGHT BLUE intercepts from the Middle East; and an insufficient number of Wrens to cope with the new Bombes. In conclusion, it was believed generally "that the importance of the work is not being impressed with sufficient force upon those outside authorities with whom we have to deal." At least Churchill took the matter seriously, for General Ismay, the Prime Minister's staff officer and personal representative on the Chiefs of Staff Committee, was ordered the following day to "make sure they have all they want on extreme priority"; four weeks later, Menzies was in a position to confirm that all the necessary steps had been taken to rectify the situation.

Ismay's intervention, on behalf of the Prime Minister, removed the bottlenecks that had jeopardized Bletchley's performance. The action was not a moment too soon, for in December 1941 two momentous events took place: the United States declared war on the Axis, and Dilly Knox cracked the Abwehr's Enigma key.

6

Clandestine Signals

The DNI asked officially "whether cryptography would be of any use in the next war" and the head of GC&CS expressed extremely defeatist terms in reply.

—WILLIAM F. CLARKE in *History of Room 40*

In spite of Henry Stimson's closure of the U.S. State Department's so-called Black Chamber at the end of October 1929, the SIGINT field had not been neglected entirely by the American military authorities. Just as Herbert Yardley was deciding to publish his controversial memoirs, and then sell his services as an adviser to the Chinese Nationalist government for $7,000, the Signal Corps was in the planning stage of a Signal Intelligence Service. The civilian chosen to head the embryonic organization was William Friedman, a Jewish refugee from Bucharest who had run the Signal Corps' Code and Cipher Section since his return from France at the end of the Great War. For the first seven years of its existence, Friedman's grandly titled SIS employed six assistants and operated on an annual budget of $17,400. At first, its raw material was drawn from two primitive intercept stations, at Battery Cove, Virginia, and Fort Monmouth, New Jersey, and from extra copies of telegrams made by the big commercial carriers, but by 1938 the army's network had developed to include two further bases, at Fort Sam Houston in Texas and at the Presidio in San Francisco, and three others overseas (at Quarry Heights in the Panama Canal Zone, Fort Shafter on Oahu and Fort McKinley in the Philippines). In March 1939, Fort Hancock, in New York harbor, was added and Fort Hunt, in Virginia, came on stream the following October.

In addition to the American SIS, the United States Navy had long maintained a Communications Security section, designated OP-20-G, which also had a secret cryptographic role and ran several intercept stations at four Navy Department establishments at home (on Bainbridge Island, Puget Sound; Winter Harbor, Maine; Jupiter, Florida; Cheltenham, Maryland) and abroad (at Corregidor in the Philippines and at Aiea on Oahu). The Tokyo-Washington traffic was monitored jointly at Bainbridge Island and San Francisco, where the intercepts were transcribed for onward relay to Washington along a regular Bell Telephone Teletype line, while the Tokyo-Berlin and Tokyo-Moscow circuits were kept under surveillance from the army unit in the Philippines. Together these two concentrated on Tokyo's wireless traffic, which consisted in the main of two varieties: the Imperial Navy's traffic in a code designated the "JN" series and diplomatic communications in a code referred to simply as "J." Whenever a new procedure was introduced for either system, a new numerical suffix was added. Thus, individual codes were known by such names as "J-16" and "JN-25." Both versions were based on a book of some 45,000 five-figure groups, which corresponded to a word or phrase in Kana, the phonetic symbols of written Japanese. Before transmission, the groups were changed by applying them to a subtraction table and, in order to prevent corruption, all the resulting numbers were immediately divisible by three. European countries had abandoned this type of hand cipher in 1917, so they presented few difficulties for the cryptographers at either SIS or, for that matter, GCHQ. However, their decryption had become progressively more difficult during the 1930s as the Japanese experimented with machines to super-encipher the texts of messages between Tokyo and certain missions abroad.

By 1935, the Signal Intelligence Service had achieved considerable success against the *Angooki Taipu A*, the Type A machine cipher used by the Japanese naval attachés. Like his British counterparts some years later, Friedman had color-categorized the traffic, and these first machine decrypts became known as RED. They were circulated discreetly in Washington under the code name MAGIC, until March 20, 1939, when a more sophisticated, electric version of the naval machine, the Type B, was brought into service by the Japanese Foreign Ministry. Only twenty-five were actually built, but were distributed to a selection of Japan's most important overseas missions, including Washington. As a result, the flow of the MAGIC decrypts to and from Washington stopped overnight, and work was begun on the new cipher, code-named PURPLE. This improved cipher was generated on an entirely novel device that bore no resemblance to the rotor-based European machines, such as the familiar Swedish-built Hagelin or the Engima, and resisted all attack until September 25, 1940, when the first complete text was solved. PURPLE's basis was a relatively straightforward plugboard, combined with an extraordinary array of Strowger electronic stepping switches or telephone exchange relays. So how was it possible to solve PURPLE's complex output without help from a device such as the electromechanical Bombe?

The answer seems to lie in two useful cribs, which had been revealed after lengthy analysis of the RED decrypts. Japanese diplomatic telegrams invariably conformed to predictable patterns and conventions. Protocol demanded certain routine introductory formulae, such as the phrase "I have the honor to inform your excellency." There were also certain words and sentences that could be expected to appear frequently, and these "probable words" gave valuable clues to the key chosen for a particular day's messages. But perhaps the best crib of all was the reluctance of Japanese diplomats to paraphrase their formal Notes. Whenever a telegram was received from Tokyo for delivery to the U.S. State Department, the Japanese diplomats in Washington handed in the text in its exact form. No effort was made to alter the original wording, so a comparison with the ciphered version sometimes revealed a daily key. Once the PURPLE cipher had been cracked, Friedman and his team were able to reconstruct the theory of its intricate internal wiring and then draw a plan from which two unnamed technicians were able to build a duplicate. The final breakthrough has sometimes been attributed to "an intuitive flash of genius" by Harry Larry Clark, one of Friedman's assistants. Although this explanation, which is the version that all the written accounts agree with, sounds farfetched, given the difficulties experienced by the Poles and GCHQ in their pursuit of the German Enigma, it should be remembered that there was a plentiful supply of Hagelin machines in the United States for the cryptographers to experiment with, and not a few cipher machines that had been invented (and patented) by Friedman himself. The fact that in December 1940 Friedman underwent a nervous breakdown is an indication of the cerebral power he had expended on the exercise, which had lasted for more than twenty months. Another possible aid to the cryptographers was a clandestine entry into a Japanese consular office which, it is alleged, went undetected and enabled the exterior switches of the PURPLE machine to be photographed.

The American SIS's first PURPLE replica was used as a model to create others, and by the end of 1940 a second had been delivered to OP-20-G in Washington. A third is known to have gone to Bletchley late in January 1941, aboard HMS *King George V*, the battleship that had recently delivered Lord Halifax as Britain's new ambassador to the neutral

United States. The machine had been escorted by two U.S. Navy officers, Lieutenant Robert H. Weeks and Ensign Prescott H. Currier, two FBI special agents (of whom one is believed to have been the powerful future assistant director, Hugh Clegg) and two representatives from the Signal Intelligence Service, Major Abraham Sinkov and Captain Leo Rosen. Overtly the group had represented a technical mission to establish their country's needs and to identify profitable areas of cooperation, but in reality the mission had conducted a somewhat one-sided exchange of SIGINT developments. The Admiralty had presented the American visitors with the latest Marconi-Adcock direction-finding system and, in return, had received a treasure trove of information: a list of the current PURPLE keys and a complete copy of its three-letter code; two RED machines with a solution manual; two Japanese consular codes; two Japanese fleet codes with their current keys; two Japanese merchant shipping codes and radio call signs; and details of American work on German and Italian cipher systems. The (third) PURPLE machine eventually found its way to the Far East Combined Bureau, then temporarily accommodated in Singapore. The four U.S. servicemen soon returned to America, but the two G-men were placed on temporary attachment to the Secret Intelligence Service headquarters in Broadway to learn more of the intelligence war.

The fourth PURPLE went to the U.S. Army base at Cavite in the Philippines; the fifth was scheduled for Hawaii, but the Japanese attack on Pearl Harbor interrupted matters, and it too was sent to Bletchley. The remarkable generosity of the U.S. authorities in donating a pair of PURPLE machines to GCHQ before issuing one to Pearl Harbor is, on the face of it, an indication of the close political relationship between President Roosevelt and Winston Churchill. In practical terms it has to be recognized that, for all the strategic importance of its geographic location, Hawaii was not seriously considered as a likely target for the Japanese. Nor, at that stage, did the islands possess even the most rudimentary decryption capacity which, of course, was essential if the intercepts were to be processed locally. All such facilities had been centralized in Washington. In spite of these considerations, the decision to pass two PURPLE units to the British subsequently became a matter of some controversy, although at the time only a handful of very senior officers had been made aware of it.

Throughout 1940 and 1941, there were continuous, but secret, negotiations between Britain and the neutral United States on the subject of mutual cooperation and the exchange of technical information. The first major Allied mission to America had been led by Sir Henry Tizard in August 1940, in his capacity as a member of the British Air Council, and this had paved the way for further visits by experts in various fields of interest, such as proximity fuses, radar and bomb-aiming devices. Major General George V. Strong of the U.S. Army Department's War Plans Division had reciprocated in October 1940, and later had become a permanent U.S. liaison officer in London, with the uninformative title of "Special Observer." Exact details of these exchanges, or the quality of the information that was passed, remain obscure as no written records survive, but both sides must have been anxious to discover what progress the other had made against the Japanese. What is certain is that Strong had been informed of Friedman's success with PURPLE shortly before his departure for London, and it seems likely that he was the first to disclose details of the coup to his British contacts. In any event, Strong's visit was the first, tentative step in what was to be an ambitious Anglo-American pact to swop SIGINT material.

For their part, the British had substantial assets in the Pacific theater with which to trade. Quite apart from the many accumulated secrets held by Captain Shaw's Far East Combined Bureau's offices at Singapore and Hong Kong, the Empire boasted an impressive capacity to intercept Japanese signals. In Australia alone there were no less than four stations: at HMAS Harman, near Canberra; the Royal Australian Navy's facility at Coonawarra, near Darwin; and two bases in Melbourne: Commander T.E. Nave's cryptographic unit at the Naval Intelligence headquarters at St. Kilda Road, and the Defense Signals Division headquarters at Watsonia. In addition, the Dutch government in exile had evacuated a clandestine wireless intercept station from Java in the Netherlands East Indies to a new location near Darwin. Considering America's relatively late entry into the cryptographic field, these facilities were of inestimable value to the United States. From the British point of view, any American help on the Japanese machine ciphers would have been most welcome. Work on the RED and PURPLE machines had merited a low priority in comparison to the Imperial Navy's hand ciphers, which had begun to yield results in England in September 1939. Japanese territorial gains in the Far East during the winter of 1941, culminating in the surrender of Singapore on February 15, 1942, were later to highlight the escalating need for reliable information about the enemy.

The principal item that the Americans had to trade was their access to the PURPLE cipher and, in particular, Friedman's reconstructed machine. The fact that this even existed was part luck, for in April 1941

MAGIC had been jeopardized by a leak, which eventually had been traced to the Under-Secretary of State, Sumner Welles. He had disclosed the contents of a PURPLE decrypt to Constantin Oumansky, the Soviet ambassador in Washington, in a well-intentioned but futile attempt to alert Moscow to the impending Nazi invasion. The decrypt had consisted of a telegram from Ambassador Oshima in Berlin addressed to Tokyo, and had given advance notice of Hitler's intention to invade Russia the following June. Oumansky had pretended to ignore Welles's advice, but had promptly challenged Dr. Hans Thomsen, the German envoy in Washington, with the text. Predictably, Thomsen had denounced the State Department's action as a provocation, but had wasted no time in warning Ribbentrop's ministry that the Berlin-Tokyo wireless circuit had been compromised. He had also alerted the Japanese ambassador in Washington, Admiral Kichisaburo Nomura. The disquieting news was promptly sent to Tokyo, where a major investigation had been launched by Foreign Minister Matsuoka:

> *From*: Washington (Nomura)   May 20, 1941
> *To*: Tokyo   #327
>
> INTELLIGENCE
>
> Though I do not know which ones, I have discovered that the United States is reading some of our codes. As for how I got the intelligence, I will inform you by courier or another safe way.[1]

Naturally, OP-20-G had monitored the exchange and translated it within twenty-four hours. To the incredulity of the Americans, the responsible authorities in Tokyo decided that no significant breach of PURPLE's security had occurred, and that in all probability the relevant text had been repeated in error in a low-grade cipher which had been intercepted by the Americans. Thus, even when the Japanese had been presented with incontrovertible evidence of PURPLE's insecurity, they had clung to an insupportable faith in the integrity of the key, which was altered every ten days, and had actively sought alternative explanations rather than face the unpalatable truth. Matsuoka's response had been limited to a tightening up of the regulations governing the use of the code employed for important dispatches, and an order that only one named telegraph clerk in the Washington embassy should be entrusted with future cipher work. This latter precaution was never implemented because of the obvious impracticability of employing just one clerk to handle such a large (and growing) volume of crucial signals traffic.

The Japanese Foreign Ministry consistently displayed great confidence in the security of its cipher machines, even though it was itself actively engaged in the interception of signals. It had run a secret station at Owada, near Tokyo, since 1937, and another site near Shanghai, and had bought large supplies of American radio equipment to expand its intercept program. In fact, numerous internal memoranda recovered after the war reveal that Foreign Minister Matsuoka really suspected only the Germans and Italians of attacking his sensitive communications.

In the light of American mastery of the Japanese diplomatic ciphers, it is astonishing that the entire administration could have been caught unawares by a single massed air raid on the Pacific Fleet's protected anchorage at Pearl Harbor. That the warships themselves should have been surprised in their home port is equally remarkable, but can be explained by the very limited SIGINT dissemination at that time. The American military establishment had been left to deduce for itself the strategic significance of the deteriorating political situation. MAGIC was such a closely guarded secret that it had gone "to only a few of the highest-level United States officials." Neither the senior U.S. Army nor Navy commanders in Hawaii, General Walter Short or Admiral Husband Kimmel, had been among this privileged circle, even though much of the Japanese wireless traffic had been intercepted from locations nominally under their control. Because they had not been made privy to the MAGIC material, or even to the existence of such a source, they had deployed their forces in accordance with a general war alert which had been issued from Washington on November 27, 1941. In General Short's case, this had involved a decision to concentrate his aircraft together so that they could be guarded effectively against sabotage. It was widely believed that local subversives of Japanese origin posed the greatest threat. This failure to disperse his planes meant that the Japanese bombers found easy targets on the ground when, on the morning of December 7, the raid was mounted. As a direct consequence, only a tiny number of fighters were able to defend Pearl Harbor and the mighty Pacific Fleet was eliminated within a matter of minutes.

The raid on Pearl Harbor was a defeat of immense proportions for the U.S. Navy, but it was to have two crucial consequences for the development of SIGINT. America's formal entry into the war opened the way for a closer relationship with the British cryptographers, and the recovery of documents from a crashed enemy aircraft disclosed vital information about the Japanese, including a complete list of the Imperial

Navy's operational call signs. In addition, the catastrophe had served to alert the American authorities to the importance of SIGINT. The numerous official investigations that followed the debacle had all reinforced the view that sufficient intelligence had been available before December 7 to have alerted Hawaii to the possibility of an attack if only this information had been disseminated to those in command. The lack of any such warning was the result of neither incompetence nor conspiracy (although some historians would have it otherwise), but simply of the administration's inability to assess, collate and disseminate the available intelligence. Lack of manpower, for example, had prevented many of the clues from being examined until the attack was over, and the limited resources available to the cryptographers had, on occasion, meant a delay of up to two weeks before a low-grade cipher was examined in Washington. One particularly significant J-19 signal, dated September 24, 1941, had been addressed to Nagao Kita, the Japanese consul in Honolulu. Kita had been instructed to divide Pearl Harbor into five subareas and to report on the exact number of warships moored in each. In retrospect, the text clearly indicates that Kita had been required to begin work on what amounted to an aerial bombardment grid. On November 15, Kita had been ordered to double his reports and transmit his latest observations twice a week. His last signal, dated December 6, after detailed requests for reconnaissance on December 4 and 5, had confirmed the presence of all nine of the U.S. Pacific Fleet's battleships at anchor in Pearl Harbor, as well as three light cruisers, three submarine tenders, four heavy-cruisers and seventeen destroyers. The consul had also remarked on the absence of any barrage balloons or torpedo nets, and had concluded that "there is considerable opportunity left to take advantage of a surprise attack."

The September 24 intercept did not actually reach Washington until October 6, and even then there was a further three-day delay in decrypting and translating it. Similarly, the November 15 intercept, which demanded "extreme secrecy," was not decoded until December 3. The deteriorating political situation between America and Japan had increased the pressure on the cryptographers who had opted, understandably, to concentrate on the high-priority PURPLE messages passing between Tokyo and Washington. This had necessitated less attention being paid to the lower-grade cipher traffic, so that when Kita had burned his J-19 code books on December 2, in accordance with a directive from Tokyo, his wireless traffic had become less of a priority. Ironically, it had also become easier to read, for now he had only an out-of-date code, known as PAK2, in which to cipher his messages. Because PAK2 was considered inferior even to the J-19, the intercepts were thought to be unlikely to contain any information of immediate value and were thus virtually the last to be processed. As a consequence, the full SIGINT picture only emerged at the postmortem conducted by a joint congressional committee in 1942, and by that time America had joined the war and learned the relevance of signals intelligence.

The committee's inquiry established that there had indeed been plenty of evidence to indicate that the Japanese had intended to launch a surprise attack on Hawaii. The decrypts of Consul Kita's signals proved especially eloquent. The committee also discovered that only nine individuals within the U.S. administration had been cleared for MAGIC (although several others had occasional access). The source had been regarded as so secret that it had been decided not to risk jeopardizing it by allowing its distribution by radio to Hawaii. One particular consideration had been the fear that the Japanese might have intercepted and decrypted Washington's advice. Consequently, neither Kimmel nor Short was ever in a position to judge the threat to his command.

It was always extremely difficult to maintain a balance between keeping knowledge of SIGINT confined to as few people as possible for fear of endangering its source and disseminating it for appropriate action. Pearl Harbor was an extreme example of excessive secrecy denying vital information to those in greatest need. In Britain a compromise had been reached by the creation of a small, secret organization whose sole purpose was the channeling of "special intelligence" to the appropriate recipients in the field. The foundations of the Special Liaison Units had been laid during the BEF's campaign in France in 1940, when Robert Gore-Browne, Tubby Long and Humphrey Plowden had used one-time pads to bypass the usual channels and communicate directly with Whaddon. By the end of 1941, the arrangement had become altogether more sophisticated.

The Pearl Harbor fiasco had highlighted two significant pitfalls that had already been dealt with by the British Secret Intelligence Service. The first was the assessment of the relative importance of each decrypt. The second was the secure routing of the resulting summaries to the correct addressees. The first problem had been overcome by a method of "starring" each decrypt. As has been explained, the highest priority signals bore the legend "ZZZZZ" at the top, and the number of Zs decreased in relation to the significance of the decrypt's content. Before June 1941, the summaries had been circulated under the code name BONIFACE, the implication being that the information had been supplied by a secret agent. After that date the classification Ultra SECRET was employed, and Ultra became a generic term for Enigma-based SIGINT. The question of conveying the material to its recipient within the British Isles was simply a matter of advising an indoctrinated liaison officer by landline teleprinter, but overseas the matter was altogether more complex. As already mentioned, Freddie Jacob had opened the Combined Bureau Middle East, Bletchley's branch in the Middle East, in November 1940, but as GCHQ's output had increased, so had the need to supply substantial quantities of Ultra to the commanders on the ground in North Africa. At first, paraphrased messages were transmitted over an RAF circuit to Heliopolis in Egypt, on an average of one a day, and Jacob had the sole responsibility for deciphering them and ensuring their safe delivery to the relevant service headquarters. After two months, in May 1941, Jacob had obtained permission to indoctrinate two assistants to help with the ever-growing volume of signals and eventually, in August 1941, the first Special Communications Unit (SCU) had been established to ease the burden.

SCU No. 1 was a development of the SLU idea and consisted of a team headed by Kenneth MacFarlan, the GCHQ liaison officer with the French and the Poles, who had been evacuated from the Château de Vignolles the previous year. MacFarlan's outfit, which operated under "A Detachment, Special Signals Unit," contained six branches: Drivers (led by Corporal Watt); Operators (Corporal Ware); Technical (Sergeant Sall); Administration (Lieutenant Pemberton); and Ciphers. The latter was the most important and had twelve cipher officers, including Robert Gore-Brown and Ronald Crawshaw. From Abbassia, a location conveniently close to the CBME at Heliopolis, a direct link was established with Whaddon's satellite transmitter at Windy Ridge, and further substations or Special Liaison Units were added in September 1941 at Malta, Beirut, Baghdad, Jerusalem, Alexandria, Eighth Army Headquarters and the Tactical Air Force. The SCU/SLU organization, under Fred Winterbotham's overall direction in London, was eventually to attach temporary representatives (usually specially selected RAF personnel) to headquarters all over the world, with permanent posts in Brisbane and Delhi. By using a network entirely separated from the routine military traffic, and employing one-time pads and specially adapted TypeX machines, Bletchley could distribute its valuable product with a measure of safety and, at the same time, avoid the bitter American experience.

During the course of 1941, GCHQ continued to expand, but its new status as Whitehall's most reliable source of intelligence created many complications. Before the arrival of the first electromagnetic Bombes, the Enigma solutions had been painstakingly developed by hand with the help of John Jeffrey's perforated sheets. These had established, in May 1940, the value of testing many thousands of possibilities to identify the correct combination of the enemy's Enigma rotor settings. Transforming this theoretical advance into a working machine was a problem of mechanical and electrical engineering rather than pure cryptography, so the matter had been handed over to the British Tabulating Machinery Company (BTMC).

The British Tabulating Machinery Company had previously concentrated on electromechanical office equipment, such as calculators and punch-card sorters which could undertake repetitious, logical functions. There was no machine already in existence that conformed to the very unusual specifications required for the testing of thousands of Enigma rotor settings, so a secret contract code-named CANTAB was negotiated by Edward Travis with BTMC's managing director, Mr. Bailey, and his chief researcher, Harold Keen. CANTAB required the construction of a device based on a complicated wiring diagram prepared by Gordon Welchman and Alan Turing. The idea was to pass an electrical current through 676 terminals, corresponding to the 26×26 holes in the original perforated sheets, and then to employ a series of revolving drums to reproduce the effect of the Enigma's rotors. The drums were to duplicate every possible alphabetical setting of the rotors in a matter of seconds instead of hours, and identify particular combinations which would transform samples of intercepted texts selected from a table of "probable words" in message preambles into recognizable German. When the right consistency had been achieved, the machine was supposed to cease operating, so the resulting "stop" could be compared to the remainder of the intercepted text to see if the setting worked equally well. By using the probable-word system as a crib, and building 104 connections (equivalent to four complete alphabets) into each drum, the Bombe could race through some half-a-million combinations in just a few hours.

The first prototype Bombe, dubbed *Agnes*, took just six weeks to build and was assembled with Hollerith relays at the BTMC's factory at Ignield Way, Letchworth. It was delivered to Hut 11 at Bletchley Park late in August 1940, and during the course of the next twelve months a further twenty were manufactured. The overall project was coordinated by Harold Fletcher, the Cambridge mathematician, but he soon found that there was insufficient space at Station X to accommodate the bulky, eight-foot-tall machines. Accordingly, three neighboring manor houses which had been used as billets by MI6 personnel, at Wavendon, Adstock and Little Horwood, were taken over. At Adstock Manor the stables, previously used for the Prior family's hunters, were transformed into a "Bombe hut," and at Wavendon House an extra wing was added. As the thirst for additional Bombe capacity increased, room for a further sixteen Bombes was needed, and another neighboring estate, at Gayhurst, was requisitioned by the Admiralty at the request of Commander Malcolm Saunders, the head of Hut 3. The house itself, a magnificent Elizabethan mansion, continued to be occupied by its owners, Sir Walter and Lady Carlile, who played host to hundreds of Wrens, but a special windowless building was hastily constructed at the rear to house the Bombes. Forty years later the mysterious Bombe hut lies dilapidated and empty, with no clue as to its original purpose.

The escalation in the use of Bombes had caused a further staffing problem, as each machine needed constant attention and maintenance. They were tended in eight-hour watches by teams of volunteers from the Women's Royal Naval Service. Altogether some seven hundred Wrens were assigned to HMS *Pembroke V*, the Admiralty's cover shore station designation for GCHQ. Each Bombe was given the name of a port, and at the beginning of each watch a special document known as a menu was delivered to assist the setting up of a machine. Once the drums had been inserted and the connections cleaned to prevent short circuits, the Bombe would be put into operation. The thirty-two drums would spin noisily, all at different speeds, until they all suddenly stopped. Readings would be taken from each and then fed into a checking machine, which had already been programmed with the complete menu. If the figures and letters matched up in the required sequence, the news was telephoned to Station X where another menu was in preparation. This procedure, conducted in conditions of extraordinary secrecy, had helped GCHQ to exploit the RED, BLUE, BROWN and VIOLET Luftwaffe traffic as well as ONION, MUSTARD and LEEK. However, as soon as Whitehall and, in particular, the War Office had grasped the significance of GCHQ's output, interdepartmental conflict erupted. In retrospect, the cause of the crisis seems to have been the disproportionate amount of intelligence material emanating from Bletchley in comparison with the amount of resources committed by individual services. The army was particularly sensitive on this issue because to date the main beneficiary of intercept work had been the RAF. The fact that GCHQ was still essentially a civilian organization prompted the Director of Military Intelligence, Major-General F.H.N. Davidson, to try and rationalize control of all the intercept stations, though he was principally concerned with the three services, and GCHQ.

The War Office's inordinate contribution to the intercept program was largely the work of a secret body known as the Special Wireless Group, whose origins were to be found in the British Expeditionary Force's direction-finding team, led by Major A. E. Barton. This unit had been evacuated from Chartres in May 1940 along with the remainder of the mobile company that had been engaged on intercept duties. In the aftermath of Dunkirk, the Special Wireless Group had been created by Barton from the remnants of No. 2 GHQ Signals at the recently vacated barracks of the Wiltshire Regiment at Trowbridge. In addition, a small radio station had been built in North Wales at a holiday camp near Prestatyn requisitioned from Billy Butlin. SWG 1 subsequently moved to Rothamsted Manor, just outside Harpenden in Hertfordshire, where it had concentrated on the interception of wireless signals from the Continent. Known as Y1, Rothamsted played an important part in the reconstruction of the Luftwaffe's list of call signs, which was referred to as the BIRD book. In the absence of any useful Wehrmacht traffic, SWG 1 had homed in on Luftwaffe intercepts and had even devoted its training center at Farleigh Hungerford to monitoring the enemy air force.

As well as the regular radio operators who logged the intercepts and relayed them to Bletchley, SWG 1 eventually accommodated a large number of intelligence officers who "had a talent for solving crossword puzzles." Some supervised the watches, switching men from covering one frequency to monitoring traffic on another. "Drop MUSTARD for LIGHT BLUE" was a familiar instruction from the duty officers who were responsible for judging which traffic was the more important. An SWG 1 offshoot, designated Y3, was later installed in the basement of St. Anne's Mansions near Broadway under the leadership of John Rendle to provide Menzies and the Prime Minister with a convenient and quick supply of RED intercepts. Y3's function was to shortcut GCHQ's normal channel of handling some of the more current decrypts so as to save time. Because the daily key to the Luftwaffe's RED traffic was usually available by eleven o'clock in the morning, Y3 became RED experts. Thus, the War Office's main, specialized wireless unit found itself dealing with material that some believed ought to have been handled by the RAF. The same was also true in North Africa, where the land war was being waged in earnest.

Soon after the creation of SWG 1, a second Special Wireless Group, SWG 2, had been formed in a disused brush factory in the center of

Trowbridge under Major C.A. Oliver. It had consisted of a mobile unit about 150 strong, and three direction-finding units, totaling about forty operators. Late in 1940, SWG 2 had been dispatched around the Cape to the Middle East to reinforce No. 2 Wireless Company at Sarafand in Palestine and, by March 1941, had established a second base in the King Farouk Museum at Heliopolis, next door to the RAF's signals station.

In 1940, command of No. 2 Wireless Company had passed from Major W. Scott to Major H. Winterbotham, and although the main base remained at Sarafand throughout the war, numerous smaller intercept units had sprung up under its control throughout the Middle East. The North African theater, however, remained under SWG 2's control from Heliopolis, with special wireless sections distributed among the three army corps headquarters. Each section was equipped with twenty HRO receivers and ten S27 sets for VHF work. In addition, the 110 Special Wireless Section had the use of three Decca Loop direction-finding vans.

Major Oliver's first task was the erection of a combined high-frequency and long-frequency remote direction-finding station out in the desert, about five miles east of the Heliopolis Museum and connected to it by a landline. Sixteen copper earth mats were placed six feet under the aerial array, which was built on four masts, each exactly three hundred feet apart, by a team of Italian prisoners of war. Once this work had been completed, SWG 2 began intercepting the enemy's signals, concentrating on the Luftwaffe's RED traffic which had already yielded. It was inevitable that SWG 2 should have begun with an easily identifiable set of enemy signals, but it meant that apart from a little tactical activity both Special Wireless Groups were effectively "taking in washing" for the RAF.

Meanwhile, further out in the desert, the mobile direction-finding vans were posted to the 4th Indian Division, which had been ordered to the Middle East in August 1939 and had fought the Italians in Eritrea. One particularly enterprising Signals officer attached to the 4th Indian Division at Bagush was a Lieutenant Barkworth, who had made considerable progress on some of the Wehrmacht's low-grade ciphers. He discovered that many of the Germans' battlefield communications were conducted in three-letter groups, which were easily breakable. Furthermore, it seemed that these signals were transmitted in a range between 1.2 and 3 megahertz and were, therefore, susceptible to interception by standard British army receivers. As a countermeasure the Germans had developed a special security grid for map references, but because the Afrika Korps tended to rely on British maps, it was a relatively simple matter to reconstruct the grid. The daily change in the grid was calculated by bringing down an artillery barrage on selected German positions and then intercepting the resulting wireless traffic. The German forward units invariably reported the position of the shelling to headquarters, and once Barkworth had discovered the grid reference he could break the rest of the three-letter code.

SWG 2 was quickly indoctrinated into the enemy's routine and learned all kinds of useful tips. The Italians, for example, kept good signals security and changed their call signs almost every day. However, their individual "fists" were so recognizable that such security measures were irrelevant. One important source of early intelligence was a daily report transmitted by the mobile repair workshop attached to the 15th Panzer Division. Each message included a special group of figures which never varied: number of tanks running, number under repair and number written off. For good measure the workshop included an estimate of anticipated fuel requirements compared to fuel stocks held. Such intelligence was invaluable to the British corps commanders. With help such as this, it did not take SWG 2 long to start work on their main task: the reconstruction of the enemy's list of call signs.

Once SWG 2 had taken delivery of some extra Adcock direction-finding equipment, it began operating in earnest by building substations at Siwa and Jarabub, the latter, technically, being located behind enemy lines. The DF results were so accurate that the positions of the powerful eighty-watt transmitters used by the Afrika Korps headquarters could be plotted with an accuracy of one hundred yards. SWG 2 later learned from experience that the best plots were obtained when the Germans used vertical radio masts, rather than the more complicated horizontal and center-fed dipoles. This itself was useful intelligence because it tended to indicate the impending departure of a particular unit; the vertical aerials were telescopic and could be dismantled at short notice. The bigger arrays were used by stations which did not expect to be on the move.

One of the first successes of the signals war in the desert took place at Sidi Rezegh, when the 4th Indian Division captured intact a German Horch *funkwagen* communications vehicle, complete with radio transmitter and Enigma machine. The Enigma was promptly delivered to Heliopolis for examination, along with a collection of clear-text messages which would provide the cryptanalysts with some useful clues to breaking old traffic. Such were the prizes available to the smaller SIGINT sections focusing on local, tactical traffic.

However, not everything worked in favor of the Allies. When Tobruk fell, No. 111 Special Wireless Section was captured by Italian troops although, miraculously, the enemy appeared not to realize the unit's significance. In any event, the Afrika Korps failed to spot that Major Oliver's men had succeeded in building up an impressively accurate list of their call signs which was incorporated into a document known as the ELEPHANT book. But while interservice SIGINT cooperation was good in North Africa, the situation was reversed at home, where the military intelligence bureaucrats in the War Office felt increasingly anxious about SWG 1's continued preoccupation with the Luftwaffe.

Stewart Menzies, as titular chief of GCHQ, had been locked for months in constant conflict with the DMI, Major-General Davidson. This was in part a struggle for control of Station X, which Davidson believed could operate with greater efficiency under the jurisdiction of the War Office. Menzies acknowledged that the arrangement of civilians working alongside service personnel, the two being subject to different standards of discipline, was unsatisfactory, but resisted Davidson's takeover bid.

In theory, the day-to-day administration of Bletchley had been left to Alastair Denniston, but in reality the reins of power were firmly in the hands of Captain E. G. G. Hastings RN, Menzies's personal representative at the park. Eddie Hastings had retired from the Royal Navy in 1937, having served as the DNI's liaison officer in Canada for the previous five years. In 1939, he had been invited to join SIS and, as Menzies's nominee, had been appointed to Denniston's Joint Committee of Control, GCHQ's governing board which drew its members from GCHQ (Travis and Tiltman) and SIS (Fred Winterbotham and Richard Gambier-Parry). Unfortunately, Denniston did not excel as a personnel manager, and a series of internal disputes arose following the famous letter to Churchill of October 21, 1941, which had catalogued many of the difficulties that were handicapping the work at Bletchley. Hastings played a masterly rearguard action for SIS, but the pressure for reform had been too great. In Davidson's view, the War Office had devoted a considerable amount of its resources to the interception program, but had gained relatively little in terms of hard intelligence.

Menzies's compromise with Davidson was a secret inquiry, which was conducted into GCHQ's efficiency by a former Deputy DMI, Major General K.J. Martin, during the winter of 1941. The dissension had been aggravated by the growing number of self-styled intelligence "professionals" who had been drafted into Bletchley to translate and analyze the ever-increasing volume of Enigma decrypts. Although these officers were technically attached to the Secret Intelligence Service for the du-

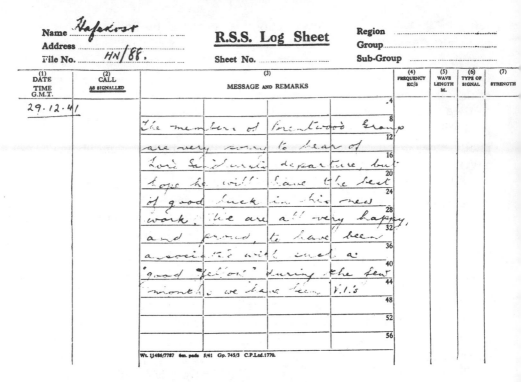

ration of their posting to Station X, their loyalties lay with the service organizations from whence they had come; they were soon in conflict with the civilian "old hands" who had hitherto been responsible for selecting particular decrypts for distribution. It had been the well-established practice for the individual sections to study the translated decrypts and then issue appreciations or summaries, instead of circulating the exact text of the originals. This, of course, had developed from the view held by those who had served in Room 40 that release of unexpurgated decoded messages invariably led to faulty assessment by the recipients. The new arrivals disapproved of this supervisory role, which was believed to be mischievous interference, and demanded complete operational control for themselves, arguing that they understood the requirements of the client departments rather better than their civilian counterparts. Inevitably, Denniston resented this attitude, but Menzies attempted to keep the peace by transferring responsibility for the assessment sections to the respective senior Air and Military Intelligence representatives on the site. This system lasted only a short period, for they both fell out among themselves, as well as with Denniston.

The internal wrangling reached a peak in December 1941, with several officers hardly speaking to each other. Ironically, the unpleasantness had been caused by GCHQ's success with the German and Italian machine-cipher traffic, which had led to a merger between the German and Italian sections on August 21, 1941. Frank Birch had been placed in charge of the new section, with Wilfred Bodsworth as his deputy. The latter was a fine cryptographer, but a poor organizer, and not a little in awe of Professor Vincent who had once taught him, but was now his junior. Vincent had virtually taken command of the Italian subsection, along with a linguist named Crighton, whom William Clarke regarded as "useless and idle."

The political struggle had been particularly bitter in the Naval Section, which had been led by Clarke for many years. The atmosphere had not been helped by the personal antagonism between Clarke and Stewart Menzies. The feud had originated over Clarke's belief that Menzies held Clarke's father responsible for some embarrassment suffered by his wife's family during the Tranby Croft baccarat affair. Sir Edward Clarke QC had acted for the unsuccessful plaintiff, Sir William Gordon-Cumming, during this famous libel case, and Arthur Wilson, Menzies's relation by marriage, had been ruthlessly cross-examined in court. Clarke was apparently convinced that because Wilson had been ridiculed in court, Menzies held a grudge against him and was determined to destroy his career.

When Clarke fell ill late in November, Birch took the opportunity to persuade Denniston that the Admiralty should be allowed to have the complete texts of decrypts, rather than the summaries. Under the new system (Professor Sir) Harry Hinsley, from St. John's College, Cambridge, acted as an intelligence supremo and a group of NID staff, headed by Commander Gorley Putt RNVR, analyzed the current traffic. It was then all passed to Walter Ettinghausen (later Walter Eytan, Israel's ambassador to Paris) for collating before final delivery to the Admiralty.

Major-General Martin completed his inquiry into GCHQ late in January 1942, and his recommendations were accepted by Stewart Menzies the following month. The Joint Committee of Control was scrapped, and the Diplomatic and Commercial Sections were transferred to Berkeley Street in Mayfair, under Denniston, who was given the title Deputy Director (C). The various service sections remained at Station X under Travis, who became Deputy Director (S). Thus, in one swift move the somewhat hidebound Denniston had been removed to London and Travis had been handed complete control of Bletchley Park. In addition, the individual heads of section, including those who were civilians, were granted full operational control of their service contingents.

The spring of 1942 proved to be a crucial period for GCHQ, which had now grown to comprise some 1,500 staff and was handling an average of 25,000 Wehrmacht and Luftwaffe decrypts, and around 14,000 German navy signals a month. Among the new recruits were such figures as Leonard Palmer (later Professor of Comparative Philology at Oxford), Henry Reed, the poet, two future politicians, Roy Jenkins and (Sir) Edward Boyle, Asa (now Lord) Briggs, Dennis Babbage, the writer (Sir) Angus Wilson and (Lord) Noel Annan.

In his capacity as Deputy Director (C), Denniston led a small delegation to Washington, hot on the heels of a party from the Y Committee, consisting of high-echelon members of the three services and the Foreign Office. The Y Committee took the political decisions, such as the division of responsibility for the interception of signals on an international basis and the general coordination of effort in the SIGINT field. Once these formalities had been completed, Denniston was able to brief the Americans on the progress achieved against the German Enigma with Station X's bank of forty-nine Bombes and to persuade them to concentrate on the Japanese. Accompanying him was Hugh Foss, then GCHQ's principal Japanese cryptographer. Although Denniston had much to boast about, there had been certain developments earlier in the year which had given cause for concern.

The year had begun well with three further Luftwaffe keys (GADFLY, HORNET and WASP) succumbing on January 1. These had turned out to be the operational signal traffic for Fliegerkorps X, IV and IX respectively, and they shed important light on the enemy's air movements on the eastern front and in North Africa. COCKROACH, LOCUST, FOXGLOVE and PRIMROSE followed within a matter of days, the two insects being keys used by the Luftwaffe in France and Sicily. Then, without warning, disaster had struck.

The success of the U-boat fleet in the Atlantic had been declining steadily, thanks largely to the Admiralty's policy of routing convoys away from the known positions of enemy submarines. Regular signals reporting current positions enabled the Operational Intelligence Center to issue very precise sailing instructions to merchant shipping before embarkation, and any subsequent alterations were transmitted by wireless from London, but always citing a plausible pretext and never quoting intercepts as a reason for changing course. This precaution was wise because, as has already been seen, the Royal Navy's main ciphers had been thoroughly compromised and most of the Admiralty's traffic was being read on a regular basis. The Allied convoys thus largely avoided making contact with the U-boat packs. For a two-month period, about this time, the Naval Section in Hut 8 had beaten every record and had read the enemy's DOLPHIN traffic within an hour of transmission. Although the Germans did not know this, they had become increasingly uneasy about the security of their communications; in June 1941, they introduced a special grid system to improve the method of position reporting, and two months later references to individual U-boat numbers in messages were scrapped in favor of the names of their commanders. This precaution caused a few problems for Hut 4, where the Naval Section's processing was undertaken, but a massive nominal card index of personalities had dealt with this difficulty except for an occasional hiccup when a commander was transferred to a new submarine. A month later, in September 1941, DOLPHIN had been replaced by another key, which hardly interrupted Bletchley's work. U-boat performance, however, was still deteriorating at such a dramatic rate that by mid-November Admiral Doenitz decided to impose a radical measure: henceforth his U-boats would be issued with a special Enigma machine, the "Schlüssel 4M," equipped with an extra internal rotor, bringing the total to four. It was to be known as Triton, and the prefix of Beta Beta in message preambles would indicate its use.

This modified machine was code-named SHARK by GCHQ, and its general introduction was greatly feared at Station X. Eventually, on February 1, 1942, the dreaded Beta Beta preambles materialized, and the subsequent U-boat traffic resisted virtually all attack, with appalling consequences for Allied merchant fleets. In November 1942, 190 Allied ships totaling 729,000 tons were sunk. The U-boat arm was also more numerous. Doenitz had begun the year with just 91 operational submarines; by the end, his construction program had increased the number to 212. Furthermore, various technical improvements had greatly increased the range and time spent at sea by the fleet, and the new "milch-cow" boats were enabling U-boat packs to be refueled and replenished at sea. The only effective defense against the marauding submarines was "special intelligence," but Bletchley had been baffled by SHARK. At first it had been assumed that the extra rotor on the Schlüssel 4M meant that there was now a choice of four out of a possible nine rotors, in place of the conventional three out of eight. Such a development would have involved a staggering increase in the permutations available from the current level. Instead of racing through 16,900 rotor settings, the Bombes were apparently confronted with an additional factor of some 234.

Clearly a shortcut was needed and the Naval Section, which had grown to nearly one thousand people, assigned several of its most talented cryptographers to the German subsection dealing with the enemy's hand ciphers. As well as the various Enigma keys, the German navy also employed some twenty-seven different hand ciphers, of which six were high grade. One, the *Reservehandverfahren*, was used whenever an Enigma machine broke down, and this had been solved manually by James Hogarth, a Sorbonne and Edinburgh University educated recruit from the Scottish Department of Health. He was part of a team that included (Sir) John H. Plumb, later Professor of Modern English History at Cambridge, Bentley Bridgewater, then the Assistant Keeper of the British Museum, and Charles Carr, later Professor of German Language and Literature at St. Andrews. Carr had become an accomplished cryptographer through his experience with the three-letter *Seenotfunksignaltafel*, the enemy's air-sea rescue service's radio code. Designed to be read with speed and to identify the position of downed Luftwaffe crews, the system had been tapped since July 1940 and had enabled British patrol craft to reach many of the enemy airmen in the Channel before the Germans.

Together the hand-cipher section studied the intercepted manual traffic for possible cribs into the machine traffic and developed an ingenious aid known as "gardening." This involved the Royal Navy undertaking provocative operations with the intention of generating predictable wireless traffic. A particular favorite was the laying of mines in areas thought by the Germans to have been cleared. Once a new mine was discovered, it would be reported and minesweepers would be deployed until the short signal for "route cleared" was transmitted. Interception of this single message was often enough for the Bletchley analysts to isolate the text and discover the daily change in the cipher.

The clues to SHARK were obtained on just two occasions in February when, due to a breach of German security, particular texts appeared exactly to match the length of other DOLPHIN messages. The relative complexity of SHARK was demonstrated by the time needed to isolate each of the three daily keys by working backward through these texts. No less than six (three-rotor) Bombes had to be left in continuous operation for seventeen days. This reverse procedure gave the Hut 8 cryptanalysts a startling discovery. The fourth rotor was permanent, and because the short signal book was still in use for certain routine messages, such as meteorological reports, and had been based on the old three-letter groups, the extra rotor had been put into neutral. This arrangement was confirmed with the aid of a decrypt dated March 14, 1942, announcing

Admiral Doenitz's promotion, which had been duplicated to U-boat commanders and those in home waters using DOLPHIN. If the SHARK texts employing just three moving rotors could be isolated, the same daily settings with the fourth rotor could be attacked with relative ease. The problem, of course, was spotting these signals, and as there did not seem to be any obvious traffic analysis method of doing this, the cryptographers went back to the drawing board to design another electromagnetic relay machine capable of handling the vast number of permutations. Even if the fourth rotor was fixed (and not interchangeable with the others), it still had the effect of multiplying the permutations by twenty-six and raising the number of possible settings to 439,000 separate possibilities.

Bletchley's only consolation was that the new units had not been distributed to the surface fleet. SHARK's entry into service heralded an impressive improvement in the fortunes of the U-boats, and this was the cause of the unease expressed by the Americans when Denniston made his first visit to Washington. How could he expect the U.S. Navy to leave Enigma decryption work to GCHQ if the U-boat menace threatened to sever Allied shipping links across the Atlantic? Denniston had pointed out that no less than twenty-six Luftwaffe and Wehrmacht keys (out of a total of fifty) had been tackled. He had also expressed some optimism about the prospects of breaking SHARK, which was not entirely justified.

If SHARK was a major headache for GCHQ, FISH seemed like a terminal illness. FISH was GCHQ's generic code name for a distinctive enemy signal that had been intercepted on a regular basis since the beginning of the war at the two Foreign Office bases at Grove Park and Sandridge. Traffic analysts had studied the system, which the Germans had called *Sägefisch*, and concluded that the traffic was a non-Morse radio Teletype. GCHQ's inability to break into the complicated cipher had become an increasing cause for concern, especially since there was always the possibility that the *Sägefisch* might replace the Enigma. The daily volume of messages exchanged had been escalating steadily, and there seemed little prospect of decryption. A small team, led by Major Tester, had been concentrating on the problem at Bletchley for many months in an outhouse known as the Testery. Among those who worked there were Roy Jenkins and Peter Benenson (later of Amnesty International), and although considerable progress on the theory of FISH had been made by the mathematicians W.H. Tutte and Peter Hilton (later Professor of Mathematics at Cornell University), it was only the capture of two complete machines in North Africa that transformed the somewhat gloomy situation.

FISH had been generated on several highly sophisticated ciphering teleprinters known to the Germans as *Geheimschreiber* or "secret writers." Some had been manufactured by Siemens (code-named STURGEON) and others by Lorenz (code-named TUNNY). Both models were much more bulky than the Enigma and worked at very high speed, employing an alternative to Morse known as the Baudot telegraph code, completely automatically. The operator simply typed a message on to the conventional keyboard of the machine, which enciphered it by passing the text through no less than ten coding rotors, and then transmitted the resulting groups at a rate of sixty-two words a minute. The receiving unit, with the decode switch selected, decrypted the message automatically and printed it on to a long paper tape, which was then cut up and pasted on to standard military telegram forms.

The capture of two *Geheimschreiber* by units of the Eighth Army enabled Major Tester to pass on the mechanical problem of creating a FISH Bombe to three eminent academics who were accommodated in Hut F: Max Newman (then University Lecturer in Mathematics at Cambridge), Donald Michie (later Professor of Machine Intelligence at Edinburgh) and Jack Good (later Professor of Statistics at the University of West Virginia), who was brought in from Hut 8. Later they were joined by as impressive a collection of mathematical brainpower as could be found anywhere in Station X. Among the new transfers were Shaun Wylie (a hockey international and president of the popular Bletchley Park Amateur Dramatics Society, as well as a brilliant topologist), Arthur Chamberlain, Michael Ashcroft, John H. Whitehead (later Professor of Pure Mathematics at Cambridge) and Michael Crum, son of the Canon of Canterbury. Together they designed a machine to process the paper tape generated by STURGEON and TUNNY and were then able to run through the mathematical sequence required to isolate the original cipher key. Most of the work on the first experimental device was undertaken by Dr. C.E. Wynn-Williams, a brilliant Cambridge physicist who had been seconded to GCHQ from the Telecommunications Research Establishment to help with the four-rotor Bombe needed for the SHARK intercepts. Later, additional assistance was obtained from four members of the GPO's Engineering Research Station at Brook Road, Dollis Hill: D.A. Campbell, Arthur Lynch, F.O. Morrell and E.A. Speight. This little-known branch of the Post Office had previously concentrated on developing high-speed electromagnetic trunk switching gear for telephone exchanges. Dollis Hill was already part of the Allied SIGINT effort as it was the location of one of the GPO's direction-finding networks (the other two stations being at Burnham and Baldock), and it also possessed many of the technical facilities needed to build a prototype. It had the added advantage of being completely secure, for the engineering staff (particularly W. W. Chandler and A. W. M. Coombs), under T. H. Flowers and S. W. Broadhurst, were familiar with secret projects. The Dollis Hill site, which had once formed part of Neasden golf course, had been considered so safe that an alternative Cabinet War Room code-named PADDOCK had been constructed in the grounds during the summer of 1940 in case the seat of government needed to be evacuated in an emergency. All in all, the Research Station fulfilled every qualification for it to become GCHQ's clandestine workshop.

Dollis Hill's first FISH Bombe was delivered to Bletchley early in June 1942 and became known as the Robinson because its extraordinary construction, with wheels and pulleys guiding loops of perforated paper tape, resembled one of the bizarre and impractical contraptions inspired by the cartoonist Heath Robinson. Its objective was to pass two tapes at synchronized speed through two photoelectric readers which, when working properly, were capable of scanning two thousand telegraphic characters a second, and then to feed the information onto a series of electronic binary counters for comparison. The results were printed out on a sort of early electric typewriter. In spite of its odd appearance, novel design (incorporating nearly eighty valves) and temperamental behavior (it occasionally got too hot and began to smolder), it produced excellent results and a further twenty-four machines were ordered. The only limitation on the Robinsons seemed to be the loops of paper tape, which frequently broke under prolonged pressure. The problem was eventually overcome by linking five machines together and running them in tandem. Some 425 Wrens and engineers were to be employed by GCHQ's latest unit, the Fish Machine Section, but even as the extra machines were being built, Tommy Flowers had turned his attention to a mammoth super-Bombe, equipped with more than 1,500 valves and carrying the appropriate code name COLOSSUS.

The proliferating FISH traffic caused the Foreign Office's interception work to be transferred, under Commander Kenworthy's leadership, to an entirely new, purpose-built station known as the Foreign Office Research and Development Establishment. This was located at Ivy Farm, high on the Downs just outside Knockholt Pound in Kent, where more than six hundred skilled operators were eventually employed to log FISH traffic and relay it by landline teleprinter to Bletchley. The intercepts from Knockholt were considered to be of excellent quality, especially those logged at night, and the site continued in operation for more than a decade before moving to Culmhead, outside Taunton. The first non-Morse signals from Knockholt to be broken proved to be high-grade Wehrmacht communications on a TUNNY link between Vienna and Athens, and confirmed the suspicion that top echelon messages, especially those with the greatest strategic content, were reserved for this particular "secure" Teletype channel. Henceforth, it was to be GCHQ's most valued source.

It was not until December 13, 1942, that the optimism expressed by Denniston earlier in the year in Washington was to be justified. On that date SHARK, the four-rotor Enigma U-boat traffic, finally surrendered. This breakthrough resulted not from the painstaking development of the four-rotor Bombe, but from the capture of documents on a submarine sunk in the Mediterranean off Port Said six weeks earlier.

Soon after dawn on October 30, a Sunderland flying boat had spotted a Type VIIC oceangoing submarine some seventy miles north of the Nile Delta. HMS *Hero* had been alerted by radio and the destroyers *Pakenham*, *Petard*, *Dulverton* and *Hawarth* had raced to the scene from Port Said. Although the *U-559* had failed to notice the flying boat, it had detected the *Hero*'s approach and had promptly submerged.

The hunt continued for sixteen hours, during which the elusive submarine was constantly depth charged, but it was not forced to the surface until much later the same night. The *U-559* was so close, when it was picked out in a searchlight, that HMS *Petard* could not depress her main armaments enough, but instead opened up with Oerlikons. The *U-559*'s commander, Korvettleutnant Hans Heidtmann, promptly gave the order to abandon ship and the *Petard*'s captain, Mark Thornton, maneuvered his destroyer to within sixty yards. While the Germans jumped into the water and swam for the *Petard*'s whaleboat, Lieutenant Tony Fasson and Able Seaman Colin Grazier stripped off their clothes, dived naked into the sea and made their way to the submarine's conning tower which, by this time, was only just visible above the waves. Fasson and Grazier clambered down into the deserted pressure hull where, much to their surprise, they were joined by a young NAAFI canteen assistant, Tommy Brown. On the spur of the moment, and without orders, Brown had decided to give them a hand. Inside, the submarine's lights were still burning, and the three men succeeded in grabbing a four-rotor Enigma machine from the radio room and an armful of charts and a list of what turned out to be current SHARK keys. These items were handed to Brown who remained close to the hatch, and he just managed to transfer them to the whaler before the submarine went under. The U-boat's engineer, one of the forty Germans rescued, later confirmed that he had opened the submarine's seacocks before his departure with the intention of sinking the *U-559* straightaway. The slight delay had given Fasson and Grazier an opportunity to recover the Enigma prize, but at the last moment neither had been able to escape.

In guarded terms HMS *Petard* reported its find by radio and was ordered to sail for Haifa at full speed, escorted by HMS *Dulverton*. There the destroyer was met by Naval Intelligence officers, who sent the *U-559*'s Enigma and a list of SHARK keys by courier to London. Fasson and Grazier were posthumously awarded George Crosses for their bravery, although no details were released of the exact circumstances of their deaths. Tommy Brown was also decorated with the George Medal, but subsequent inquiries by the Admiralty revealed that he was then only sixteen years old and had lied about his age to join the navy. This made him the youngest recipient of the George Medal. He was immediately discharged and sent home to North Shields, where two years later he was killed in another act of heroism, attempting to rescue his younger sister who had been trapped by fire in their slum tenement after an air raid.

Brown probably had little idea of the value of the material he had helped recover from the *U-559*, but his contribution had been overwhelming. Suddenly, after all the disappointments of the previous six months, Station X was poised, once again, to dominate the Allied intelligence scene.

7

GCHQ

GCHQ had made a crucial contribution to the Allied execution of the war in several theaters, not the least of which was North Africa and the Battle of the Atlantic. In the world at large, only a tiny handful knew the extent of the secret wireless war, but the Prime Minister was one of them and, after the relief of Malta early in 1942, Churchill made a second visit to his "most secret source" to congratulate Bletchley Park's staff. He rarely made any public mention of his "most secret source," but after the war he commented, somewhat obliquely, in *Their Finest Hour*:

> This was the secret war, whose battles were lost or won unknown to the public; and only with difficulty comprehended, even now, by those outside the small high scientific circles concerned. No such warfare had ever been waged by mortal men. The terms in which it could be recorded or talked about were unintelligible to ordinary folk. Yet if we had not mastered its profound meaning and used its mysteries even while we only saw them in the glimpse, all the efforts, all the prowess of the fighting airmen, all the bravery and sacrifices of the people, would have been in vain.

Many of the earliest Enigma keys broken at Bletchley were directly relevant to the Afrika Korps. LIGHT BLUE, for example, was particularly useful in revealing the Luftwaffe's plans and its later derivatives, for individual Fliegerkorps, proved of tremendous value to the commanders in the field. In December 1941, Hitler had appointed the Luftwaffe general, Albrecht Kesselring, as Commander in Chief South, so many of the Luftwaffe's compromised channels yielded important information about the Wehrmacht's intentions. One memorable signal from Kesselring was a long-awaited, top-priority message, which was decoded with ease at Bletchley. It turned out to be an order for the Commander in Chief's silk pajamas. Such decrypts were destroyed to prevent indiscreet dinner-party gossip.

During Operation CRUSADER in the Western Desert, a wealth of enemy documents was captured from the 15th Panzer Division at Tobruk, including the keys to CHAFFINCH and PHOENIX. CHAFFINCH had consisted of three separate Enigma channels advising store depots at Salonika and Rome on the Afrika Korps's logistical requirements. PHOENIX had turned out to be Rommel's main method of communicating with his units, a prize of inestimable value for the Eighth Army. Analysis of CHAFFINCH and PHOENIX betrayed Rommel's complete order of battle, and General Montgomery was kept informed, on a daily basis, of the enemy's losses and reserves. Routine SIGINT operations, such as direction finding and call sign analysis, also played a vital role on the battlefield. SWG2 direction-finding stations often identified the various Panzer divisional headquarters and monitored their movements. When Rommel found himself outmaneuvered by his opponent, he voiced his anxiety about German signal security to the High Command in Berlin, where he was scorned.

Allied experience in the desert was to pay dividends later. It was soon learned that Italian infantry commanders had a standard surrender message which usually read: "We will defend the sacred soil of Africa with our last drop of blood. Long live the King. Long live the Duce." Such a message invariably indicated that a particular unit was ready to capitulate immediately and could be captured without a fight. The nearest Allied unit was advised, and the Italians invariably surrendered without a shot being fired! Another useful text was the daily garrison medical report. Like most soldiers in the desert, the Italians were prone to hemorrhoids, but their prudish code book had no single cipher group for the word. Consequently, the operators had to spell the word out in full every day, which immediately compromised the daily subtraction number used to alter the original code-numbers.

Further information concerning the enemy had also been supplied by a specialist organization, the Combined Services Detailed Interrogation

Center (CSDIC), which supervised the questioning of enemy prisoners of war. Designated MI19, CSDIC was headed by A. R. (Dick) Rawlinson, who reported to Norman Crockatt of MI9, the Deputy DMI in charge of the Secret Intelligence Service's escape and evasion arm. Although head-quartered in England, CSDIC built several local camps in North Africa. During the course of CRUSADER, a Wehrmacht signals sergeant had been captured and taken to CSDIC's regional cage at Bir Quadem, where he had supplied answers to a number of questions concerning the enemy's radio procedures. This intelligence had been relayed by CSDIC to Bletchley, where it had been gratefully received. On another occasion, one of Rommel's radio intelligence companies, designated Unit 621, was surprised by the Australian 9th Division at Tel El Eisa. The German officer in charge, Captain Seebohm, had been killed in the fighting, but his second in command, Leutnant Hertz, had surrendered and supplied CSDIC with valuable information, including details of Allied inefficiency and lack of security. Hertz once remarked that the Afrika Korps did not have to bother with breaking Eighth Army codes: "All we really need is linguists, the sort who were waiters at the Dorchester before the war." His advice was relayed to Montgomery's staff, who were reminded that the enemy listened in to virtually every radio telephone conversation.

A greater embarrassment for GCHQ was its possession of VUL-TURE, the Wehrmacht's Enigma key used generally throughout the Russian front. This had been broken on June 27, 1941, five days after the Nazi invasion of the Soviet Union, and had been followed a fortnight later by KESTREL, the combined Wehrmacht/Luftwaffe key employed on joint operations. The British government had long known of the Nazi plan, code-named BARBAROSSA, to invade Russia, but the Soviet authorities, and Stalin in particular, had refused to heed the warnings. An indoctrinated MI6 officer, Cecil Barclay, was one of only a few of the British Embassy staff in Moscow to know of Bletchley Park (having served in the Foreign Office's Communications Department before the war with Henry Maine and Harold Eastwood). His task was to deliver timely warnings to his Soviet counterpart, General F.F. Kuznetsov, without compromising his source. However, it now seems likely that official attempts to alert the Kremlin were matched by decidedly unofficial sources—the NKVD's sources within the intelligence community in London. Kim Philby, Guy Burgess, Anthony Blunt, John Cairncross and Leo Long were (to name but a few) all actively engaged in secret intelligence operations and all were, to a greater or lesser extent, privy to the Station X material. Cairncross and Long were in especially useful positions for the Soviets, as they were interpreting SIGINT data relevant to Germany's eastern flank and developing a comprehensive assessment of the enemy's order of battle. Cairncross undertook these duties from Hut 6, the heart of Bletchley's activities, while Long, another self-confessed Soviet mole, concentrated on the identification of individual German formations. Both had access to the broad picture drawn by the Enigma decrypts (rather than the narrower, Abwehr field studied by Philby and Blunt) and communicated regularly with Soviet case officers operating under diplomatic cover from the Embassy in London.

GCHQ's relative position of influence within the Allied intelligence structure was in part a reflection of the poor performance by the other organizations. The Secret Intelligence Service had largely been reduced to a liaison department, exploiting information from foreign networks that had taken refuge in England. The Vichy French, for example, boasted excellent contacts in enemy-occupied territory, and André Bonfouce had actually been given accommodation in Bletchley Park so that he could keep in touch with the sections run by Knox and Strachey which were concentrating on the Abwehr's communications. Paul Paillole had remained in Provence until January 1942 when he had fled to Rabat, complete with his cryptographic files hidden in tennis-ball cartons. Paillole continued to operate from North Africa, and SIS maintained a link with him via Tangier.

Stewart Menzies must have recognized the weakness of his organization's position but, ever the shrewd manipulator, he consolidated his relationship with the Prime Minister by purveying personally the Ultra summaries and continued to exercise almost complete control over Allied SIGINT at Bletchley through Captain Hastings. Certainly, it was the only field where Menzies could demonstrate some success. His agents in France, initially at least, were actually part of an independent Polish stay-behind network. Based in Paris, the INTERALLIE group were directed from London by the Polish Director of Military Intelligence, Colonel Stefan Mayer. He had relocated the Polish Deuxième Bureau-in-exile in the Rubens Hotel and, with Menzies's approval, had built a powerful receiving and transmitting station at Woldingham, in Surrey. The Poles had also taken over a small electronics factory in Letchworth, where they had built a series of experimental, clandestine radios, known as the BP3 and the AP4. None of the Polish models was ready for operational use until 1943, so in the meantime SIS supplied INTERALLIE with a Mark XV set from Whaddon. This was delivered in December 1940, but the link had proved unsatisfactory until May the following year when a regular schedule had been established. Three more Mark XVs had followed, but by the end of 1941 INTERALLIE's entire network had been penetrated by the enemy and all the sets came under German control. Neither Whaddon nor Woldingham realized the scale of the deception until early in 1942, when several well-planned operations went wrong and it became clear that INTERALLIE's security had been thoroughly compromised by the Abwehr.

The elimination of INTERALLIE as a source of reliable information left only ALLIANCE, an embryonic resistance group working under the protection of the Vichy Deuxième Bureau. Wireless contact had been started with Whaddon in March 1941 via a French operator named Laroche, who had been trained in London by SIS and then parachuted back into Vichy territory near Clermont-Ferrand equipped with a Mark XV set. Several more agents had followed, but in August another operator, a Londoner with a French background, had turned out to be a Fascist sympathizer and had defected to the Abwehr almost as soon as he had landed. Using the call sign SHE, the traitor had maintained his schedule for the benefit of the Abwehr and had thereby compromised virtually all the ALLIANCE members. Once again, the Abwehr had taken control of an SIS radio circuit and had successfully manipulated it for its own ends.

This, then, was the background of the struggle that was waged between Menzies and Hastings on the one hand and their recently created rival, Special Operations Executive, on the other. SOE was justified in its skepticism of the performance of its "professional" elder and felt inhibited by the restrictions imposed in the communications field. Such radio links as existed with the Continent were firmly in SIS's grip. Menzies argued forcefully to keep SOE dependent upon Whaddon, but in March 1942 SOE's recently knighted director, Sir Charles Hambro, finally triumphed and acquired the right for SOE's French Section to use its own code and ciphers. Brigadier F. W. Nicholls, who had formerly commanded No. 2 Wireless Company in Sarafand, was installed in Baker Street as Director of Communications, and by May 1942 SOE was operating seven F Section wireless sets in France. Nicholls wasted no time in constructing his own organization and took over four estates in Oxfordshire to train wireless agents and run receiving stations. Thame Park was designated "Special Training School No. 52" and used to accommodate French Section volunteers, while Grendon Underwood and Poundon House became STS 53A and 53B respectively. A large transmitter was built on Signal Hill (STS 53C), just outside Poundon (which is still used by the Diplomatic Wireless Service), and an operator-training center,

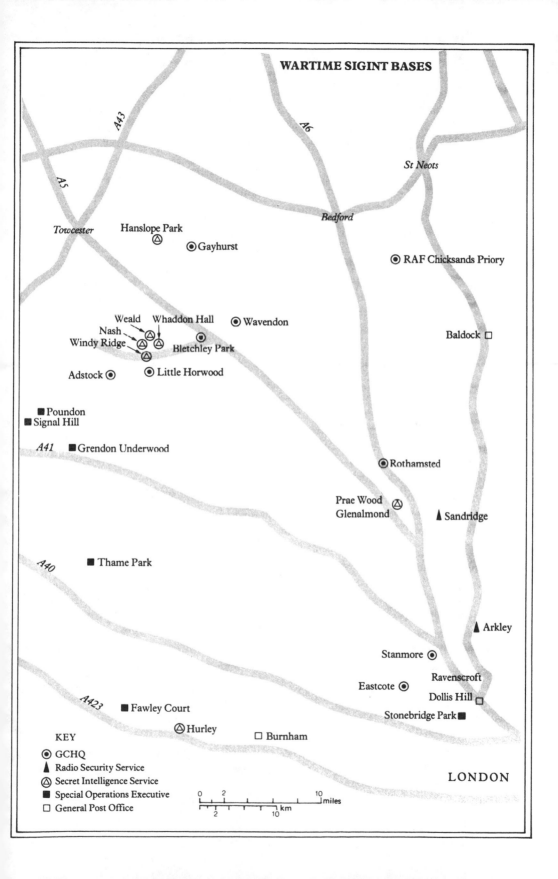

STS 54, was established at Fawley Court, near Henley. In addition, Belhaven House, General Orde Wingate's Scottish home in Dunbar, was requisitioned as STS 52D for signaling to Scandinavia. Within a year of his appointment, Nicholls had developed a sophisticated network and was in touch with some thirty SOE wireless sets in occupied Europe. SOE's demand for suitable equipment was unable to be met by Whaddon, so Nicholls also established a small factory at Stonebridge Park, north London, under the direction of a talented prewar radio amateur, John Brown, who subsequently designed and developed the B3, SOE's main clandestine set, of which more than seven hundred were eventually built and which set the standard for the rest of the world in portable transceivers.

One of the agreements made by Denniston during his first visit to Washington in 1942 had concerned the division of cryptographic labor he had advocated. The deal involved the exchange of a Bombe for the U.S. Navy in return for the U.S. Army's promise to concentrate on Japanese signals. The idea was to avoid wasteful duplication, and in June 1942 three American cryptanalysts arrived at Bletchley railway station to be escorted to the Park by Bill Marchant. Paul K. Whitaker, Selmer Norland and Arthur Levenson were the first three Americans to be introduced into the marvels of Bletchley Park. Later, they were to be followed by numerous distinguished figures, such as William Bundy (later an Assistant Secretary of State and editor of *Foreign Affairs*); Alfred Friendly (the *Washington Post*'s former managing editor); Lewis Powell (a future Supreme Court judge); Langdon Van Norden (president of the Metropolitan Opera Guild); and Inser Wyatt (a New York judge).

These selected Americans were allowed to learn the secrets of Ultra, although the full implications were only grasped by a handful who somehow gained access to all the many facets of the British SIGINT picture —the Y services, the Radio Security Service (now under new management following Lord Sandhurst's transfer to SCU 1 in January 1942), Fred Winterbotham's SLU, Gambier-Parry's SCUs, the Special Wireless Groups, and the rest. But even if relatively few Americans knew the full range of the secret wireless war, enough was known of MI6's failures to make the embryonic American intelligence organization, the Office of Strategic Services (OSS), very wary. OSS boasted what seemed by comparison to MI6's meager resources to be an unlimited supply of men and material. As had happened in the case of SOE, Menzies made a skillful attempt to dominate the fledgling OSS by demanding that the Americans restrict their secret communications to codes supplied by GCHQ. The negotiations continued until January 1943, when Menzies was obliged to admit defeat and OSS exercised its right to make and use its own ciphers.

From Menzies's viewpoint 1943 had got off to a poor start. The assertion of American independence at OSS was followed the next month by Dilly Knox's death and the closure of the intercept station at Murmansk. This had operated since the Nazi invasion in support of the Arctic convoys, but somehow word had leaked to Moscow that its activities had not been limited to German traffic. As soon as the Soviets realized that their own signals had been monitored, it was summarily closed down and the Admiralty's Y team repatriated.

Owing to this mutual suspicion, relations with the Soviets became somewhat strained in the SIGINT field. Now, of course, that we know the Russians possessed their own *sub rosa* sources within the British intelligence community, it is possible to see how skeptical they must have been of their new Allies, knowing as they did that the British explanations for the source of the Ultra material were bogus. Sometimes they were told that the information had come from a disgruntled Austrian prisoner of war; at other times the cover was an unnamed spy in the German War Office. Neither story showed much trust by Britain in her Soviet ally. Both stories were intended to conserve Station X's integrity, because GCHQ was dubious, for its part (and with plenty of justification), of the standards of Soviet security. Bletchley argued that if a substantial proportion of the Red Army's traffic was being read by friendly forces with only minimal effort, what results might be being achieved by the Nazis who would obviously have targeted the Soviets? The closure of the Murmansk station tended to frost the inter-Allied atmosphere further, although Anglo-American relations were becoming more friendly all the time and, on May 17, 1943, culminated in the BRUSA pact.

BRUSA was the cryptonym given to the world's first major SIGINT agreement between two foreign powers, Britain and the USA. In the past there had been several examples of cooperation, such as the tripartite exchanges between Paris, London and Warsaw in the prewar era. These, of course, had been of an informal nature and had diplomatically omitted any discussion of mutual monitoring. This was just as well as GCHQ had been tapping French communications with considerable success for years, and Denniston would never have consented to an agreement limiting his organization. In any event, such a ban would be difficult to enforce, and it could always be said that mutual monitoring is an essential ingredient of mutual trust. Far better to be advised of a security weakness by a friend than discover it too late from an enemy.

BRUSA's purpose was to eliminate wasteful duplication of effort, establish secure means for the exchange and distribution of information (including the general introduction of the CCM, the Combined Cipher Machine) and create spheres of SIGINT interest. The historic agreement was negotiated with the Foreign Office and GCHQ by William Friedman (who had recovered from his breakdown); the author Telford Taylor (representing U.S. Military Intelligence) and Colonel Alfred McCormack, a New York lawyer and head of the newly formed Signal Corps Special Branch. Since Pearl Harbor, McCormack had been engaged on a review of America's SIGINT capability and its numerous shortcomings. He found that the entire area was a story of neglect and interservice rivalry. He noted that on the outbreak of the war in Europe, the still neutral U.S. Signal Intelligence Service had increased its full-time strength from 7 to 19, and that on the day Pearl Harbor had been attacked the service still had a staff of only 331. At his recommendation the Signal Intelligence Service underwent a speedy expansion and an entirely new branch of the War Department was created to evaluate and assess enemy decrypts. Known at first as the Signal Security Division, the new group employed twenty-eight officers and fifty-five civilians, and underwent several name changes until it acquired the title Signal Security Agency (which it retained until July 1943, when it was renamed the Signal Security Service). At the end of 1942, the agency had established itself at Arlington Hall, an imposing mansion in Virginia, just across the Potomac from Washington, that had formerly accommodated an expensive girls' school. In addition, a major intercept base was built at Vint Hill Farm, outside the small town of Warrenton, in the same state. Under the terms of BRUSA, the new organization was to collaborate with the British in India and examine the as yet untapped Japanese military traffic.

Once the political and bureaucratic niceties had been disposed of, the SIGINT experts could get down to the business of synchronizing their procedures. In official jargon, the secret BRUSA agreement provided for "a full exchange of cryptographic systems, cryptanalytical techniques, direction finding, radio interception and other technical communication matters." In practical terms, it was an exercise in standardizing the SIGINT work of the two countries. Both sides adopted the code word Ultra as a generic standard and harmonized three lesser classifications: DEXTER, CORRAL and RABID for U.S. forces, while GCHQ stuck to PEARL, THUMB and ZEAL. German and Italian Enigma traffic was to be left to GCHQ's Bombes, with the U.S. Navy integrating its effort against the U-boat signals with Bletchley. This left the U.S. War Department to concentrate on the Japanese military ciphers and to liaise with GCHQ's intercept assets in the Far East. Friedman, Taylor and McCormack were to spend two months in England, and while they were there it became known that Admiral Isoroku Yamamoto, the Commander in Chief of the Imperial Navy, who had masterminded the raid on Pearl Harbor, had been ambushed in the air over the South Pacific on his way to inspect a garrison on the island of Rabaul. How did the Americans know Yamamoto's itinerary? It had been revealed four days earlier in a decrypted signal. Sixteen Lightnings shot down his bomber and escort, but in doing so jeopardized MAGIC, or at least risked the Japanese changing the particular JN cipher used in that sector. In the event, the Japanese did not attribute Yamamoto's death to poor signal security, but it was Station X's firmly held opinion that such coups should be avoided. Friedman's party continued its survey of GCHQ's "security principles and methods," and it is not surprising that they were impressed by GCHQ's organization.

By June 1943, the number of staff employed at GCHQ had grown to 5,052, of which rather more than half, 2,635, were civilians. Many had been recruited by word of mouth, by relatives at Bletchley Park, but the demand for linguists was sufficiently great to justify the placing of discreet advertisements in *The Times*. The Naval Section, which had begun the war with a strength of 24, had now reached 1,000. Not all, of course, were based at Station X, where the huts had been supplemented by new brick blocks identified with letters. Thus Block D took in the old Huts 3, 6 and 8. Two brand new estates, at Canon's Corner in Stanmore and Lime Grove at Eastcote, were acquired as satellite stations to house the growing number of Bombes and handle the traffic. Both sites were, in many respects, similar to the new single-story buildings that had sprung up around the original wooden huts at Bletchley. Each block consisted of a dozen suites, every one of which had a pair of Bombe bays. Each bay gave access to a decoding room named after a country, a machine room which housed a Bombe, a workshop equipped with an electronic rectifier, and an engineering room staffed in shifts by specially selected Post Office engineers and RAF personnel. Although the decoding rooms and Bombes bore the names of Allied countries and ports, such as Trondheim and Narvik in the Norway bay, the work was all on German Enigma texts. The system had the dual purpose of introducing an element of healthy competition between the bays and giving the entire arrangement some cover in the unlikely event of an indiscretion. To be overheard discussing "Toulon" would not jeopardize security. The blocks themselves were grouped together in a compound, surrounded by high barbed-wire fences and guarded by armed Royal Marines. The Bombes were operated by hundreds of Wrens, all sworn to secrecy and billeted together in the neighborhood. At Eastcote the site occupied part of Eastcote Place, a property owned by the elderly widow of Sir John Anderson, formerly the chief executive of Guthrie & Co., the Far East merchants. She was never allowed to know the nature of the very secret work undertaken next door, which was simply referred to as "No. 2 Temporary Office Buildings, Lime Grove."

In accordance with the BRUSA pact, the Americans were not only privy to these arrangements, but actively participated in them. Indeed, John Tiltman, who had headed GCHQ's General Cryptographic Section, was appointed as a permanent liaison officer to the U.S. War Department in order to encourage profitable cross-fertilization. A tented U.S. Army encampment was put up in Ruislip Woods, close to Eastcote, and teams of American Signals Security cryptographers underwent indoctrination courses at Bletchley. The exchange also worked in reverse, with groups of GCHQ cryptographers moving to Washington to assist in tackling some Japanese hand ciphers. Thus George McVittie (later Professor of Mathematics at London University), Bletchley Park's expert on meteorological codes, crossed the Atlantic with Philip Howse and James Gillis to head a special section concentrating on JN36 and JN37, two of the Japanese Imperial Navy's keys used for weather reports.

Gradually the BRUSA pact forced a greater measure of cooperation among the Allies, and in November 1943 a second inter-Allied conference was convened in Washington, taking in the two original participants, with Canadian and Australian representatives. The venue was Arlington Hall, and the gathering that followed involved some thirty Allied officers, including many of the leading figures of the postwar SIGINT scene. Among them were Travis (who was to head GCHQ until his retirement in March 1952), Tiltman (subsequently GCHQ's liaison officer at the British Embassy in Washington until 1954) and L.J. (Joe) Hooper, later GCHQ's Director-General until his transfer to the Cabinet Office as the Intelligence Coordinator in 1973. The Canadian SIGINT organization, the Examination Unit of the National Research Council, sent Edward W. Drake, a Saskatchewan and subsequently its director. S.R. Clark, an Australian, represented the Central Bureau in Brisbane. Together these negotiators carved up the Allied SIGINT world and laid the foundations of BRUSA's successor, the UKUSA Treaty of 1947.

If there had been any lingering doubts anywhere in the Allied intelligence community concerning the comparative importance of SIGINT as a reliable source, they must surely have disappeared during 1943. Station X's expansion continued at a breathtaking rate, with around 150 new faces joining GCHQ each month. New Enigma keys were being identified and solved every week; there were also painful reminders that the human alternative to SIGINT was tragically fallible.

Evidence that even the best trained and best prepared of agents could be turned into instruments of counterproductive disinformation was uncovered by MI6 during the summer of 1943. Two SOE Dutch volunteers, who had parachuted back into Holland in March 1943, had been captured on arrival but had managed to escape from German custody and had reported that the previous year the Abwehr had coerced an SOE radio operator to exchange signals with London. The initial communications had led to a sophisticated deception campaign in which SOE's London Dutch Section had been persuaded of the existence of a large resistance organization covering most of the Netherlands and extending into Belgium and France. In reality, the entire network, which at one point boasted seventeen transmitters, had been run entirely by the Abwehr's counter-intelligence department. The *Englandspiel*, or English game, as it was known to the Germans, had begun in March 1942 soon after the arrest of an SOE agent, Hubertus Lauwers, who had been caught with his wireless set in The Hague. Lauwers later testified that he had only agreed to operate his transmitter, call sign RLS, because he had not compromised his security checks, the telltale prearranged warnings concealed in the texts of all messages that confirmed whether or not the operator was working at liberty or under duress. Lauwers was confident that London would spot that he had come under enemy control, but to his consternation SOE had acknowledged all his signals without apparently noting the absence of the secret security checks. By August 1941, the Germans had caught a further seven wireless operators and were running them in harness. Each of these operators had been trained either at one of MI6's training schools at Sloane Square in London or at TS7 St. Albans, or at one of SOE's radio centers at Fawley Court or at Thame Park in Oxfordshire. Here they had all been taught to give security checks and double checks to prove that their messages were authentic. To their astonishment, despite their *not* using these checks, SOE headquarters continued to maintain contact as if nothing had happened; some thought this was a deliberate maneuver to save their lives. Several agents tried to alert SOE to the situation by inserting words (at considerable risk to themselves) like "caught" into the texts prepared by the Germans, but their hints were ignored by inexperienced controllers who evidently could not bring themselves to believe that they had been duped. Indeed, on some occasions the SOE receiving station at Grendon Underwood actually reminded individual agents to include the security checks in their texts. During the eighteen months that the deception lasted, more than two thousand messages were exchanged between SOE stations in Oxfordshire and agents in German hands. The catastrophe led to hundreds of arrests and the execution of forty-seven SOE volunteers at Mauthausen concentration camp.

Exactly how quickly SOE responded to MI6's news that its Dutch organization was under enemy control remains a subject of controversy to this day. SOE subsequently suspended all its activities in Holland while the position was clarified, but similar penetrations were experienced elsewhere. In France, for example, skillful manipulation of key resistance cells led to thousands of arrests. In June 1943, another SOE agent, Gilbert Norman, was captured and he too maintained a radio link to London under German control. As a consequence, some 1,500 activists were rounded up by the Gestapo and several F Section circuits were decimated.

In defense of SOE and, indeed, of MI6, who were responsible for handling the first of the *Englandspiel* messages on behalf of SOE's Dutch Section before the creation of SOE's Signals Directorate in June 1942, there were considerable problems encountered when communicating with an agent working in hostile territory. The standard-issue transceivers could manage only a weak, twenty-watt signal, and conditions in the field were often far from ideal. Nervous tension often caused individual operators to make mistakes in coding their messages, and garbled texts were the norm rather than the exception. The texts also passed through several hands before reaching the relevant intelligence officer in London: the signal was received and acknowledged by the home station operator, who would pass it to cipher staff for decoding. It was then relayed by teleprinter to the final addressee in the appropriate organization's country section. In SOE's case, the teleprinters from the three main stations at Poundon, Grendon Underwood and Fawley Court in Oxfordshire terminated at the Directorate of Signals headquarters at 83 Baker Street. If one includes the possibility of an error in the original coding or transmitting, there were usually five separate opportunities for a message to be corrupted. It was therefore a matter of some fine judgment for the ultimate recipient to decide whether an agent, working under stress, had deliberately omitted a security check or had simply been a trifle careless. As often as not the controllers gave their agents the benefit of the doubt, a practice which had terrible implications for security. Inevitably SOE desperately wanted to believe in its agents, and it was not unknown for a home station operator to keep a listening schedule for weeks or even (on at least one occasion) months for a particular transmitter to make contact. The fact that a net had been established so late in the day, and against all the odds, was discounted in the elation that followed what purported to be news of an agent's safety. To make matters worse, some SOE personnel, especially in F Section, considered the verification checks superfluous and a bureaucratic waste of time, and some case officers even argued that the verification procedures were counterproductive, in that they might guarantee the authenticity of a traitor who had switched sides and betrayed all his checks. Attitudes like these caused SOE's security staff much concern. On February 1, 1945, a security officer wrote in a memo to SOE's Director of Security, Air Commodore Archie Boyle: "Many members of the security directorate have never been happy about the bland way Country Sections and Signals dismissed identity checks and certain mutilations." Boyle subsequently recommended a permanent security review of all traffic on a daily basis, but the belated proposition was only made six months after the cessation of hostilities in Europe.

Technical methods of confirming the identity of suspect operators were promoted from time to time; there was a process known as "radio finger-printing," in which the particular characteristics of each individual transmitter were recorded separately. Another system, code-named TINA, made a permanent recording of an agent's Morse technique so it could be compared to his (or her) later messages. It was widely believed that the system, which made a unique visual record of an agent's procedure, would highlight any change in a subject's transmitting characteristics. Unfortunately, TINA failed to live up to expectations. The resulting Morse "signatures" varied widely and sometimes did not indicate that a Sicherheitsdienst operator had been substituted even when this was known to be the case. Instead, cipher methods were updated with the more general introduction of one-time pads, in the place of antiquated double transposition tables, and regular schedules were abandoned in favor of less predictable timetables. SOE also changed to the Royal Naval system of avoiding a radio dialogue by sending and receiving messages at different times and on changing frequencies.

In spite of these precautions, the enemy took a heavy toll of SOE agents. Those who survived were obliged to make greater use of personal messages broadcast by the BBC from its two main sites at Crowborough and Rugby. This method was known to be monitored by the German B-Dienst, but it had the virtue of concealing the hidden message without compromising the location of any single clandestine set. MI6, on the other hand, still had to rely on passing lengthy cipher signals containing specific information, so an ingenious electronic cover was developed to deceive the opposition. Long before a new wireless circuit was placed in occupied territory, a duplicate "phantom" was given an airing in England, in the hope that the enemy's direction-finding services would log its appearance without noticing that some weeks later it had moved across the Channel. There was some evidence to suggest that the scheme achieved a measure of success, although the true winner of the secret wireless war waged over France was unquestionably Dr. Josef Goetz, a former schoolmaster who became the Sicherheitsdienst's radio expert in Paris. He was detained by MI5 in 1945 and interrogated, but was eventually released without charge, having given a very full account of his wartime activities and perhaps having earned some grudging respect from the Allied SIGINT experts anxious to discover the mistakes made by their predecessors. Certainly, not all the Allied clandestine services realized the skill of their opponents during the last months of the war, for Ernst Vogt, a former Sicherheitsdienst counterintelligence official, later recalled that "at the end of January 1945 English or American agents were still being parachuted into our hands through our radio-link with London. . . . We still had in Germany at the end of 1944 and in the beginning of 1945 two radio-links with London."

The net result of the demonstrable vulnerability of clandestine communications was a further battle in the struggle for supremacy waged between MI6 and SOE. SOE's misfortunes had a painful relevance for MI6, which, after all, was the traditional agent-running organization. MI6 had taken over the Radio Security Service from MI5 and had tried (and failed) to get a grip on the signal divisions of both SOE and OSS. German success at penetrating rings of Allied agents had confirmed many of the anti-MI6 prejudices nurtured by the services, so early in 1944 Stewart Menzies confounded his critics by strengthening his hold on the one area of MI6 operations which met with general approval—GCHQ. In February 1944, he shook up Bletchley's senior echelons, of which only a minority could probably recall the last coup—Birch's "palace revolution" of January 1942—by taking the style director-general and appointing Travis as his deputy. By June 1944, GCHQ's staff had grown to a wartime peak of 6,812. The following month, Combined Bureau Middle East at Heliopolis closed down and Freddie Jacob transferred to Washington as a liaison officer. One of the people most affected by these changes was Denniston, who had been treated for a stone in his bladder while on this third (and last) visit to Washington and had subsequently gone into hospital in Luton. Ill-health was the excuse for his premature retirement but, as was the case with Ewing some twenty-five years earlier, he felt bitter about his rejection. His son later observed:

> He got quite bad depression, which my mother called Scotch blight, in which he found it impossible to say anything for hours. . . . After he was fired from Bletchley he suffered enormously. . . . He was very irritable. He had lost confidence in himself, betrayed as he saw it, and so did many, by his friends—by Travis, his subordinate for so many years who now took his job—no evidence at all that he behaved badly—by de Grey, presumably they put Menzies up to it, and he never liked Menzies. . . . The privacy of his temperament, the secretness of the job meant not only total security but no delegation. He found delegation very difficult not because he was possessive (I don't think he was), he was a good and experienced cryptographer, but others like Knox and Cooper and Strachey might have been better and he knew it, and of course he readily acknowledged and supported the recruitment of the great mathematicians and chess players—areas in which he did not pretend to compete.[1]

It would seem that Menzies was utterly determined to exercise complete control over GCHQ, the issue becoming all the more urgent as GCHQ notched up triumph after triumph, while MI6 endured setbacks at the hands of the enemy. Clearly the business of infiltrating agents and saboteurs into a hostile environment was fraught with risk, but there was no obvious letup in the volume of operations during the last year of the war. Before D-Day, there was a considerable increase in the number of clandestine flights made into France, as might be expected, and there was a commensurate escalation in wireless traffic. For the Americans, who had played a relatively minor role in this particular field during 1943, the position changed in March 1944 when two special home stations were opened to communicate with clandestine U.S. forces, particularly teams of specially trained OSS agents, who were to act as pathfinders for the invasion. The first home station to begin operations was code-named VICTOR and was located at Ladye Place, a small country house in the picturesque village of Hurley in Berkshire. Initially, the base was staffed by forty-six experienced British operators, but gradually American technicians took over; the second home station, code-named CHARLIE, was at SOE's station at Signal Hill, Poundon.

During the weeks before the invasion, all the Allied radio nets shouldered a double responsibility: to maintain security surrounding the date and intended target area of the landings, and simultaneously to engage in the overall deception plan that had been conceived to confuse the enemy. Wireless played an important part in the Allied deception campaign since it was known, courtesy of the B-Dienst's Enigma traffic, that the enemy monitored all Allied tactical communications. Accordingly, a sophisticated plan was executed with the intention of misleading the opposition. Special equipment was developed to simulate the wireless traffic of dozens of different military formations, and located in areas that might have been used to concentrate forces in anticipation of an assault across the shortest part of the Channel, to the Pas-de-Calais. The ruse worked well, with the B-Dienst making continuous direction-finding reports from triangulation bearings indicating a buildup of troops in southeast England and East Anglia.

The sheer cunning exercised by some of the more skilled SIGINT practitioners was truly astonishing in its audacity. On occasions when the Luftwaffe's Y service selected a particularly elusive Enigma setting, the RAF would arrange to broadcast a coded message in a low-grade cipher, known to be compromised, with the sole intention of having it intercepted and decrypted by the enemy. As soon as a text of the same length appeared on the relevant German radio circuit, the cryptanalysts extracted it and, by working backward, identified the troublesome new key. Similar shortcuts proved highly effective in the Mediterranean theater, where two B-Dienst stations, at Noto and Erice in Sicily, were judged to be particularly susceptible to such ploys. Indeed, it was not unknown for a signal to be repeated at a slower speed if a German operator had reported difficulty in copying the Morse first time around. Between June 1943 and June 1944, no less than fifteen separate Luftwaffe keys were broken by Station X, and most succumbed to Bombe treatment within a few days of the traffic being isolated and identified.

GCHQ's continuing rate of success was in part due to the first COLOSSUS, which had been installed at Bletchley in December 1943. In March, the initial results were considered so promising that a second machine was ordered from Dollis Hill, with the stipulation that it should be delivered before June 1. This was an impossible task, but virtually half the entire Research Station's facilities were switched to the job, and the Mark II went into operation exactly on schedule. This version was largely the design of Donald Michie and Jack Good, and was an extraordinary feat of engineering, being capable of reading the Baudot code punch tape at a rate of five thousand characters per second. It functioned completely automatically and performed numerous binary arithmetical and logical functions. The output was printed on to an electric typewriter at fifteen characters per second. Truly, it was no object of beauty, but it was the most advanced equipment of its kind in the world. The actual programming was set up by means of a plugboard, and once the process had begun, the COLOSSUS sifted through the millions of logical branch functions at an unprecedented speed. All the circuitry was in quintuplicate, so the actual reading power of the photoelectric sensors was 25,000 bits per second—or the kind of performance not reached by later, commercial computers for another decade. The analytical process was supervised by the machine operator, who watched the typewriter output and called suitable adjustments to the Wren handling the plugboard program. All those with access to the secret of COLOSSUS were invited to suggest improvements, and there was a daily tea party in the Research Room at which suggestions were thrashed out on a large blackboard. With the general success of the super-Bombe, the pressure returned to the intercept stations.

Cheadle, Montrose and West Kingsdown continued to monitor the Luftwaffe's Northern European Enigma traffic, and Professor Arthur Humphreys's Air Section at Bletchley allocated such code names as LION, LEOPARD, HYENA and JAGUAR to the resulting decrypts. Meanwhile, in the Mediterranean, LLAMA, YAK, MAYFLY and SQUIRREL were kept under surveillance from a secret coordinating center designated No. 380 Wireless Unit, which was constructed in November 1943 in the grounds of the Château Beraud at Draria, just outside Algiers. This station acted in concert with the old-established organization at Heliopolis and communicated with Whaddon via its own Special Liaison Unit. It also supervised the work of two other large RAF intercept stations, No. 351 Wireless Unit at Gibraltar and No. 371 Wireless Unit at Freetown, Sierra Leone. Other, more localized, enemy wireless signals were watched by two RAF units known as 276 and 329 Wings. They comprised a total of 113 receivers concentrating on tactical wireless, with some thirty sets logging the German radio-telephony traffic. Each Wing consisted of several field units of some two hundred men and these Wings were spread right across North Africa and the Near East, from No. 23 at a coastal site on Cap Bon in Tunisia to No. 3 on Maqab airfield at Habbaniyah, some distance outside Baghdad in Iraq. Others were located at Amriyah, Alexandria (No. 2); Siggiewi on Malta (No.10); Nerab, near Aleppo (No. 6); and on the Greek island of Kos (No. 9). After the invasion of Italy, more stations were erected in Calabria, in Sicily (No. 25) and at Conversano and Bitonto, near Bari. These ground facilities were reinforced further by two airborne detachments from the Wireless Intelligence Development Unit at Wyton, operating in the region under 192 and 162 Squadron cover, at the west and east ends of the Mediterranean respectively; 192 Squadron was based at Maison-Blanche outside Algiers, with its companion outfit moving between airstrips in the Canal Zone.

At this point a review of the Allied intercept assets elsewhere around the world might be appropriate. As might be expected, the Admiralty had made a heavy investment in traffic analysis, even though much of the German navy's Enigma traffic had resisted attack. In the sphere of naval operations, direction finding and call sign analysis had proved rather more valuable than cryptanalysis. The exact position of enemy vessels at sea and the positive identification of their call signs was the main concern of the Naval Intelligence Division, and access to the exact texts of their messages was only of secondary importance. Direction finding, of course, was a priority, and no fewer than twenty stations in the British Isles were connected to the central control at Scarborough. A further sixty-nine covered the rest of the globe with a heavy concentration in the Atlantic. In the South Atlantic, the network included stations on the islands of Tristan da Cunha, St. Helena and Ascension, with additional land-based units in West Africa at Freetown and Accra and in South Africa at Simonstown. All the enemy's maritime channels were routinely scanned, and the skill of the operators was such that the position of a suspect signal could be calculated by triangulation with considerable accuracy and communicated to London within seconds of a transmission. The only area of comparative weakness was the Mediterranean, where circumstances prevented the Royal Navy from operating more than the three big stations at Gibraltar, at Dingli on Malta, at Lieutenant Commander David Johnson's NID 9 outpost at Alexandria, and at the two units at Benghazi and Crete which, due to enemy action, were only occasionally mobile. Local, tactical traffic was also monitored afloat with some assistance from the RAF, who seemed at times to have had a monopoly of German-speaking Jewish volunteers from Palestine and Italian linguists from England. Several warships, including HMS *Hilary* and HMS *Bulolo*, were temporarily transformed into SIGINT-gathering platforms, but only to support particular operations such as the amphibious landings at Anzio and Salerno.

The British army's overt SIGINT effort was divided between the two big fixed home stations at Beaumanor and Wincombe, near Shaftesbury, focused on the Wehrmacht's Enigma traffic, and the more mobile

Special Wireless Groups. In 1946, the War Office discreetly changed the latter's name to Special Wireless Regiment and three years later the term "Special" was dropped altogether. On the covert side the military officially ran the Special Communications Units, but in reality SCU 1 headed by Lord Sandhurst remained MI6's "Main Line" radio conduit from Whaddon to its interests abroad. Radio links with the Special Liaison Units entrusted with distributing Ultra remained in the hands of Gambier-Parry at Windy Ridge. By the end of the war, he had established SLUs in Delhi, Brisbane, Algiers, Beirut, Cairo, Malta and Italy. MI6's empire also included the old Radio Security Service network based at Barnet, now headed by Jack Hester, and encompassed the GPO's Interference Investigation Unit. SCU 1 also ran the highly secret intercept station hidden on the top floor of the Passport Office in Petty France, which kept an ear open for ground-wave signals radiating from London's growing number of foreign embassies. During the previous four years, Arkley, the dormitory village near Barnet, had become a hive of undercover activity. The vital discrimination tasks were undertaken at Arkley View; not far away were The Granary and Arkley Lodge, where two direction-finding control centers were linked by landline to smaller RSS sites at St. Erth, Forfar, Thurso, Wymondham and Gilnahirk. A large intercept station handling Central European diplomatic traffic had been constructed in the grounds of Ravenscroft, opposite the gates to Ravenscroft Park, Barnet, and staffed by around twenty operators from the GPO's Engineering Department. SCU3, located at Hanslope Park (with a substation at The Lawns, Arkley), kept Europe's diplomatic traffic under surveillance, and smaller, mobile SCUs later traveled to the Continent after the invasion. One unit went to Gibraltar, while SCU 10 made its way slowly, with the advancing armies, through France to Holland and Germany where semi-permanent bases were erected at Eindhoven, Bad Salzuflen, Bad Oeynhausen and Bad Godesberg. SCU11 went to Palestine and set up a satellite at Habbaniyah.

The magnitude of the Allied SIGINT effort during the final year of the war in Europe was truly extraordinary. Quite apart from the numerous American Signal Intelligence Service units on the scene, which will be described later, each of the three British services maintained a vast intercept organization to catch enemy signals, and the traditional intelligence arms of the various forces had been transformed into nothing more than SIGINT conveyors, comparing new developments to the knowledge already gleaned from the ether. The scale of knowledge was such that the style, habits and eccentricities of virtually every enemy wireless op-

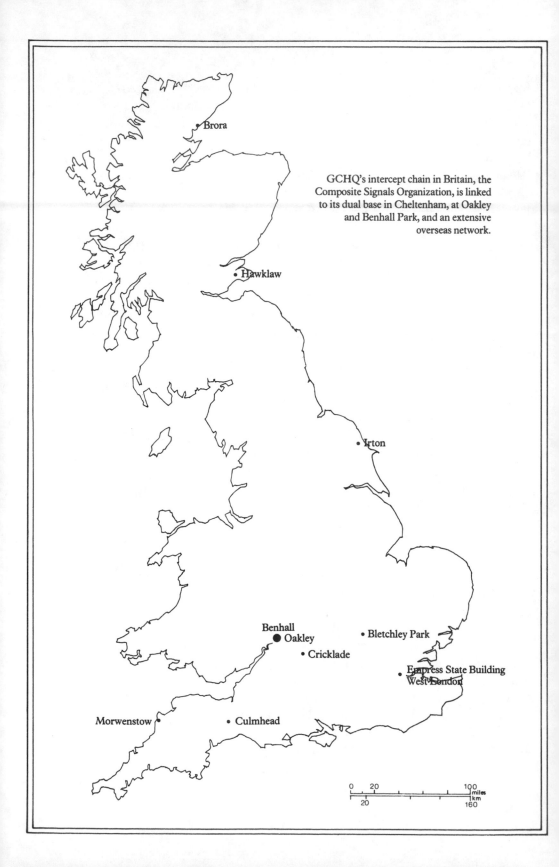

GCHQ's intercept chain in Britain, the
Composite Signals Organization, is linked
to its dual base in Cheltenham, at Oakley
and Benhall Park, and an extensive
overseas network.

Brora

Hawklaw

Irton

Benhall
Oakley

Bletchley Park

Cricklade

Empress State Building
West London

Morwenstow

Culmhead

erator were recorded somewhere on a card index. Each individual was linked to his unit, and the ceaseless recording of even the most trivial bits of information led to a detailed picture of every German military unit, its composition, its location, and sometimes the proclivities of its members. Suddenly, with the end of the hostilities, the sophisticated apparatus appeared redundant, or might have done so if an extraordinary discovery had not been made in Australia.

8

Russian Adventures

The Bolsheviks are our superior in only one field—espionage.

—ADOLF HITLER, May 17, 1942

The news from Australia that caused such a stir in London was the reported interception of Soviet diplomatic traffic at an Allied base at Coonawarra, near Darwin. The station had been operating since 1939, but the Japanese surrender had enabled it to concentrate more of its resources on the Russian long-distance Morse. That signals to and from Moscow had been picked up on the other side of the world was not entirely a surprise. Atmospheric conditions and other effects, such as a radio wave's tendency to bounce back and forth between the ionosphere and the earth's surface, often produced such phenomena. Royal Air Force listening posts in North Africa had often monitored low-power transmissions thousands of miles away on the Russian front after the Nazi invasion in 1941. But what was unexpected was the nature of the traffic, code-named VENONA, and GCHQ's ability to read a substantial part of it. If the organization's peacetime future had ever been in doubt, the discovery in Darwin put such doubts to rest.

The Soviets had long been regarded as thoroughly insecure, and they had for years been propagating absurdly long messages. To some of GCHQ's operators, it seemed that Soviet officialdom preferred to communicate by radio Teletype than letter. On occasions, the length of the message seemed to reflect the status of the sender. The greater his verbosity, the more important his standing within the party. The volume of material, with frequent repetition, familiar call signs and frequencies, and plenty of operator chat, ensured easy interception. Most of it was copied by Allied stations and then filed as RA (Russian Air) or RM (Russian Military). Unfortunately, most of the content was very tedious and of little or no strategic value. Naturally, the intercept series designated RI, for Russian Intelligence, was of the greatest interest, but here at least the Soviets exercised some caution. All the high-grade traffic was enciphered with one-time pads.

That GCHQ might not have a peacetime role had never really been a matter for serious argument within the British intelligence community, but the exact nature and structure of that role was not discussed at senior level until the early weeks of 1945, when Sir Findlater Stewart, the chairman of the wartime Home Defense Executive, was commissioned by Churchill to review Britain's future needs and recommend any organizational changes that might be needed. Evidence submitted to Sir Findlater has never been released, but it is known that MI5 and MI6's responsibilities remained unchanged. GCHQ, which absorbed RSS, itself remained under the umbrella of the Foreign Office, but was at last able to shake off Sir Stewart Menzies. That the MI6 chief had succeeded in exercising control over the department for so long was itself quite an achievement, but unlike the gray area of counterintelligence, where both MI5 and MI6 had a mandate to operate, there was a very clear demarcation line between the kind of work that MI6 might be expected to undertake in the postwar era and the interests of GCHQ. It could be argued (and it probably was) that in certain well-defined fields GCHQ was the prime source of reliable information. The various Y services and the cryptographers had played a critical role in combating German espionage at home and abroad, and if it could be assumed that hostile undercover agents would continue to rely on wireless as a means of communication, then they would be needed again. No doubt GCHQ resisted this line by pointing out the difference between close cooperation with independence, which is evidently what Travis sought, and complete control, which Menzies wished to keep. In any event, the compromise was a Foreign Office umbrella and the creation of a Counter Clandestine Committee, a subbranch of the Y Committee, on which both MI5 and MI6 would have permanent representatives. W.F. Clarke, the head of the Naval Section who retired in October 1945, had taken this view of what he termed "the greatest problem" of GCHQ's organization and control in peacetime the previous January:

> It may be assumed that it will not be much larger than the establishment of 1919 and that its main function will be on the civil side. It would

be quite impossible to have two separate bodies. The volume of service traffic will be in all probability not more than a fifth of the total traffic and this is a generous estimate. . . . The codes and ciphers of most countries will probably be prepared by one central authority and the experience of cryptographers dealing with the civil traffic should be pooled with that of those dealing with service traffic.[1]

GCHQ's very existence, and its secret function in the civil and military fields, was to remain a secret for many years to come, which, in some measure, contradicted Clarke's stated opinion that "the existence of a Government Code and Cypher School is not and cannot be a secret, the great secret is its measure of success." But how could the hierarchy expect complete discretion when so many thousands of people had served at Bletchley, Stanmore, Eastcote and Station X's numerous other satellites? The answer lies in the compartmentation policy enforced, originally by Denniston, and pursued with equal vigor by Travis. Only a tiny handful of individuals had an inkling of the complete picture. Few were in a position to grasp the massive scale of the Allied SIGINT effort. Those working in a particular hut at Bletchley avoided discussing their work with staff from other sections. Sometimes the discipline proved counter-productive, as was once noted: "The early results of Hut 3 were not communicated to other sections to which they would have been priceless. This was only due to a false idea of security tinged by selfishness."[2]

From time to time words of encouragement were delivered to groups who had made a significant contribution to a successful operation, such as the sinking of the *Bismarck*, but such morale-boosting sessions were rare and restricted only to those directly involved. Thus, personnel working on Luftwaffe traffic were never able to learn the achievements gained by others. Similarly, the cryptographers and analysts were generally prevented from acquiring knowledge of other aspects of the SIGINT art, such as interception techniques or methods of disseminating the final processed intelligence product. This was not a matter of seniority and should not be interpreted as reflecting a lack of trust. It was a sensible security precaution, universally accepted at all levels. Late in 1944, Alan Turing returned from a series of conferences in America and sought help from Jack Good on a technical question. Both men had been at the very heart of Bletchley Park's decision-making for some years, but Good later recalled that Turing had been unable to disclose details of the practical application of the subject of his work and he had only realized much later that Turing had been involved in researching the atomic bomb. Turing had given no clue to it during their talks, and Good accepted, without hesitation, that he should be kept in ignorance if there was not a need for him to know. Internally, security restrictions were tight, and the voluntary system of self-regulation and self-discipline generally respected by all. Indeed, the atmosphere often took its toll and there were several nervous breakdowns brought on by overwork and excessive strain. All were told repeatedly of their heavy responsibility and reminded that one mistake in a decrypt could cost the lives of thousands; an indiscretion might jeopardize the entire operation. This was the reason for the destruction of the more entertaining decrypts. One amusing anecdote to impress a friend might compromise everything. For some of the young, brilliant "crossword puzzle-solvers," the burden forced them to concentrate exclusively on their work and become rather too bound up in it. For others, the task was simply too much.

In the area of technical achievements, the actual methods of interception, analysis and interpretation were (and still are) regarded as having greater significance than the use to which SIGINT information has been put. In other words, the fact that a certain event was caused, prevented or influenced by SIGINT is altogether less important than the details of the system employed. In the light of this, it is perhaps a little odd to report, forty years later and more than a decade after the release of the first accounts of Station X's wartime role, that there never really was an "Ultra secret" as such. Contrary to the claims of many writers and historians, the Enigma cipher machine itself was not completely mastered by the cryptographers. Some dozens of different books have either stated that all the German Enigma traffic was solved, or implied that the invention of the Bombe enabled the keys to be isolated automatically. Neither claim is correct, and of the various authors who actually served at Bletchley Park, only Gordon Welchman has ventured into the sensitive area of the technical means employed by GCHQ. His unauthorized account in 1982, *The Hut Six Story*, which nearly resulted in an Official Secrets Act prosecution, was the first to spell out the message that "the machine as it was would have been impregnable if it had been used properly." The important phrase is the condition of proper use, which was met rather more times than not. But enemy operators did ignore their instructions, and it was those lapses in security which made so many of the Enigma keys vulnerable to attack. As Welchman stated, "At any time during the war, enforcement of a few minor security measures could have defeated us completely." This, then, was the true secret of Ultra:

> That we managed to stay in the game until the end of the war was made possible only by a comedy of errors committed by the Germans,

who failed in many ways to do what could and should have been
done to protect the security of their command communications. . . .
Looking back, it is amazing that so much could hang on such slender
threads.[3]

On the issue of the Bombes, the same principle applied:

Our Bombes, if we could ever have justified their development, would
have been useless without cribs, and we would never have found our
cribs if the Germans had not made a number of errors in procedure.[4]

In short, when the procedures were operated correctly, the Enigma
keys resisted all attack. No wonder GCHQ's management was so anxious
to suppress Welchman's memoirs. In the end, the decision was taken not
to take legal action for three reasons. Welchman had become an American
citizen and was then living in Massachusetts. Litigation would have caused
great resentment among his former colleagues and, perhaps most important of all, would have generated further interest in the very subject that
GCHQ wished to play down. Sir Brian Tovey, then GCHQ's Director,
confirmed in April 1982 that ''Welchman's book, published without official sanction, did in fact contravene'' the guidelines on disclosures of
technical details and, more ominously, ''appropriate official action is still
being considered.'' The cat, however, was already out of the bag in
America, and when *The Hut Six Story* was released in England, Sir Stuart
Milner Barry, another Hut 6 veteran, confirmed the gist of Welchman's
recollections and commented that ''fortunately [the German] operators
continued to make sufficient procedural mistakes to keep us in business.''

Millions of man-hours had been spent on futile attempts to break
the *Ausserheimisch* key, the German navy's Distant Waters cipher, code-
named PIKE, which never succumbed. There are plenty of other examples, including BARRACUDA, the key used for the highest grade of
fleet messages. Similarly, the SS key known as MEDLAR was only rarely
tackled, and the Luftwaffe's PURPLE key was glimpsed on just one day.
If there was anything that could be fairly described as an Ultra secret, it
was simply that human failure was at the heart of cryptographic success,
and relatively straightforward (and inexpensive) precautions could have
been taken to render hostile cryptanalysis harmless. GCHQ's secret was
not its overwhelming mastery of the Enigma's traffic, but rather its recognition of the machine's relative invulnerability, given the right conditions: hence the need to make the maximum use of every crib, error,
slip and plain-language indiscretion that was spotted.

A recurring feature of GCHQ's postwar history is not so much the organization's prowess at cracking codes, but rather its tendency to suppress systems that threatened to reduce the chances of finding a successful solution or jeopardize the ''slender threads.'' Inventors of new, innovative ciphering systems have often been encouraged to surrender their ideas to GCHQ. Since it was widely known that the Soviets had switched to the use of one-time pads, it was therefore, in SIGINT terms, a matter of cosmic importance to prevent Moscow from discovering that a route into their supposedly watertight communications had been found.

Firm details of the breakthrough are still closely guarded, but evidently the material, code-named VENONA, came on stream through Darwin, Australia, in the latter part of 1944. What it revealed was the existence of a worldwide Soviet spy network containing literally hundreds of enthusiastic volunteer agents. It was the first glimpse of the Kremlin's long-denied commitment to international subversion since the decrypts of the 1920s, and the source was to prove a powerful incentive for the Americans to expand their global SIGINT capability.

That VENONA should ever have succumbed to GCHQ is remarkable, considering that the Soviets were known to be heavily reliant on one-time pads. Soviet espionage in Western Europe during the war had largely flopped due to poor security procedures, and no doubt Moscow had received plenty of advice on the issue from its covert sources within the British intelligence community. Two cases in particular had highlighted Russian susceptibility to inadequate wireless security: the LUCY ring in Switzerland, and the network known to the Germans as the *Rote Kapelle*, or Red Chapel.

The *Rote Kapelle* had been broken up by the Abwehr following the arrest in June 1942 of Johann Wenzel, a Russian-trained wireless operator whose copious transmissions had been monitored by German goniometric stations at Nuremberg, Augsburg and Brest. The triangulation azimuths had narrowed the illicit signals to Brussels, and thereafter it had simply been a matter of time before the clandestine operator had been caught. When arrested, Wenzel was found with a shortwave transmitter, still warm, and a quantity of coding paraphernalia. He had subsequently cooperated with his captors and participated in another *funkspiel* at Moscow's expense. Hundreds of Soviet agents throughout occupied Europe were rounded up and executed, and the Germans used the turned network's five wirelesses to convey disinformation until March 1944 when the Soviets realized they had been duped.

The penetration of the *Rote Kapelle* was followed, in October and November 1943, by the capture of three clandestine Soviet radio sets operating from Geneva and Lausanne. The Swiss federal security police, the Bundespolizei, had been monitoring the traffic for about a month before they moved in, and the three principal operators, all committed Communists, made detailed statements about their activities. Once again, it was the poor training received by those responsible for communicating with Moscow that had jeopardized their spy rings. As a consequence of these two catastrophes, the Soviet intelligence authorities had equipped their agents with one-time pads and instructed their networks to send their messages via locally based intelligence personnel masquerading as diplomats. This avoided the use of poorly trained wireless operators trying to contact Moscow with low-powered sets and indifferent aerials. Instead, the networks were guaranteed access to the overt, high-powered transmitters located at most Soviet diplomatic missions. This apparently welcome development improved reception by the Russian intelligence controllers—and the British and American intercept stations. Everything now depended on the integrity of the one-time pads and, unknown to the Soviets, these had been compromised by nothing more complicated than a bureaucratic mixup. The result was the signal series code-named VENONA which provided the West with the best insight into the NKVD's foreign operations ever known.

The mistake that led to the VENONA material was the reissue of the same one-time pads. In theory at least, the one-time pad is invincible, but the system loses all of its built-in security if the same randomly selected letters are used in the same sequence more than once. It can be argued that the critical definition of a one-time pad is the random nature of the selection process. Machine logic, as practiced by modern computers, can discern a pattern in any series of numbers or figures chosen by human intellect. In other words, unless a one-time pad has been constructed by a machine process, it will ultimately be susceptible to a machine.

The Soviets employed several different hand-cipher systems, of which the most sophisticated was a combination of them all with the one-time pads. Many routine messages were simply encoded with a code book containing a list of five-figure groups, which corresponded to frequently used words or phrases. This, of course, was a well-tried arrangement and could only be compromised by access to a copy of the code book, or a reconstruction. This latter route had often been used in the past, as has been seen, and generally promised good results if the cryptographers could find a worthwhile crib. Such aids ranged from frequency tables, which indicated the words or letters most used in particular types of texts, to conventions that had proved so profitable on the prewar Japanese traffic. The best shortcut was always the duplicate text sent in plain language or by a known cipher, and once even the smallest fragment of a message had been solved, the rest might be expected to follow with relative ease.

In the Soviet case, many of the five-figure groups had been acquired during several FBI-sponsored break-ins at a diplomatic mission in New York. This had assisted with the low-grade diplomatic traffic that had been super-enciphered, but it was not much help with the NKVD texts which were subjected to a further encipherment based on one-time pads. However, in 1948, the Americans spotted a similarity between two separate messages—one an NKVD text, the other a telegram that had been exchanged between President Truman and Winston Churchill three years earlier.

GCHQ's ability to reach into its records and extract the texts of messages intercepted months and even years earlier is testimony to the scale of its activities and its close relationship with the American, Australian and Canadian SIGINT organizations. All were secretly involved in the VENONA operation.

The Canadian wartime cover had been the Examination Unit of the National Research Council and had operated four intercept bases: at Rockville in Ottawa (which had monitored the Vichy Embassy's diplomatic traffic), West Point Barracks, Victoria, Amherst, Nova Scotia, and on the west coast at Riske Creek, British Columbia. The unit had initially hired Herbert Yardley as an adviser, but he was fired in November 1941 following objections from GCHQ which offered Oliver Strachey as a replacement. By 1945, they were all intercepting Soviet signals, and the Canadian traffic analysts are believed to have made a valuable contribution to the overall operation. In the postwar era, the unit was renamed the Communications Branch of the National Research Council and is now known as the Communications Security Establishment.

The Australian SIGINT body, the Defense Signals Division (DSD), also survived the war and absorbed the old Central Bureau's cryptographic sections. As well as providing useful intercept sites in the Far East, the DSD also provided staff for GCHQ's installations at Coonawarra and Hong Kong.

After such a late wartime start, the American Signal Security Service had grown rapidly and had developed in close parallel with the British Special Wireless Groups. By the end of hostilities, the Signal Security Agency had changed its title, once again, to the Army Security Agency, and as such retained responsibility for intercepting wireless traffic around the world from more than nine hundred sites. In addition, the Federal Bureau of Investigation (FBI), U.S. Navy, Air Force, the Federal Communications Commission and even the Coast Guard maintained their own separate intercept divisions, and their workload was supervised by a Communications Intelligence Board which had been formed in June 1946.

The following year, the terms of the BRUSA pact had been confirmed and extended into the peace by another secret treaty, known as the United Kingdom–United States of America Security Agreement and invariably referred to by the acronym UKUSA. The exact terms of UKUSA remain secret and neither government has ever acknowledged its existence. Other parties to the treaty included Canada, Australia and New Zealand, and their objectives were to define areas of interest and to standardize working methods and security procedures. It also allowed for the exchange of SIGINT representatives, known as Special Liaison Officers, who operated under the acronyms SUSLO and SUKLO so as to avoid confusion with MI5's overseas representatives who enjoyed the cover title Security Liaison Officer, or SLO. The cement of the agreement was the VENONA material intercepted in Australia and a common interest in thwarting Communist hegemony.

Britain's contribution to UKUSA was twofold: convenient sites in secure, garrisoned locations all over the world, from Hong Kong to Iraq, from Austria to Ascension; and in addition to the product from the three service intercept organizations, which continued their activities into the peace, GCHQ could also offer useful SIGINT facilities within the United Kingdom. At that time some 64 percent of long-distance communications was still sent by cable, and a substantial proportion was carried on systems run by Cable & Wireless. Copies of all Cable & Wireless traffic routinely went to GCHQ's new postwar home at Eastcote and were thus available, either in their unprocessed raw state, or in the form of summaries, to the SUSLO. The volume of material was vast, and in due course the RAF bases at Chicksands Priory and Waddington were transferred to American control and began relaying SIGINT material back to Arlington Hall. By far the most important of these intercepts was the VENONA material, the worldwide collection of which was code-named Operation BRIDE.

If there had ever been any doubt about the importance of VENONA, the defection in September 1945 of Igor Gouzenko, a young cipher clerk from the Soviet Embassy in Ottawa, had confirmed Moscow's true intentions. Before his departure, he had removed sufficient documents from the embassy's cipher room to indicate the existence of dozens of ideologically motivated Soviet agents, including the atomic physicist Alan Nunn May. Nunn May had subsequently been arrested in London and convicted of passing secrets to a Soviet intelligence officer.

The identification of Nunn May had been relatively straightforward, for much of the evidence against him had come from Gouzenko's purloined papers. More complex was the case of the first Soviet spy identified from the VENONA source, code-named HOMER. He had betrayed the text of a telegram from President Truman to the then Prime Minister, Winston Churchill, and while the analysts sifted through thousands of intercepts they came across traces of another agent. The clues leading to him were gleaned from several different intercepts, which revealed that the spy had access to secret atomic experiments and had a sister at an American university on the East Coast. This narrowed the field to Klaus Fuchs, another physicist who had become a naturalized British subject after fleeting the Nazi regime in Germany before the war. The VENONA clues left no doubt about his commitment to the Soviet cause, but how could he be arrested and tried on SIGINT evidence? To acknowledge publicly the VENONA breakthrough would cause Moscow instantly to suspend its compromised communications. The problem was made all the more serious because Fuchs had been transferred to the Atomic Energy Authority's highly sensitive establishment at Harwell, and was working on classified research. The news that Fuchs was a Soviet asset was passed from Arlington Hall early in October 1949, via the SUSLO to GCHQ's liaison officer in MI5, Arthur Martin. Martin was a SWG 1 veteran, who had been invited to stay in GCHQ's postwar organization after having worked in the field in North Africa. His job in MI5's headquarters was to handle all the SIGINT material and, on this occasion, provide the counterespionage, B Division, with all the relevant VENONA information which, for added security, was referred to obliquely as simply "U" or "V" material. It was now up to MI5 to bluff an admission from Fuchs without betraying the source of the evidence against him. Exercising great skill, Harwell's security officer, Wing Commander Henry Arnold, persuaded Fuchs to make a full confession without ever hinting at VENONA's existence.

The Fuchs case demonstrated how the VENONA material could best be exploited, but it was not for another two years that the pursuit of the original agent, HOMER, neared its end. Working on the assumption that the Truman telegram had been copied from the British Embassy in Washington, a lengthy investigation of all those who might have had access to it had produced several suspects. It was only when it was noticed that

HOMER had conducted regular meetings with his Soviet controller in Manhattan that the field was narrowed to Donald Maclean, whose American wife was pregnant and was living in New York. He was the only member of the embassy staff who had enjoyed the right access and had made regular, twice-weekly visits to New York. Arrangements were made for him to be interrogated in London, where he had been appointed head of the Foreign Office's American Department, but in May 1951 he escaped abroad just hours before he was due to meet MI5.

Maclean's disappearance sparked off a huge mole hunt for his fellow conspirators, and also marked the end of Operation BRIDE, but analysis of the VENONA material was to continue for a further twenty years. In the meantime, Eastcote and Arlington Hall had other preoccupations, including the invasion of South Korea in June 1950.

On May 20, 1949, the U.S. Army Security Agency had undergone a further name change, to the Armed Forces Security Agency, a reflection of the growing interest in SIGINT expressed by all three American services. Traffic analysis and cryptographic processing continued to be undertaken at Arlington Hall, but responsibility for communications security had been switched to the Naval Security Group at its headquarters on Nebraska Avenue, Washington, D.C. The combined AFSA strength amounted to 4,921 civilians and 1,948 military personnel. Yet these impressive numbers, and the ever-increasing network of intercept stations (of which there were 1,821), failed to give adequate warning of the Korean invasion. The AFSA made the point that only with greater resources in manpower and facilities could it have given advance notice, and this view evidently prevailed. During the next twelve months, the AFSA suddenly mushroomed and received authority to increase its civilian establishment to 6,613, making a total of 8,500 with a budget of $60.9 million.

In SIGINT terms the Korean conflict was a sideshow to the main event, the secret wireless war conducted throughout the late 1940s over the Soviet Union. The demand in the Far East was for tactical signals intelligence relevant to the increasingly bitter conflict on the ground, but GCHQ's main interest continued to be the strategic traffic passing to and from the Eastern Bloc, and the covert transmissions to Soviet agents around the world. This material was acquired from fixed stations in Allied territory in Europe, such as the now well-established intercept bases in West Germany, Turkey, Cyprus and, before the withdrawal in March 1948, Palestine. In April the following year, the North Atlantic Treaty Organization (NATO) was formed and the signatories undertook ''separately and jointly, by means of continuous and effective self-help and mutual aid, to maintain and develop their individual and collective capacity to resist armed attack." To date, the most practical method of assessing a potential enemy's intentions had been the interception and analysis of his communications. In practice, this meant additional SIGINT sites becoming available in Italy, Norway, Iceland and Portugal. The following year Turkey and Greece joined NATO, giving legitimacy to the bases already operated under diplomatic cover on the Black Sea and paving the way for the construction of two new U.S. communications bases in Greece, at Suda Bay in Crete and at Marathon on the mainland.

These events were political in nature, and it should be borne in mind that only a few individuals in the countries concerned were ever indoctrinated into the secrets of SIGINT. The terms of the UKUSA pact, which had already delineated the various spheres of SIGINT interest between GCHQ and the Americans, remained unaffected by NATO. The new treaty simply gave greater scope for the construction of overt listening posts. Bletchley Park was to remain within GCHQ's umbrella (and, even to the present day, accommodates GCHQ's training section), but the details of its work were kept restricted. Nevertheless, there were occasions when the public glimpsed the secret wireless war.

On April 8, 1950, a United States Navy bomber, a Consolidated PB4Y-2 Privateer from Wiesbaden on a flight to Copenhagen, was lost over the Baltic. The crew of ten were killed, of whom no less than six were radio technicians. No hint was given in the bland official public statements that in fact the aircraft was a specially adapted intercept platform, and that it had been shot down over Latvia. The plane's mission was one of electronic surveillance, recording Soviet signals that could not be picked up by the AFSA-sponsored station on the ground at Bremerhaven. The Privateer was a patrol version of the old B-24 Liberator and was unarmed at the time of the attack. The Russians protested that the "B-29 Superfortress bomber" had violated Soviet airspace and had been shot down. The SIGINT experts concluded that the wireless war had hotted up. In October and November the following year, two more U.S. planes on eavesdropping missions were shot down: the first, another Privateer from Wiesbaden, was brought down in Siberia with the loss of ten lives. This was followed by a U.S. Navy P2V Neptune which was shot down by MiGs, killing all ten crew, near Vladivostok. The true nature of these operations was carefully concealed, and no admissions were made about these "routine navigational flights" or "training missions." The Swedish air force, which also regularly indulged in such flights, lost a Dakota in June 1952. Naturally, GCHQ was an active participant in similar operations, using Lincolns from 162 Squadron at RAF Wyton, and specially modified Canberra bombers from 51 Squadron operated on behalf of the Central Signals Establishment at RAF Watton.

The purpose of these flights was to scoop up as much electronic information about Eastern Bloc communications as possible. Experience had shown that traffic analysis could reveal valuable information, even if the cryptographers failed to crack any codes. The greater the volume of traffic intercepted, the greater the chances of making progress. By April 1952, the AFSA had taken delivery of the first of a series of sophisticated number-crunching machines capable of processing intercepts at high speed. Code-named ABNER, it was a direct descendant of the original COLOSSUS machines, the wartime computers that were still in service at Eastcote and Arlington Hall.

ABNER's introduction was one of several significant events in the Allied SIGINT community during 1952. Commander Travis, who had been knighted in 1944, retired at the end of March and was succeeded by Eric Jones, Jones, who was just a few days short of his forty-fifth birthday, had not been to university; in fact, he had been a textile merchant before joining the Air Ministry in 1939. He had subsequently been attached to Bletchley and had been promoted to the rank of group captain in 1944, when he took over the leadership of Hut 3. In *Ultra in the West*, a former Hut 3 colleague, Ralph Bennett, has remarked on the value at Bletchley of Jones's "steadying temperament and business experience." But perhaps more significant was the appointment of Major-General Ralph Canine, who had only been posted to the AFSA in August the previous year, to be the first director of an entirely new federal body, the National Security Agency (NSA). President Truman's executive authorization of the NSA's creation is known to be dated November 4, 1952, but little else is known about "National Security Council Intelligence Directive No. 6." That the NSA's official charter covers seven pages has been disclosed, but only in a successful attempt to block its publication. Even the security classification of the document is a secret. Compared to the huge quantities of published material on American intelligence organizations, relatively little has been written about the NSA. The U.S. Government Organization Manual simply states: "The National Security Agency performs highly specialized technical and coordinating functions relating to the national security."

The NSA's internal organization is not unlike that of GCHQ (see charts on pages 16–18). It acquires its raw intelligence from two parallel intercept sources: the listening posts spread around the world which are under the NSA's direct control, and those operated by three surrogate service branches: the Naval Security Group, the U.S. Army Security and Intelligence Command, and the USAF's Electronic Security Command (formerly the USAF Security Service). All filter unprocessed signals to the NSA's headquarters in much the same way that the Composite Signals Organization, which GCHQ formed at the time of UKUSA in 1947, coordinated the collection program for Eastcote.

Yet, for all its secrecy, the NSA has been the heart of the U.S. intelligence structure and has consistently employed more staff, and enjoyed a greater budget, than both the CIA and the FBI put together. There were no public announcements concerning the NSA in 1952, yet during the first two years of its existence planes flying missions on its behalf did receive some attention. During that period, five SIGINT reconnaissance flights were prematurely terminated because of Soviet attacks and sixteen crew members were killed. The scale of incidents ranged from a brief dogfight on March 15, 1953, over Kamchatka, which resulted in a badly damaged aircraft limping back to Elmendorf Air Force Base in Alaska, to the destruction of a Boeing RB-50 in the Sea of Japan with the loss of sixteen airmen on July 19, 1953. Few outside observers realized that these events, occurring at the height of the Cold War, were directly linked to the NSA because only those inside the U.S. intelligence community knew the agency's true role.

This was wireless espionage of the most overt variety, but the Soviets were clearly interested in the alternatives, as was demonstrated by the recruitment in Moscow of William Marshall, a twenty-three-year-old wireless operator at the British Embassy. Marshall had been a member of SWG 2's successor, the No. 2 Special Wireless Regiment in Palestine and Egypt, and had joined the Diplomatic Wireless Service (DWS) when he had been demobbed in 1948. The latter body had been founded after the war as a peacetime successor to the Special Communications Unit and was based at the two old SCU stations, Hanslope Park and Poundon. Although the DWS was responsible for handling all the Foreign Office's overseas radio traffic, it also provided a useful cover, complete with immunity, for clandestine interception. Through his access to Hanslope, and his Royal Signals experience, Marshall must have been an extremely useful source for the Soviets. He had done a twelve-month tour of duty as a cipher clerk at the embassy in Moscow and had returned to Hanslope in December 1951. The following April he was spotted by MI5 in London with a Soviet intelligence officer and was arrested on June 13, 1952, after a lengthy surveillance operation. The Soviet, a second secretary named

Pavel Kusnetsov, turned out to have diplomatic immunity, so he was released, but Marshall was prosecuted for selling DWS secrets and sentenced to five years' imprisonment.

Marshall had spent nearly five years at the business end of wireless interception and certainly knew a great deal about British SIGINT activities in the Middle East and procedures in the British Embassy in Moscow. GCHQ's postwar signal collection program had been divided between the three services, which concentrated on their particular areas of expertise or access, leaving GCHQ to do the rest. Thus the Admiralty had largely taken over direction finding, and the British Army of the Rhine had provided suitable facilities at five sites in Germany and the odd corner in its overseas garrisons. The RAF confined itself to airborne collection and the provision of sites on well-located airfields abroad. For its part, GCHQ collaborated with the Americans at NSA sites, manned clandestine stations under civilian covers, or simply took over rooms in embassies and high commissions. Because Marshall knew all about the military end as well as GCHQ's role, he would have been in a position to explain how DWS personnel were routinely seconded to GCHQ for special duties at diplomatic missions overseas.

The question of exactly how much he told his Soviet contacts is something only he and the KGB know. The prevailing view was that Marshall had been a naïve young man and had been talent-spotted by the Soviets as a likely ideological recruit during his period in Moscow. In short, he had been arrested before GCHQ or the DWS had sustained any lasting damage. It was, nevertheless, a reminder that everyone connected with SIGINT, at every level, was a potentially useful source for the opposition, and new security procedures were introduced at GCHQ. Similar checks were imposed in other Allied intelligence organizations, and in America a routine query on an NSA analyst's foreign correspondence revealed that he was in regular contact with a Dutch intelligence official.

Joseph Petersen, a forty-year-old scientist, had spent the war at Arlington Hall working on Japanese diplomatic traffic and had become friendly with a Dutch liaison officer and noted cryptologist, Colonel J.A. Verkuyl. At the end of the war, Verkuyl and Petersen had continued to exchange letters; during the course of the correspondence, Petersen had disclosed details of the NSA's progress on the Hagelin B-211, the very machine used by the Dutch government for its postwar communications. Petersen had also given copies of various secret documents to Giacomo Stuyt, an official at the Netherlands Embassy in Washington. As soon as the NSA's security section discovered Petersen's illicit activities, he was sacked and then arrested on a charge of espionage. Petersen was sentenced to seven years' imprisonment, and the NSA's true function was suddenly thrust into the public domain. Indeed, there was a double danger of attracting unwelcome attention to at least two of GCHQ's secrets: the eavesdropping on "friendly" traffic (which was justified on the grounds that the continued security of Allied systems depended upon mutual monitoring to identify lapses) and the vulnerability of elderly cipher machines. Much of GCHQ's work was still concentrated on traffic generated by Enigma machines that had been discreetly reconditioned by GCHQ and placed on the commercial market, or even supplied direct to certain Commonwealth countries. The Swedish Hagelin, which had been mastered during the war when the Italians had relied upon it, was particularly vulnerable to the NSA and GCHQ, and both organizations were anxious to avoid tipping off the many other Hagelin users.

The Petersen case was an awkward embarrassment for the NSA, and apparently some thought was given to the idea of dropping all the charges to avoid publicity. But in spite of the public revelations, and the nature of the evidence presented in court, which included documents bearing such titles as "Routing of North Korean Political Security Traffic as Indicated by Group A2," the disclosure in no way harmed the NSA's most ambitious project to date, and one that GCHQ actively participated in: the Utility 2 program.

The plane now known as the U-2 is notorious, but in its heyday the project code-named ACQUATONE was considered the most exciting development to date in the secret wireless war. The objective was to exploit an extraordinary discovery made by the RAF's Canberra bombers which had, by 1955, been overflying large parts of the Soviet Union without interference for more than six years. These high-speed incursions had shown that the Russians had neither the aircraft nor the guided-missile technology to shoot down the Canberras. Provided the RAF flew sufficiently high, and 541 Squadron announced a record 63,668 feet in May 1953, the Canberras were practically invulnerable to attack. The MiG-15, the only Soviet fighter capable of even posing a threat to the high-flying PR3 reconnaissance version of the Canberra, had a very short duration at maximum height and required constant radar guidance and ground control. The SIGINT Canberras had little trouble in detecting the radar signals and listening to the ground vectoring, and were thus able to avoid interception. Frustrated, the impotent Soviet air defenses were obliged to limit their activities to harassing slower SIGINT platforms.

Occasionally their enthusiasm led to incidents like the shooting down in East Germany, on March 12, 1953, of an RAF Avro Lincoln from 192 Squadron. Six of the seven crew were killed. In another, more embarrassing incident, the Soviets attacked a U.S. Navy Neptune in international airspace over the Bering Sea on June 22, 1955. Badly damaged, the plane managed to limp back to its base near Gambell, on St. Lawrence Island, and Moscow subsequently paid up $724,947 in compensation.

ACQUATONE was the rushed development of a plywood and plastic jet-powered glider that could cruise for more than eight hours at an astonishing 450 mph and well over the ceiling of hostile interceptors. The first U-2s, built in California in 1955 under conditions of great secrecy by Lockheed, were extremely flimsy and the elongated wings were thought to have a life expectancy of just two years. Because the plane was intended to operate over long periods at heights of around 90,000 feet, an altitude considered almost impossible in those days, a special engine was adapted by Pratt & Whitney from the new Super Sabre jet fighter and Shell Oil invented a special kerosene fuel, known as JPTS, which reduced the danger of "flameouts," the power failures caused by lack of oxygen.

After a series of test flights at a secret site on the Groom Dry Lake in the Nevada desert, the first U-2 arrived at RAF Lakenheath near Newmarket, early in 1956, to begin flights over the Iron Curtain. A U.S. Air Force cover was introduced locally, the "1st Weather Reconnaissance Squadron (Provisional)," although in reality all the personnel involved were employees of the Central Intelligence Agency (CIA). In a rare breach of security *Flight* magazine reported, on June 1, 1956, the arrival of a "mysterious stranger" over Suffolk. The data collected by the U-2 and its twenty sisters, all packed with the most sophisticated electronic intelligence-gathering equipment, was passed through a special liaison body entitled the National Reconnaissance Office to the NSA and other interested organizations, such as the State Department and the White House. During the next five years, the CIA made thirty penetration flights, some from bases in England, others from either Incirli in Turkey or Atsugi in Japan. CIA-trained pilots would take off from one of these airfields and would ditch their undercarriage as soon as they were airborne so as to reduce the plane's radar profile and save weight. For long endurance flights, refueling stops were scheduled at a limited number of secure airfields in West Germany, Norway or Pakistan. En route the pilots would activate the highly sophisticated electronic and photographic equipment packed into the unmarked, mat-black planes and record everything. It was not unusual for the pilots to report the ineffective detonation of Soviet surface-to-air missiles at much lower altitudes, and the occasional vain attempt of a MiG fighter to climb to more than 70,000 feet. On one occasion, it was believed that the air defenses had actually succeeded in shooting down their own interceptors.

While the U-2 overflight program was under way, and GCHQ was reaping the benefit of flight recordings of low-powered Soviet signals out of range of the fixed intercept stations, the British suffered their first SIGINT defector. On July 2, 1956, Brian Patchett, a twenty-five-year-old corporal in the Intelligence Corps, failed to report for his watch at the secret listening post at Gatow, Berlin's military airfield. Patchett had been on intercept duties in Germany since the previous November and was known to have acquired an East German girlfriend. His disappearance was followed by the discovery of a letter announcing his intention to defect, and soon afterward the official East German news agency released a statement reporting Patchett's avowed disgust with his radio interception duties. Although a member of the Intelligence Corps, and not a full-time employee of GCHQ, he had been fully indoctrinated into GCHQ's procedures. He had enjoyed access to hundreds of highly classified SIGINT instructions and was aware of the scale of the Allied interception program in Germany. The British army's No. 2 Wireless Regiment (which had dropped the epithet "Special" in 1949 as a security measure) had become No. 13 Signal Regiment and had installed detachments in permanent bases at Birgelen, Jever and Teufelsberg. In addition, the RAF had its Signals Units stationed at Gatow, Schafoldenorf, Celle and Dannenberg. Patchett's revelations to the East Germans, and presumably the KGB, may have given an interesting insight into Britain's intercept activities, but the public at large was none the wiser and the U-2 was uncompromised.

Patchett's defection was followed by another awkward episode in February 1957, when two Oxford undergraduates, Paul Thompson and William Miller, wrote an account of their eavesdropping activities while doing their National Service in the Royal Navy. Their article, entitled "Foreign Incident—Exposure" in a special nuclear disarmament edition of *Isis*, reported that,

> All along the frontier between east and west from Iraq to the Baltic, perhaps further, are monitoring stations manned largely by National Servicemen trained in Morse and Russian, avidly recording the last squeak from Russian transmitters. In order to get information the West has been willing to go to extraordinary lengths of deception.

> British embassies usually contain monitoring spies. When the fleet
> paid a "goodwill" visit to Danzig in 1955 they were on board. And
> since the Russians do not always provide the required messages, they
> are sometimes provoked. A plane "loses its way." There is no con-
> trolling the appetite of the statistical analyzers at Cheltenham.

This unwelcome disclosure caused consternation in Whitehall, for it was
the first authoritative public comment on the secret wireless war and,
though it omitted to mention GCHQ by name, it did mention Cheltenham,
GCHQ's new location following its move from Eastcote three years earlier. Efforts to conceal GCHQ's true activities had been relaxed slightly
in January 1954, when the publicly available Diplomatic List mentioned,
for the first time, the existence of the Foreign Office "Signals Department
(Government Communications Headquarters)" and identified three of its
most senior staff: Eric Jones as the Director, Clive Loehnis as his deputy,
and Gildart Jackson as GCHQ's Principal Establishment Officer. GCHQ's
address in Cheltenham was not to be disclosed in an official document
for a further fourteen years. The two authors of the *Isis* article were
promptly arrested and, in July 1958, tried at the Old Bailey on several
charges under the Official Secrets Act. Both pleaded guilty to the single
charge of communicating classified information and were sentenced by
the Lord Chief Justice, Lord Goddard, to three months' imprisonment.

The *Isis* article was probably of little interest to the Soviets because
they certainly knew about the overflight program. This they demonstrated
two months later, on September 2, 1958, when an USAF EC-130 Hercules
from Incirli in Turkey was brought down near Jerevan in Armenia, with
a loss of all seventeen crew. The Americans simply announced the loss
of the EC-130 as the crash of an unarmed plane researching "radio-wave
propagation" in Turkey, not far from the Soviet frontier. Ten days later,
the Soviets confirmed that the EC-130 had come down in their territory,
and returned the bodies of six air-force crewmen. So what had happened
to the remaining eleven? Initially, the Soviets denied all knowledge of
the circumstances of the crash, and because there seemed a chance that
there were eleven prisoners behind the Iron Curtain, the State Department
released a tape and transcript of messages intercepted between five MiG
fighter pilots and their ground control. The NSA was not credited as the
source for this incriminating evidence, but the exchanges had been monitored at the NSA's listening post at Trabzon and the recordings made it
clear that the MiGs had deliberately attacked the unarmed American
aircraft, albeit one that had strayed into Soviet airspace. The Kremlin

denounced the speech recordings and transcript as forgeries, and then remained silent on the fate of the missing eleven crew. Curiously, the State Department did not actually announce them to be "presumed dead" for more than four years, until November 1962. In the meantime, the wireless war continued to be waged from higher altitudes.

The overflights over Russia continued until May 1, 1960, when a mat-black, unmarked U-2 piloted by Francis Gary Powers, on a routine mission from Peshawar in Pakistan to Bodö in Norway, was brought down near Sverdlovsk. The Soviets had fired several missiles at the U-2, as had become their custom, and none had made contact, but one had exploded close enough to send Powers's fragile plane into a spin. Unable to correct his course, Powers parachuted to the ground where he was captured.

The Kremlin's announcement that the U-2 had been shot down omitted to mention that Powers had escaped the crash and had been arrested. That item came soon after President Eisenhower's spokesmen had publicly stated that the downed U-2 was a civilian aircraft on a weather research flight. Apparently, the CIA had assured the White House that its pilot could never have survived, but it had been unaware that Powers had not used his ejection seat. Instead, he had managed to jettison the U-2's perspex canopy, clamber out of the cockpit and float to the ground on his parachute. Because he had decided against using his ejection seat, he failed to activate the U-2's automatic self-destruct mechanism and much of the plane's equipment had survived the ensuing crash.

Powers's arrest and subsequent trial were events of excruciating embarrassment for Eisenhower's administration, for it became clear that Powers was a contract employee of the CIA and that his plane was not engaged in meteorological research as claimed, but espionage. Large portions of the U-2's remains were put on public display in Moscow, including the photographic equipment and the electronic recording devices. The latter material was of great concern to the NSA for several electronic companies were identified as having supplied the U-2's receiving sets. Among them were such specialist firms as Micro Labs Inc., Huggins Labs of Menlo Park, California, Raytheon, General Electric, Hewlett-Packard and Transco Products. A Soviet SIGINT expert testified that

the radio apparatus examined is a system of airborne radio reconnaissance equipment, intended for the collection of information on the structure of the radio-technical service of the antiaircraft defense system of the Soviet Union, its individual towns, big industrial and administrative centers, as well as data on separate radio stations in this system. These data on the radio-technical service of the antiaircraft defense system of the Soviet Union were recorded on a ferromagnetic tape which was found to contain signals of ground radar stations of the Soviet Union.

Powers's own confession left little room for the U.S. administration to maneuver. He admitted his CIA links and confirmed that the flight had been authorized at the highest level and was intended to cross 4,700 kilometers of Soviet territory. The political fallout necessarily put an end to the overflights, but there was also a further loss of a more technical nature. For the first time, the Soviets had acquired the very latest Allied radio interception equipment, complete with their wave-guide assemblies, high-frequency amplifiers and complex antennae. After studying the captured apparatus, the Soviets would be able to make an accurate assessment of the NSA's capability and interests. In short, they could begin to plan suitable countermeasures. Such concerns, of course, were not shared by Powers, who expressed remorse for his part in the affair and received ten years' confinement, the first three to be served in prison. In fact, he was released early and was swopped for the Soviet spy Rudolf Abel on February 10, 1962.

The Soviets were naturally delighted by their success in capturing Powers and exposing the CIA's involvement, but they were unable to duplicate the U-2's impressive performance for another two years until they introduced their own version of the Canberra, the Yakovlev 25, code-named *Mandrake* by NATO. At the time, the Soviets extracted the maximum capital from the Powers affair and used the resulting propaganda to their advantage. However, in contrast to their public outrage and professed surprise at the U-2's incursion, they had certainly known about the overflights for some considerable time, as had been demonstrated by their futile rocket attacks on previous flights. There was also some evidence that Soviet diplomats had been spotted in parked cars close to the USAF airfield at Wiesbaden that serviced the U-2s. In addition, there was the odd case of the defection, in October 1959, of an American who had previously served in the U.S. Marine Corps as a radar operator with an air-control squadron at Atsugi in Japan, another of the U-2's airbases. It is probable that he too supplied the KGB with some information about the mysterious plane and its capabilities. The former marine private was named Lee Harvey Oswald, and was later to achieve some notoriety as the alleged assassin of President Kennedy.

The U-2 fiasco was to have a profound effect on the conduct of the secret wireless war; it left the Allies in a state of considerable anxiety. In other circumstances, the NSA might have abandoned the overflight intercept program and concentrated on its latest secret project, the construction of SIGINT platforms in space, but the Soviets had already established an impressive lead in the space race.

The first Soviet Sputnik had been launched in 1957, and the Americans had followed with the *Discoverer* program two years later. *Discoverer*'s objective was to place a series of satellites in orbit 567 miles over the Soviet Union and then return whatever information they collected to earth in special capsules. The project performed poorly, with only twenty-six of the thirty-eight attempted launches actually reaching their designated position. And of those, only twenty-three managed to eject the capsules. Unfortunately, the weak link was the method of recovering the ejected capsules which weighed around three hundred pounds each. The plan called for a specially modified C-119 plane to catch their parachutes in midair over the Pacific, but in total only twelve capsules were ever recovered and, in 1962, the *Discoverer* program was abandoned.

However, before giving up the project, some excellent material had been obtained from the first of the twelve successfully ejected and recovered capsules. This had occurred in August 1960, three months after the President had ordered a ban on all future U-2 overflights over the Soviet Union. On that occasion, the capsule contained no less than 6,200 photographic frames; when they were developed, each individual frame showed an area of 115 square miles in extraordinary detail. The intelligence authorities were elated at the quality of the pictures, in which single buildings could be identified and enlarged, but the celebrations were short-lived. On September 6, 1960, while Powers was beginning his prison term in Russia and the CIA's analysts were giving slide shows of the first *Discoverer* "takes," the NSA suffered its first defections.

9

A Prime Mole

In the last resort there is no procedure of personnel or physical security which will offer complete protection against the ill-disposed public servant who has access to secret information.

—Report of the Committee on Security Procedures in the Public Service, April 1962

Even before William Martin and Bernon Mitchell joined the NSA in July 1957, both had acquired considerable SIGINT experience. They had served together in the U.S. Navy where Martin, then aged twenty-nine and a chess champion, had been assigned to the Naval Security Group as a cryptographer at an intercept station in Alaska and had then moved on to another at Kamiseya in Japan. When Martin's period of service expired in 1954, he had briefly switched to the Army Security Agency as a mathematician. Mitchell, who was two years older, returned to his studies in 1954 and was recruited into the NSA while still at Stanford University.

Mitchell and Martin progressed through the NSA's training school and were posted to the Office of Research and Development where, in September 1959, they learned the true purpose of the EC-130 Hercules that was shot down in Soviet Armenia. Horrified that no one outside the intelligence community seemed to be aware of its mission for the NSA, the two cryptographers approached a congressman from Ohio and told him that far from being an innocent stray, the USAF transport had actually been a SIGINT "ferret," deliberately deployed with orders to test Soviet air defenses and to record any interesting electronic emissions. The congressman, Wayne Hays, subsequently decided to drop the matter and, disillusioned, Mitchell and Martin planned their defection during their summer vacation. On June 25, 1960, they flew to Mexico and the next day caught a plane to Havana. The NSA listed them as missing on August

1 when they failed to report for work, and five days later, after the briefest of investigations, the Department of Defense announced that "it must be assumed that there is a likelihood that they have gone behind the Iron Curtain."

Nothing more was heard of the two defectors until their appearance at a press conference in Moscow, at which they made the most damaging allegations, which included several disclosures about GCHQ and its close relationship with the NSA. Mitchell and Martin claimed that the NSA possessed "over two thousand manual intercept positions" and had broken the codes of more than forty countries, including "Italy, Turkey, France, Yugoslavia, the United Arab Republic, Indonesia and Uruguay." The two Americans angrily denounced the U-2 overflight program and described the crashed EC-130's real mission.

Perhaps as bad as the Mitchell-Martin affair was the aftermath of their defection. In the belated investigation into their backgrounds, it was discovered that neither should ever have been cleared for access to classified information. Both had probably been homosexuals and had openly associated with members of the Communist party. They had actually joined the party in February 1958 and, in December the following year, had taken a vacation in Cuba in violation of the NSA's regulations. It was also revealed that during a routine NSA polygraph test, Mitchell had once confessed to having indulged in some adolescent sexual experiments with dogs and chickens. Martin was believed to be a masochist. As if all this was not bad enough, the NSA's Director of Personnel, Maurice Klein, was found to have fabricated important parts of his own employment record and had been assisted by the NSA's Director of Security, a former FBI special agent named S. Wesley Reynolds, who had discovered the forgery but decided "it did not have a security significance." Both men were asked to resign immediately, as were twenty-six other NSA officials who were found to be "sexual deviates," and just one Communist who had previously been refused employment by three federal agencies because of his political views.

The Mitchell-Martin scandal sparked off a lengthy review of security procedures in the United States, and was matched in London by the continuing mole hunt into the numerous contacts of the Soviet spies, Burgess and Maclean. In 1960, the directorship of GCHQ had passed from Sir Eric Jones to his long-serving deputy, Commander Clive Loehnis RN. The son of a barrister, Loehnis had been educated at the Royal Naval Colleges at Osborne, Dartmouth and Greenwich, and had qualified in signal duties in 1928. He had retired from the navy in 1935, but had been reemployed in the Admiralty's Signals Division three years later. In 1942, he had been transferred to Bletchley and, at the end of the war, had formally joined GCHQ. Jones had appointed him as his deputy in 1952, and he had been knighted ten years later.

As well as processing all the current Cold War signals, GCHQ was still preoccupied with the clues contained in the old Soviet decrypts. MI5 was still in pursuit of the high-level spies who had appeared in the VENONA traffic more than a decade earlier, and to date the best suspects had been Kim Philby, the MI6 liaison officer in Washington who had been sacked immediately after the defections of Burgess and Maclean in 1951, and John Cairncross, another former wartime MI6 officer who had served in Hut 6 at Bletchley. Neither Philby nor Cairncross had made any admissions, so the atmosphere in British counterintelligence circles was one of general mutual suspicion, although on the surface it appeared as if GCHQ had escaped the damaging breaches of security that had bedeviled its American partners and both MI5 and MI6.

In fact, throughout this period the NSA was hemorrhaging secrets on a vast scale through Sergeant Jack Dunlap, although his treachery only came to light after his suicide in July 1963. Dunlap had joined the NSA as a chauffeur in April 1958 and had later become a courier, carrying sensitive NSA documents between the agency's various different buildings. He was also selling copies to the KGB, although nobody was ever able to establish exactly how much he compromised. However, judging by the estimated $60,000 paid to Dunlap in cash by the KGB, it seems likely that he photographed and sold virtually every classified item he handled. Dunlap's newfound, hard-to-explain wealth, which included three cars, two boats and an expensive mistress, led to his suspension in May 1963 and to two suicide attempts. He finally succeeded in taking his own life on July 22, an event which was followed by his widow's discovery of a cache of NSA documents.

On the very same day that Dunlap died, *Izvestia* published a letter from yet another disillusioned former NSA official. This time it was an Arab named Hindali, a graduate of the American University in Beirut, who had been forced to resign from the NSA in June 1959 following a bout of mental illness. Hindali had changed his name to Victor Hamilton after his marriage to an American whom he had met in Libya, and he had been hired by the NSA in June 1957 as an analyst researching Middle Eastern ciphers. In his Soviet letter, Hindali omitted to mention that he had been diagnosed as approaching a paranoid schizophrenic breakdown, but he gave a detailed description of his work at Fort Meade. Hindali stated that the wireless traffic of "Syria, Iraq, Lebanon, Jordan, Saudi Arabia, Yemen, Libya, Morocco, Tunisia, Turkey, Iran, Greece and Ethiopia" was routinely examined by the NSA's ALLO division. He was, he said, an

> expert on the Near East Sector in the office designated ALLO, which means All Other Countries. . . . The duties of my colleagues in ALLO included the study and breaking of military ciphers of these countries, and also the deciphering of all correspondence reaching their diplomatic representatives in any part of the world. . . . I knew for a fact that the State Department and the Defense Department systematically read, analyzed and utilized in their own interests the enciphered correspondence between the United Arab Republic embassies in Europe and the UAR government in Cairo.

Hindali's disclosures added further discomfort to the beleaguered NSA, but there were still instances when the organization could demonstrate its extraordinary skills. Chief among them was the opportunity granted by the war of nerves that became known as the Cuban missile crisis.

Following President Eisenhower's ban on Soviet overflights in 1960 and the switch of emphasis to new satellite systems such as the *Discoverer*, the NSA came under increasing scrutiny from Soviet SIGINT-collecting ships. By 1962, the Soviets had just four such oceangoing vessels operational, all converted trawlers which could spend long periods at sea. Within fifteen years more than 160 were to be spotted by Western naval observers. Designated AGIs, for "Auxiliary Vessel, Intelligence Gatherer," these floating Soviet SIGINT platforms first appeared around the NSA base on Johnston Island in the Pacific during the American atmospheric testing of nuclear weapons in 1958 and the *Discoverer* experiments in 1960. The NSA responded by building its own secret fleet of AGTRs (Auxiliary General Technical Research vessels), of which the first was the *Private Jose F. Valdez*, a rusting hulk of a 1944-vintage Liberty ship which was packed with electronic receiving gear and sent down to cruise in the South Atlantic off the coast of Africa. All the freighter's holds had been transformed into large, secure "crypto and communication spaces," filled with the very latest SIGINT recording apparatus. The *Valdez*'s sister ship, the *Joseph E. Muller*, also underwent a similar conversion and, in August 1962, picked up the first signs of Soviet military rockets in Cuba. Based in Port Everglades in Florida, the *Muller* and another AGTR, the *Oxford*, relayed the intercepted Russian traffic to Fort Meade, where it was confirmed that the Soviets had begun installing offensive ballistic missiles around San Cristóbal. A U-2 obtained further proof during a series of reconnaissance flights which, incidentally, cost the life of the pilot, Major Rudolf Anderson, who was shot down on August 27. Altogether nine separate missile sites were identified by the *Muller* and photographed by U-2s operating from Texas and Florida. Confronted with the visual proof (but not the SIGINT evidence), Khrushchev announced on October 28 that the missile bases were to be dismantled and shipped home.

The success of the *Muller* and *Oxford* encouraged the NSA to expand its fleet, and in 1963 the *Georgetown* and *Jamestown* were taken out of mothballs and commissioned. The *Georgetown* concentrated on Latin America, while the *Jamestown* joined the *Valdez* off South Africa. Finally, late in 1964, the *Liberty* and *Belmont* were deployed around the West African coastline and off the coast of South America, respectively. Two regular warships also fitted out with SIGINT equipment, the destroyers *Turner Joy* and *Maddox*, were involved in a brief skirmish in 1964 off the Gulf of Tonkin. In retaliation, the United States launched its first air attack on North Vietnam.

At the end of May 1967, the *Liberty* was ordered to make for the U.S. naval facility at Rota, in southern Spain, where she was to be joined by a group of NSA linguists who were to replace the French-speaking personnel. The leisurely cruise in West African waters had been canceled and, instead, the *Liberty* had been ordered to monitor the tension-filled airwaves of the eastern Mediterranean. The *Liberty* arrived on station, in international waters off the Sinai Peninsula, on June 7, 1967, and proceeded to move slowly up and down the Egyptian coast, listening constantly to the Arab-Israeli conflict that had erupted suddenly just three days earlier.

Although of May 1945 vintage, the *Liberty* contained some of the most sophisticated radio equipment afloat, and was in constant touch with the NSA's secret annex at the U.S. Naval Communications Station at Asmera, in Eritrea, and the two signals centers at Port-Lyautey in Morocco and another in Greece. Throughout most of the morning of June 8 the ship was buzzed by a single Israeli jet and several reconnaissance aircraft, so the skipper, Commander William McGonagle, sent the crew to action stations. Because they were in relatively shallow waters, all unnecessary classified documents were destroyed, a routine precaution. It was a wise one, for at exactly 1400 two Dassault Mirage fighters launched a rocket attack on the *Liberty*. The coordinated incendiary bombing and strafing that followed during the next few minutes left the ship with three major fires and eight crewmen dead or dying. A further seventy-five were wounded by shrapnel or blast. It was subsequently established that the *Liberty*'s hull and superstructure had been hit 821 times. When most of the ship's radio masts had been shot away, and only a voice channel survived, McGonagle reported his situation to the U.S. Sixth Fleet. He also ordered a signalman to replace the tattered remains of the American flag with the holiday ensign, the largest flag aboard which measured 7 × 13 feet. No sooner had this been hauled up than three Israeli torpedo boats were spotted closing in. They strafed the ship with machine-gun fire and launched two torpedoes, one of which holed the hull under the waterline and killed twenty-five of the crew, including Allen Blue, one of the three NSA civilians who had joined the ship at Rota.

Though listing badly, the *Liberty* survived the Israeli attacks and sixteen and a half hours later was just able to limp to a rendezvous with two destroyers from the Sixth Fleet. The casualties were evacuated to a military hospital in Naples, but Commander McGonagle, though wounded himself, remained with the *Liberty* and, in company with a naval tug, steered it to Malta for repairs. Two boats from the destroyers remained in the area, searching the sea for classified material that might have washed out of the gaping thirty-nine-foot gash in the *Liberty*'s hull. They were watched by a Soviet Kildin class guided-missile destroyer, but it was not seen to pick anything out of the water.

The day after the incident, the Israelis apologized and claimed that they had mistaken the *Liberty* for an Egyptian ship, the *El-Kasir*, an explanation that the NSA's deputy director called "a nice whitewash." An Israeli court of inquiry later absolved its personnel from any blame, although the Israeli government was to pay $3.3 million in compensation to the families of the thirty-four crew members killed and $3.5 million to those wounded. Eventually, on December 18, 1980, a further $6 million was paid to the United States for "material damage" to the *Liberty*.

In 1981, the NSA commissioned a top-secret report on the incident from William D. Gerhard, the long-serving chief librarian at Fort Meade. Gerhard's painstaking account was partly declassified in July 1983, and those sections that were released uncensored added little to the story, except to confirm that virtually no one really believed the official version of an "Israeli miscalculation."

No sooner had the NSA recovered from the *Liberty* affair than it became embroiled in another incident afloat which, in SIGINT terms, was of far more lasting damage. On January 23, 1968, another merchantman converted into an NSA floating platform, the USS *Pueblo*, came under attack from North Korean torpedo boats.

The *Pueblo* was on its first SIGINT mission, having been commissioned the previous year, and was lying stationary in international waters sixteen miles off the Korean coast when three fast patrol vessels approached and ordered the *Pueblo*'s skipper, Commander Lloyd Bucher, to heave to. Bucher assumed that he was about to experience the kind of routine harassment that the *Pueblo*'s sister ship, the *Banner*, had been subjected to on most of its sixteen missions. He reported the situation to Camp Fuchinobe, the NSA base outside Tokyo, via the Naval Communications Station at Kamiseya, and set a course out to sea at a speed of five knots. Suddenly, at 1330, the Koreans opened fire with a cannon and hit Bucher and two crewmen. They then ordered the *Pueblo* to sail under escort to the North Korean port of Wŏnsan. Bucher indicated that he would comply, and for the next hour trailed behind the Koreans, destroying as much classified material as could be burned. After an hour, the convoy stopped and the *Pueblo* was boarded by just eight Koreans. The *Pueblo*'s crew of eighty-two offered no resistance and the ship's last radio message simply stated, "Ship being boarded at this time. Four men injured, one critically. Going off the air now and destroying this gear." All the crew were bound and blindfolded for the remainder of the journey into Wŏnsan, where the *Pueblo* docked later the same night.

Both the crew and ship remained captives of the North Koreans for the following eleven months, during which time there was ample opportunity to interrogate in depth the cryptographic personnel and to study all the ship's classified wireless equipment, of which more than a ton was removed from the communication spaces. Commander Bucher was coerced into making a confession in which he falsely admitted having violated North Korea's territorial waters, and a similar document was signed by some of his crew. Following the release of the bogus confessions, the U.S. government published the text of its own apology, the Koreans' precondition for the release of the crew. In it President Johnson's administration confirmed that the *Pueblo*

> had illegally intruded into the territorial waters of the Democratic People's Republic of Korea on many occasions and conducted espionage activities of spying out important military and state secrets of the Democratic People's Republic of Korea.

Bucher and his men were set free at Panmunjom on December 23, 1968. The *Pueblo* fiasco sealed the fate of the NSA's secret fleet, and all the remaining vessels were returned to Norfolk, Virginia, where they were unceremoniously stripped of their equipment and turned into scrap. Only one AGTR survived the program: the *Pueblo*, which, while officially attached to the U.S. Seventh Fleet, actually still remains in North Korean hands and is used as a coastal freighter based at Najin, uncomfortably close to the Soviet border.

While the NSA coped with its woes, the hierarchy at Cheltenham was equally beleaguered. The *Liberty* and *Pueblo* affairs had drawn unwelcome attention to the secret wireless war, but it was a newspaper story published in the *Daily Express* on February 21, 1967, that really set the cat among the SIGINT pigeons.

The story had originated five days earlier when a disenchanted young telegraphist, named Robert Lawson, formerly employed by two big firms, Commercial Cables and Western Union, visited Fleet Street in an attempt to interest various newspapers in his claim that the Ministry of Defense routinely collected copies of all the company's incoming and outgoing cable traffic, and returned them forty-eight hours later. At the *Daily Mail*, Lawson was seen by Celia Haddon and Angus Macpherson and the allegation was checked with the Ministry of Defense's Press Office. The story, Macpherson was assured, "was nonsense," but he was unconvinced. Nevertheless, his newspaper was persuaded by Colonel Sammy Lohan, the secretary of the Ministry of Defense's D-Notice Committee, not to publish.

Lawson, evidently disappointed by the *Daily Mail*'s decision, was subsequently turned away from the *Manchester Evening News*. But at the *Daily Express* building he was directed to Chapman Pincher, the newspaper's veteran defense correspondent who also happened to be a close friend of Colonel Lohan. Pincher made two telephone calls to check the telegraphist's story and received two startlingly different replies. His call to the Ministry of Defense's Press Office elicited the same kind of flat denial as had been given to Macpherson, but the Post Office reluctantly agreed that some overseas cables were submitted to the security authorities on a regular basis.

The contradiction between the two replies irresistibly attracted the newspaperman, and he was subsequently advised that the government had been granted the right to inspect the contents of overseas cables by Section 4 of the 1920 Official Secrets Act. His sensational story was published on the front page of the *Daily Express* five days after Lawson's visit to the paper and sparked off a major political row. The Prime Minister, Harold Wilson, insisted that the paper had published in spite of a legitimate request not to do so because of the damage it might cause to national security. The *Daily Express* responded by pointing out that routine, large-scale interception was a matter of genuine public concern and quite different from an isolated case connected with an individual counterespionage investigation. In fact, the entire area was covered by a blanket ban, itself a closely guarded secret, issued under the Defense Notices convention, in which newspaper editors were requested not to comment publicly on certain subjects. Ten days after the *Express* story, D-Notice No. 2, dated October 30, 1961, was published. It demanded silence about

> the various methods used in the interception of foreign communications for secret intelligence purposes. In this connection the Committee request that you will not refer to the fact that on occasions it is necessary in the interest of defense for the services to intercept such communications.

The emphasis of the original *Express* article had been Pincher's claim that the large-scale interception of overseas cables had been quite a recent event:

> Most of the original cables and telegrams go out through the Post Office, which owns the former Cable & Wireless Company. Cables passed through private companies—mainly branches of foreign concerns operating in Britain—are collected in vans or cars each morning and taken to the Post Office security department.
> It has not been possible to establish when this routine cable probe was introduced but I understand it has been in operation for several years.

On the day after the storm broke, Pincher defended his decision to publish on the grounds that the relevant D-Notice covered only the occasional interception of communications and did not refer to the general principle of wholesale "vetting." "My inquiries show that though sporadic checks of cables had always been permissible under the Official Secrets Acts, the *routine* vetting of all cables is more recent." The SIGINT community was now in considerable difficulties and was presented with an awkward choice. It could either admit that Pincher was forty years late with his revelation, and confirm that virtually every overseas cable had been routinely passed to GCHQ since 1920, or it could try to cover its tracks by concentrating on the question of whether or not the *Daily Express* had breached a D-Notice. The cryptanalysts took the latter course, and the argument centered on the behavior of the *Express* which was in sharp contrast to the attitude originally taken by the *Daily Mail*. It also called into question exactly what had taken place during a lunch at which Lohan and Pincher had debated the issue of publishing Lawson's claims. Lohan thought he had persuaded Pincher to drop the story; Pincher insisted that Lohan had given him the go-ahead. A government inquiry subsequently concluded that there had been no breach of the convention, but the Prime Minister disagreed and issued a White Paper criticizing Pincher and his newspaper. The net result was to deflect attention away from the central issue of the intercepts and to bring the antiquated D-Notice Committee system into general disrepute. The oddest feature of the entire affair is that in all the parliamentary debates and the dozens of newspaper comments, GCHQ's name was never once mentioned, nor was that of Sir Clive Loehnis's successor as Director, Leonard Hooper.

Hooper, who had taken over from Sir Clive in 1965, had originally joined Bletchley from the Air Ministry in 1942. A graduate of Worcester College, Oxford, Hooper was actually knighted in the New Year Honors just a few weeks before the storm broke. Yet, in spite of the furor, GCHQ escaped unscathed, in part because there was little danger of anyone within the traditionally close-lipped British intelligence community speaking up. Even the embittered Alastair Denniston, who died in 1961, had gone to his grave without revealing any of GCHQ's wartime secrets. Furthermore, there was no chance of any senior figure from within the communications industry making any public comment. The big British companies had all willingly collaborated with GCHQ, and many senior GCHQ officials like Henry Maine had taken consultancy posts on their retirement with such firms as Standard Telephone & Cables. Indeed, many insiders knew GCHQ's relationship with Cable & Wireless to be so close that it was often difficult to determine where a liaison section ended and a commercial department began. It was common knowledge that the company gave commercial cover to GCHQ intercept operators in hostile environments; and in certain key sites, such as Ascension Island and St. Helena, the Cable & Wireless operators were obliged to undergo the government's Positive Vetting procedure for a security clearance. In some locations the commercial operators were even billeted in GCHQ buildings. Cable & Wireless's two postwar chairmen, Sir Stanley Angwin and Sir Leslie Nicholls, had both enjoyed distinguished careers in the Royal Corps of Signals before their peacetime appointments, and were no strangers to intelligence work. Even Cable & Wireless's American competitors maintained a discreet silence on the *Daily Express*'s revelations. They had good reason to, for the NSA had been following GCHQ's example, as will soon be seen.

In fact, Hooper was a past master at protecting his organization from unwelcome attention. A year earlier, in 1966, word had reached MI6 that an American academic was planning a major book on cryptography entitled *The Codebreakers*. The author, David Kahn, was approached to delete three brief paragraphs, which described GCHQ and disclosed its location in Cheltenham . . . and the identity of its director. Both John Tiltman, the SUKLO in Washington, and Geoffrey Evans, a senior GCHQ official, told Kahn's American publishers that the deletion was essential to national security, and Kahn gave his consent. Accordingly, *The Codebreakers* was published in the United States and in Britain and became the standard textbook on the subject, but omitted all mention of GCHQ or its predecessor, GC&CS.

The American intervention on GCHQ's behalf was not entirely unselfish. The NSA was anxious to limit the public's knowledge about its own organization, and to date very little had been disclosed about it. The two most persistent journalists in the intelligence field, David Wise and Thomas Ross, had briefly referred to the NSA in three of their books, *The U-2 Affair* (1962), *The Invisible Government* (1964) and *The Espionage Establishment* (1967), but each had contained only the briefest of references to the NSA's existence. Despite their controversial reputation in Washington, the two authors had "voluntarily omitted certain information, particularly dealing with current intelligence operations, in the belief that the national interest would best be served by withholding it." One example of their patriotism is to be found in their statement that the U-2 had "an altitude no higher than 58,000 feet," which was amended by the equally fictitious comment in a footnote that "advanced models of the U-2, such as the one flown by Powers, actually had a ceiling of over 80,000 feet." In fact, "over 90,000 feet" would have been nearer the mark, but the CIA had pointed out that at the time of publication the U-2 was still undertaking missions over hostile (though not necessarily Soviet) territory.

The NSA was concerned to preserve GCHQ's anonymity because it too was involved in secret surveillance of overseas communications in an operation code-named SHAMROCK. Ever since 1945, the American Army Security Agency (ASA) had required the three biggest U.S.-based international commercial carriers, RCA Global, ITT World Communications and Western Union, to copy all their traffic and send it to the ASA. This procedure, in parallel with GCHQ's cable-copying program, was in violation of the 1934 Federal Communications Act, but the ASA had assured the companies concerned that there was no chance of prosecution and that anyway the law was open to several different interpretations if the intercepted traffic was to, or from, an overseas destination.

While Britain was debating Chapman Pincher's revelation, the White House authorized an extension of SHAMROCK to cover American domestic traffic and, in particular, communications to and from names on a list of civil rights and antiwar activists compiled by the FBI. Within the NSA this highly illegal project was code-named MINARET and was put into operation with GCHQ's passive assistance. Most of America's overseas communications were then channeled across the Atlantic via one of two Intelsat satellites in permanent geosynchronous high orbit, 22,375 miles over the ocean. The ground bases for the transatlantic traffic are located at Andover, Maine, and Etam, West Virginia, on America's eastern seaboard, and at Madley in Herefordshire and Goonhilly in Cornwall in the British Isles. Each of the two satellites could handle up to four thousand telephone circuits and rather more telex or data channels. By the end of 1967, the NSA had secretly constructed two identical receiving stations at Winter Harbor, Maine, and Sugar Grove, West Virginia. Coincidentally, two similar bases were built in England, at Menwith Hill in Yorkshire and at Morwenstow in north Cornwall. The first site, five hundred acres of windswept Yorkshire moorland outside the market town of Harrogate, had been occupied by the U.S. Army Security Agency's 13th Field Station since 1955, although it only came under the NSA's direct control in August 1966. The second, on the cliffs of Morwenstow, remains within GCHQ's Composite Signals Organization.

By initiating the MINARET program on British territory, the NSA hoped to avoid breaking the 1934 statue. Once intercepted, the resulting product (which required no decryption as it was generally in plain language) was relayed via a secure NSA channel to Fort Meade for processing by an IBM 7090 computer, which boasted a capacity of 230,000 separate calculations per second. However, the project was to be short-lived, for it was hastily abandoned in the wake of the Watergate investigations and the numerous congressional inquiries into illegal intelligence operations.

No sooner had the "cable vetting scandal" died down in Britain than GCHQ discovered its first major case of Soviet espionage. Few details were made public at the time, but the spy was Douglas Britten, a senior RAF SIGINT expert who held the rank of chief technician. He was arrested at RAF Digby in September 1968, as a result of MI5's routine surveillance of the Soviet Consulate in London. Britten was spotted attempting to contact his Soviet controller and subsequently confessed to having been recruited in 1962, thirteen years after he had joined the RAF. Britten held an amateur radio license and had first been approached in the Science Museum in South Kensington. There he had agreed to sell a Soviet intelligence officer an obsolete RAF 1154 wireless. The Soviet had kept in touch, and when Britten had been posted to the RAF's 33 Signals Unit at Pergamos, inside the British Sovereign Base at Dhekelia, Cyprus, other Soviet agents had paid him for information. He had served in Cyprus for four years, during which period he had ample opportunity to compromise the Pergamos station and the three other British SIGINT installations in Cyprus: the No. 9 Signal Regiment's sites at Ayios Nikolaos, Episkopi and the big complex on top of Mount Olympus in the Troodos Mountains. In October 1966, Britten had returned to resume his duties at RAF Digby in Leicestershire, the very heart of the RAF's SIGINT organization in Europe which controlled the old wartime station at RAF Cheadle, 2 Signals Unit at RAF Bampton Castle and 9 Signals Unit at RAF Boddington, as well as the RAF's numerous overseas installations. Britten pleaded guilty to espionage at the Old Bailey on November 4, 1968, and was sentenced to twenty-one years' imprisonment by the Lord Chief Justice, Lord Parker.

The exact extent of Britten's treachery remains unknown, but clearly there were few secrets in the SIGINT field to which he was not privy. He had served in Cyprus and RAF Digby, and enjoyed the highest security clearance. What he did not have a direct knowledge of, he could certainly have found out during the five years he traded with the KGB. RAF Digby was, and remains today, the center of the RAF's intercept network, and Britten was certainly aware of the technical details of the RAF's intercept procedures.

Britten's belated arrest came in time to prevent him from compromising the West's latest generation of SIGINT interception platforms, the satellite successors to the ill-fated *Discoverer* series. The first of these was the huge, forty-nine-foot-long *Big Bird* platform, built by Lockheed and launched in June 1971. It was designed to relay SIGINT material to ground stations connected to the *Skynet* system, like the satellite control facilities at RAF Oakhanger in Hampshire and Pine Gap, near Alice Springs in Australia. Unlike the geostationary satellites, *Big Bird* had a relatively short life-span and burned up on reentering the earth's atmosphere after an existence lasting between 90 and 180 days. While *Big Bird* was in orbit, particularly sensitive intercepts could be recorded on tape and then be jettisoned in up to six recoverable canisters, in much the same way that the first *Discoverer* tapes were retrived. In addition to its SIGINT equipment, *Big Bird* contained a giant camera built by the Perkin-Elmer Corporation, with a lens the size of a man, capable of a resolution of 8 inches from a height of 110 miles. Since 1971, there have been an average of two *Big Bird* launches a year, and the resulting information has been received at five locations around the globe: Guam, the Seychelles, Oahu, Ascension and New Boston. Guidance signals are transmitted from two control stations, at Kodiak Island in Alaska and Vandenberg Air Force Base in California.

Big Bird was followed, in March 1973, by the most sophisticated of all platforms, and arguably the most successful, the RHYOLITE. Uniquely, the RHYOLITE proved that it was possible to monitor high-frequency and VHF transmissions from space, and this proved to be of inestimable value for analyzing the telemetry data of Soviet missile tests. The Soviets had not bothered to encrypt their telemetry broadcasts because they believed the low-power transmissions could be received only in the immediate vicinity of the launch. The RHYOLITE was able to keep all the operational rocket proving grounds under surveillance, but details of the RHYOLITE were betrayed to the Soviets almost as soon as the design work had been completed, and so they hastily introduced telemetry encryption into their tests.

The first evidence that the Soviets had succeeded in penetrating RHYOLITE came on January 6, 1977, when a twenty-five-year-old convicted drug peddler named Andrew Daulton Lee was arrested in Mexico when he was spotted by the local police throwing a package into the Soviet Embassy's compound. When searched, he was found to be carrying Minox films of classified documents from the TRW Corporation of Redondo Beach, the Californian defense contractor which had constructed the RHYOLITE satellite. The miniaturized films were of top-secret plans for a third generation of communications satellites, code-named PYRAMIDER by the CIA, which would enable undercover agents to exchange high-frequency radio signals "in denied areas" without risk of discovery by hostile direction finding. Ten days later, on January 17, Lee was handed over to the FBI and revealed that for the past two years he had been supplied with secret information from TRW's code room by a boyhood friend, Christopher Boyce. Because of TRW's specialist work for the CIA and the NSA, it had been equipped with a secure communications chamber, known as the black vault, where Boyce had access to several coding machines and scrambled voice channels to the CIA's headquarters at Langley, Virginia, and several of the NSA's satellite control facilities. The two had financed their drug habit by selling photographs taken by Boyce to the KGB. Among the compromised TRW documents were the operating manuals for the RHYOLITE satellite.

Boyce was arrested on January 16, 1977. A month earlier, he had resigned from his post at the TRW Corporation so that he could return to college, at the University of California at Riverside. During his two years of espionage, he had passed Lee dozens of copies of secret documents, including many concerned with the RHYOLITE and PYRAMIDER projects, and an even more sensitive SIGINT satellite which was still in the development stage, code-named ARGUS. Boyce and Lee were convicted of espionage in April 1977, but the prosecution was handicapped by the government's reluctance to allow the compromised secret documents to be released in evidence. Both men were eventually found guilty, and Lee received a life sentence. Boyce got forty years. (Their story was recently made into a film, *The Falcon and the Snowman*.)

While the CIA and NSA instituted a damage-control exercise to establish how much of the Allied SIGINT satellite program had been compromised by Boyce, a further security breach was uncovered. On August 17, 1978, a former junior CIA officer, William Kampiles, was arrested in Hammond, Indiana, and charged with the theft of a satellite operating manual nine months earlier. Kampiles, a twenty-three-year-old graduate of the University of Indiana, had been recruited into the CIA on the strength of his fluency in Greek, which he had learned from his immigrant parents. During his brief spell at the CIA's headquarters in Langley, he had undertaken routine watch-officer duties in the Operations Center and had removed copy No. 155 of a classified sixty-four-page technical manual on the KH-11 SIGINT satellite code-named KEYHOLE. In November 1977, he had resigned from the agency and, the following March while on holiday in Athens, had sold the manual for $3,000 to a Soviet intelligence officer. He had then volunteered to go back to work for the CIA, but as soon as he revealed his contacts with the Soviets he was arrested. After failing two polygraph tests, Kampiles gave his FBI interrogators a full confession.

KEYHOLE was a low-altitude SIGINT platform, which was first

launched into orbit on December 19, 1976. Its operating height of three hundred miles gave it a duration of two years, a considerable advance on *Big Bird*. KEYHOLE was equipped with infrared and multispectral photographic apparatus, and boasted "advanced sensor and data transmission techniques." In the language of laymen, it was the very latest surveillance satellite, and one far in advance of anything the Soviets had built.

During the course of Kampiles's trial, it was disclosed that no less than thirteen copies of the secret KEYHOLE manual were unaccounted for at the CIA's headquarters. This revelation had little impact on the jury, and Kampiles was declared guilty and sentenced to forty years' imprisonment.

That KEYHOLE had been betrayed was extremely worrying, for low-altitude SIGINT platforms were particularly important during the 1970s as secure land-based intercept stations became vulnerable to the increasingly volatile political climate in the Middle and Far East. Four clandestine GCHQ operators working under Cable & Wireless cover were killed by Turkish terrorists at Sinop, on the Black Sea coast, in 1972. Even the weather seemed against GCHQ. In December 1974, Cyclone Tracy hit the Coonawarra station at Darwin and the base had to be temporarily evacuated and then rebuilt thirty-two kilometers south of Darwin on the Stuart Highway. In 1971, the election of President Allende's Popular Socialist party in Chile forced the closure of an NSA installation on Easter Island. The NSA's huge station at Kagnew, near Asmera, in Eritrea, was forced to close in May 1977 following the overthrow of the Ethiopian emperor, while in July 1975 the Turkish government had suspended the NSA's installations along the Soviet frontier in retaliation for the arms embargo imposed by Washington, an act that was itself a response to the Turkish invasion of Cyprus. In December 1979, the listening post at Behshahr was evacuated pending the collapse of the shah's regime in Iran, and the NSA's civilian staff at the Kabkan monitoring station experienced some agonizing days when they realized that the incoming revolutionary government had no idea of their continued presence in Iran. The Kabkan base had functioned normally until the Iranian unit charged with guarding the perimeter fence mutinied and denounced the Americans to the mullahs in Tehran. Embarrassed by the appearance of this uncharted American radio installation, the new regime allowed the NSA discreetly to evacuate all its personnel. However, not all the political developments of the period were of a negative nature. Following President Nixon's historic visit to Peking, secret negotiations were entered into with the People's Republic of China, who granted the NSA permission to build two intercept bases, at Korla and Qitai, high in the Himalayas in the autonomous region of Xinkiang, close to the Soviet border.

The Soviets, who had also made a heavy investment in the SIGINT field, had opted for mobile platforms, with a heavy emphasis on purpose-built, seagoing intercept vessels. By 1979, the number of Warsaw Pact AGIs had reached nearly 200. They also ran a sizable airborne fleet of long-range "ferrets" with which to probe Western defenses. These, combined with an average of no less than 329 satellites in orbit at any one moment, gave the Soviets a numerical, though not a technical, advantage over NATO. With the construction plans and operating details of the various different systems supplied by Boyce and Kampiles, the Allied SIGINT experts assumed that what the KGB lacked more than anything else was the overview, which might show Moscow how all the elements were put together and how clear a picture it all provided of Soviet activities. What the Soviets needed more than anything was information from that rarest of sources, the well-informed Russian specialist who had access to virtually every type of SIGINT material relating to the Soviet Union from both sides of the Atlantic. That source was to be Geoffrey Prime.

Prime was eighteen when he joined the RAF in 1956. He volunteered for a language course and qualified as a Russian linguist. In 1964, following a tour of duty in Kenya, he was posted to the receiving station at Gatow, Berlin's military airfield, from where Brian Patchett had deserted nine years earlier. Prime remained at Gatow for four years during which time he worked in a section supplying RAF Digby, where Douglas Britten was then based, with tactical Eastern Bloc intercepts. He then returned to England to join GCHQ, which was still under Sir Leonard Hooper's directorship. His first appointment, at the end of September 1968, was to the Joint Technical Language Service. Prime proved a diligent worker and in March 1976 was assigned to the Soviet section of J Division, the special SIGINT unit handling the most sensitive of Soviet intercepts. On November 1, 1976, Prime was again promoted to head a J Division subsection and was even made a Personnel Security Supervisor, charged with responsibility for submitting annual security reports on his colleagues. The pressure of his double life clearly took its toll and, having divorced his first wife and remarried, he resigned from GCHQ in September 1978 and became a taxi driver in Cheltenham. Although out of the organization, he kept in touch with his colleagues and often collected them from the railway station for the short ride to either Oakley or Benhall Park, GCHQ's two sites on the outskirts of the town.

Prime would probably have remained undiscovered if he had not begun to sexually assault young schoolgirls. In April 1982, the police obtained the description of a car used by the attacker in three incidents. The owner of every car fitting the description was visited, and on April 27 it was Prime's turn. Two detectives took a statement from him at his home, and though he denied having molested the schoolchildren, he made a full confession to his wife the same evening. The following day Prime repeated his confession to the police and admitted having been responsible for three attacks on children in the area. He was promptly arrested and, once again, matters might have rested there if, while still in custody, he had not confided in his wife. She reported his duplicity and surrendered a cache of espionage paraphernalia she had found hidden under his bed. Three weeks after her husband had been taken into custody, Rhona Prime called the police back to her home and sparked off one of the most intensive espionage investigations ever known in England. On June 26, when confronted with the evidence of his work for the KGB—a stack of preaddressed envelopes marked with the name of a contact in East Berlin and two polythene sachets containing one-time pads—Prime finally agreed to make a full confession which took him nine hours. In it he told how he volunteered his services to the Soviets while still in Berlin with the RAF, and how he had held several meetings with his Russian contacts, including a lengthy debriefing session with them in Vienna in 1980 and another in East Germany in 1981. The damage caused by Prime to the Allied SIGINT community was unequaled. Between the date of his re-cruitment in January 1968 and his retirement from GCHQ a decade later, Prime had told the Soviets everything he knew: GCHQ's internal struc-ture, its operating procedures, its personalities, the location of its intercept sites in Britain and overseas, the performance of its mobile platforms, the commercial and diplomatic covers used by clandestine intercept op-erators, the relative quality of the two major satellite systems to which he had had access, *Big Bird* and RHYOLITE, and numerous other details. For more than ten years, the Soviets had enjoyed a source at the very heart of the Allied SIGINT effort. At the time of Prime's retirement, GCHQ directly employed rather less than 10 percent of the NSA's total of 68,203, but the organization was nevertheless regarded as an equal partner in many joint projects and accorded privileged access to numerous secret activities.

Prime's crime was matched by the severity of the sentence meted out by the Lord Chief Justice, Lord Lane, at the Old Bailey in November 1982: thirty-five years for espionage and three years for his sexual as-saults, to run consecutively. The task before GCHQ and the NSA was to repair the damage, or at least assess if such a feat was possible. The scale of Prime's betrayal was truly hard to grasp. His time in GCHQ had spanned the stewardship of three directors: Sir Leonard (Joe) Hooper had been appointed Intelligence Coordinator to the Cabinet in 1972, and early in the following year his deputy, Arthur (Bill) Bonsall, one of Josh Cooper's wartime recruits from the Air Ministry, had succeeded him. Upon his retirement five years later, Brian Tovey had taken over. A graduate of St. Edmund Hall, Oxford, and the School of Oriental and African Studies at London University, Tovey had not joined GCHQ until 1950. It became his responsibility to pick up the pieces left by the Prime affair, to liaise with the inevitable Security Commission inquiry and to handle the consequent political fallout.

GCHQ had suddenly become notorious and was constantly referred to in the media as the "spy center in Cheltenham." Much of the trouble taken throughout the early 1970s to discourage open discussion about Britain's most secret intelligence body had been in vain. In 1973, the Independent Broadcasting Authority had stepped in to prevent publication of a brief film segment shot outside Oakley's main gate in Prior's Road. In May 1976, following the publication of a controversial article on SIGINT by Mark Hosenball and Duncan Campbell entitled "The Eavesdroppers" in *Time Out*, a former Intelligence Corps corporal, John Berry, had approached two radical journalists, Crispin Aubrey and Duncan Campbell, and had given an account of his service with the No. 9 Signal Regiment at its intercept base at Ayios Nikolaos in Cyprus. All three were arrested and prosecuted, but the case became a *cause célèbre* when the identity of the prosecution's principal witness, Colonel Hugh Johnstone, was revealed in the House of Commons. The Crown had tried to conceal "Colonel B's" true name in an ill-conceived attempt to protect what was alleged to be the interests of national security. The defense pointed out that Colonel Johnstone's position was well known to all the readers of the (unclassified) regimental journal, *The Wire*. It also demonstrated that almost all of the documentary material offered as evidence of espionage had been gleaned from legitimate, open sources, freely available to all journalists and researchers. All three defendants were convicted of minor breaches of the Official Secrets Act, but six of the original nine charges were dropped. The Crown was obliged to content itself with a deportation order on Mark Hosenball, who was American, and a banning order on his source, a former American employee at Chicksands Priory, Perry Fellwock.

GCHQ's troubles now seemed to follow thick and fast. In May 1980, a disillusioned former wireless supervisor, Jock Kane, made a series of damaging allegations concerning widespread corruption within GCHQ and the penetration by hostile agents of the Little Sai Wan base in Hong Kong. His book, *GCHQ: The Negative Asset*, became the subject of a High Court injunction in May 1984, which effectively prevented its publication in England. Kane insisted that he had been forced to leave GCHQ, after thirty-two years' service. Unwelcome attention was focused on the relationship between the NSA and GCHQ, and in particular the exchange of SIGINT material, following the Argentine invasion of the Falkland Islands in April 1982. That episode led to a damaging disclosure by a former Foreign Office Minister of State, Ted Rowlands, who told the House of Commons that GCHQ "had been reading the Argentine's diplomatic traffic for years." It was an unprecedented admission from so senior figure, albeit a politician, and once again GCHQ found itself in the headlines. The British government also found itself in difficulties when attempting to reconstruct certain events of the Falklands conflict which had been largely based on intelligence supplied by the NSA. To admit American involvement in particularly sensitive operations would have had serious consequences for the State Department and would have been contrary to the unattributable basis on which the NSA and GCHQ freely exchanged the most valuable SIGINT.

Sir Brian Tovey retired from his hot seat in 1983 and was succeeded by his deputy, Peter Marychurch, who had joined the organization from the RAF in 1948. But within a few months of moving into his new office at Oakley, Marychurch was enveloped in controversy as a result of the government's decision to ban trade unions inside GCHQ. This decision, which was reached in secret by the Cabinet's inner Defense and Overseas Policy Committee on the advice of the Secretary to the Cabinet, Sir Robert Armstrong, was broken to the Civil Service unions in January 1984. From 1979 onward, the Civil Service unions had taken prolonged, disruptive action in support of a pay claim. Largely unknown to the British public, branches of the Society of Civil and Public Servants inside GCHQ had participated in the disruption and had created a good deal of administrative chaos. This situation continued in the face of growing international tension created by the Soviet invasion of Afghanistan and the imposition of martial law in Poland. The uninterrupted supply of intelligence became of critical importance, not least to restore the NSA's confidence in its partner, and Sir Robert Armstrong advised that the best method of restoring order was to ban trade-union membership. Various alternatives had been debated, including the suggestion of a formal no-strike contract, but it was reluctantly acknowledged that such an agreement was unenforceable and, anyway, left the trade-union structure intact, in a position to renege at any time.

The main argument against a blanket trade-union ban was the probability of yet more publicity and prolonged staff resistance. However, GCHQ's senior management had predicted that only a handful of staff would hold out against the ban provided it was packaged with appropriate incentives, and this view proved largely correct. All GCHQ personnel were offered either a tax-free bonus of £1,000 to surrender their right to union membership, or promised a transfer to an outside post if anyone wished to retain their membership. In addition, it was recommended that a staff association, unaffiliated to any external body, should be formed. All these suggestions were incorporated into the ultimatum, which was announced on January 2, 1984. On that date the Foreign Secretary, Sir Geoffrey Howe, broke the news that the trade-union ban would come into effect on March 1, 1984.

Both GCHQ and the inner Cabinet anticipated some publicity, but probably not on such a scale. Since Geoffrey Prime's conviction in November 1978, GCHQ had become highly newsworthy. Minor events that had hardly rated a mention in the past acquired the status of national importance if a link could be made with GCHQ. The accidental death of Jack Wolfenden, a senior GCHQ official, in a gliding accident in the Cotswolds in July 1982, ten days after Prime's arrest, hit the headlines. This was followed by the suicides of two GCHQ employees in Cheltenham, Ernest Brockway, who died at his home in November 1982, and twenty-five-year-old Stephen Drinkwater, who asphyxiated himself with a plastic bag over his head in September 1983. In April 1984, George Franks, one of thirty-eight wireless operators based at GCHQ's intercept station atop the Empress State Building in west London, died of a heart attack alone in his Brighton flat and became front-page news. Two weeks later, Stephen Oake, a thirty-five-year-old traffic handler with eleven years' experience, also committed suicide. He had been attached to the CSO station at Morwenstow in Cornwall. The authorities denied any security implications in any of these cases, but the press was characteristically undeterred by routine denials from the Foreign Office. Even the most trivial matter, such as the news that two airmen had been charged with the possession of a small quantity of cannabis, which happened in July 1984, acquired added significance when it was mentioned that both men were stationed at RAF Digby.

If there was a miscalculation in the British government's decision to ban trade unions at GCHQ, it was in the assessment of the trade-union movement's determination to exploit the position to cause the maximum embarrassment. When the Foreign Secretary, Sir Geoffrey Howe, visited Oakley on July 13, 1984, he was met by Peter Marychurch . . . and twenty placard-waving demonstrators. A High Court application was made to have the trade-union ban declared illegal, and in July Mr. Justice Glidewell ordered that the ban was "invalid and of no effect" because there had been insufficient consultation with the unions. The following month the Court of Appeal overturned this judgment, acknowledging that the courts had no power to interfere with government decisions taken in the interests of national security. This effectively defused the confrontation, and the position of the remaining handful of protesters was further undermined in December 1985 by GCHQ's amalgamation of the Joint Speech Research Unit with the Royal Signals and Radar Establishment at Malvern. Because the new RSRE body was to continue operating under the jurisdiction of the Ministry of Defense, any GCHQ personnel would have their right to membership of a trade union reinstated automatically.

Proof that the secret wireless war was still being waged in earnest long after Prime had settled into his prison life was provided in September 1983, by the arrest of Paul Davies. A telegraphist with the rank of senior aircraftsman, the twenty-one-year-old Davies was alleged to have passed carbon copies of secret teleprinter messages to his Hungarian-born girlfriend while serving in the military communications section of RAF Episkopi in Cyprus. Davies had originally been questioned about the theft of some cash, but once his relationship with his married girlfriend, Mrs. Eva Jaafar, became known, the emphasis shifted perceptibly. When evidence was given about her at the Old Bailey in July 1984, she was characterized as a Soviet agent and was likened to the legendary Mata Hari. When, to everyone's amazement, she flew in from Beirut to appear as a surprise defense witness and refuted the allegations made against her, she seemed the most unlikely of espionage suspects; the prosecution's case collapsed and Davies was acquitted.

In a similar case a few months later, seven airmen attached to the No. 9 Signals Regiment in Cyprus were similarly accused of having traded SIGINT secrets for sex. Once again, there were allegations of unfair tactics employed by the RAF Provost and Security Service investigators, and all seven denied the written confessions attributed to them. The trial, which was largely held in camera, lasted a record 116 days before the first two defendants were acquitted. Gradually, the jury brought in not guilty verdicts on the remaining airmen, and the government announced two official inquiries—one into the handling of the investigations in Cyprus, and the other, conducted by the Security Commission, to establish whether there had ever been any lapses in security in the first place. From such evidence as did become public after the conclusion of the trials, it seemed likely that the counterintelligence officials in the field who had undertaken the preliminary interrogations had been so anxious to plug any possible leak of information that, in their enthusiasm, they had ruined whatever chances they had ever had of obtaining enough evidence to persuade a jury to convict. It was almost as though Geoffrey Prime, the unsurpassed SIGINT spy, had managed to exert an influence even from his maximum security prison cell.

10

Recent Developments

I further declare that I understand that all information relating to COMINT may only be discussed with persons whom I know to be COMINT indoctrinated.

—Clause 3 of the Official Secrets Act declaration signed by all
Allied SIGINT personnel

Soviet attempts to penetrate the inner sanctums of GCHQ and the West's SIGINT community continue unabated. GCHQ's own security manual warns new recruits that they have probably become targets for KGB entrapment. The security purge that followed the acquittals of the Cyprus telegraphists in 1985 received scant notice compared to the publicity that surrounded the trials themselves. A total of eighty-three signalers were subsequently discharged prematurely.

But what of the less publicized crises? When Morris and Lona Cohen, alias Peter and Helen Kroger, were arrested in January 1962 there was considerable anxiety because the house in which they had been living since October 1955 was only a short distance from GCHQ's postwar headquarters at Eastcote. Had this been a coincidence, or was the explanation altogether more sinister? There was never any evidence to indicate that secrets had been leaked from Eastcote, but the Cohens' modest bungalow contained sophisticated wireless transmitters and clandestine receiving equipment. Had they obtained secrets from anyone other than the two Portland naval base employees who were convicted with them?

Another disagreeable conundrum was posed in 1977, during a lengthy investigation into Leslie James Bennett, a recently retired member of the Royal Canadian Mounted Police's Security Service. Jim Bennett had joined the Special Wireless Group as a wireless operator in May 1940 and had subsequently been posted to Malta and Heliopolis. After the war, he had joined GCHQ and worked in intercept stations in Austria and, under consular cover, in Istanbul. In 1950, he did a tour of duty in Melbourne, as a Traffic Liaison Officer with the Australian Defense Signals Division, followed by another at Little Sai Wan in Hong Kong. He was later promoted to the head of GCHQ's Middle East Section and was then transferred to the General Search Section.

During the austere years of the late 1940s and early 1950s, many of GCHQ's personnel lost confidence in their organization. The wartime camaraderie had been lost, and Bennett was not alone in finding the atmosphere uncomfortable. The work was undertaken in conditions of extreme secrecy which, on occasion, seemed to frustrate their objectives. The old spirit of RSS, with its emphasis on voluntary effort, had been replaced by a bureaucracy of civil servants who preferred to stifle, rather than encourage, initiative. In March 1954, Bennett resigned from GCHQ and, armed with nothing more than a glowing reference from the personnel department signed by Robert Amys, emigrated to Canada where he joined the counterintelligence division of the Royal Canadian Mounted Police's Security Service. Twenty-two years later, as one of the Security Service's most senior and influential officers, Bennett was secretly taken into custody and interrogated for five days. The charge against him was that he had been a long-term Soviet agent and Communist sympathizer. Bennett denied the accusation, but was retired with immediate effect on medical grounds. News of Bennett's sudden departure, and his subsequent decision to start a new life in Australia, led to questions in the Canadian Parliament and divided opinion inside the Security Service. Was Bennett a lifelong mole who had willingly moved from Cheltenham to Ottawa on KGB instructions, or the innocent victim of a conspiracy?

The Bennett case is remarkable because news of it eventually surfaced and reached the public. In the espionage world "smoking gun evidence" is a rarity, as was pointed out by Peter Wright, one of MI5's mole hunters who spent a career in pursuit of the elusive owners of the code names mentioned in the VENONA decrypts. Geoffrey Prime is the sole GCHQ official known definitely to have spied for Moscow, but it is unlikely that he was the only one. Indeed, it is known that one of his tasks was to supply his Soviet controllers with a comprehensive "order of battle" for GCHQ, complete with details of the personalities known to him. One possible motive for such a talent-spotting exercise is to save time when starting a recruiting campaign.

The NSA, like its British partner, is wary of any kind of media attention. It managed to avoid scrutiny until 1969, when the Washington-based columnist Andrew Tully published *The Super Spies*. That he managed to accumulate so much, even from public sources, was an achievement, but the book highlighted the difficulties faced by those wishing to document the darkest corners of the intelligence establishment which governments of all political complexions, whatever their public protestations, use to their profit and protect accordingly. Any review of the West's postwar SIGINT experience is bound to concentrate on those episodes that have become public knowledge, and most are failures of one kind or another. No intelligence service would willingly compromise its sources by proclaiming a success. When propaganda or political considerations dictate otherwise, the claims made can turn out to be deceptive. Sometimes, though, the dogged researcher can beat the system. In 1982, a determined young lawyer from Boston, James Bamford, published *The Puzzle Palace*, the results of his own study into the NSA. Luck seems to have been on his side, because although at first he could find few declassified papers, he did discover that the NSA sponsored a staff newsletter which was taken home by NSA personnel. This meant it was available to be read by people who had not been granted a security clearance and was not, therefore, a secret document. Unwilling to challenge Bamford in court, the NSA reluctantly gave him a measure of cooperation. He was even able to discover the exact number of the NSA's employees by obtaining the records of the NSA's credit union which, by law, is obliged to disclose its actual membership and its full potential membership.

Details such as employment figures are of considerable value to those wishing to assess a SIGINT organization's capability. Both the NSA and GCHQ employ many times more people than the total engaged on more familiar duties with their country's respective intelligence agencies, the CIA and MI6. One of the principal lessons of the secret wireless war is the relative value of SIGINT as compared to other secret sources. By and large, SIGINT is more accurate, easier to verify, less risky and cheaper to acquire than old-fashioned espionage. The prizes attainable through good signals intelligence can help to win campaigns. Certainly SIGINT is no substitute for numerical superiority in armed forces, but if skillfully exploited, can tip the balance and more. But the prizes hang by a slender thread and are easily placed in jeopardy. A slight indiscretion, a mere whisper of an electronic origin, and the source can be terminated. The simplest of rules can eliminate the risk of a security breach, but fortunately (or unfortunately, depending upon your point of view) wireless operators will always indulge in "chatter" and the most experienced of signalers will make the occasional mistake, thereby giving the vigilant eavesdropper an opportunity.

Since the development of the Bombes, GCHQ has been in the

forefront of computer development. The old principles of cryptanalysis remain much the same today as they were in 1941. Repetition, probable words and frequency tables have been programmed in data processors that are several years ahead of anything openly available on the commercial market. In 1972, the most advanced computer in the world was the Cray-1, designed by the reclusive Seymour Cray, the founder of Control Data and, latterly, Cray Research. When the first Cray-1 was sold openly to an approved buyer (other than the NSA), it cost $8 million and Cray Research Inc. of Chippewa Falls, Wisconsin, sold only three machines in two years. Cray has an unsurpassed reputation for innovation, and when he worked for the Sperry Rand Corporation he built the first computer to use transistors instead of vacuum tubes. The latest model, the Cray-3, is the first of a generation of supercomputers and is thoroughly classified. Nevertheless, it is known to generate such heat that the core is permanently immersed in a liquid fluorocarbon compound. The Cray-1 installed at Fort Meade is known to have an operating capacity of one hundred "megaflops." Each megaflop is a million floating point operations per second. By comparison, the largest IBM mainframe has a maximum speed of just three or four megaflops. The new Cray-3 boasts one thousand megaflops. No cipher system, however ingeniously constructed, can withstand the application of such power. The ability to perform complex, repetitive logical functions at this unprecedented rate makes the NSA and its partner the world leaders in number-crunching. The Cray-1's only known disadvantage was its unreliability: it would break down every three hundred hours. It remains to be seen if the Cray-3 gives a better performance.

Soviet industry cannot match such quantum leaps in technology, so the KGB is forced to improvise and take shortcuts. In 1985, a father and son spy team, John and Michael Walker, were arrested and convicted of selling U.S. naval secrets to Soviet contacts. Michael Walker was a neophyte in the business compared to his father's seventeen years of undetected espionage. John Walker, then aged forty-eight, had spent most of his naval career as a communications specialist, handling the most highly classified cipher equipment; he agreed to make a full confession in return for a life sentence. The Justice Department approved the deal so as to enable the U.S. Navy and the NSA to make a full evaluation of the damage inflicted by the Walkers. Among the revelations made during Walker senior's debriefing was the admission that he had betrayed many of the operating manuals and crypto-keys of the hardware lost on the *Pueblo*. The NSA's hope that the silence of the *Pueblo*'s crew had prevented the Soviets from discovering all the ship's secrets proved too optimistic. Walker had supplied the KGB with exactly the information they would have needed.

Soviet inferiority in the SIGINT field had been confirmed, with tragic results, in September 1983, when a Korean Airlines Boeing 747-230B en route from New York to Seoul was shot down over Sakhalin Island. The civilian airliner, with 269 passengers and crew aboard, had strayed from a recognized international flight path and overflown the Soviet peninsula of Kamchatka. Thereafter, it had continued in Soviet airspace over the Sea of Okhotsk before being intercepted by four fighters from the Dolinsk-Sokol airfield on Sakhalin.

After some initial denials, Moscow eventually admitted that KAL Flight 007 had indeed been attacked and destroyed. The American administration produced incontrovertible proof of Soviet responsibility: the tape recording and transcript of the exchanges between the four interceptors and their ground controllers. Two questions remained unanswered: how had it been possible for an experienced commercial pilot to have flown his airliner over three hundred miles off course without apparently noticing, and why had Soviet fighters attacked?

There is no immediate answer to the first question, although human error or a mechanical failure in the inertial navigation systems are both possible explanations. However, the Soviets themselves provided the solution to the second. Flight KAL 007 had been tracked as a hostile intruder for more than an hour before the fatal interception. In fact, the plane had been identified as an RC-135 reconnaissance plane from Shemya, on a "ferret" mission for the NSA. According to Soviet statements, radar blips from two aircraft appeared to merge on the screens of the air defense controllers before they separated. One plane was seen to land at the well-known USAF base on Shemya Island in the Aleutians. The other set a course which was to take it over numerous Soviet military installations. Because the Soviet radar operators were unable to differentiate between the RC-135 and the much larger Boeing 747, the interceptors were instructed that their target was a hostile ferret. Although both aircraft are manufactured by Boeing, that is about all the two have in common. Their silhouettes are easily distinguished, especially to trained personnel, and the wingspans of each differ by nearly sixty-five feet. But once the fighter pilots had been vectored on to the target, their concern, as demonstrated by the dialogue recorded by the NSA, was simply to complete their mission. There was no mention of the type or role of the airliner in the intercepted traffic, just references to it as "the target."

The Soviet ground controllers were convinced that the aircraft was the familiar RC-135 being deliberately provocative, and the four pilots executed their instructions without question. No doubt they had previously been briefed about some of the twenty-eight similar, but less serious, incidents that had occurred between 1945 and 1960.

Lack of technical expertise has also led the People's Republic of China to indulge in shortcuts. Attacks on airborne ferrets operating from Japan and Taiwan almost became routine affairs during the 1950s, and both the CIA and GCHQ have experienced penetration by agents working for Peking. In 1961, Chan Tak Fei, a linguist at the Little Sai Wan installation, was repatriated after he had been caught passing GCHQ's secrets to his Chinese contacts, and as recently as 1973 two Taiwanese specialists defected to the People's Republic.

None of these cases, nor those of Geoffrey Prime, Christopher Boyce, William Kampiles, Jack Dunlap or the Walkers, were detected by good counterintelligence. Chan Tak Fei was identified by accident during a customs search; Prime would probably have escaped completely but for his sexual deviation. His wife denounced him, as did John Walker's wife and Jack Dunlap's widow. Boyce was only caught after his partner had named him, and Kampiles actually volunteered enough incriminating information to the CIA to convict him. The SIGINT field is a fertile area for the recruitment of agents, and a profitable one for hostile intelligence services. Despite the lessons, embarrassments and scandals of more than eighty years, there is no reason to believe that any of the participants in the wireless war are any the wiser. This was demonstrated by the arrest in November 1985 of Ronald Pelton, a fourteen-year veteran of the NSA, on a charge of having sold Allied secrets to the KGB over a period of six years.

Security scandals are invariably followed by reviews of internal procedures and the introduction of new measures, such as the polygraph test. Such exercises are useful deterrents, but little else. Counterintelligence officials have come to accept that agent penetration is an occupational hazard and, after too many years of complacency, realize that the only effective weapon against hostile penetration is constant vigilance. The trick is to balance the precautions so that they do not become counterproductive and damage morale or performance. The secret wireless war will continue for as long as there are communications to be intercepted and signals to be interpreted. Accordingly, GCHQ will remain an invaluable source . . . and a tempting target.

Appendix 1

GCHQ'S WARTIME
WIRELESS TRAFFIC CODE NAMES

GCHQ Code name	Enemy Service	Enemy Code name	Subject of Contents	Date of First Break
ALBATROSS	Wehrmacht		Italy	6/2/43
ASTER	Luftwaffe		Western Front	5/12/43
BANTAM	Wehrmacht		Western Front	3/1/44
BARNACLE	Kriegsmarine	Offizier	Berlin-Tokyo	9/10/43
BARRACUDA	Kriegsmarine	NEPTUN	Secret Info	Unbroken
BEETLE	Luftwaffe		Luftflotte 6	3/4/42
BLACK JUMBO	Diplomatic			
BLUE	Luftwaffe		Exercise	
BONITO	Kriegsmarine	Eichendorff	Small naval units	5/10/44
BREAM	Wehrmacht		Berlin–Italy	
BROWN	Luftwaffe		Navigation	
BULLFINCH	Wehrmacht		Tunis: Panzers	11/20/42
BUZZARD	Wehrmacht		S.E. Europe	5/16/43
CELERY	Luftwaffe		Weather Reports	9/2/42
CHAFFINCH	Wehrmacht		N. Africa	1/12/41
CHICKEN	Wehrmacht		France: Logistics	2/27/44
CLAM	Kriegsmarine	Offizier	Black Sea	10/10/43
CHUB	Wehrmacht			
CLOVER	Luftwaffe		Western Front	3/1/43
COCKLE	Kriegsmarine	Offizier	U-Boats in Med	6/10/43
COCKROACH	Luftwaffe		Fighters	1/7/42
CODFISH	Wehrmacht		Strasbourg–	
CORMORANT	Wehrmacht		Rome–Sardinia	5/8/43
CORNCRAKE	Wehrmacht		V-Weapons	5/13/44
COWRIE	Kriegsmarine	Offizier	Small naval units	5/10/44
CRAB	Luftwaffe		Luftflotte 1	9/24/42
CRICKET	Luftwaffe		Europe	4/24/44

GCHQ Code name	Enemy Service	Enemy Code name	Subject of Contents	Date of First Break
DACE	Wehrmacht		Königsberg– Golssen	
DAFFODIL	Luftwaffe		Western Front	5/9/42
DODO	Wehrmacht		Tunis: Panzers	2/8/43
DOLPHIN	Kriegsmarine	Heimisch	Ships	8/1/41
DRAGONFLY	Luftwaffe		Tunis	3/5/43
DUCK	Wehrmacht		7th Army France	6/9/44
ERMINE	Luftwaffe		Russian Front	2/25/43
FISH	Geheimschreiber		Radio Teletype	
FLORADORA	Diplomatic			
FLOUNDER	Wehrmacht		Radio-Rhodes	
FOXGLOVE	Luftwaffe		Russian Front	1/12/42
FREYA	Kriegsmarine		B-Dienst	6/10/44
GADFLY	Luftwaffe		Fliegerkorps X	1/1/42
GANNET	Wehrmacht		Norway	1/2/41
GARLIC	Luftwaffe		Weather Reports	4/8/42
GGG	Abwehr		Berlin–Gibraltar	2/10/42
GNAT	Luftwaffe		Fliegerkorps X	5/1/44
GOLDFINCH	Wehrmacht		Rome–Tunis	12/2/42
GORSE	Luftwaffe		Russian Front	9/20/43
GRAMPUS	Kriegsmarine	POSEIDON	Black Sea	10/10/43
GRAPEFRUIT	SS		Camps Admin.	8/21/44
GRAYLING	Wehrmacht		Königsberg–	
GREEN	Wehrmacht	Wehrkries	Home Admin.	1/18/40
GREENSHANK	Wehrmacht		Home Admin.	
GRILSE	Wehrmacht		Strausberg–	
GURNARD	Wehrmacht		Strausberg–	
HEDGEHOG	Luftwaffe		Joint Operations	2/21/43
HERRING	Wehrmacht		Strausberg–Tunis	
HORNET	Luftwaffe		Fliegerkorps IV	1/1/42
HYENA	Luftwaffe		Luftflotte Reich	3/10/44
INDIGO	Luftwaffe		Secret info.	10/3/43
ISK	Abwehr		Enigma key	12/10/41
ISOS	Abwehr		Hand ciphers	
JAGUAR	Luftwaffe		Luftflotte 3	2/11/44
JELLYFISH	Wehrmacht		Strausberg–	
KESTREL	Wehrmacht		Russian Front	7/9/41
KINGFISHER	Wehrmacht		14th Army Italy	5/30/44
KITE	Wehrmacht		Russian Front	1/2/42
LEEK	Luftwaffe		Weather	7/31/41

GCHQ Code name	Enemy Service	Enemy Code name	Subject of Contents	Date of First Break
LEOPARD	Luftwaffe		Italy	2/5/44
LIGHT BLUE	Luftwaffe		N. Africa	2/28/41
LILY	Luftwaffe		France, Belgium	5/1/43
LIMPET	Kriegsmarine	Offizier	U-Boats	12/10/42
LION	Luftwaffe		Norway	6/14/43
LLAMA	Luftwaffe		Albania	2/9/44
LOCUST	Luftwaffe		Sicily	1/12/42
MAGPIE	Wehrmacht		Dodecanese	11/29/43
MALLARD	Wehrmacht		Rome Admin	11/20/42
MAYFLY	Luftwaffe		Mediterranean	6/30/43
MEDLAR	SS		Radio cross-work	5/29/44
MERLIN	Wehrmacht		Balkan Staff	2/10/43
MOORHEN	Wehrmacht		Italy: Logistics	Unknown
MOSQUITO	Luftwaffe		Russian Front	6/8/42
MULLET	Wehrmacht		Strausberg–Norway	
MUSTARD	Luftwaffe		Y Service	6/27/41
NARCISSUS	Luftwaffe		Norway	8/10/42
NARWHAL	Kriegsmarine	NIOBE	U-Boats in North	9/10/44
NIGHTJAR	Wehrmacht		France Occup.	3/17/44
NUTHATCH	Wehrmacht		Berlin–Belgrade	2/13/43
OCELOT	Luftwaffe		Western Front	5/31/44
OCTOPUS	Wehrmacht		Königsberg–Russia	
ONION	Luftwaffe		Navigation	5/8/41
ORANGE	SS		General	12/10/40
ORCHID	Luftwaffe		Russian Front	3/1/43
OSPREY	Todt/Organization		Enigma key	9/30/42
OWL	Wehrmacht		Crimea	2/14/44
OYSTER	Kriegsmarine		U-Boats	Unbroken
PARR	Wehrmacht		Salzburg–Königsberg	
PELICAN	Wehrmacht		Panzers	3/27/44
PERCH	Wehrmacht		Königsberg–	
PEREGRINE	SS Panzers		Yugoslavia	8/24/43
PHOENIX	Wehrmacht		Panzers	11/23/41
PIKE	Kriegsmarine	Auserheimisch	Ships	Unbroken
PINK	Luftwaffe		Secret info.	1/1/42

GCHQ Code name	Enemy Service	Enemy Code name	Subject of Contents	Date of First Break
PLAICE	Kriegsmarine	POTSDAM	Baltic	1/1/44
POLLACK	Wehrmacht		Golssen–Salzburg	
POPPY	Luftwaffe		Luftgau XII	9/13/43
PORCUPINE	Luftwaffe		South Russia	1/21/43
PORPOISE	Kriegsmarine	SUD	U-Boats	8/10/42
PRIMROSE	Luftwaffe		Mediterranean	1/17/42
PUCE	Luftwaffe		Russian Front	Unbroken
PUFFIN	Wehrmacht		Sicily–Italy	7/23/43
PULLET	Wehrmacht		Enigma Y key	6/11/44
PUMA	Luftwaffe		Luftflotte 2	8/1/43
PUMPKIN	SS		Rome–Berlin	4/1/44
PURPLE	Luftwaffe			5/26/40
QUINCE	SS		Main key	8/14/42
RAVEN	Wehrmacht		Balkans	2/20/42
RED	Luftwaffe		General	1/29/40
ROACH	Wehrmacht		Königsberg–	
ROCKET	Reichbahn		Railways	2/10/41
ROULETTE	Polizei		Police Enigma	/44
SCORPION	Luftwaffe		Africa	4/22/42
SEAHORSE	Kriegsmarine	BERTOK	Berlin–Tokyo	9/10/43
SHAD	Wehrmacht		Königsberg– Ukraine	
SHAMROCK	Luftwaffe		Exercise	3/9/43
SHARK	Kriegsmarine	TRITON	U-Boats	12/10/42
SHRIKE	Wehrmacht		Italy	8/23/43
SKATE	Wehrmacht			
SKUNK	Luftwaffe		Russian Front	5/10/42
SKYLARK	Wehrmacht		Channel Isles	5/18/42
SMELT	Wehrmacht		Ukraine–	
SNOWDROP	Luftwaffe		France	4/7/42
SPARROW	Wehrmacht		Med: Y Service	4/6/43
SQUID	Wehrmacht		Königsberg– N. Ukraine	
SQUIRREL	Luftwaffe		Bombers	7/3/43
STICKLEBACK	Wehrmacht		Königsberg– S. Ukraine	
STURGEON	Siemens T52		Radio Teletype	
SUNFISH	Kriegsmarine	TIBET	Far East U-Boats	9/10/43
TARPON	Wehrmacht		Strausberg–Ru- mania	

GCHQ Code name	Enemy Service	Enemy Code name	Subject of Contents	Date of First Break
TGD	Gestapo		Main Enigma Key	Unbroken
THRASHER	Wehrmacht		Radio Teletype	Unbroken
THRUSH	Wehrmacht		Italy–Greece	7/23/42
TOUCAN	Wehrmacht		Logistics: Italy	11/10/43
TROUT	Wehrmacht		Strausberg–Memel	
TRUMPETER	Kriegsmarine	URANUS	Mediterranean	4/10/44
TULIP	Luftwaffe		Holland	3/1/43
TUNNY	Schlüssel- zusatz 40		Radio Teletype	
TURBOT	Wehrmacht		Strausberg– Denmark	
TURTLE	Kriegsmarine	MEDUSA	U-Boats in Med	6/10/43
VIOLET	Luftwaffe		General	12/24/40
VULTURE	Wehrmacht		Russian Front	6/27/41
WASP	Luftwaffe		Fliegerkorps IX	1/1/42
WEASEL	Luftwaffe		Russian Front	7/15/42
WHELK	Kriegsmarine	Offizier	Baltic	1/1/44
WHITING	Wehrmacht		Königsberg–	
WOOD- PECKER	Wehrmacht		S.E. Europe	11/16/43
WRYNECK 1	SS Panzer		Yugoslavia	9/18/43
YAK	Luftwaffe		Croatia	10/22/43
YELLOW	Wehrmacht		Norway	4/10/40

Appendix 2

PRINCIPAL WARTIME SIGINT STATIONS IN BRITAIN

RADIO SECURITY SERVICE
Sandridge, Herts
Wymondham, Norfolk
Bridgwater, Somerset
Forfar, Angus
Thurso, Caithness
Gilnahirk, Belfast
St. Erth, Cornwall

GENERAL POST OFFICE
Sandridge, Herts
Cupar, Fife
Brora, Sutherland

RAF Y SERVICE
RAF Montrose, Scotland
RAF Cheadle, Staffordshire
RAF Chicksands Priory, Bedfordshire
RAF Waddington, Lincolnshire

ADMIRALTY Y SERVICE
Irton Moor, Scarborough
Leafield, Oxon

ARMY Y SERVICE
Fort Bridgewoods, Kent
Flowerdown, Hampshire
Beaumanor, Leicestershire
Shaftesbury, Dorset
Rothamsted, Harpenden, Herts

SECRET INTELLIGENCE SERVICE
Hanslope Park, Bucks
Knockholt, Kent
Whaddon Hall, Bucks
Windy Ridge, Bucks
Nash, Bucks

SPECIAL OPERATIONS EXECUTIVE
STS 52, Thame Park, Oxon
STS 53A, Grendon Underwood, Oxon
STS 53B, Poundon House, Poundon, Oxon
STS 53C, Signal Hill, Poundon, Oxon
STS 53D, Belhaven House, Dunbar, Lothian
STS 54, Fawley Court, Henley-on-Thames, Oxon

OFFICE OF STRATEGIC SERVICES
CHARLIE, Signal House, Poundon, Oxon
VICTOR, Layde Place, Hurley, Berkshire

Appendix 3

CORRESPONDENCE
NATIONAL SECURITY AGENCY
CENTRAL SECURITY SERVICE
Fort George G. Meade, Maryland 20755

MITRE
21 May 1982

Mr. Gordon Welchman
167 Water Street
Newburyport, MA 01950

Dear Gordon,

The attached guidance is intended solely to provide protection to classified cryptologic sources or methods which are protected under United States law, specifically 18 USC 798, and to related information which may jeopardize classified cryptologic sources and methods.

I am sure that the guidance contained will be useful for any interviews or discussions you may have relative to your publication, ''The Hut Six Story''.

Sincerely,

Robert J. Roberto, Manager
Corporate Security Office

RJR/fem

18 May 1982
Guidance for Mr. Gordon Welchman
If questioned or interviewed by the media or others relative to the information contained in The Hut Six Story;

You may discuss:

—the history, organization, geographic setting of Bletchley Park;
—the identities of persons involved in the wartime effort at Bletchley;
—the "Enigma" machine in broad generalities;
—the effect of the "breaking" of the "Enigma" on the war effort;
—cryptologic collaboration between December 7, 1941 and May 8, 1945;
—the significance of communications in military or other operations.

You may not discuss:

—technical details of the structure, logic or operation of the "Enigma" machine, or other similar machines;
—weaknesses of German or other communications systems and the methods of exploitation of such weaknesses;
—methodologies which cryptanalysts use to successfully exploit code or cipher systems, except for those which have been officially declassified by the United States;
—methodologies used to provide protection to U.S. or Allied communications;
—details of any cryptanalytic or cryptographic methods, except for those officially declassified by the United States.

167 Water Street
Newburyport, Mass. 01950
May 28, 1982

Mr. Robert J. Roberto
Corporate Security – A210
The MITRE Corporation
Burlington Road
Bedford, Massachusetts 01730

Dear Bob:

Thank you for your letter of 21 May 1982, enclosing a one-page document headed "Guidance for Mr. Gordon Welchman."
In the letter you make the following statement:

The attached guidance is intended solely to provide protection to classified cryptologic sources or methods which are protected under

United States Law, specifically 18USC798, and to related information
which may jeopardize classified cryptologic sources and methods.

I would like to be assured that this statement reflects the official attitude. If it
does, the "guidance" should be made more specific. I enclose a copy with
suggested modifications, which I hope will be acceptable. The added words are
underlined.

I would also like to know what is implied by the words "or others" in the
opening sentence of the "guidance." I certainly hope to have discussions with
senior personnel in MITRE about the implications of Part Four of my book for
our role in advanced military planning and procurement. I will be emphasizing
the extreme importance of what I have come to think of as *The Three C's,* namely
communication, collaboration, and coordination. In particular I will be trying
to establish the theme that, for the security and survival of our military capabilities
in war, we must adopt a true "combined arms" approach that extends to many
clandestine activities as well as to all branches of the military services. For this
purpose it will not be essential to elaborate on what I have said about Enigma
in the book, but for such discussions a rigid curtain would be unfortunate.
Moreover, it does seem important to establish two of my contentions; first that
the German failure was largely due to the isolation of the designers of the Enigma
machine from the many people who would be involved in its uses, and second
that the British success was largely due to excellent communication, collaboration
and coordination among the many specialized activities that were involved. These
two contentions can hardly be regarded as cryptological ones.

I hope you will be able to confirm that I was not shown section 18USC§798
until last month, when it was brought to my attention both by my lawyer, John
Stevens, and by you. Since receiving your letter I have looked again at this
section and have noticed that, according to the footnote on page 422, it must
have been prepared before 31 October 1951. It seems extraordinary that disclosure of information of great value to our future national security should still be
governed by attitudes to cryptology of more than 30 years ago.

A great deal has happened since 1951. Almost everything that I have said
about Enigma in the book has already been made public. For example, several
Enigma machines are now available for public inspection, the sheet-stacking
method has been fully described, the purpose of the Polish Bomba has been
revealed, and a published picture of an American version of the British Bombe
makes it possible to guess the purpose of that machine. Moreover, in a very real
sense, cryptology has gone public. Relevant lessons from history are now badly
needed for the fight against electronic crime as well as for the protection of our
military and political secrets.

In view of the information that is now in the public domain, it seems that
the only possible case against me lies in the account of my invention of the
diagonal board late in 1939. This account contains significant lessons for today's

efforts to guard against crime in the civil sphere as well as against enemy cryptanalysis in the military and political spheres. Moreover, 18USC§798 starts with the statement,

The term "classified information" means information which, at the time of a violation of this section, is, for reasons of national security, specifically designated by a United States Government Agency for limited or restricted dissemination or distribution.

Perhaps you will be able to prove that no such specific designation of my diagonal board idea exists. I am hoping, also, that MITRE will support me in what I am trying to contribute to our future national security.

Yours sincerely,

Gordon Welchman

Enclosure – Modified Guidelines
cc: John Stevens

Serial: Q4-608-82
30 June 1982

Mr. Gordon Welchman
167 Water Street
Newburyport, Massachusetts 01950

Dear Mr. Welchman:

This will serve to confirm information provided during our telephone conversation of Friday, 18 June 1982.

Mr. Robert J. Roberto of the MITRE Corporation has requested that I respond to questions raised by you concerning the guidance provided, at your request, under cover of MITRE letter of 21 May 1982. As you may be aware, the guidance was originated by the National Security Agency, and thus does reflect an official U.S. government viewpoint.

You ask what is implied by the words "or others" in the opening sentence of the guidance. This was intended to extend the guidance beyond contacts with the media, *per se,* to anyone in the public or private sectors wherein the contact is not protected in a government approved classified environment. It is not intended in any way to inhibit your contacts or discussions with appropriately cleared MITRE personnel, subject to whatever groundrules MITRE may apply.

Relative to your suggested modifications of the guidance, it would appear that there is a definitional problem which precludes our acceptance of those modifications. Cryptology encompasses signals intelligence and communications security. Communications security includes all measures taken to deny unauthorized persons information from communications and ensure authenticity of communications. It is not limited to cryptographic security; it includes, transmission security, emission security, and other measures intended for the protection of sensitive communications. Public discussion of the technical details of any of these measures would not be in the national interest. In this light your suggested modifications would provide an unintended liberalization of the guidance which would not be acceptable.

Comments on other points raised in your letter (i.e. the age, current applicability, and your knowledge of the law, and your follow-on discussions with MITRE) are not germane to the question of guidance on public contacts and thus are not covered here. They can, perhaps, be best addressed by MITRE or your counsel.

Should additional questions arise concerning the guidance (or on future publications) we are prepared to assist you in answering them.

Sincerely,

M. J. LEVIN
Chief, Information Security Division

Copy Furnished:
  Mr. Roberto, MITRE
  Mr. Fedor, ODUSDP

167 Water Street
Newburyport, Mass. 01950

July 16, 1982

Mr. M.J. Levin
National Security Agency
Central Security Service
Fort George G. Meade
Maryland 20755

Dear Mr. Levin,

Thank you for your letter of 30 June 1982, confirming information that you gave me during our telephone conversation of 18 June 1982. Your third paragraph clears up what you intended to imply by "or others". But I do have further questions.

I enclose a copy of the MITRE letter of 21 May 1982 to which you refer. From what you now tell me, it seems that Mr. Roberto's statement of the purpose of the guidance does in fact reflect the official attitude, provided that "cryptology" is understood to include SIGINT and all aspects of COMSEC. Is this correct?

In any discussion of information contained in *The Hut Six Story*, I will want to focus on the content of Part Four—TODAY—which I and many others regard as the most important part of my book. What I have said about the Enigma of World War Two will be used only as means of illustrating some of the major problems and dangers that badly need to be faced now in our advanced planning. I cannot alter what is in my book, but I will be very careful, in any public discussion, not to go beyond what I have said about signals intelligence and the various aspects of communications security. This, I believe, is what you really want me to do.

Of the six subjects that I am allowed to discuss in public, the only one that really interests me is the sixth, namely "the significance of communications in military or other operations." As is evident from my Part Four, I am concerned with a wide range of human and non-military problems of communication as well as military ones. But I cannot talk about this subject intelligently if I am not allowed to discuss weaknesses of communication systems.

I cannot believe that you want to prevent me from discussing historical evidence, such as the disastrous failures of British tactical communications in the desert campaigns, described in my Chapter 14. So could you please make it clear that I may discuss both strengths and weaknesses of communications systems in public, provided that I stay away from SIGINT and COMSEC? I see why you could not accept my suggested modification restricting what I may not discuss to "cryptographic" weaknesses. Would you be willing to substitute the word "cryptological," which seems to include all the types of weakness that you do not want me to talk about in public?

The last three of the prohibited subjects are ones that I would not wish to discuss in public. But the first one, telling me that I may not discuss "technical details of the structure, logic, or operation of the Enigma," has already put me in an awkward position.

Early in June, while attending a function at the Digital Computer Museum near here, I was examining the two German Enigmas that they have on public display for anyone to play with. Someone, knowing that I had written *The Hut Six Story,* asked me what the plugs in front of the machine were for. I had to explain that I am not allowed to discuss details of the Enigma, even though the answers to simple questions such as his can be found in my book and elsewhere in open literature. Brian Randell, who has written about Colossus, was there and answered the question with more detail than I could have supplied. He has his own German Enigma, a 1940 model, at his home in England and has taken it apart, whereas I had not seen an Enigma since the war, and even then was not too familiar with details. (The description of the Enigma in my book was based on my memory, and I now find that it is incorrect in some matters of detail.) I had to cancel a seminar at the Museum, scheduled for June 27, because I was expected to make some remarks on their Enigmas.

There must be a misunderstanding here. Perhaps the trouble lies in the word "technical." Could you please tell me what types of detail you regard as dangerous? Surely a simple explanation of the purpose of the plugs would have been innocuous.

Finally, I am having to delay talks to the local Rotary Club and other groups until it is made clear that your guidance is not intended to cover *all* the information contained in *all* parts of *The Hut Six Story*. Here it seems that you may after all be willing to accept my suggested modification, because I use the word "cryptological" which covers all the areas of SIGINT and COMSEC with which you are concerned. In fact, I am still hoping that the opening sentence of your guidance can be modified to read:

"If questioned or interviewed . . . relative to the *cryptological* information contained in *The Hut Six Story*."

Yours sincerely,

Gordon Welchman

CC: Mr. Roberto
    Mr. Fedor

GW:sos

PERSECUTION OF AN AUTHOR
Gordon Welchman
October 22, 1982

Readers of my book *The Hut Six Story—Breaking the Enigma Codes* will be aware that in the last twenty years I have become more and more convinced that the story of what I did during the first year of the war—virtually unknown to anyone else because I was working alone at the start—is badly needed in areas of advanced military planning in which I have been working. In April of this year, when the book had just been published, I was looking forward to more leisure and to writing about other matters than our military needs. But on April 20 I began to be investigated by special agents for having allegedly disclosed information about cryptanalytical activities in World War Two that is still considered to be classified in this country. I was confronted with a legal document, 18 USCS § 798, which threatened me with a fine of not more than $10,000 or imprisonment for not more than ten years, or both. Pressure on my employer, The MITRE Corporation, resulted in an interruption of my consulting services and consequent loss of income. My health was seriously affected, as was that of my wife. Now, six months later, and after a second investigation by special agents in June, I have not yet been told exactly what I am thought to have done amiss. Moreover, in the two investigations, there was little if any mention of the value to this country of what I did in the war, of what I have done since, or of what I could still contribute.

Let me explain briefly why I feel that I should have been encouraged to continue my work, not prevented from doing so.

At age 76 I can look back with some pride to my wartime activities as a temporary civil servant at Bletchley Park, Britain's cryptological headquarters. Indeed the astonishing success of Ultra intelligence, derived from decodes of Enigma traffic during the war against Hitler's Germany, was largely due to the personal contributions that I was able to make in the first year of that war.

After the war I emigrated to this country and am now a United States citizen. Since 1962, when I joined the technical staff of The MITRE Corporation, I have taken part in many studies of military needs. To acquire the necessary realism I did a lot of reading, both of military history and of the forward-looking views of today's military thinkers. I took advantage of every opportunity to talk to people with actual experience of battle. Since my retirement in 1971, I have been employed as a MITRE consultant for eleven years, which is evidence that my work on a variety of military research and development projects has been considered valuable.

In my twenty years at MITRE I have been trying to determine what should be done now in preparation for the many types of land/air conflict in which we may become involved in the future. The focus has usually been on the needs of commanders and combat units on a battlefield. I have been particularly concerned with communications, intelligence, and security—areas in which my wartime experience is applicable. Furthermore, as a result of my private reading, I have become convinced that recent disclosures of the many clandestine activities of World War Two, and of the intelligence activities on both sides, are very important for our advanced planning.

In the last four years I have expended about one third of my effort in consulting for MITRE and two thirds on trying to make my book as valuable as possible to people concerned with our future national security. My main contention is that, in military planning and system development, there must be effective communication and collaboration among imaginative thinkers drawn from many fields of expertise. Otherwise there will be little chance of achieving the close coordination of all capabilities that will be so vital on battlefields of the future.

In particular I have learned that, in the procurement of new military systems for use on those battlefields, the importance of tactical communications is often underestimated, and that communications security, if considered at all, is only tackled as an afterthought, when system design is pretty well frozen. In fact the importance of the contribution that NSA experts should make at all stages of system development is not recognized by people in the military, let alone by politicians and the general public. This situation, if allowed to persist, could be extremely dangerous to our national security.

Because my book was aimed at the general reader rather than the student of military affairs, I could not say much about my ideas of what should be done. However, I tried to establish three important themes. First that the German cryptographic failure was largely due to the isolation of the designers of the Enigma machine from the many people who would be involved in its use. Second, that the British success was due to excellent communication, collaboration, and cooperation among the many specialized activities that were involved. Third that, as I had realized around 1976, the security and survival of our military capabilities will depend on a true "combined arms" approach that extends to many clandestine activities (including cryptology) as well as to all branches of the military services.

At the end of my first recorded interview with special agents, on April 22, I was warned that, as a result of the publication of my book, I might become a target for enemy agents looking for further revelations. I should therefore be on the lookout for leading questions in any public appearance, and for suspicious inquiries in the mail. This was reasonable, and I thought that I could handle the matter. To be on the safe side, however, I asked for a definition of what particular revelations would be considered dangerous. This led to a most unsatisfactory correspondence.

The first result was a one-page document, "Guidance for Mr. Gordon Welchman," a copy of which is attached. My lawyer, when I showed it to him, remarked that I was being treated like a schoolboy. The author turned out to be the Chief, Information Security Division, Central Security Service, National Security Agency (NSA). Note that he allowed me to discuss "cryptologic collaboration between December 7, 1941, and May 8, 1945." He should have known that, as Assistant Director for Mechanization at Bletchley Park, I visited this country in 1944 and 1945 for top-level discussions concerned with the development of new cryptanalytical equipment. I would not dream of revealing the subject matter of these discussions, and it seems ridiculous that a senior official of NSA has given me permission to do so in public. In subsequent correspondence with this official I have tried, without success, to get a satisfactory definition of the underlying principles that should govern what I may and may not discuss.

During both interviews with special agents, in April and June, I was asked to give an account of how I came to write *The Hut Six Story,* and to have it published without first obtaining permission from the Department of Defense. After the second interview I decided to check the statements that I had made from memory. I went through old papers and notebooks and wrote a somewhat more accurate account entitled, *The Story of My Story,* dated July 30, 1982.

At this point I am trying to recover from the ordeal of the last six months. I am just beginning to think again of what I hope to do in the future. But my first need is to be freed from the threat that is still hanging over my head, a threat that I believe to be undeserved. As far as I can make out this threat comes from NSA, which is somewhat ironical because I have been trying very hard to convince all concerned that cooperation with NSA experts is badly needed at all stages of military research and development programs.

Bibliography

Aart, Dick van der, *Aerial Espionage* (Airlife, Shrewsbury, 1984)

Andrew, Christopher, *The Missing Dimension* (Macmillan, London, 1984)

Andrew, Christopher, *Secret Service* (Heinemann, London, 1985)

Arcangelis, Mario de, *Electronic Warfare* (Blandford Press, Dorset, 1985)

Baglehole, K. C., *A Century of Service* (Cable & Wireless, London, 1969)

Baker, W. J., *The History of the Marconi Company* (Methuen, London, 1970)

Ball, Desmond, *A Suitable Piece of Real Estate* (Hall & Iremonger, Sydney, 1980)

Bamford, James, *The Puzzle Palace* (Houghton Mifflin, Boston, 1982)

Barker, Wayne (ed.), *History of Codes and Ciphers in the U.S. during World War I* (Aegean Park Press, California, 1979)

Beesley, Patrick, *Very Special Intelligence* (Hamish Hamilton, London, 1977)

Beesley, Patrick, *Very Special Admiral* (Hamish Hamilton, London, 1980)

Bennett, Ralph, *Ultra in the West* (Hutchinson, London, 1979)

Bergamini, David, *Japan's Imperial Conspiracy* (William Morrow, New York, 1971)

Bertrand, Gustave, *Enigma* (Librairie Plon, Paris, 1975)

Block, Jonathan, *British Intelligence and Covert Action* (Junction Books, London, 1983)

Boucard, Robert, *Revelations from the Secret Service* (Hutchinson, London, 1930)

Brett-James, Anthony, *Report My Signals* (Harrap, London, 1948)

Brownrigg, Admiral Sir D., *Indiscretions of the Naval Censor* (Doran, London, 1920)

Bucher, Lloyd M., *Pueblo & Bucher* (Michael Joseph, London, 1971)

Bywater, Hector, *Their Secret Purposes* (Constable, London, 1932)

Bywater, Hector, and Ferraby, H. C., *Strange Intelligence* (Constable, London, 1931)

Cain, Frank, *The Origins of Political Surveillance in Australia* (Angus & Robertson, London, 1983)

Calvocoressi, Peter, *Top Secret Ultra* (Cassell, London, 1980; Pantheon Books, New York, 1980)

Campbell, Duncan, *The Unsinkable Aircraft Carrier* (Michael Joseph, London, 1984)

Cave Brown, Anthony, *Bodyguard of Lies* (W. H. Allen, London, 1976; Harper & Row, New York, 1975)

Churchill, Winston, *The Second World War* (Cassell, London, 1948)

Churchill, Winston, *The World Crisis* (Hamlyn, London, 1974)

Clarke, Ronald, *The Man Who Broke Purple* (Weidenfeld & Nicolson, London, 1977; Little, Brown, Boston, 1977)

Clarke, William F., *History of Room 40* (Unpublished, Clarke Papers, Churchill College, Cambridge)

Clarke, W., and Birch, F., *A Contribution to the History of German Naval Warfare* (Unpublished, Clarke Papers, Churchill College, Cambridge)

Clayton, Aileen, *The Enemy Is Listening* (Hutchinson, London, 1980)

Clubb, Oliver, *KAL Flight 007* (Permanent Press, New York, 1985)

Collier, Basil, *Hidden Weapons* (Hamish Hamilton, London, 1982)

Collier, Richard, *The Road to Pearl Harbor* (Bonanza, New York, 1985)

Costello, John, *The Pacific War* (William Morrow, New York, 1981)

Dallin, Alexander, *Black Box* (University of California Press, Berkeley, 1985)

Dallin, David, *Soviet Espionage* (Yale University Press, New Haven, 1955)

Davis, Burke, *Get Yamamoto* (Random House, New York, 1969)

Day, E. G. (ed.), *Through to 1970* (RSI, London, 1970)

Deacon, Richard, *The Silent War* (David & Charles, Devon, 1978; Hippocrene Books, New York, 1978)

Deavours, Cipher A., *Machine Cryptography and Modern Cryptanalysis* (Adtech, London, 1985)

Denniston, Alastair, *Autobiographical Notes* (Unpublished, Denniston Papers, Churchill College, Cambridge)

Department of Defense, *The MAGIC Background of Pearl Harbor* (Washington, DC, 1977)

Dilks, David (ed.), *The Diaries of Sir Alexander Cadogan* (Cassell, London, 1971)

Donaldson, Frances, *The Marconi Scandal* (Hart-Davis, London, 1962)

Ennes, James M., *Assault on the Liberty* (Random House, New York, 1970)

Ewing, Alfred W., *The Man of Room 40* (Hutchinson, London, 1939)

Farago, Ladislas, *The Broken Seal* (Arthur Barker, London, 1967; Random House, New York, 1967)

Farago, Ladislas, *Game of the Foxes* (Hodder & Stoughton, London, 1972; McKay, New York, 1971)

Fitzgerald, Penelope, *The Knox Brothers* (Coward-McCann, New York, 1977)

Friedman, William F., *Solving German Codes in World War I* (Aegean Park Press, 1977)

Friedman, William F., *The Zimmermann Telegram* (Aegean Park Press, 1976)

Gaines, Helen, *Cryptanalysis* (Dover, New York, 1956)

Galley, Admiral Daniel, *The Pueblo Incident* (Doubleday, New York, 1970)

Garlinski, Jozef, *Intercept* (Dent, London, 1979)

Gill, E. W. B., *War, Wireless and Wangles* (Blackwells, Oxford, 1934)
Gleason, Norma, *Crytograms and Spygrams* (Dover, New York, 1981)
Grant, Robert M., *U-Boat Intelligence* (Archon, Connecticut, 1969)
Haldane, R. A., *The Hidden World* (Robert Hale, London, 1976)
Hall, Richard, *The Secret State* (Cassell, London, 1978)
Hancock, H. E., *Wireless at Sea* (Marconi, London, 1950)
Harris, L. H., *Signal Venture* (Gale & Polden, Aldershot, 1951)
Hedley, Peter, *The D-Notice Affair* (Michael Joseph, London, 1967)
Hendrick, B. J., *The Life and Letters of Walter Hines Page* (Heinemann, London, 1922)
Hezlet, Admiral Sir Arthur, *Electronics and Sea Power* (Stein & Day, New York, 1975)
Hinsley, F. H., *British Intelligence in the Second World War* Vols I, II, III (HMSO, London, 1979, 1981, 1984; Cambridge University Press, New York, 1979, 1981, 1984)
Hitt, Parker, *Manual for the Solution of Military Ciphers* (Army Service Press, Kansas, 1916)
Hobart-Hampden, E., *A Brief Account of Diplomatic Events in Manchuria* (1927)
Hobart-Hampden, E., *English–Japanese Dictionary of the Spoken Word* (1928)
Hochman, Sandra, *Satellite Spies* (Bobbs-Merrill, Indianapolis, 1976)
Hodges, Andrew, *Alan Turing: The Enigma* (Hutchinson, London, 1983)
Höhne, Heinz, *Codeword: Direktor* (Secker & Warburg, London, 1971)
Holmes, W. J., *Double-Edged Secrets* (Naval Institute Press, Maryland, 1979)
Hoy, Hugh Cleland, *40 O.B.* Hutchinson, London, 1932)
Infield, Glenn, *Unarmed and Unafraid* (Macmillan, New York, 1973)
James, Admiral Sir William, *The Eyes of the Navy* (Methuen, London, 1955)
Johnson, Brian, *The Secret War* (BBC, London, 1978)
Jones, R. V., *Most Secret War* (Hamish Hamilton, London, 1978; as *The Wizard War*, Putnam, New York, 1978)
Kahn, David, *The Codebreakers* (Weidenfeld & Nicolson, London, 1966; Macmillan, New York, 1967)
Kahn, David, *Hitler's Spies* (Hodder & Stoughton, London, 1978; Macmillan, New York, 1978)
Kahn, David, *Kahn on Codes* (Macmillan, New York, 1983)
Kahn, David, *Two Soviet Spy Ciphers* (Great Neck, New York, 1960)
Kesaris, Paul, *ULTRA* (University Publications of America, 1980)
Kesaris, Paul, *The Rote Kapelle* (University Publications of America, 1979)
Kessler, Michael, *Wiretapping and Electronic Surveillance* (Commission Studies, Loompanics, Washington, 1983)
Kozaczuk, Wladyslaw, *Enigma* (University Publications of America, 1984)

Laffin, John, *Codes and Ciphers* (Abelard-Schuman, London, 1964)

Landau, Henry, *The Enemy Within* (Putnam, New York, 1937)

Landau, Henry, *Spreading the Spy Net* (Jarrold's, New York, 1938)

Langhorne, Richard (ed.), *Diplomacy & Intelligence during the Second World War* (Cambridge University Press, 1985)

Leigh, David, *The Frontiers of Secrecy* (Junction Books, London, 1980)

Lewin, Ronald, *The Other Ultra* (Hutchinson, London, 1982)

Lewin, Ronald, *Ultra Goes to War* (Hutchinson, London, 1978; McGraw-Hill, New York, 1979)

Lorain, Pierre, *Clandestine Operations* (Macmillan, New York, 1983)

McLachlan, Donald, *Room 39* (Weidenfeld & Nicolson, London, 1968)

Marben, Rolf, *Zeppelin Adventures* (John Hamilton, London, 1935)

May, Ernest R., *Knowing One's Enemies* (Princeton University Press, Princeton, 1985)

Montagu, Ewen, *Beyond Top Secret U* (Peter Davies, London, 1977; as *Beyond Top Secret Ultra*, Coward-McCann, New York, 1977)

Moore, Dan T., *Cloak and Cipher* (Harrap, London, 1965)

Morgan, Richard E., *Domestic Intelligence* (University of Texas Press, Austin, 1978)

Morris, Joseph, *The German Air Raids on Great Britain* (Sampson Low, London)

Mure, David, *Practise to Deceive* (William Kimber, London, 1977)

Murphy, Edward R., *Second in Command* (Holt, Rinehart & Winston, New York, 1971)

Nalder, Major–General R. F., *Royal Corps of Signals* (RSI, London, 1958)

Norman, Bruce, *Secret Warfare* (David & Charles, Devon, 1973)

Padfield, Peter, *Dönitz* (Gollancz, London, 1984; Harper & Row, New York, 1984)

Paine, Lauran, *Britain's Intelligence Service* (Robert Hale, London, 1979)

Paul, Doris A., *The Navajo Code–Talkers* (Dorrance, Philadelphia, 1973)

Perrault, Gilles, *The Red Orchestra* (Arthur Barker, London, 1968; Simon & Schuster, New York, 1969)

Pincher, Chapman, *Their Trade Is Treachery* (Sidgwick & Jackson, London, 1981; Bantam, New York, 1982)

Pincher, Chapman, *Too Secret Too Long* (Sidgwick & Jackson, London, 1984)

Poolman, Kenneth, *Zeppelins over England* (White Lion, 1975)

Powers, F. Gary, *Operation Overflight* (Holt, Rinehart & Winston, New York, 1970)

Prange, Gordon W., *Target Tokyo* (McGraw-Hill, New York, 1984)

Pratt, Fletcher, *Secret and Urgent* (Robert Hale, London, 1942)

Prime, Rhona, *Time of Trial* (Hodder & Stoughton, London, 1984)

Rawlinson, A., *The Defence of London* (Melrose, Maryland, 1923)

Read, Anthony, *Colonel Z* (Hodder & Stoughton, London, 1984)
Read, Anthony, and Fisher, David, *Operation Lucy* (Hodder & Stoughton, London, 1980; Coward-McCann, New York, 1981)
Rimmel, Raymond L., *Zeppelin!* (Conway, 1984)
Robinson, Douglas, *The Zeppelin in Combat* (G. T. Foulis, 1962)
Rohwer, Jürgen, *Axis U-Boat Successes* (US Naval Institute, 1983)
Roskill, Stephen, *Hankey: Man of Secrets* (Collins, London, 1972)
Sawatsky, John, *For Services Rendered* (Doubleday, New York, 1982)
Sawatsky, John, *Men in the Shadows* (Doubleday, New York, 1980)
Seale, Patrick, *Philby* (Hamish Hamilton, London, 1973)
Secret Codes and Ciphers (Desert Publications, Arizona, 1982)
Sinkov, Abraham, *Elementary Cryptanalysis* (Singer, New York, 1968)
Smith, Laurence, *Cryptography* (W. W. Norton, New York, 1943)
Spector, Ronald H., *Eagle Against the Sun* (Vintage Books, New York, 1985)
Stanley, Rupert, *Textbook on Wireless Telegraphy* (Longman Green, London, 1914)
Taylor, John W. R., *Spies in the Sky* (Scribners, New York, 1972)
Theoharris, Athan, *Spying on Americans* (Temple University Press, Philadelphia, 1978)
Thomson, Sir Basil *The Scene Changes* (Collins, London, 1939)
Thompson, James, *Secret Diplomacy* (Frederick Ungar, New York, 1963)
Thorpe, Elliott R., *East Wind, Rain* (Gambit, Massachusetts, 1969)
Toland, John, *Infamy* (Methuen, London, 1982; Doubleday, New York, 1982)
Tuchman, Barbara, *The Zimmermann Telegram* (Macmillan, New York, 1958)
Tuck, Michael, *High-Tech Espionage* (Sidgwick & Jackson, London, 1986)
Tully, Andrew, *Inside the FBI* (McGraw-Hill, New York, 1980)
Tully, Andrew, *The Super Spies* (William Morrow, New York, 1969)
Tuohy, Ferdinand, *The Secret Corps* (Thomas Seltzer, New York, 1920)
Van Der Rhoer, E., *Deadly Magic* (Robert Hale, London, 1978)
Verrier, Anthony, *Through the Looking Glass* (Cape, London, 1983)
Wark, Wesley K., *The Ultimate Enemy* (I. B. Tauris, London, 1975)
Welchman, Gordon, *The Hut Six Story* (McGraw-Hill, New York, 1982)
Westwood, David, *The Type VII U-Boat* (Naval Institute Press, Maryland, 1984)
Whiting, Charles, *The Spymasters* (Dutton, New York, 1975)
Winston, T. E., *Forewarned Is Forearmed* (Hodge & Co., London, 1948)
Winterbotham, Fred, *The Nazi Connection* (Weidenfeld & Nicolson, London, 1978; Harper & Row, New York, 1978)
Winterbotham, Fred, *The Ultra Secret* (Weidenfeld & Nicolson, London, 1974; Harper & Row, New York, 1974)

Wise, David, *The American Police State* (Random House, New York, 1976)

Wise, David, and Ross, Thomas, *The Espionage Establishment* (Cape, London, 1968)

Wise, David, and Ross, Thomas, *The Invisible Government* (Random House, New York, 1964)

Wise, David, and Ross, Thomas, *The U-2 Affair* (Random House, New York, 1962)

Yardley, Herbert, *The American Black Chamber* (Bobbs-Merrill, New York, 1931)

Yardley, Herbert, *Exposition on the Solution of American Diplomatic Codes* (unpublished)

Zacharias, Ellis M., *Secret Missions* (Putnam, New York, 1946)

Zim, Herbert S., *Codes and Secret Writing* (William Morrow, New York, 1948)

Source Notes

1: The Empire Chain
1. Edmonds Memoirs, King's College, London
2. GPO Archive
3. *Ibid.*
4. CID Memorandum, June 25, 1914
5. *Ibid.*
6. Admiralty War Staff Paper, June 10, 1914
7. CID Minutes, June 21, 1914
8. Sir Basil Thomson, *Queer People*, p. 39
9. Colonel Kell, November 18, 1914; GPO Archive
10. Ferdinand Tuohy, *The Secret Corps*, p. 133

2: The Great War
1. Major-General R. F. Nalder, *Royal Corps of Signals*, p. 97
2. GPO Archive, October 31, 1914
3. *Ibid.*
4. William F. Clarke, *History of Room 40*
5. Denniston Papers, Churchill College, Cambridge
6. PRO: ADM 137/203
7. Alfred Ewing, *The Man of Room 40*, p. 198
8. Richard W. Rowan, *The Story of Secret Service*, p. 623
9. Admiral Hall's letter to Pershing's staff, October 25, 1917, quoted in *ibid.*, p. 773
10. Stephen Roskill, *Hankey: Man of Secrets*, p. 247
11. Eckhardt telegram quoted in Burton J. Hendrick, *The Life and Letters of Walter Hines Page*, p. 150
12. *Ibid.*
13. *Ibid.*
14. Parker Hitt, *Manual for the Solution of Military Ciphers*, p. v
15. *Ibid.*, p. vi
16. Herbert Yardley, *The American Black Chamber*, p. 40
17. *Ibid.*, p. 212
18. PRO: FO 366/800

3: GC&CS

1. PRO: ADM 1/8577
2. R. H. Ullman, *Anglo-Soviet Relations*, Vol. 3, p. 284
3. PRO: CAB 63/29
4. PRO: FO 366/800
5. *Ibid.*
6. Tuohy, *op. cit.*, p. 150
7. Yardley, *op. cit.*, p. 217
8. *Ibid.*
9. H. Bywater and H. C. Ferraby, *Strange Intelligence*, p. 208
10. Hugh Cleland Hoy, *40 O.B.*, p. 20
11. Walter Gill, *War, Wireless and Wangles*, p. 19
12. Denniston Papers, Churchill College, Cambridge
13. F. H. Hinsley, *British Intelligence in the Second World War*, Vol. 1, p. 55
14. Gustave Bertrand, *Enigma*, p. 57
15. PRO: FO 366/1059

4: The Radio Security Service

1. Ladislas Farago, *Game of the Foxes*, p. 128
2. *Ibid.*
3. Lord Sandhurst, *The Hunt*, No. 15, July 12, 1941
4. *Ibid.*, No. 5, December 31, 1940
5. PRO: FO 366/1110

5: War

1. Denniston Papers, Churchill College, Cambridge
2. Lord Sandhurst, *The Hunt*, No. 7, January 28, 1941
3. *Ibid.*, No. 9, March 23, 1941

6: Clandestine Signals

1. Nomura telegram, May 20, 1941 (PURPLE No. 75), Department of Defense, *The MAGIC Background of Pearl Harbor*, Vol. 1, Appendix A-53

7: GCHQ

1. Denniston Papers, Churchill College, Cambridge

8: Russian Adventures

1. Clarke Papers, Churchill College, Cambridge
2. *Ibid.*
3. Gordon Welchman, *The Hut Six Story*, p. 163
4. *Ibid.*, p. 164

INDEX

S